Winston Churchill

Richard Carvel

Winston Churchill

Richard Carvel

ISBN/EAN: 9783743308985

Manufactured in Europe, USA, Canada, Australia, Japa

Cover: Foto ©ninafisch / pixelio.de

Manufactured and distributed by brebook publishing software (www.brebook.com)

Winston Churchill

Richard Carvel

CONTENTS

CHAPTER		PAGE
I.	Lionel Carvel, of Carvel Hall	1
II.	Some Memories of Childhood	6
III.	Caught by the Tide	16
IV.	Grafton would heal an Old Breach	27
V.	"If Ladies be but Young and Fair"	41
VI.	I first suffer for the Cause	50
VII.	Grafton has his Chance	61
VIII.	Over the Wall	70
IX.	Under False Colours	78
X.	The Red in the Carvel Blood	91
XI.	A Festival and a Parting	103
XII.	News from a Far Country	116
XIII.	Mr. Allen shows his Hand	125
XIV.	The Volte Coupe	136
XV.	Of which the Rector has the Worst	144
XVI.	In which Some Things are made Clear	154
XVII.	South River	159
XVIII.	The *Black Moll*	164
XIX.	A Man of Destiny	174
XX.	A Sad Home-coming	184
XXI.	The Gardener's Cottage	195
XXII.	On the Road	203

CONTENTS

CHAPTER		PAGE
XXIII.	London Town	215
XXIV.	Castle Yard	227
XXV.	The Rescue	234
XXVI.	The Part Horatio played	244
XXVII.	In which I am sore tempted	253
XXVIII.	Arlington Street	264
XXIX.	I meet a very Great Young Man	271
XXX.	A Conspiracy	279
XXXI.	"Upstairs into the World"	290
XXXII.	Lady Tankerville's Drum-major	303
XXXIII.	Drury Lane	313
XXXIV.	His Grace makes Advances	323
XXXV.	In which my Lord Baltimore appears	329
XXXVI.	A Glimpse of Mr. Garrick	337
XXXVII.	The Serpentine	344
XXXVIII.	In which I am roundly brought to task	354
XXXIX.	Holland House	362
XL.	Vauxhall	372
XLI.	The Wilderness	380
XLII.	My Friends are proven	389
XLIII.	Annapolis once more	395
XLIV.	Noblesse Oblige	401
XLV.	The House of Memories	413
XLVI.	Gordon's Pride	422
XLVII.	Visitors	427
XLVIII.	Multum in Parvo	438
XLIX.	Liberty loses a Friend	448
L.	Farewell to Gordon's	457
LI.	How an Idle Prophecy came to pass	463

CONTENTS

CHAPTER		PAGE
LII.	How the Gardener's Son fought the *Serapis*	475
LIII.	In which I make Some Discoveries	490
LIV.	More Discoveries	500
LV.	"The Love of a Maid for a Man"	512
LVI.	How Good came out of Evil	521
LVII.	I come to my Own again	532

ILLUSTRATIONS

	PAGE
If I might kill this monster, I would die willingly *Frontispiece*	381
One fifteenth of June	11
"Why do you not come over, as you used to?"	83
"Are ye kelpie or pirate?"	174
In walked John Paul himself	192
"You ... would sell your daughter and your honour for a title!"	387
We might have tossed a biscuit aboard the *Serapis*	483
With the first strawberries of the year	536

RICHARD CARVEL

CHAPTER I

LIONEL CARVEL, OF CARVEL HALL

LIONEL CARVEL, ESQ., of Carvel Hall, in the county of Queen Anne, was no inconsiderable man in his Lordship's province of Maryland, and indeed he was not unknown in the colonial capitals from Williamsburg to Boston. When his ships arrived out, in May or June, they made a goodly showing at the wharves, and his captains were ever shrewd men of judgment who sniffed a Frenchman on the horizon, so that none of the Carvel tobacco ever went, in that way, to gladden a Gallic heart. Mr. Carvel's acres were both rich and broad, and his house wide for the stranger who might seek its shelter, as with God's help so it ever shall be. It has yet to be said of the Carvels that their guests are hurried away, or that one, by reason of his worldly goods or position, shall be more welcome than another.

I take no shame in the pride with which I write of my grandfather, albeit he took the part of his Majesty and Parliament against the Colonies. He was no palavering turncoat, like my Uncle Grafton, to cry "God save the King!" again when an English fleet sailed up the bay. Mr. Carvel's hand was large and his heart was large, and he was respected and even loved by the patriots as a man above paltry subterfuge. He was born at Carvel Hall in the year of our Lord 1696, when the house was, I am told, but a small dwelling. It was his father, George Carvel, my great-grandsire, reared the present house in the year 1720, of brick brought from England as ballast for the empty ships; he added on, in the years following, the wide wings containing the ball-room, and the banquet-hall, and the large library at the eastern end, and the offices. But it was my grandfather who built the great stables and the kennels where he kept his beagles and his fleeter hounds. He dearly loved the saddle and the chase, and taught me to love them too. Many the sharp winter day I have followed the fox with him over two counties, and lain that night, and a week after, forsooth, at the plantation of some kind friend who was only too glad to receive us. Often, too, have we stood together from early morning until dark night, waist deep, on the duck points, I with a fowling-piece I was all but too young to carry, and brought back a hundred red-heads or canvas-backs in our bags. He went with unfailing regularity to the races at Annapolis or Chestertown or Marlborough, often to see his own horses run, where the coaches of the gentry were fifty and sixty around the course; where a negro, or a hogshead of tobacco, or a pipe of Madeira was often staked at a single throw. Those times, my children, are not ours, and I thought it not strange that Mr. Carvel should delight in a good main between two cocks, or a bull-baiting, or a breaking of heads at the Chestertown fair, where he went to show his cattle and fling a guinea into the ring for the winner.

But it must not be thought that Lionel Carvel, your ancestor, was wholly unlettered because he was a sportsman, though it must be confessed that books occupied him only when the weather compelled, or when on his back with the gout. At times he would fain have me read to him as he lay in his great four-post bed with the flowered counterpane, from the *Spectator*, stopping me now and anon at some awakened memory of his youth. He never forgave Mr. Addison for killing stout, old Sir Roger de Coverley, and would never listen to the butler's account of his death. Mr. Carvel, too, had walked in Gray's Inn Gardens and met adventure at Fox Hall, and seen the great Marlborough himself. He had a fondness for Mr. Congreve's Comedies, many of which he had seen acted; and was partial to Mr. Gay's *Trivia*, which brought him many a recolection. He would also listen to Pope. But of the more modern poetry I think Mr. Gray's *Elegy* pleased him best. He would laugh over Swift's gall and wormwood, and would never be brought by my mother to acknowledge the defects in the Dean's character. Why? He had once met the Dean in a London drawing-room, when my grandfather was a young spark at Christ Church, Oxford. He never tired of relating that interview. The hostess was a very great lady indeed, and actually stood waiting for a word with his Reverence, whose whim it was rather to talk to the young provincial. He was a forbidding figure, in his black gown and periwig, so my grandfather said, with a piercing blue eye and shaggy brow. He made the mighty to come to him, while young Carvel stood between laughter and fear of the great lady's displeasure.

"I knew of your father," said the Dean, "before he went to the colonies. He had done better at home, sir. He was a man of parts."

"He has done indifferently well in Maryland, sir," said Mr. Carvel, making his bow.

"He hath gained wealth, forsooth," says the Dean, wrathfully, "and might have had both wealth and fame had his love for King James not turned his head. I have heard much of the colonies, and have read that doggerel 'Sot Weed Factor' which tells of the gluttonous life of ease you lead in your own province. You can have no men of mark from such conditions, Mr. Carvel. Tell me," he adds contemptuously, "is genius honoured among you?"

"Faith, it is honoured, your Reverence," said my grandfather, "but never encouraged."

This answer so pleased the Dean that he bade Mr. Carvel dine with him next day at Button's Coffee House, where they drank mulled wine and old sack, for which young Mr. Carvel paid. On which occasion his Reverence endeavoured to persuade the young man to remain in England, and even went so far as to promise his influence to obtain him preferment. But Mr. Carvel chose rather (wisely or not, who can judge?) to come back to Carvel Hall and to the lands of which he was to be master, and to play the country squire and provincial magnate rather than follow the varying fortunes of a political party at home. And he was a man much looked up to in the province before the Revolution, and sat at the council board of his Excellency the Governor, as his father had done before him, and represented the crown in more matters than one when the French and savages were upon our frontiers.

Although a lover of good cheer, Mr. Carvel was never intemperate. To the end of his days he enjoyed his bottle after dinner, nay, could scarce get along without it; and mixed a punch or a posset as well as any in our colony. He chose a good London-brewed ale or porter, and his ships brought Madeira from that island by the pipe, and sack from Spain and Portugal, and red wine from France when there was peace. And puncheons of rum from Jamaica and the Indies for his people, holding that no gentleman ever drank rum in the raw, though fairly supportable as punch.

Mr. Carvel's house stands in Marlborough Street, a dreary mansion enough. Praised be Heaven that those who inherit it are not obliged to live there on the memory of what was in days gone by. The heavy green shutters are closed; the high steps, though stoutly built, are shaky after these years of disuse; the host of faithful servants who kept its state are nearly all laid side by side at Carvel Hall. Harvey and Chess and Scipio are no more. The kitchen, whither a boyish hunger oft directed my eyes at twilight, shines not with the welcoming gleam of yore. Chess no longer prepares the dainties which astonished Mr. Carvel's guests, and which he alone could cook. The coach still stands in the stables where Harvey left it, a lumbering relic of those lumbering times when methinks there was more of goodwill and less of haste in the world. The great brass knocker, once resplendent from Scipio's careful hand, no longer fantastically reflects the guest as he beats his tattoo, and Mr. Peale's portrait of my grandfather is gone from the dining-room wall, adorning, as you know, our own drawing-room at Calvert House.

I shut my eyes, and there comes to me unbidden that dining-room in Marlborough Street of a gray winter's afternoon, when I was but a lad. I see my dear grandfather in his wig and silver-laced waistcoat and his blue velvet coat, seated at the head of the table, and the precise Scipio has put down the dumb-waiter filled with shining cut-glass at his left hand, and his wine chest at his right, and with solemn pomp driven his black assistants from the room. Scipio was Mr. Carvel's butler. He was forbid to light the candles after dinner. As dark grew on, Mr. Carvel liked the blazing logs for light, and presently sets the decanter on the corner of the table and draws nearer the fire, his guests following. I recall well how jolly Governor Sharpe, who was a frequent visitor with us, was wont to display a comely calf in silk stocking; and how Captain Daniel Clapsaddle would spread his feet with his toes out, and settle his long pipe between his teeth. And there were besides a host of others who sat at that fire whose names have passed into Maryland's history, — Whig and Tory alike. And I remember a tall slip of a lad who sat listening by the deep-recessed windows on the street, which somehow are always covered in these pictures with a fine rain. Then a coach passes, — a mahogany coach emblazoned with the Manners's coat of arms, and Mistress Dorothy and her mother within. And my young lady gives me one of those demure bows which ever set my heart agoing like a smith's hammer of a Monday.

CHAPTER II

SOME MEMORIES OF CHILDHOOD

A TRAVELLER who has all but gained the last height of the great mist-covered mountain looks back over the painful crags he has mastered to where a light is shining on the first easy slope. That light is ever visible, for it is Youth.

After nigh fourscore and ten years of life that Youth is nearer to me now than many things which befell me later. I recall as yesterday the day Captain Clapsaddle rode to the Hall, his horse covered with sweat, and the reluctant tidings of Captain Jack Carvel's death on his lips. And strangely enough that day sticks in my memory as of delight rather than sadness. When my poor mother had gone up the stairs on my grandfather's arm the strong soldier took me on his knee, and drawing his pistol from his holster bade me snap the lock, which I was barely able to do. And he told me wonderful tales of the woods beyond the mountains, and of the painted men who tracked them; much wilder and fiercer they were than those stray Nanticokes I had seen from time to time near Carvel Hall. And when at last he would go I clung to him, so he swung me to the back of his great horse Ronald, and I seized the bridle in my small hands. The noble beast, like his master, loved a child well, and he cantered off lightly at the captain's whistle, who cried "bravo" and ran by my side lest I should fall. Lifting me off at length he kissed me and bade me not to annoy my mother, the tears in his eyes again. And leaping on Ronald was away for the ferry with never so much as a look behind, leaving me standing in the road.

And from that time I saw more of him and loved him better than any man save my grandfather. He gave me a pony on my next birthday, and a little hogskin saddle made especially by Master Wythe, the London saddler in the town, with a silver-mounted bridle. Indeed, rarely did the captain return from one of his long journeys without something for me and a handsome present for my mother. Mr. Carvel would have had him make his home with us when we were in town, but this he would not do. He lodged in Church Street, over against the Coffee House, dining at that hostelry when not bidden out, or when not with us. He was much sought after. I believe there was scarce a man of note in any of the colonies not numbered among his friends. 'Twas said he loved my mother, and could never come to care for any other woman, and he promised my father in the forests to look after her welfare and mine. This promise, you shall see, he faithfully kept.

Though you have often heard from my lips the story of my mother, I must for the sake of those who are to come after you, set it down here as briefly as I may. My grandfather's bark *Charming Sally*, Captain Stanwix, having set out from Bristol on the 15th of April, 1736, with a fair wind astern and a full cargo of English goods below, near the Madeiras fell in with foul weather, which increased as she entered the trades. Captain Stanwix being a prudent man, shortened sail, knowing the harbour of Funchal to be but a shallow bight in the rock, and worse than the open sea in a southeaster. The third day he hove the *Sally* to; being a stout craft and not overladen she weathered the gale with the loss of a jib, and was about making topsails again when a full-rigged ship was descried in the offing giving signals of distress. Night was coming on very fast, and the sea was yet running too high for a boat to live, but the gallant captain furled his topsails once more to await the morning. It could be seen from her signals that the ship was living throughout the night, but at dawn she foundered before the *Sally's* boats could be put in the water; one of them was ground to pieces on the falls. Out of the ship's company and passengers they picked up but five souls, four sailors and a little girl of two years or thereabouts. The men knew nothing more of her than that she had come aboard at Brest with her mother, a quiet, delicate lady who spoke little with the other passengers. The ship was *La Favourite du Roy*, bound for the French Indies.

Captain Stanwix's wife, who was a good, motherly person, took charge of the little orphan, and arriving at Carvel Hall delivered her to my grandfather, who brought her up as his own daughter. You may be sure the emblem of Catholicism found upon her was destroyed, and she was baptized straightway by Doctor Hilliard, my grandfather's chaplain, into the Established Church. Her clothes were of the finest quality, and her little handkerchief had worked into the corner of it a coronet, with the initials "E de T" beside it. Around her neck was that locket with the gold chain which I have so often shown you, on one side of which is the miniature of the young officer in his most Christian Majesty's uniform, and on the other a yellow-faded slip of paper with these words: "*Elle est la mienne, quoiqu'elle ne porte pas mon nom.*" "She is mine, although she does not bear my name."

My grandfather wrote to the owners of *La Favourite du Roy*, and likewise directed his English agent to spare nothing in the search for some clew to the child's identity. All that he found was that the mother had been entered on the passenger-list as Madame la Farge, of Paris, and was bound for Martinico. Of the father there was no trace whatever. The name "la Farge" the agent, Mr. Dix, knew almost to a certainty was assumed, and the coronet on the handkerchief implied that the child was of noble parentage. The meaning conveyed by the paper in the locket, which was plainly a clipping from a letter, was such that Mr. Carvel never showed it to my mother, and would have destroyed it had he not felt that some day it might aid in solving the mystery. So he kept it in his strong-box, where he thought it safe from prying eyes. But my Uncle Grafton, ever a deceitful lad, at length discovered the key and read the paper, and afterwards used the knowledge he thus obtained as a reproach and a taunt against my mother. I cannot even now write his name without repulsion.

This new member of the household was renamed Elizabeth Carvel, though they called her Bess, and of a course she was greatly petted and spoiled, and ruled all those about her. As she grew from childhood to womanhood her beauty became talked about, and afterwards, when Mistress Carvel went to the Assembly, a dozen young sparks would crowd about the door of her coach, and older and more serious men lost their heads on her account.

Her devotion to Mr. Carvel was such, however, that she seemed to care but little for the attention she received, and she continued to grace his board and entertain his company. He fairly worshipped her. It was his delight to surprise her with presents from England, with rich silks and brocades for gowns, for he loved to see her bravely dressed. The spinet he gave her, inlaid with ivory, we have still. And he caused a chariot to be made for her in London, and she had her own horses and her groom in the Carvel livery.

People said it was but natural that she should fall in love with Captain Jack, my father. He was the soldier of the family, tall and straight and dashing. He differed from his younger brother Grafton as day from night. Captain Jack was open and generous, though a little given to rash enterprise and madcap adventure. He loved my mother from a child. His friend Captain Clapsaddle loved her too, and likewise Grafton, but it soon became evident that she would marry Captain Jack or nobody. He was my grandfather's favourite, and though Mr. Carvel had wished him more serious, his joy when Bess blushingly told him the news was a pleasure to see. And Grafton turned to revenge; he went to Mr. Carvel with the paper he had taken from the strong-box and claimed that my mother was of spurious birth and not fit to marry a Carvel. He afterwards spread the story secretly among the friends of the family. By good fortune little harm arose therefrom, since all who knew my mother loved her, and were willing to give her credit for the doubt; many, indeed, thought the story sprang from Grafton's jealousy and hatred. Then it was that Mr. Carvel gave to Grafton the estate in Kent County and bade him shift for himself, saying that he washed his hands of a son who had acted such a part.

But Captain Clapsaddle came to the wedding in the long drawing-room at the Hall and stood by Captain Jack when he was married, and kissed the bride heartily. And my mother cried about this afterwards, and said that it grieved her sorely that she should have given pain to such a noble man.

After the blow which left her a widow, she continued to keep Mr. Carvel's home. I recall her well, chiefly as a sad and beautiful woman, stately save when she kissed me with passion and said that I bore my father's look. She drooped like the flower she was, and one spring day my grandfather led me to receive her blessing and to be folded for the last time in those dear arms. With a smile on her lips she rose to heaven to meet my father. And she lies buried with the rest of the Carvels at the Hall, next to the brave captain, her husband.

And so I grew up with my grandfather, spending the winters in town and the long summers on the Eastern Shore. I loved the country best, and the old house with its hundred feet of front standing on the gentle slope rising from the river's mouth, the green vines Mr. Carvel had fetched from England all but hiding the brick, and climbing to the angled roof; and the velvet green lawn of silvery grass brought from England, descending gently terrace by terrace to the waterside, where lay our pungies and barges. There was then a tiny pillared porch framing the front door, for our ancestors never could be got to realize the Maryland climate, and would rarely build themselves wide verandas suitable to that colony. At Carvel Hall we had, to be sure, the cool spring house under the willows for sultry days, with its pool dished out for bathing; and a trellised arbour, and octagonal summer house with seats where my mother was wont to sit sewing while my grandfather dreamed over his pipe. On the lawn stood the oaks and walnuts and sycamores which still cast their shade over it, and under them of a summer's evening Mr. Carvel would have his tea alone; save oftentimes when a barge would come swinging up the river with ten velvet-capped blacks at the oars, and one of our friendly neighbours — Mr. Lloyd or Mr. Bordley, or perchance little Mr. Manners — would stop for a long evening with him. They seldom came without their ladies and children. What romps we youngsters had about the old place whilst our elders talked their politics.

ONE FIFTEENTH OF JUNE

SOME MEMORIES OF CHILDHOOD 11

In childhood the season which delighted me the most was spring. I would count the days until St. Taminas, which, as you know, falls on the first of May. And the old custom was for the young men to deck themselves out as Indian bucks and sweep down on the festivities around the Maypole on the town green, or at night to surprise the guests at a ball and force the gentlemen to pay down a shilling, and sometimes a crown apiece, and the host to give them a bowl of punch. Then came June. My grandfather celebrated his Majesty's birthday in his own jolly fashion, and I had my own birthday party on the tenth. And on the fifteenth, unless it chanced upon a Sunday, my grandfather never failed to embark in his pinnace at the Annapolis dock for the Hall. Once seated in the stern between Mr. Carvel's knees, what rapture when at last we shot out into the blue waters of the bay and I thought of the long summer of joy before me. Scipio was generalissimo of these arrangements, and was always at the dock punctually at ten to hand my grandfather in, a ceremony in which he took great pride, and to look his disapproval should we be late. As he turned over the key of the town house he would walk away with a stern dignity to marshal the other servants in the horse-boat.

One fifteenth of June two children sat with bated breath in the pinnace, — Dorothy Manners and myself. Mistress Dolly was then as mischievous a little baggage as ever she proved afterwards. She was coming to pass a week at the Hall, her parents, whose place was next to ours, having gone to Philadelphia on a visit. We rounded Kent Island, which lay green and beautiful in the flashing waters, and at length caught sight of the old windmill, with its great arms majestically turning, and the cupola of Carvel House shining white among the trees; and of the upper spars of the shipping, with sails neatly furled, lying at the long wharves, where the English wares Mr. Carvel had commanded for the return trips were unloading. Scarce was the pinnace brought into the wind before I had leaped ashore and greeted with a shout the Hall servants drawn up in a line on the green, grinning a welcome. Dorothy and I scampered over the grass and into the cool, wide house, resting awhile on the easy sloping steps within, hand in hand. And then away for that grand tour of inspection we had been so long planning together. How well I recall that sunny afternoon, when the shadows of the great oaks were just beginning to lengthen. Through the greenhouses we marched, monarchs of all we surveyed, old Porphery, the gardener, presenting Mistress Dolly with a crown of orange blossoms, for which she thanked him with a pretty courtesy her governess had taught her. Were we not king and queen returned to our summer palace? And Spot and Silver and Song and Knipe, the wolf-hound, were our train, though not as decorous as rigid etiquette demanded, since they were forever running after the butterflies. On we went through the stiff, box-bordered walks of the garden, past the weather-beaten sun-dial and the spinning-house and the smoke-house to the stables. Here old Harvey, who had taught me to ride Captain Daniel's pony, is equerry, and young Harvey our personal attendant; old Harvey smiles as we go in and out of the stalls rubbing the noses of our trusted friends, and gives a gruff but kindly warning as to Cassandra's heels. He recalls my father at the same age.

Jonas Tree, the carpenter, sits sunning himself on his bench before the shop, but mysteriously disappears when he sees us, and returns presently with a little ship he has fashioned for me that winter, all complete with spars and sails, for Jonas was a shipwright on the Severn in the old country before he came as a king's passenger to the new. Dolly and I are off directly to the backwaters of the river, where the new boat is launched with due ceremony as the *Conqueror*, his Majesty's latest ship-of-the-line. Jonas himself trims her sails, and she sets off right gallantly across the shallows, heeling to the breeze for all the world like a real man-o'-war. Then the King would fain cruise at once against the French, but Queen Dorothy must needs go with him. His Majesty points out that when fighting is to be done, a ship of war is no place for a woman, whereat her Majesty stamps her little foot and throws her crown of orange blossoms from her, and starts off for the milk-house in high dudgeon, vowing she will play no more.

And it ends as it ever will end, be the children young or old, for the French pass from his Majesty's mind and he runs after his consort to implore forgiveness, leaving poor Jonas to take care of the *Conqueror*.

How short those summer days! All too short for the girl and boy who had so much to do in them. The sun rising over the forest often found us peeping through the blinds, and when he sank into the bay at night we were still running, tired but happy, and begging patient Hester for half an hour more.

"Lawd, Marse Dick," I can hear her say, "you an' Miss Dolly's been on yo' feet since de dawn. And so's I, honey."

And so we had. We would spend whole days on the wharves, all bustle and excitement, sometimes seated on the capstan of the *Sprightly Bess* or perched in the nettings of the *Oriole*, of which ship old Stanwix was now captain. He had grown gray in Mr. Carvel's service, and good Mrs. Stanwix was long since dead. Often we would mount together on the little horse Captain Daniel had given me, Dorothy on a pillion behind, to go with my grandfather to inspect the farm. Mr. Starkie, the overseer, would ride beside us, his fowling-piece slung over his shoulder and his holster on his hip; a kind man and capable, and unlike Mr. Evans, my Uncle Grafton's overseer, was seldom known to use his firearms or the rawhide slung across his saddle. The negroes in their linsey-woolsey jackets and checked trousers would stand among the hills grinning at us children as we passed; and there was not one of them, nor of the white servants for that matter, that I could not call by name.

And all this time I was busily wooing Mistress Dolly; but she, little minx, would give me no satisfaction. I see her standing among the strawberries, her black hair waving in the wind, and her red lips redder still from the stain. And the sound of her childish voice comes back to me now after all these years. And this was my first proposal: —

"Dorothy, when you grow up and I grow up, you will marry me, and I shall give you all these strawberries."

"I will marry none but a soldier," says she, "and a great man."

"Then will I be a soldier," I cried, "and greater than the Governor himself." And I believed it.

"Papa says I shall marry an earl," retorts Dorothy, with a toss of her pretty head.

"There are no earls among us," I exclaimed hotly, for even then I had some of that sturdy republican spirit which prevailed among the younger generation. "Our earls are those who have made their own way, like my grandfather." For I had lately heard Captain Clapsaddle say this and much more on the subject. But Dorothy turned up her nose.

"I shall go home when I am eighteen," she said, "and I shall meet his Majesty the King."

And to such an argument I found no logical answer.

Mr. Marmaduke Manners and his lady came to fetch Dorothy home. He was a foppish little gentleman who thought more of the cut of his waistcoat than of the affairs of the province, and would rather have been bidden to lead the assembly ball than to sit in council with his Excellency the Governor. My first recollection of him is of contempt. He must needs have his morning punch just so, and complained whiningly of Scipio if some perchance were spilled on the glass. He must needs be taken abroad in a chair when it rained. And though in the course of a summer he was often at Carvel Hall he never tarried long, and came to see Mr. Carvel's guests rather than Mr. Carvel. He had little in common with my grandfather, whose chief business and pleasure was to promote industry on his farm. Mr. Marmaduke was wont to rise at noon, and knew not wheat from barley, or good leaf from bad; his hands he kept like a lady's, rendering them almost useless by the long lace on the sleeves, and his chief pastime was card-playing. It was but reasonable therefore, when the troubles with the mother country began, that he chose the King's side alike from indolence and contempt for things republican.

Of Mrs. Manners I shall say more by and by.

I took a mischievous delight in giving Mr. Manners every annoyance my boyish fancy could conceive. The evening of his arrival he and Mr. Carvel set out for a stroll about the house, Mr. Marmaduke mincing his steps, for it had rained that morning. And presently they came upon the windmill with its long arms moving lazily in the light breeze, near touching the ground as they passed, for the mill was built in the Dutch fashion. I know not what moved me, but hearing Mr. Manners carelessly humming a minuet while my grandfather explained the usefulness of the mill, I seized hold of one of the long arms as it swung by, and before the gentlemen could prevent was carried slowly upwards. Dorothy screamed, and her father stood stock still with amazement and fear, Mr. Carvel being the only one who kept his presence of mind. "Hold on tight, Richard!" I heard him cry. It was dizzy riding, though the motion was not great, and before I had reached the right angle I regretted my rashness. I caught a glimpse of the Bay with the red sun on it, and as I turned saw far below me the white figure of Ivie Rawlinson, the Scotch miller, who had run out. "O haith!" he shouted. "Haud fast, Mr. Richard!" And so I clung tightly and came down without much inconvenience, though indifferently glad to feel the ground again.

Mr. Marmaduke, as I expected, was in a great temper, and swore he had not had such a fright for years. He looked for Mr. Carvel to cane me stoutly. But Ivie laughed heartily, and said: "I wad ye'll gang far for anither laddie wi' the spunk, Mr. Manners," and with a sly look at my grandfather, "Ilka day we hae some sic whigmeleery."

I think Mr. Carvel was not ill pleased with the feat, or with Mr. Marmaduke's way of taking it. For afterwards I overheard him telling the story to Colonel Lloyd, and both gentlemen laughing over Mr. Manners's discomfiture.

CHAPTER III

CAUGHT BY THE TIDE

It is a nigh impossible task on the memory to trace those influences by which a lad is led to form his life's opinions, and for my part I hold that such things are bred into the bone, and that events only serve to strengthen them. In this way only can I account for my bitterness, at a very early age, against that King whom my seeming environment should have made me love. For my grandfather was as stanch a royalist as ever held a cup to majesty's health. And children are most apt before they can reason for themselves to take the note from those of their elders who surround them. It is true that many of Mr. Carvel's guests were of the opposite persuasion from him: Mr. Chase and Mr. Carroll, Mr. Lloyd and Mr. Bordley, and many others, including our friend Captain Clapsaddle. And these gentlemen were frequently in argument, but political discussion is Greek to a lad.

Mr. Carvel, as I have said, was most of his life a member of the Council, a man from whom both Governor Sharpe and Governor Eden were glad to take advice because of his temperate judgment and deep knowledge of the people of the province. At times, when his Council was scattered, Governor Sharpe would consult Mr. Carvel alone, and often have I known my grandfather to embark in haste from the Hall in response to a call from his Excellency.

'Twas in the latter part of August, in the year 1765, made memorable by the Stamp Act, that I first came in touch with the deep-set feelings of the times then beginning, and I count from that year the awakening of the sympathy which determined my career. One sultry day I was wading in the shallows after crabs, when the Governor's messenger came drifting in, all impatience at the lack of wind. He ran to the house to seek Mr. Carvel, and I after him, with all a boy's curiosity, as fast as my small legs would carry me. My grandfather hurried out to order his barge to be got ready at once, so that I knew something important was at hand. At first he refused me permission to go, but afterwards relented, and about eleven in the morning we pulled away strongly, the ten blacks bending to the oars as if their lives were at stake.

A wind arose before we sighted Greensbury Point, and I saw a bark sailing in, but thought nothing of this until Mr. Carvel, who had been silent and preoccupied, called for his glass and swept her decks. She soon shortened sail, and went so leisurely that presently our light barge drew alongside, and I perceived Mr. Zachariah Hood, a merchant of the town, returning from London, hanging over her rail. Mr. Hood was very pale in spite of his sea-voyage; he flung up his cap at our boat, but Mr. Carvel's salute in return was colder than he looked for. As we came in view of the dock, a fine rain was setting in, and to my astonishment I beheld such a mass of people assembled as I had never seen, and scarce standing-room on the wharves. We were to have gone to the Governor's wharf in the Severn, but my grandfather changed his intention at once. Many of the crowd greeted him as we drew near them, and, having landed, respectfully made room for him to pass through. I followed him a-tremble with excitement and delight over such an unwonted experience. We had barely gone ten paces, however, before Mr. Carvel stopped abreast of Mr. Claude, mine host of the Coffee House, who cried: —

"Hast seen his Majesty's newest representative, Mr. Carvel?"

"Mr. Hood is on board the bark, sir," replied my grandfather. "I take it you mean Mr. Hood."

"Ay, that I do; Mr. Zachariah Hood, come to lick stamps for his brother-colonists."

"After licking his Majesty's boots," says a wag near by, which brings a laugh from those about us. I remembered that I had heard some talk as to how Mr. Hood had sought and obtained from King George the office of Stamp Distributor for the province. Now, my grandfather, God rest him! was as doughty an old gentleman as might well be, and would not listen without protest to remarks which bordered sedition. He had little fear of things below, and none of a mob.

"My masters," he shouted, with a flourish of his stick, so stoutly that people fell back from him, "know that ye are met against the law, and endanger the peace of his Lordship's government."

"Good enough, Mr. Carvel," said Claude, who seemed to be the spokesman. "But how if we are stamped against law and his Lordship's government? How then, sir? Your honour well knows we have naught against either, and are as peaceful a mob as ever assembled."

This brought on a great laugh, and they shouted from all sides, "How then, Mr. Carvel?" And my grandfather, perceiving that he would lose dignity by argument, and having done his duty by a protest, was wisely content with that. They opened wider the lane for him to pass through, and he made his way, erect and somewhat defiant, to Mr. Pryse's, the coachmaker opposite, holding me by the hand. The second storey of Pryse's shop had a little balcony standing out in front, and here we established ourselves, that we might watch what was going forward.

The crowd below grew strangely silent as the bark came nearer and nearer, until Mr. Hood showed himself on the poop, when there rose a storm of hisses, mingled with shouts of derision. "How goes it at St. James, Mr. Hood?" and "Have you tasted his Majesty's barley?" And some asked him if he was come as their member of Parliament. Mr. Hood dropped a bow, though what he said was drowned. The bark came in prettily enough, men in the crowd even catching her lines and making them fast to the piles. A gang-plank was thrown over. "Come out, Mr. Hood," they cried; "we are here to do you honour, and to welcome you home again." There were leather breeches with staves a-plenty around that plank, and faces that meant no trifling. "McNeir, the rogue," exclaimed Mr. Carvel, "and that hulk of a tanner, Brown.

And I would know those smith's shoulders in a thousand."
"Right, sir," says Pryse, "and 'twill serve them proper when the King's troops come among them for quartering." Pryse being the gentry's patron, shaped his politics according to the company he was in: he could ill be expected to seize one of his own ash spokes and join the resistance. Just then I caught a glimpse of Captain Clapsaddle on the skirts of the crowd, and with him Mr. Swain and some of the dissenting gentry. And my boyish wrath burst forth against that man smirking and smiling on the decks of the bark, so that I shouted shrilly: "Mr. Hood will be cudgelled and tarred as he deserves," and shook my little fist at him, so that many under us laughed and cheered me. Mr. Carvel pushed me back into the window and out of their sight.

The crew of the bark had assembled on the quarterdeck, stout English tars every man of them, armed with pikes and belaying-pins; and at a word from the mate they rushed in a body over the plank. Some were thrust off into the water, but so fierce was their onset that others gained the wharf, laying sharply about them in all directions, but getting full as many knocks as they gave. For a space there was a very bedlam of cries and broken heads, those behind in the mob surging forward to reach the scrimmage, forcing their own comrades over the edge. McNeir had his thigh broken by a pike, and was dragged back after the first rush was over; and the mate of the bark was near to drowning, being rescued, indeed, by Graham, the tanner. Mr. Hood stood white in the gangway, dodging a missile now and then, waiting his chance, which never came. For many of the sailors were captured and carried bodily to the "Rose and Crown" and the "Three Blue Balls," where they became properly drunk on Jamaica rum; others made good their escape on board. And at length the bark cast off again, amidst jeers and threats, and one-third of her crew missing, and drifted slowly back to the roads.

From the dock, after all was quiet, Mr. Carvel stepped into his barge and rowed to the Governor's, whose house was prettily situated near Hanover Street, with ground running down to the Severn. His Excellency appeared much relieved to see my grandfather; Mr. Daniel Dulany was with him, and the three gentlemen at once repaired to the Governor's writing-closet for consultation.

Mr. Carvel's town house being closed, we stopped with his Excellency. There were, indeed, scarce any of the gentry in town at that season save a few of the Whig persuasion. Excitement ran very high; farmers flocked in every day from the country round about to take part in the demonstration against the Act. Mr. Hood's storehouse was burned to the ground. Mr. Hood getting ashore by stealth, came, however, unmolested to Annapolis and offered at a low price the goods he had brought out in the bark, thinking thus to propitiate his enemies. This step but inflamed them the more.

My grandfather having much business to look to, I was left to my own devices, and the devices of an impetuous lad of twelve are not always such as his elders would choose for him. I was continually burning with a desire to see what was proceeding in the town, and hearing one day a great clamour and tolling of bells, I ran out of the Governor's gate and down Northwest Street to the Circle, where a strange sight met my eyes. A crowd like that I had seen on the dock had collected there, Mr. Swain and Mr. Hammond and other barristers holding them in check. Mounted on a one-horse cart was a stuffed figure of the detested Mr. Hood. Mr. Hammond made a speech, but for the laughter and cheering I could not catch a word of it. I pushed through the people, as a boy will, diving between legs to get a better view, when I felt a hand upon my shoulder, bringing me up suddenly. And I recognized Mr. Matthias Tilghman, and with him was Mr. Samuel Chase.

"Does your grandfather know you are here, lad?" said Mr. Tilghman.

I paused a moment for breath before I answered: "He attended the rally at the dock himself, sir, and I believe enjoyed it."

Both gentlemen smiled, and Mr. Chase remarked that if all the other party were like Mr. Carvel, troubles would soon cease. "I mean not Grafton," says he, with a wink at Mr. Tilghman.

"I'll warrant, Richard, your uncle would be but ill pleased to see you in such company."

"Nay, sir," I replied, for I never feared to speak up, "there are you wrong. I think it would please my uncle mightily."

"The lad hath indifferent penetration," said Mr. Tilghman, laughing, and adding more soberly: "If you never do worse than this, Richard, Maryland may some day be proud of you."

Mr. Hammond having finished his speech, a paper was placed in the hand of the effigy, and the crowd bore it shouting and singing to the hill, where Mr. John Shaw, the city carpenter, had made a gibbet. There nine and thirty lashes were bestowed on the unfortunate image, the people crying out that this was the Mosaic Law. And I cried as loud as any, though I knew not the meaning of the words. They hung Mr. Hood to the gibbet and set fire to a tar barrel under him, and so left him.

The town wore a holiday look that day, and I was loth to go back to the Governor's house. Good patriots' shops were closed, their owners parading as on Sunday in their best, pausing in knots at every corner to discuss the affair with which the town simmered. I encountered old Farris, the clockmaker, in his brown coat besprinkled behind with powder from his queue. "How now, Master Richard?" says he, merrily. "This is no place for young gentlemen of your persuasion."

Next I came upon young Dr. Courtenay, the wit of the Tuesday Club, of whom I shall have more to say hereafter. He was taking the air with Mr. James Fotheringay, Will's eldest brother, but lately back from Oxford and the Temple. The doctor wore five-pound ruffles and a ten-pound wig, was dressed in cherry silk, and carried a long, clouded cane. His hat had the latest cock, for he was our macaroni of Annapolis. "Egad, Richard," he cries, "you are the only other loyalist I have seen abroad to-day."

I remember swelling with indignation at the affront. "I call them Tories, sir," I flashed back, "and I am none such."
"No Tory!" says he, nudging Mr. Fotheringay, who was with him; "I had as lief believe your grandfather hated King George." I astonished them both by retorting that Mr. Carvel

might think as he pleased, that being every man's right; but that I chose to be a Whig. "I would tell you as a friend, young man," replied the doctor, " that thy politics are not over politic." And they left me puzzling, laughing with much relish over some catch in the doctor's words. As for me, I could perceive no humour in them.

It was now near six of the clock, but instead of going direct to the Governor's I made my way down Church Street toward the water. Near the dock I saw many people gathered in the street in front of the "Ship" tavern, a time-honoured resort much patronized by sailors. My curiosity led me to halt there also. The "Ship" had stood in that place nigh on to three-score years, it was said. Its latticed windows were swung open, and from within came snatches of "Tom Bowling," "Rule Britannia," and many songs scarce fit for a child to hear. Now and anon some one in the street would throw back a taunt to these British sentiments, which went unheeded. "They be drunk as lords," said Weld, the butcher's apprentice, "and when they comes out we'll hev more than one broken head in this street." The songs continuing, he cried again, "Come out, d—n ye." Weld had had more than his own portion of rum that day. Spying me seated on the gate-post opposite, he shouted: "So ho, Master Carvel, the streets are not for his Majesty's supporters to-day." Other artisans who were there bade him leave me in peace, saying that my grandfather was a good friend of the people. The matter might have ended there had I been older and wiser, but the excitement of the day had gone to my head like wine. "I am as stout a patriot as you, Weld," I shouted back, and flushed at the cheering that followed. And Weld ran up to me, and though I was a good piece of a lad, swung me lightly onto his shoulder. "Harkee, Master Richard," he said, " I can get nothing out of the poltroons by shouting. Do you go in and say that Weld will fight any mother's son of them single-handed."

"For shame, to send a lad into a tavern," said old Robbins, who had known my grandfather these many years. But the desire for a row was so great among the rest that they silenced him. Weld set me down, and I, nothing loth, ran through the open door.

I had never before been in the "Ship," nor, indeed, in any tavern save that of Master Dingley, near Carvel Hall. The "Ship" was a bare place enough, with low black beams and sanded floor, and rough tables and chairs set about. On that September evening it was stifling hot; and the odours from the men, and the spilled rum and tobacco smoke, well-nigh overpowered me. The room was filled with a motley gang of sailors, mostly from the bark Mr. Hood had come on, and some from H.M.S. *Hawk*, then lying in the harbour.

A strapping man-o'-war's-man sat near the door, his jacket thrown open and his great chest bared, and when he perceived me he was in the act of proposing a catch; 'twas "The Great Bell o' Lincoln," I believe; and he held a brimming cup of bumbo in his hand. In his surprise he set it awkwardly down again, thereby spilling full half of it. "Avast," says he, with an oath, "what's this come among us?" and he looked me over with a comical eye. "A d—d provincial," he went on scornfully, "but a gentleman's son, or Jack Ball's a liar." Whereupon his companions rose from their seats and crowded round me. More than one reeled against me. And though I was somewhat awed by the strangeness of that dark, ill-smelling room, and by the rough company in which I found myself, I held my ground, and spoke up as strongly as I might.

"Weld, the butcher's apprentice, bids me say he will fight any man among you single-handed."

"So ho, my little gamecock, my little schooner with a swivel," said he who had called himself Jack Ball, "and where can this valiant butcher be found?"

"He waits in the street," I answered more boldly.

"Split me fore and aft if he waits long," said Jack, draining the rest of his rum. And picking me up as easily as did Weld he rushed out of the door, and after him as many of his mates as could walk or stagger thither.

In the meantime the news had got abroad in the street that the butcher's apprentice was to fight one of the *Hawk*'s men, and when I emerged from the tavern the crowd had doubled, and people were running hither in all haste from both directions. But that fight was never to be. Big Jack Ball had scarce set me down and shouted a loud defiance, shaking his fist at Weld, who stood out opposite, when a soldierly man on a great horse turned the corner and wheeled between the combatants. I knew at a glance it was Captain Clapsaddle, and guiltily wished myself at the Governor's. The townspeople knew him likewise, and many were slinking away even before he spoke, as his charger stood pawing the ground.

"What's this I hear, you villain," said he to Weld, in his deep, ringing voice, "that you have not only provoked a row with one of the King's sailors, but have dared send a child into that tavern with your fool's message?"

Weld was awkward and sullen enough, and no words came to him.

"Your tongue, you sot," the captain went on, drawing his sword in his anger, "is it true you have made use of a gentleman's son for your low purposes?"

But Weld was still silent, and not a sound came from either side until old Robbins spoke up.

"There are many here can say I warned him, your honour," he said.

"Warned him!" cried the captain. "Mr. Carvel has just given you twenty pounds for your wife, and you warned him!"

Robbins said no more; and the butcher's apprentice, hanging his head, as well he might before the captain, I was much moved to pity for him, seeing that my forwardness had in some sense led him on.

"'Twas in truth my fault, captain," I cried out. The captain looked at me, and said nothing. After that the butcher made bold to take up his man's defence.

"Master Carvel was indeed somewhat to blame, sir," said he, "and Weld is in liquor."

"And I'll have him to pay for his drunkenness," said Captain Clapsaddle, hotly. "Get to your homes," he cried. "Ye are a lot of idle hounds, who would make liberty the excuse for riot." He waved his sword at the pack of them, and they scattered like sheep until none but Weld was left. "And as for you, Weld," he continued, "you'll rue this pretty business, or Daniel Clapsaddle never punished a cut-throat." And turning to Jack Ball, he bade him lift me to the saddle, and so I rode with him to the Governor's without a word; for I knew better than to talk when he was in that mood.

The captain was made to tarry and sup with his Excellency and my grandfather, and I sat perforce a fourth at the table, scarce daring to conjecture as to the outcome of my escapade. But as luck would have it, the Governor had been that day in such worry and perplexity, and my grandfather also, that my absence had passed unnoticed. Nor did my good friend the captain utter a word to them of what he knew. But afterwards he called me to him and set me upon his knee. How big, and kind, and strong he was, and how I loved his bluff soldier's face and blunt ways. And when at last he spoke, his words burnt deep in my memory, so that even now I can repeat them.

"Richard," he said, "I perceive you are like your father. I love your spirit greatly, but you have been overrash to-day. Remember this, lad, that you are a gentleman, the son of the bravest and truest gentleman I have ever known, save one; and he is destined to high things." I know now that he spoke of Colonel Washington. "And that your mother," — here his voice trembled, — "your mother was a lady, every inch of her, and too good for this world. Remember, and seek no company, therefore, beyond that circle in which you were born. Fear not to be kind and generous, as I know you ever will be, but choose not intimates from the tavern." Here the captain cleared his throat, and seemed to seek for words. "I fear there are times coming, my lad," he went on presently, "when every man must choose his side, and stand arrayed in his own colours. It is not for me to shape your way of thinking. Decide in your own mind that which is right, and when you have so decided," — he drew his sword, as was his habit when greatly moved, and placed his broad hand upon my head, — "know then that God is with you, and swerve not from thy course the width of this blade for any man."

We sat upon a little bench in the Governor's garden, in front of us the wide Severn merging into the bay, and glowing like molten gold in the setting sun. And I was thrilled with a strange reverence such as I have sometimes since felt in the presence of heroes.

CHAPTER IV

GRAFTON WOULD HEAL AN OLD BREACH

Doctor Hilliard, my grandfather's chaplain, was as holy a man as ever wore a gown, but I can remember none of his discourses which moved me as much by half as those simple words Captain Clapsaddle had used. The worthy doctor, who had baptized both my mother and father, died suddenly at Carvel Hall the spring following, of a cold contracted while visiting a poor man who dwelt across the river. He would have lacked but three years of fourscore come Whitsuntide. He was universally loved and respected in that district where he had lived so long and ably, by rich and poor alike, and those of many creeds saw him to his last resting-place. Mr. Carroll, of Carrollton, who was an ardent Catholic, stood bareheaded beside the grave.

Doctor Hilliard was indeed a beacon in a time when his profession among us was all but darkness, and when many of the scandals of the community might be laid at the door of those whose duty it was to prevent them. The fault lay without doubt in his Lordship's charter, which gave to the parishioners no voice in the choosing of their pastors. This matter was left to Lord Baltimore's whim. Hence it was that he sent among us so many fox-hunting and gaming parsons who read the service ill and preached drowsy and illiterate sermons. Gaming and fox-hunting, did I say? These are but charitable words to cover the real characters of those impostors in holy orders, whose doings would often bring the blush of shame to your cheeks. Nay, I have seen a clergyman drunk in the pulpit, and even in those freer days their laxity and immorality were such that many flocked to hear the parsons of the Methodists and Lutherans, whose simple and eloquent words and simpler lives were worthy of their cloth. Small wonder was it, when every strolling adventurer and soldier out of employment took orders and found favour in his Lordship's eyes, and were given the fattest livings in place of worthier men, that the Established Church fell somewhat into disrepute. Far be it from me to say that there were not good men and true in that Church, but the wag who writ this verse, which became a common saying in Maryland, was not far wrong for the great body of them: —

"Who is a monster of the first renown?
A lettered sot, a drunkard in a gown."

My grandfather did not replace Dr. Hilliard at the Hall, afterwards saying the prayers himself. The doctor had been my tutor, and in spite of my waywardness and lack of love for the classics had taught me no little Latin and Greek, and early instilled into my mind those principles necessary for the soul's salvation. I have often thought with regret on the pranks I played him. More than once at lesson-time have I gone off with Hugo and young Harvey for a rabbit hunt, stealing two dogs from the pack, and thus committing a double offence. You may be sure I was well thrashed by Mr. Carvel, who thought the more of the latter misdoing, though obliged to emphasize the former. The doctor would never raise his hand against me. His study, where I recited my daily tasks, was that small sunny room on the water side of the east wing; and I well recall him as he sat behind his desk of a morning after prayers, his horn spectacles perched on his high nose and his quill over his ear, and his ink-powder and pewter stand beside him. His face would grow more serious as I scanned my Virgil in a faltering voice, and as he descanted on a passage my eye would wander out over the green trees and fields to the glistening water. What cared I for "Arma virumque" at such a time? I was watching Nebo afishing beyond the point, and as he waded ashore the burden on his shoulders had a much keener interest for me than that Æneas carried out of Troy.

My Uncle Grafton came to Dr. Hilliard's funeral, choosing this opportunity to become reconciled to my grandfather, who he feared had not much longer to live. Albeit Mr. Carvel was as stout and hale as ever. None of the mourners at the doctor's grave showed more sorrow than did Grafton. A thousand remembrances of the good old man returned to him, and I heard him telling Mr. Carroll and some other gentlemen, with much emotion, how he had loved his reverend preceptor, from whom he had learned nothing but what was good. "How fortunate are you, Richard," he once said, "to have had such a spiritual and intellectual teacher in your youth. Would that Philip might have learned from such a one. And I trust you can say, my lad, that you have made the best of your advantages, though I fear you are of a wild nature, as your father was before you." And my uncle sighed and crossed his hands behind his back. "'Tis perhaps better that poor John is in his grave," he said. Grafton had a word and a smile for every one about the old place, but little else, being, as he said, but a younger son and a poor man. I was near to forgetting the shilling he gave Scipio. 'Twas not so unostentatiously done but that Mr. Carvel and I marked it. And afterwards I made Scipio give me the coin, replacing it with another, and flung it as far into the river as ever I could throw.

As was but proper to show his sorrow at the death of the old chaplain he had loved so much, Grafton came to the Hall drest entirely in black. He would have had his lady and Philip, a lad near my own age, clad likewise in sombre colours. But my Aunt Caroline would none of them, holding it to be the right of her sex to dress as became its charms. Her silks and laces went but ill with the low estate my uncle claimed for his purse, and Master Philip's wardrobe was twice the size of mine. And the family travelled in a coach as grand as Mr. Carvel's own, with panels wreathed in flowers and a footman and outrider in livery, from which my aunt descended like a duchess. She embraced my grandfather with much warmth, and kissed me effusively on both cheeks.

"And this is dear Richard?" she cried. "Philip, come at once and greet your cousin. He has not the look of the Carvels," she continued volubly, "but more resembles his mother, as I recall her."

"Indeed, madam," my grandfather answered somewhat testily, "he has the Carvel nose and mouth, though his chin is more pronounced. He has Elizabeth's eyes."

But my aunt was a woman who flew from one subject to another, and she had already ceased to think of me. She was in the hall. "The dear old home!" she cries, though she had been in it but once before, regarding lovingly each object as her eye rested upon it, nay, caressingly when she came to the great punch-bowl and the carved mahogany dresser, and the Peter Lely over the broad fireplace. "What memories they must bring to your mind, my dear," she remarks to her husband. "'Tis cruel, as I once said to dear papa, that we cannot always live under the old rafters we loved so well as children." And the good lady brushes away a tear with her embroidered pocket-napkin. Tears that will come in spite of us all. But she brightens instantly and smiles at the line of servants drawn up to welcome them. "This is Scipio, my son, who was with your grandfather when your father was born, and before." Master Philip nods graciously in response to Scipio's delighted bow. "And Harvey," my aunt rattles on. "Have you any new mares to surprise us with this year, Harvey?" Harvey not being as overcome with Mrs. Grafton's condescension as was proper, she turns again to Mr. Carvel.

"Ah, father, I see you are in sore need of a woman's hand about the old house. What a difference a touch makes, to be sure." And she takes off her gloves and attacks the morning room, setting an ornament here and another there, and drawing back for the effect. "Such a bachelor's hall as you are keeping!"

"We still have Willis, Caroline," remonstrates my grandfather, gravely. "I have no fault to find with her housekeeping."

"Of course not, father; men never notice," Aunt Caroline replies in an aggrieved tone. And when Willis herself comes in, auguring no good from this visit, my aunt gives her the tips of her fingers. And I imagine I see a spark fly between them.

As for Grafton, he was more than willing to let bygones be bygones between his father and himself. Aunt Caroline said with feeling that Dr. Hilliard's death was a blessing, after all, since it brought a long-separated father and son together once more. Grafton had been misjudged and ill-used, and he called Heaven to witness that the quarrel had never been of his seeking,—a statement which Mr. Carvel was at no pains to prove perjury. How attentive was Mr. Grafton to his father's every want. He read his *Gazette* to him of a Thursday, though the old gentleman's eyes are as good as ever. If Mr. Carvel walks out of an evening, Grafton's arm is ever ready, and my uncle and his worthy lady are eager to take a hand at cards before supper. "Philip, my dear," says my aunt, "thy grandfather's slippers," or, "Philip, my love, thy grandfather's hat and cane." But it is plain that Master Philip has not been brought up to wait on his elders. He is curled with a novel in his grandfather's easy chair by the window. "There is Dio, mamma, who has naught to do but serve grandpapa," says he, and gives a pull at the cord over his head which rings the bell about the servants' ears in the hall below. And Dio, the whites of his eyes showing, comes running into the room.

"It is nothing, Diomedes," says Mr. Carvel. "Master Philip will fetch what I need." Master Philip's papa and mamma stare at each other in a surprise mingled with no little alarm, Master Philip being to all appearances intent upon his book.

"Philip," says my grandfather, gently. I had more than once heard him speak thus, and well knew what was coming. "Sir," replies my cousin, without looking up. "Follow me, sir," said Mr. Carvel, in a voice so different that Philip drops his book. They went up the stairs together, and what occurred there I leave to the imagination. But when next Philip was bidden to do an errand for Mr. Carvel my grandfather said quietly: "I prefer that Richard should go, Caroline." And though my aunt and uncle, much mortified, begged him to give Philip another chance, he would never permit it.

Nevertheless, a great effort was made to restore Philip to his grandfather's good graces. At breakfast one morning, after my aunt had poured Mr. Carvel's tea and made her customary compliment to the blue and gold breakfast china, my Uncle Grafton spoke up.

"Now that Dr. Hilliard is gone, father, what do you purpose concerning Richard's schooling?"

"He shall go to King William's school in the autumn," Mr. Carvel replied.

"In the autumn!" cried my uncle. "I do not give Philip even the short holiday of this visit. He has his Greek and his Virgil every day."

"And can repeat the best passages," my aunt chimes in. "Philip, my dear, recite that one your father so delights in."

However unwilling Master Philip had been to disturb himself for errands, he was nothing loth to show his knowledge, and recited glibly enough several lines of his Virgil verbatim; thereby pleasing his fond parents greatly and my grandfather not a little.

"I will add a crown to your savings, Philip," says his father.

"And here is a pistole to spend as you will," says Mr. Carvel, tossing him the piece.

"Nay, father, I do not encourage the lad to be a spendthrift," says Grafton, taking the pistole himself. "I will place this token of your appreciation in his strong-box. You know we have a prodigal strain in the family, sir." And my uncle looks at me significantly.

"Let it be as I say, Grafton," persists Mr. Carvel, who liked not to be balked in any matter, and was not overpleased at this reference to my father. And he gave Philip forthwith another pistole, telling his father to add the first to his saving if he would.

"And Richard must have his chance," says my Aunt Caroline, sweetly, as she rises to leave the room.

"Ay, here is a crown for you, Richard," says my uncle, smiling. "Let us hear your Latin, which should be purer than Philip's."

My grandfather glanced uneasily at me across the table; he saw clearly the trick Grafton had played me, I think. But for once I was equal to my uncle, and haply remembered a line Dr. Hilliard had expounded, which fitted the present case marvellously well. With little ceremony I tossed back the crown, and slowly repeated those words used to warn the Trojans against accepting the Grecian horse: —

"*Timeo Danaos et dona ferentes.*"

"Egad," cried Mr. Carvel, slapping his knee, "the lad hath beaten you on your own ground, Grafton." And he laughed as my grandfather only could laugh, until the dishes rattled on the table. But my uncle thought it no matter for jesting.

Philip was also well versed in politics for a lad of his age, and could discuss glibly the right of Parliament to tax the colonies. He denounced the seditious doings in Annapolis and Boston Town with an air of easy familiarity, for Philip had the memory of a parrot, and 'twas easy to perceive whence his knowledge sprang. But when my fine master spoke disparagingly of the tradesmen as at the bottom of the trouble, my grandfather's patience came to an end.

"And what think you lies beneath the wealth and power of England, Philip?" he asked.

"Her nobility, sir, and the riches she draws from her colonies," retorts Master Philip, readily enough.

"Not so," Mr. Carvel said gravely. "She owes her greatness to her merchants, or tradesmen, as you choose to call them. And commerce must be at the backbone of every great nation. Tradesmen!" exclaimed my grandfather. "Where would any of us be were it not for trade? We sell our tobacco and our wheat, and get money in return. And your father makes a deal here and a deal there, and so gets rich in spite of his pittance."

My Uncle Grafton raised his hand to protest, but Mr. Carvel continued: —

"I know you, Grafton, I know you. When a lad it was your habit to lay aside the money I gave you, and so pretend you had none."

"And 'twas well I learned then to be careful," said my uncle, losing for the instant his control, "for you loved the spendthrift best, and I should be but a beggar now without my wisdom."

"I loved not John's carelessness with money, but other qualities in him which you lacked," answered Mr. Carvel.

Grafton shot a swift glance at me; and so much of malice and of hatred was conveyed in that look that with a sense of prophecy I shuddered to think that some day I should have to cope with such craft. For he detested me threefold, and combined the hate he bore my dead father and mother with the ill-will he bore me for standing in his way and Philip's with my grandfather's property. But so deftly could he hide his feelings that he was smiling again instantly. To see once, however, the white belly of the shark flash on the surface of the blue water is sufficient.

"I beg of you not to jest of me before the lads, father," said Grafton.

"God knows there was little jest in what I said," replied Mr. Carvel, soberly, "and I care not who hears it. Your own son will one day know you well enough, if he does not now. Do not imagine, because I am old, that I am grown so foolish as to believe that a black sheep can become white save by dye. And dye will never deceive such as me. And Philip," the shrewd old gentleman went on, turning to my cousin, "do not let thy father or any other make thee believe there cannot be two sides to every question. I recognize in your arguments that which smacks of his tongue, despite what he says of your reading the public prints and of forming your own opinions. And do not condemn the Whigs, many of whom are worthy men and true, because they quarrel with what they deem an unjust method of taxation."

Grafton had given many of the old servants cause to remember him. Harvey in particular, who had come from England early in the century with my grandfather, spoke with bitterness of him. On the subject of my uncle, the old coachman's taciturnity gave way to torrents of reproach. "Beware of him as has no use for horses, Master Richard," he would say; for this trait in Grafton in Harvey's mind lay at the bottom of all others. At my uncle's approach he would retire into his shell like an oyster, nor could he be got to utter more than a monosyllable in his presence. Harvey's face would twitch, and his fingers clench of themselves as he touched his cap. And with my Aunt Caroline he was the same. He vouchsafed but a curt reply to all her questions, nor did her raptures over the stud soften him in the least. She would come tripping into the stable yard, daintily holding up her skirts, and crying, "Oh, Harvey, I have heard so much of Tanglefoot. I must see him before I go." Tanglefoot is led out begrudgingly enough, and Aunt Caroline goes over his points, missing the greater part of them, and remarking on the depth of chest, which is nothing notable in Tanglefoot. Harvey winks slyly at me the while, and never so much as offers a word of correction. "You must take Philip to ride, Richard, my dear," says my aunt. "His father was never as fond of it as I could have wished. I hold that every gentleman should ride to hounds."

"Humph!" grunts Harvey, when she is gone to the house, "Master Philip to hunt, indeed! Foxes to hunt foxes!" And he gives vent to a dry laugh over his joke, in which I cannot but join. "Horsemen grows. Eh, Master Richard? There was Captain Jack, who jumped from the cradle into the saddle, and I never once seen a horse get the better o' him. And that's God's truth." And he smooths out Tanglefoot's mane, adding reflectively, "And you be just like him. But there was scarce a horse in the stables what wouldn't lay back his ears at Mr. Grafton, and small blame to 'em, say I. He never dared go near 'em. Oh, Master Philip comes by it honestly enough. *She* thinks old Harvey don't know a thoroughbred when he sees one, sir. But Mrs. Grafton's no thoroughbred; I tell 'ee that, though I'm saying nothing as to her points, mark ye. I've seen her sort in the old country, and I've seen 'em here, and it's the same the world over, in Injy and Chiny, too. Fine trappings don't make the horse, and they don't take thoroughbreds from a grocer's cart. A Philadelphy grocer," sniffs this old aristocrat. "I'd knowed her father was a grocer had I seen her in Pall Mall with a Royal Highness, by her gait, I may say. Thy mother was a thoroughbred, Master Richard, and I'll tell 'ee another," he goes on with a chuckle, "Mistress Dorothy Manners is such another; you don't mistake 'em with their high heads and patreeshan ways, though her father be one of them accidents as will occur in every stock. She's one to tame, sir, and I don't envy no young gentleman the task. But this I knows," says Harvey, not heeding my red cheeks, "that Master Philip, with all his satin smallclothes, will never do it."

Indeed, it was no secret that my Aunt Caroline had been a Miss Flaven, of Philadelphia, though she would have had the fashion of our province to believe that she belonged to the Governor's set there; and she spoke in terms of easy familiarity of the first families of her native city, deceiving no one save herself, poor lady. How fondly do we believe, with the ostrich, that our body is hidden when our head is tucked under our wing! Not a visitor in Philadelphia but knew Terence Flaven, Mrs. Grafton Carvel's father, who not many years since sold tea and spices and soap and glazed teapots over his own counter, and still advertised his cargoes in the public prints. He was a broad and charitable-minded man enough, and unassuming, but gave way at last to the pressure brought upon him by his wife and daughter, and bought a mansion in Front Street. Terence Flaven never could be got to stay there save to sleep, and preferred to spend his time in his shop, which was grown greatly, chatting with his customers, and bowing the ladies to their chariots. I need hardly say that this worthy man was on far better terms than his family with those personages whose society they strove so hard to attain.

At the time of Miss Flaven's marriage to my uncle 'twas a piece of gossip in every mouth that he had taken her for her dower, which was not inconsiderable; though to hear Mr. and Mrs. Grafton talk they knew not whence the next month's provender was to come. They went to live in Kent County, as I have said, spending some winters in Philadelphia, where Mr. Grafton was thought to have interests, though it never could be discovered what his investments were. On hearing of his marriage, which took place shortly before my father's, Mr. Carvel expressed neither displeasure nor surprise. But he would not hear of my mother's request to settle a portion upon his younger son.

"He has the Kent estate, Bess," said he, "which is by far too good for him. Never doubt but that the rogue can feather his own nest far better than can I, as indeed he hath already done. And by the Lord," cried **Mr**. Carvel, bringing his fist down upon the card-table where they sat, "he shall **never** get another farthing of my money while I live, **nor** afterwards, if I can help it! I would rather give it over **to Mr**. Carroll to found **a** nunnery."

And so that matter ended, for Mr. Carvel could not be moved from **a** purpose he had once made. **Nor** would he make **any** advances whatsoever to Grafton, or receive **those** hints which my uncle was forever dropping, **until at** length he begged **to** be allowed to come to Dr. Hilliard's funeral, a request my grandfather could **not** in decency refuse. 'Twas a pathetic letter in truth, and served **its** purpose well, though **it was** not as dust in the old gentleman's eyes. He called **me into his** bedroom and told **me that** my Uncle Grafton **was coming at** last. And seeing that I said nothing thereto, he gave me a queer look and bade **me** treat them **as** civilly **as** I knew **how**. "I well **know** thy **temper**, Richard," said he, "and I **fear** 'twill bring thee trouble enough in life. Try **to** control **it**, my lad; take an old man's advice and try to control it." **He** was in one of his gentler **moods**, and passed his arm about me, and together we stood **looking** silently through the square panes out into the rain, at the ducks paddling in the puddles until the darkness hid them.

And God knows, lad that I was, I tried to be civil to them. But my tongue rebelled at the very sight **of** my uncle ('twas bred into me, I suppose), and his fairest words seemed **to me** to contain a hidden sting. Once, when he spoke in his innuendo of my father, **I ran** from the room to restrain some **act** of violence; I know not what I should **have done**. And Willis found **me** in the **deserted** study of the doctor, where my hot tears had stained the flowered paper on the wall. She did her best **to calm me**, good **soul**, though **she** had her own troubles with my Lady Caroline to think about at the time.

I had one experience with Master Philip **before** our visitors betook themselves back **to** Kent, **which**, unfortunate as **it was**, I cannot but relate here. My cousin would enter into none of those rough amusements **in** which **I** passed my time, for fear, **I took it, of** spoiling his fine broadcloths or **of** losing a gold buckle. He never could be got to wrestle, though I challenged him more than once. And he was a well-built lad, and might, with a little practice, have become skilled in that sport. He laughed at the homespun I wore about the farm, saying it was no costume for a gentleman's son, and begged me sneeringly to don leather breeches. He would have none of the company of those lads with whom I found pleasure, young Harvey, and Willis's son, who was being trained as Mr. Starkie's assistant. Nor indeed did I disdain to join in a game with Hugo, who had been given to me, and other negro lads. Philip saw no sport in a wrestle or a fight between two of the boys from the quarters, and marvelled that I could lower myself to bet with Harvey the younger. He took not a spark of interest in the gaming cocks we raised together to compete at the local contests and at the fair, and knew not a gaff from a cockspur. Being one day at my wits' end to amuse my cousin, I proposed to him a game of quoits on the green beside the spring-house, and thither we repaired, followed by Hugo, and young Harvey come to look on. Master Philip, not casting as well as he might, cries out suddenly to Hugo:—

"Begone, you black dog! What business have you here watching a game between gentlemen?"

"He is my servant, cousin," I said quietly, "and no dog, if you please. And he is under my orders, not yours."

But Philip, having scarcely scored a point, was in a rage. "And I'll not have him here," he shouted, giving poor Hugo a cuff which sent him stumbling over the stake. And turning to me, continued insolently: "Ever since we came here I have marked your manner toward us, as though my father had no right in my grandfather's house."

Then could I no longer contain myself. I heard young Harvey laugh, and remark: "'Tis all up with Master Philip now." But Philip, whatever else he may have been, was no coward, and had squared off to face me by the time I had run the distance between the stakes. He was heavier than I, though not so tall; and he parried my first blow and my second, and many more; having lively work of it, however, for I hit him as often as I was able. To speak truth, I had not looked for such resistance, and seeing that I could not knock him down, out of hand, I grew more cool and began to study what I was doing.

"Take off your macaroni coat," said I. "I have no wish to ruin your clothes."

But he only jeered in return: "Take off thy wool-sack." And Hugo, getting to his feet, cried out to me not to hurt Marse Philip, that he had meant no harm. But this only enraged Philip the more, and he swore a round oath at Hugo and another at me, and dealt a vicious blow at my stomach, whereat Harvey called out to him to fight fair. He was more skilful at the science of boxing than I, though I was the better *fighter*, having, I am sorry to say, fought but too often before. And presently, when I had closed one of his eyes, his skill went all to pieces, and he made a mad rush at me. As he went by I struck him so hard that he fell heavily and lay motionless.

Young Harvey ran into the spring-house and filled his hat as I bent over my cousin. I unbuttoned his waistcoat and felt his heart, and rejoiced to find it beating; we poured cold water over his face and wrists. By then, Hugo, who was badly frightened, had told the news in the house, and I saw my Aunt Caroline come running over the green as fast as her tight stays would permit, crying out that I had killed her boy, her dear Philip. And after her came my Uncle Grafton and my grandfather, with all the servants who had been in hearing. I was near to crying myself at the thought that I should grieve my grandfather. And my aunt, as she knelt over Philip, pushed me away, and bade me not touch him. But my cousin opened one of his eyes, and raised his hand to his head.

"Thank Heaven he is not killed!" exclaims Aunt Caroline, fervently.

"Thank God, indeed!" echoes my uncle, and gives me a look as much as to say that I am not to be thanked for it. "I have often warned you, sir," he says to Mr. Carvel, "that we do not inherit from stocks and stones. And so much has come of our charity."

I knew, lad that I was, that he spoke of my mother; and my blood boiled within me.

"Have a care, sir, with your veiled insults," I cried, "or I will serve you as I have served your son."

Grafton threw up his hands.

"What have we harboured, father?" says he. But Mr. Carvel seized him by the shoulder. "Peace, Grafton, before the servants," he said, "and cease thy crying, Caroline. The lad is not hurt." And being a tall man, six feet in his stockings, and strong despite his age, he raised Philip from the grass, and sternly bade him walk to the house, which he did, leaning on his mother's arm. "As for you, Richard," my grandfather went on, "you will go into my study."

Into his study I went, where presently he came also, and I told him the affair in as few words as I might. And he, knowing my hatred of falsehood, questioned me not at all, but paced to and fro, I following him with my eyes, and truly sorry that I had given him pain. And finally he dismissed me, bidding me make it up with my cousin, which I was nothing loth to do. What he said to Philip and his father I know not. That evening we shook hands, though Philip's face was much swollen, and my uncle smiled, and was even pleasanter than before, saying that boys would be boys. But I think my Aunt Caroline could never wholly hide the malice she bore me for what I had done that day.

When at last the visitors were gone, every face on the plantation wore a brighter look. Harvey said: "God bless their backs, which is the only part I ever care to see of their honours." And Willis gave us a supper fit for a king. Mr. Lloyd and his lady were with us, and Mr. Carvel told his old stories of the time of the First George, many of which I can even now repeat: how he and two other collegians fought half a dozen Mohocks in Norfolk Street, and fairly beat them; and how he discovered by chance a Jacobite refugee in Greenwich, and what came of it; nor did he forget that oft-told episode with Dean Swift. And these he rehearsed in such merry spirit and new guise that we scarce recognized them, and Colonel Lloyd so choked with laughter that more than once he had to be hit between the shoulders.

CHAPTER V

"IF LADIES BE BUT YOUNG AND FAIR"

No boyhood could have been happier than mine, and throughout it, ever present with me, were a shadow and a light. The shadow was my Uncle Grafton. I know not what strange intuition of the child made me think of him so constantly after that visit he paid us, but often I would wake from my sleep with his name upon my lips, and a dread at my heart. The light — need I say? — was Miss Dorothy Manners. Little Miss Dolly was often at the Hall after that happy week we spent together; and her home, Wilmot House, was scarce three miles across wood and field by our plantation roads. I was a stout little fellow enough, and before I was twelve I had learned to follow to hounds my grandfather's guests on my pony; and Mr. Lloyd and Mr. Carvel when they shot on the duck points. Ay, and what may surprise you, my dears, I was given a weak little toddy off the noggin at night, while the gentlemen stretched their limbs before the fire, or played at whist or loo. Mr. Carvel would have no milksop, so he said. But he early impressed upon me that moderation was the mark of a true man, even as excess was that of a weak one.

And so it was no wonder that I frequently found my way to Wilmot House alone. There I often stayed the whole day long, romping with Dolly at games of our own invention, and many the time I was sent home after dark by Mrs. Manners with Jim, the groom. About once in the week Mr. and Mrs. Manners would bring Dorothy over for dinner or tea at the Hall. She grew quickly — so quickly that I scarce realized — into a tall slip of a girl, who could be wilful and cruel, laughing or forgiving, shy or impudent, in a breath. She had

as many moods as the sea. I have heard her entertain Mr.
Lloyd and Mr. Bordley and the ladies, and my grandfather, by
the hour, while I sat by silent and miserable, but proud of her
all the same. Boylike, I had grown to think of her as my possession, tho' she gave me no reason whatever. I believe I had
held my hand over fire for her, at a word. And, indeed, I did
many of her biddings to make me wonder, now, that I was not
killed. It used to please her, Ivie too, to see me go the round
of the windmill, tho' she would cry out after I left the ground.
And once, when it was turning faster than common and Ivie not
there to prevent, I near lost my hold at the top, and was thrown
at the bottom with such force that I lay stunned for a full
minute. I opened my eyes to find her bending over me with
such a look of fright and remorse upon her face as I shall never
forget. Again, walking out on the bowsprit of the *Oriole* while
she stood watching me from the dock, I lost my balance and
fell into the water. On another occasion I fought Will Fotheringay, whose parents had come for a visit, because he dared
say he would marry her.

"She is to marry an earl," I cried, tho' I had thrashed
another lad for saying so. "Mr. Manners is to take her home
when she is grown, to marry her to an earl."

"At least she will not marry you, Master Richard," sneered
Will. And then I hit him.

Indeed, even at that early day the girl's beauty was enough
to make her talked about. And that foolish little fop, her
father, had more than once declared before a company in our
dining room that it was high time another title came into his
family, and that he meant to take Dolly abroad when she was
sixteen. Lad that I was, I would mark with pain the blush
on Mrs. Manners's cheek, and clinch my fists as she tried to
pass this off as a joke of her husband's. But Dolly, who sat
next me at a side table, would make a wry little face at my
angry one.

"You shall call me 'my lady,' Richard. And sometimes, if
you are good, you shall ride inside my coroneted coach when
you come home."

Ah, that was the worst of it! The vixen was conscious of

her beauty. But her airs were so natural that young and old bowed before her. Nothing but worship had she had from the cradle. I would that Mr. Peale had painted her in her girlhood as a type of our Maryland lady of quality. Harvey was right when he called her a thoroughbred. Her nose was of patrician straightness, and the curves of her mouth came from generations of proud ancestors. And she had blue eyes to conquer and subdue, with long lashes to hide them under when she chose, and black hair with blue gloss upon it in the slanting lights. I believe I loved her best in the riding-habit that was the colour of the red holly in our Maryland woods. At Christmas-tide, when we came to the eastern shore, we would gallop together through miles of country, the farmers and servants tipping and staring after her as she laid her silver-handled whip upon her pony. She knew not the meaning of fear, and would take a fence or a ditch that a man might pause at. And so I fell into the habit of leading her the easy way round, for dread that she would be hurt.

How those Christmas times of childhood come sweeping back on my memory! Often, and without warning, my grandfather would say to me: "Richard, we shall celebrate at the Hall this year." And it rarely turned out that arrangements had not been made with the Lloyds and the Bordleys and the Manners, and other neighbours, to go to the country for the holidays. I have no occasion in these pages to mention my intimacy with the sons and daughters of those good friends of the Carvels', Colonel Lloyd and Mr. Bordley. Some of them are dead now, and the rest can thank God and look back upon worthy and useful lives. And if any of these, my old playmates, could read this manuscript, perchance they might feel a tingle of recollection of Children's Day, when Maryland was a province. We rarely had snow; sometimes a crust upon the ground that was melted into paste by the noonday sun, but more frequently, so it seems to me, a foggy, drizzly Christmas, with the fires crackling in saloon and lady's chamber. And when my grandfather and the ladies and gentlemen, his guests, came down the curving stairs, there were the broadly smiling servants drawn up in the wide hall, — all who could gather there,—and the rest on the lawn outside, to wish "Merry Chris'mas" to "de quality." The redemptioners in front, headed by Ivie and Jonas Tree, tho' they had long served their terms, and with them old Harvey and his son; next the house blacks and the outside liveries, and then the oldest slaves from the quarters. This line reached the door, which Scipio would throw open at "de quality's" appearance, disclosing the rest of the field servants, in bright-coloured gowns, and the little negroes on the green. Then Mr. Carvel would make them a little speech of thanks and of good-will, and white-haired Johnson of the senior quarters, who had been with my great-grandfather, would start the carol in a quaver. How clear and sweet the melody of those negro voices comes back to me through the generations! And the picture of the hall, loaded with holly and mistletoe even to the great arch that spanned it, with the generous bowls of egg-nog and punch on the mahogany by the wall! And the ladies our guests, in cap and apron, joining in the swelling hymn; ay, and the men, too. And then, after the breakfast of sweet ham and venison, and hot bread and sausage, made under Mrs. Willis, and tea and coffee and chocolate steaming in the silver, and ale for the gentlemen if they preferred, came the prayers and more carols in the big drawing-room. And then music in the big house, or perhaps a ride afield to greet the neighbours, and fiddling and dancing in the two big quarters, Hank's and Johnson's, when the tables were cleared after the bountiful feast Mr. Carvel was wont to give them. There was no stint, my dears,—naught but good cheer and praising God in sheer happiness at Carvel Hall.

At night there was always a ball, sometimes at Wilmot House, sometimes at Colonel Lloyd's or Mr. Bordley's, and sometimes at Carvel Hall, for my grandfather dearly loved the company of the young. He himself would lead off the minuet,—save when once or twice his Excellency Governor Sharpe chanced to be present,—and would draw his sword with the young gallants that the ladies might pass under. And I have seen him join merrily in the country dances too, to the clapping of hands of the company. That was before

"IF LADIES BE BUT YOUNG AND FAIR" 45

Dolly and I were let upon the floor. We sat with the other children, our mammies at our sides, in the narrow gallery with the tiny rail that ran around the ball-room, where the sweet odour of the green myrtleberry candles mixed with that of the powder and perfume of the dancers. And when the beauty of the evening was led out, Dolly would lean over the rail, and pout and smile by turns. The mischievous little baggage could hardly wait for the conquering years to come.

They came soon enough, alack! The season Dorothy was fourteen, we had a ball at the Hall the last day of the year. When she was that age she had near arrived at her growth, and was full as tall as many young ladies of twenty. I had cantered with her that morning from Wilmot House to Mr. Lloyd's, and thence to Carvel Hall, where she was to stay to dinner. The sun was shining warmly, and after young Harvey had taken our horses we strayed through the house, where the servants were busy decorating, and out into my grandfather's old English flower garden, and took the seat by the sundial. I remember that it gave no shadow. We sat silent for a while, Dorothy toying with old Knipe, lying at our feet, and humming gayly the burden of a minuet. She had been flighty on the ride, with scarce a word to say to me, for the prospect of the dance had gone to her head.

"Have you a new suit to wear to-night, to see the New Year in, Master Sober?" she asked presently, looking up. "I am to wear a brocade that came out this autumn from London, and papa says I look like a duchess when I have my grandmother's pearls."

"Always the ball!" cried I, slapping my boots in a temper. "Is it, then, such a matter of importance? I am sure you have danced before — at my birthdays in Marlboro' Street and at your own, and Will Fotheringay's, and I know not how many others."

"Of course," replies Dolly, sweetly; "but never with a real man. Boys like you and Will and the Lloyds do not count. Dr. Courtenay is at Wilmot House, and is coming to-night; and he has asked me out. Think of it, Richard! Dr. Courtenay!"

"A plague upon him! He is a fop!"

"A fop!" exclaimed Dolly, her humour bettering as mine went down. "Oh, no; you are jealous. He is more sought after than any gentleman at the assemblies, and Miss Dulany vows his steps are ravishing. There's for you, my lad! He may not be able to keep pace with you in the chase, but he has writ the most delicate verses ever printed in Maryland, and no other man in the colony can turn a compliment with his grace. Shall I tell you more? He sat with me for over an hour last night, until mamma sent me off to bed, and was very angry at you because I had engaged to ride with you to-day."

"And I suppose you wish you had stayed with him," I flung back, hotly. "He had spun you a score of fine speeches and a hundred empty compliments by now."

"He had been better company than you, sir," she laughed provokingly. "I never heard you turn a compliment in your life, and you are now seventeen. What headway do you expect to make at the assemblies?"

"None," I answered, rather sadly than otherwise. For she had touched me upon a sore spot. "But if I cannot win a woman save by compliments," I added, flaring up, "then may I pay a bachelor's tax!"

My lady drew her whip across my knee.

"You must tell us we are beautiful, Richard," said she, in another tone.

"You have but to look in a pier-glass," I retorted. "And, besides, that is not sufficient. You will want some rhyming couplet out of a mythology before you are content."

She laughed again.

"Sir," answered she, "but you have wit, if you can but be got angry."

She leaned over the dial's face, and began to draw the Latin numerals with her finger. So arch, withal, that I forgot my ill-humour.

"If you would but agree to stay angry for a day," she went on, in a low tone, "perhaps —"

"Perhaps?"

"Perhaps you would be better company," said Dorothy. "You would surely be more entertaining."

"Dorothy, I love you," I said.

"To be sure. I know that," she replied. "I think you have said that before."

I admitted it sadly. "But I should be a better husband than Dr. Courtenay."

"La!" cried she; "I am not thinking of husbands. I shall have a good time, sir, I promise you, before I marry. And then I should never marry you. You are much too rough, and too masterful. And you would require obedience. I shall never obey any man. You would be too strict a master, sir. I can see it with your dogs and your servants. And your friends, too. For you thrash any boy who does not agree with you. I want no rough squire for a husband. And then, you are a Whig. I could never marry a Whig. You behaved disgracefully at King William's School last year. Don't deny it!"

"Deny it!" I cried warmly; "I would as soon deny that you are an arrant flirt, Dorothy Manners, and will be a worse one."

"Yes, I shall have my fling," said the minx. "I shall begin to-night, with you for an audience. I shall make the doctor look to himself. But there is the dressing-bell." And as we went into the house, "I believe my mother is a Whig, Richard. All the Brices are."

"And yet you are a Tory?"

"I am a loyalist," says my lady, tossing her head proudly; "and we are one day to kiss her Majesty's hand, and tell her so. And if I were the Queen," she finished in a flash, "I would teach you surly gentlemen not to meddle."

And she swept up the stairs so stately, that Scipio was moved to say slyly: "Dem's de kind of ladies, Marse Richard, I jes dotes t' wait on!"

Of the affair at King William's School I shall tell later.

We had some dozen guests staying at the Hall for the ball. At dinner my grandfather and the gentlemen twitted her, and laughed heartily at her apt retorts, and even toasted her when she was gone. The ladies shook their heads and nudged one another, and no doubt each of the mothers had her notion of what she would do in Mrs. Manners's place. But when my lady came down dressed for the ball in her pink brocade with the pearls around her neck, fresh from the hands of Hester and those of her own tremulous mammy, Mr. Carvel must needs go up to her and hold her at arm's length in admiration, and then kiss her on both her cheeks. Whereat she blushed right prettily.

"Bless me!" says he; "and can this be Richard's little playmate grown? Upon my word, Miss Dolly, you'll be the belle of the ball. Eh, Lloyd? Bless me, bless me, you must not mind a kiss from an old man. The young ones may have their turn after a while." He laughed as my grandfather only could laugh, and turned to me, who had reddened to my forehead. "And so, Richard, she has outstripped you, fair and square. You are only an awkward lad, and she — why, i' faith, in two years she'll be beyond my protection. Come, Miss Dolly," says he; "I'll show you the mistletoe, that you may beware of it."

And he led her off on his arm. "The old year and the new, gentlemen!" he cried merrily, as he passed the door, with Dolly's mammy and Hester simpering with pride on the landing.

The company arrived in coach and saddle, many having come so far that they were to stay the night. Young Mr. Beall carried his bride on a pillion behind him, her red riding-cloak flung over her ball dress. Mr. Bordley and family came in his barge, Mr. Marmaduke and his wife in coach and four. With them was Dr. Courtenay, arrayed in peach-coloured coat and waistcoat, with black satin breeches and white silk stockings, and pinchbeck buckles asparkle on his shoes. How I envied him as he descended the stairs, stroking his ruffles and greeting the company with the indifferent ease that was then the fashion. I fancied I saw his eyes wander among the ladies, and not marking her he crossed over to where I stood disconsolate before the fireplace.

"Why, Richard, my lad," says he, "you are quite grown

since I saw you. And the little girl that was your playmate, — Miss Dolly, I mean, — has outstripped me, egad. She has become suddenly *une belle demoiselle*, like a rose that blooms in a night."

I answered nothing at all. But I had given much to know whether my stolid manner disconcerted him. Unconsciously I sought the bluff face above the chimney, depicted in all its ruggedness by the painter of King Charles's day, and contrasted with the bundle of finery at my side. Dr. Courtenay certainly caught the look. He opened his snuff-box, took a pinch, turned on his heel, and sauntered off.

"What did you say, Richard?" asked Mr. Lloyd, coming up to me, laughing, for he had seen the incident.

"I looked merely at the man of Marston Moor, sir, and said nothing."

"Faith, 'twas a better answer than if you had used your tongue, I think," answered my friend. But he teased me a deal that night when Dolly danced with the doctor, and my grandfather bade me look to my honours. My young lady flung her head higher than ever, and made a minuet as well as any dame upon the floor, while I stood very glum at the thought of the prize slipping from my grasp. Now and then, in the midst of a figure, she would shoot me an arch glance, as much as to say that her pinions were strong now. But when it came to the country dances my lady comes up to me ever so prettily and asks the favour.

"'Tis a monstrous state, indeed, when I have to beg you for a reel!" says she.

And so was I made happy.

E

CHAPTER VI

I FIRST SUFFER FOR THE CAUSE

In the eighteenth century the march of public events was much more eagerly followed than now by men and women of all stations, and even children. Each citizen was ready, nay, forward, in taking an active part in all political movements, and the children mimicked their elders. Old William Farris read his news of a morning before he began the mending of his watches, and by evening had so well digested them that he was primed for discussion with Pryse, of the opposite persuasion, at the Rose and Crown. Sol Mogg, the sexton of St. Anne's, had his beloved *Gazette* in his pocket as he tolled the church bell of a Thursday, and would hold forth on the rights and liberties of man with the carpenter who mended the steeple. Mrs. Willard could talk of Grenville and Townshend as knowingly as her husband, the rich factor, and Francie Willard made many a speech to us younger Sons of Liberty on the steps of King William's School. We younger sons, indeed, declared bitter war against the mother-country long before our conservative old province ever dreamed of secession. For Maryland was well pleased with his Lordship's government.

I fear that I got at King William's School learning of a far different sort than pleased my grandfather. In those days the school stood upon the Stadt House hill near School Street, not having moved to its present larger quarters. Mr. Isaac Daaken was then Master, and had under him some eighty scholars. After all these years, Mr. Daaken stands before me a prominent figure of the past in an ill-fitting suit of snuff colour. How well I recall that schoolroom of a bright morning, the sun's rays shot hither and thither, and split violet, green, and red by the bulging glass panes of the windows. And by a strange irony it so chanced that where the dominie sat — and he moved not the whole morning long save to reach for his birches — the crimson ray would often rest on the end of his long nose, and the word "rum" be passed tittering along the benches. For some men are born to the mill, and others to the mitre, and still others to the sceptre; but Mr. Daaken was born to the birch. His long, lanky legs were made for striding after culprits, and his arms for caning them. He taught, among other things, the classics, of course, the English language grammatically, arithmetic in all its branches, book-keeping in the Italian manner, and the elements of algebra, geometry, and trigonometry with their applications to surveying and navigation. He also wrote various sorts of hands, fearful and marvellous to the uninitiated, with which he was wont to decorate my monthly reports to my grandfather. I can shut my eyes and see now that wonderful hyperbola in the C in Carvel, which, after travelling around the paper, ended in intricate curves and a flourish which surely must have broken the quill. The last day of every month would I fetch that scrolled note to Mr. Carvel, and he laid it beside his plate until dinner was over. And then, as sure as the sun rose that morning, my flogging would come before it set. This done with, and another promised next month provided Mr. Daaken wrote no better of me, my grandfather and I renewed our customary footing of love and companionship.

But Mr. Daaken, unwittingly or designedly, taught other things than those I have mentioned above. And though I never once heard a word of politics fall from his lips, his school shortly became known to all good Tories as a nursery of conspiracy and sedition. There are other ways of teaching besides preaching, and of that which the dominie taught best he spoke not a word. He was credited, you may well believe, with calumnies against King George, and once my Uncle Grafton and Mr. Dulany were for clapping him in jail, avowing that he taught treason to the young. I can account for the tone of King William's School in no other way than to say that patriotism was in the very atmosphere, and seemed to exude in some mysterious way from Mr. Daaken's person. And most of us became infected with it.

The dominie lived outside the town, in a lonely little hamlet on the borders of the Spa. At two of the clock every afternoon he would drive through School Street to the Coffee House, where the hostler would have his bony mare saddled and waiting. Mr. Daaken by no chance ever entered the tavern. I recall one bright day in April when I played truant and had the temerity to go afishing on Spa Creek with Will Fotheringay, the bass being plentiful there. We had royal sport of it that morning, and two o'clock came and went with never a thought, you may be sure. And presently I get a pull which bends my English rod near to double, and in my excitement plunge waist deep into the water, Will crying out directions from the shore, when suddenly the head of Mr. Daaken's mare is thrust through the bushes, followed by Mr. Daaken himself. Will stood stock still from fright, and I was for dropping my rod and cutting, when I was arrested by the dominie calling out:—

"Have a care, Master Carvel; have a care, sir. You will lose him. Play him, sir; let him run a bit."

And down he leaps from his horse and into the water after me, and together we landed a three-pound bass, thereby drenching his snuff-coloured suit. When the big fish lay shining in the basket, the dominie smiled grimly at William and me as we stood sheepishly by, and without a word he drew his clasp knife and cut a stout switch from the willow near, and then and there he gave us such a thrashing as we remembered for many a day after. And we both had another when we reached home.

"Mr. Carvel," said Mr. Dulany to my grandfather, "I would strongly counsel you to take Richard from that school. Pernicious doctrines, sir, are in the air, and like diseases are early caught by the young. 'Twas but yesterday I saw Richard at the head of a rabble of the sons of riff-raff, in Green Street, and their treatment of Mr. Fairbrother hath set the whole town by the ears."

I FIRST SUFFER FOR THE CAUSE

What Mr. Dulany had said was true. The lads of Mr. Fairbrother's school being mostly of the unpopular party, we of King William's had organized our cohorts and led them on to a signal victory. We fell upon the enemy even as they were emerging from their stronghold, the schoolhouse, and smote them hip and thigh, with the sheriff of Anne Arundel County a laughing spectator. Some of the Tories (for such we were pleased to call them) took refuge behind Mr. Fairbrother's skirts, who shook his cane angrily enough, but without avail. Others of the Tory brood fought stoutly, calling out: "God save the King!" and "Down with the traitors!" On our side Francie Willard fell, and Archie Jennison raised a lump on my head the size of a goose egg. But we fairly beat them, and afterwards must needs attack the Tory dominie himself. He cried out lustily to the sheriff and spectators, of whom there were many by this time, for help, but got little but laughter for his effort. Young Lloyd and I, being large lads for our age, fairly pinioned the screeching master, who cried out that he was being murdered, and keeping his cane for a trophy, thrust him bodily into his house of learning, turned the great key upon him, and so left him. He made his escape by a window and sought my grandfather in the Duke of Marlboro' Street as fast as ever his indignant legs would carry him.

Of his interview with Mr. Carvel I know nothing save that Scipio was requested presently to show him the door, and conclude therefrom that his language was but ill-chosen. Scipio's patrician blood was wont to rise in the presence of those whom he deemed outside the pale of good society, and I fear he ushered Mr. Fairbrother to the street with little of that superior manner he used to the first families. As for Mr. Daaken, I feel sure he was not ill-pleased at the discomfiture of his rival, though it cost him five of his scholars.

Our schoolboy battle, though lightly undertaken, was fraught with no inconsiderable consequences for me. I was duly chided and soundly whipped by my grandfather for the part I had played; but he was inclined to pass the matter after that, and set it down to the desire for fighting common to most boyish natures. And he would have gone no farther than this had it not been that Mr. Green, of the Maryland *Gazette*, could not refrain from printing the story in his paper. That gentleman, being a stout Whig, took great delight in pointing out that a grandson of Mr. Carvel was a ringleader in the affair. The story was indeed laughable enough, and many a barrister's wig nodded over it at the Coffee House that day. When I came home from school I found Scipio beside my grandfather's empty seat in the dining-room, and I learned that Mr. Carvel was in the garden with my Uncle Grafton and the Reverend Bennett Allen, rector of St. Anne's. I well knew that something out of the common was in the wind to disturb my grandfather's dinner. Into the garden I went, and under the black walnut tree I beheld Mr. Carvel pacing up and down in great unrest, his *Gazette* in his hand, while on the bench sat my uncle and the rector of St. Anne's. So occupied was each in his own thought that my coming was unperceived; and I paused in my steps, seized suddenly by an instinctive dread, I know not of what. The fear of Mr. Carvel's displeasure passed from my mind so that I cared not how soundly he thrashed me, and my heart filled with a yearning, born of the instant, for that simple and brave old gentleman. For the lad is nearer to nature than the man, and the animal oft scents a danger the master cannot see. I read plainly in Mr. Allen's handsome face, flushed red with wine as it ever was, and in my Uncle Grafton's looks a snare to which I knew my grandfather was blind. I never rightly understood how it was that Mr. Carvel was deceived in Mr. Allen; perchance the secret lay in his bold manner and in the appearance of dignity and piety he wore as a cloak when on his guard. I caught my breath sharply and took my way toward them, resolved to make as brave a front as I might. It was my uncle, whose ear was ever open, that first heard my footstep and turned upon me.

"Here is Richard, now, father," he said.

I gave him so square a look that he bent his head to the ground. My grandfather stopped in his pacing and his eye rested upon me, in sorrow rather than in anger, I thought.

I FIRST SUFFER FOR THE CAUSE

"Richard," he began, and paused. For the first time in my life I saw him irresolute. He looked appealingly at the rector, who rose. Mr. Allen was a man of good height and broad shoulders, with piercing black eyes, reminding one more of the smallsword than aught else I can think of. And he spoke solemnly, in a deep voice, as though from the pulpit.

"I fear it is my duty, Richard, to say what Mr. Carvel cannot. It grieves me to tell you, sir, that young as you are you have been guilty of treason against the King, and of grave offence against his Lordship's government. I cannot mitigate my words, sir. By your rashness, Richard, and I pray it is such, you have brought grief to your grandfather in his age, and ridicule and reproach upon a family whose loyalty has hitherto been unstained."

I scarce waited for him to finish. His pompous words stung me like the lash of a whip, and I gave no heed to his cloth as I answered: —

"If I have grieved my grandfather, sir, I am heartily sorry, and will answer to him for what I have done. And I would have you know, Mr. Allen, that I am as able as any to care for the Carvel honour."

I spoke with a vehemence, for the thought carried me beyond myself, that this upstart parson his Lordship had but a year since sent among us should question our family reputation.

"Remember that Mr. Allen is of the Church, Richard," said my grandfather, severely.

"I fear he has little respect for Church or State, sir," Grafton put in. "You are now reaping the fruits of your indulgence."

I turned to my grandfather.

"You are my protector, sir," I cried. "And if it please you to tell me what I now stand accused of, I submit most dutifully to your chastisement."

"Very fair words, indeed, nephew Richard," said my uncle, "and I draw from them that you have yet to hear of your beating an honest schoolmaster without other provocation than that he was a loyal servant to the King, and wantonly injuring the children of his school." He drew from his pocket a copy of that *Gazette* Mr. Carvel held in his hand, and added ironically: "Here, then, are news which will doubtless surprise you, sir. And knowing you for a peaceful lad, never having entertained such heresies as those with which it pleases Mr. Green to credit you, I dare swear he has drawn on his imagination."

I took the paper in amaze, not knowing why my grandfather, who had ever been so jealous of others taking me to task, should permit the rector and my uncle to chide me in his presence. The account was in the main true enough, and made sad sport of Mr. Fairbrother.

"Have I not been caned for this, sir?" said I to my grandfather.

These words seemed to touch Mr. Carvel, and I saw a tear glisten in his eye as he answered:—

"You have, Richard, and stoutly. But your uncle and Mr. Allen seem to think that your offence warrants more than a caning, and to deem that you have been actuated by bad principles rather than by boyish spirits." He paused to steady his voice, and I realized then for the first time how sacred he held allegiance to the King. "Tell me, my lad," said he, "tell me, as you love God and the truth, whether they are right."

For the moment I shrank from speaking, perceiving what a sad blow to Mr. Carvel my words must be. And then I spoke up boldly, catching the exulting sneer on my Uncle Grafton's face and the note of triumph reflected in Mr. Allen's.

"I have never deceived you, sir," I said, "and will not now hide from you that I believe the colonies to have a just cause against his Majesty and Parliament." The words came ready to my lips: "We are none the less Englishmen because we claim the rights of Englishmen, and, saving your presence, sir, are as loyal as those who do not. And if these principles be bad," I added to my uncle, "then should we think with shame upon the Magna Charta."

My grandfather stood astonished at such a speech from me, whom he had thought a lad yet without a formed knowledge of public affairs. But I was, in fact, supersaturated with that of which I spoke, and could have given my hearers many able

I FIRST SUFFER FOR THE CAUSE

Whig arguments to surprise them had the season befitted. There was silence for a space after I had finished, and then Mr. Carvel sank right heavily upon the bench.

"A Carvel against the King!" was all he said.

Had I been alone with him I should have cast myself at his feet, for it hurt me sorely to see him so. As it was, I held my head high.

"The Carvels ever did what they believed right, sir," I answered. "You would not have me to go against my conscience?"

To this he replied nothing.

"The evil has been done, as I feared, father," said Grafton, presently; "we must now seek for the remedy."

"Let me question the lad," Mr. Allen softly interposed. "Tell me, Richard, who has influenced you to this way of thinking?"

I saw his ruse, and was not to be duped by it.

"Men who have not feared to act bravely against oppression, sir," I said.

"Thank God," exclaimed my uncle, with fervour, "that I have been more careful of Philip's associations, and that he has not caught in the streets and taverns this noxious creed!"

"There is no danger from Philip; he remembers his family name," said the rector.

"No," quoth Mr. Carvel, bitterly, "there is no danger from Philip. Like his father, he will ever believe that which best serves him."

Grafton, needless to say, did not pursue such an argument, but rising, remarked that this deplorable affair had kept him long past his dinner hour, and that his services were as ever at his father's disposal. He refused to stay, though my grandfather pressed him of course, and with a low bow of filial respect and duty and a single glance at the rector, my uncle was gone. And then we walked slowly to the house and into the dining room, Mr. Carvel leading the procession, and I an unwilling rear, knowing that my fate would be decided between them. I thought Mr. Allen's grace would never end, and the meal likewise; I ate but little, while the two gentlemen discussed parish matters. And when at last Scipio had retired, and the rector of St. Anne's sat sipping the old Madeira, his countenance all gravity, but with a relish he could not hide, my grandfather spoke up. And though he addressed himself to the guest, I knew full well what he said was meant for me.

"As you see, sir," said he, "I am sore perplexed and troubled. We Carvels, Mr. Allen, have ever been stanch to Church and King. My great-grandsire fought at Naseby and Marston Moor for Charles, and suffered exile in his name. 'Twas love for King James that sent my father hither, though he swore allegiance to Anne and the First George. I can say with pride that he was no indifferent servant to either, refusing honours from the Pretender in '15, when he chanced to be at home. An oath is an oath, sir, and we have yet to be false to ours. And the King, say I, should, next to God, be loved and loyally served by his subjects. And so I have served this George, and his grandfather before him, according to the talents which were given me."

"And ably, sir, permit me to say," echoed the rector, heartily. Too heartily, methought. And he carefully filled his pipe with choice leaf out of Mr. Carvel's inlaid box.

"Be that as it may, I have done my best, as we must all do. Pardon me, sir, for speaking of myself. But I have brought up this lad from a child, Mr. Allen," said Mr. Carvel, his words coming slowly, as if each gave him pain, "and have striven to be an example to him in all things. He has few of those faults which I most fear; God be thanked that he loves the truth, for there is yet a chance of his correction. A chance, said I?" he cried, his speech coming more rapid, "nay, he *shall* be cured! I little thought, fool that I was, that he would get this pox. His father fought and died for the King; and should trouble come, which God forbid, to know that Richard stood against his Majesty would kill me."

"And well it might, Mr. Carvel," said the divine. He was for the moment sobered, as weak men must be in the presence of those of strong convictions. My grandfather had half risen in his chair, and the lines of his smooth-shaven face deepened visibly with the pain of the feelings to which he gave utterance. As for me, I was well-nigh swept away by a bigness within me, and torn between love and duty, between pity and the reason left me, and sadly tried to know whether my dear parent's life and happiness should be weighed against what I felt to be right. I strove to speak, but could say nothing.

"He must be removed from the influences," the rector ventured, after a halt.

"That he must indeed," said my grandfather. "Why did I not send him to Eton last fall? But it is hard, Mr. Allen, to part with the child of our old age. I would take passage and go myself with him to-morrow were it not for my duties in the Council."

Eton! I would have sooner, I believe, wrought by the side of any rascally redemptioner in the iron mines of the Patapsco than have gone to Eton.

"But for the present, sir, I would counsel you to put the lad's studies in the charge of some able and learned man, that his mind may be turned from the disease which has fed upon it. Some one whose loyalty is beyond question."

"And who so fit as yourself, Mr. Allen?" returned my grandfather, relief plain in his voice. "You have his Lordship's friendship and confidence, and never has rector of St. Anne's or of any other parish brought letters to his Excellency to compare with yours. And so I crave your help in this time of need."

Mr. Allen showed becoming hesitation.

"I fear you do me greater honour than I deserve, Mr. Carvel," he answered, a strain of the pomp coming back, "though my gracious patron is disposed to think well of me, and I shall strive to hold his good opinion. But I have duties of parish and glebe to attend, and Master Philip Carvel likewise in my charge."

I held my breath for my grandfather's reply. The rector, however, had read him, and well knew that a show of reluctance would but inflame him the more.

"How now, sir?" he exclaimed. "Surely, as you love the King, you will not refuse me in this strait."

Mr. Allen rose and grasped him by the hand.

"Nay, sir," said he, "and you put it thus, I cannot refuse you."

The thought of it was too much. I ran to my grandfather crying: "Not Mr. Allen, sir, not Mr. Allen. Any one else you please, — Mr. Fairbrother even."

The rector drew back haughtily. "It is clear, Mr. Carvel," he said, "that Richard has other preferences."

"And be damned to them!" shouted my grandfather. "Am I to be ruled by this headstrong boy? He has beat Mr. Fairbrother, and shall have no skimmed-milk supervision if I can help it."

And so it was settled that I should be tutored by the rector of St. Anne's, and I took my seat beside my cousin Philip in his study the very next day.

CHAPTER VII

GRAFTON HAS HIS CHANCE

To add to my troubles my grandfather was shortly taken very ill with the first severe sickness he had ever in his life endured. Dr. Leiden came and went sometimes thrice daily, and for a week he bore a look so grave as to frighten me. Dr. Evarts arrived by horse from Philadelphia, and the two physicians held long conversations in the morning room, while I listened at the door and comprehended not a word of their talk save when they spoke of bleeding. And after a very few consultations, as is often the way in their profession, they disagreed and quarrelled, and Dr. Evarts packed himself back to Philadelphia in high dudgeon. Then Mr. Carvel began to mend.

There were many who came regularly to inquire of him, and each afternoon I would see the broad shoulders and genial face of Governor Sharpe in the gateway, completing his walk by way of Marlboro' Street. I loved and admired him, for he had been a soldier himself before he came out to us, and had known and esteemed my father. His Excellency should surely have been knighted for his services in the French war. Once he spied me at the window and shook his cane pleasantly, and in he walks to the room where I sat reading of the victories of Blenheim and Malplaquet, for chronicles of this sort I delighted in.

"Aha, Richard," says he, taking up the book, "'tis plain whither your tastes lead you. Marlboro' was a great general, and as sorry a scoundrel as ever led troops to battle. Truly," says he, musing, "the Lord often makes queer choice in his instruments for good." And he lowered himself into the easy chair and crossed his legs, regarding me very comically. "What's this I hear of your joining the burghers and barristers, and trouncing poor Mr. Fairbrother and his flock, and crying 'Liberty forever!' in the very ears of the law?" he asks. "His Majesty will have need of such lads as you, I make no doubt, and should such proceedings come to his ears I would not give a pipe for your chances."

I could not but laugh, confused as I was, at his Excellency's rally. And this I may say, that had it pleased Providence to give me dealing with such men of the King's side as he, perchance my fortunes had been altered.

"And in any good cause, sir," I replied, "I would willingly give my life to his Majesty."

"So," said his Excellency, raising his eyebrows, "I see clearly you are of the rascals. But a lad must have his fancies, and when your age I was hot for the exiled Prince. I acquired more sense as I grew older. And better an active mind, say I, than a sluggard partisan."

At this stage of our talk came in my Uncle Grafton, and bowing low to the Governor made apology that some of the elders of the family had not been there to entertain him. He told his Excellency that he had never left the house save for necessary business, which was true for once, my uncle having taken up his abode with us during that week. But now, thanking Heaven and Dr. Leiden and his own poor effort, he could report his dear father to be out of danger.

Governor Sharpe answered shortly that he had been happy to hear the good news from Scipio. "Faith," says he, "I was well enough entertained, for I have a liking for this lad, and to speak truth I saw him here as I came up the walk."

My uncle smiled deprecatingly, and hid any vexation he might have had from this remark.

"I fear that Richard lacks wisdom as yet, your Excellency," said he, "and has many of his father's headstrong qualities."

"Which you most providentially escaped," his Excellency put in.

Grafton bit his lip. "Necessity makes us all careful, sir," said he.

"Necessity does more than that, Mr. Carvel," returned the

Governor, who was something of a wit; "necessity often makes us fools, if we be not careful. But give me ever a wanton fool rather than him of necessity's handiwork. And as for the lad," says he, "let him not trouble you. Such as he, if twisted a little in the growth, come out straight enough in the end."

I think the Governor little knew what wormwood was this to my uncle.

"'Tis heartily to be hoped, sir," he said, "for his folly has brought trouble enough behind it to those who have his education and his welfare in hand, and I make no doubt is at the bottom of my father's illness."

At this injustice I could not but cry out, for all the town knew, and my grandfather himself best of all, that the trouble from which he now suffered sprang from his gout. And yet my heart was smitten at the thought that I might have hastened or aggravated the attack. The Governor rose. He seized his stick aggressively and looked sharply at Grafton.

"Nonsense," he exclaimed; "my friend Mr. Carvel is far too wise to be upset by a boyish prank which deserves no notice save a caning. And that, my lad," he added lightly, "I dare swear you got with interest." And he called for a glass of the old Madeira when Scipio came with the tray, and departed with a polite inquiry after my Aunt Caroline's health, and a prophecy that Mr. Carvel would soon be taking the air again.

There had been high doings indeed in Marlboro' Street that miserable week. My grandfather took to his bed of a Saturday afternoon, and bade me go down to Mr. Aikman's, the bookseller, and fetch him the latest books and plays. That night I became so alarmed that I sent Diomedes for Dr. Leiden, who remained the night through. Sunday was well gone before the news reached York Street, when my Aunt Caroline came hurrying over in her chair, and my uncle on foot. They brushed past Scipio at the door, and were pushing up the long flight when they were stopped on the landing by Dr. Leiden.

"How is my father, sir?" Grafton cried, "and why was I not informed at once of his illness? I must see him."

"Your vater can see no one, Mr. Carvel," said the doctor, quietly.

"What," says my uncle, "you dare to refuse me?"

"Not so lout, I bray you," says the doctor; "I tare anyting vere life is concerned."

"But I will see him," says Grafton, in a sort of helpless rage, for the doctor's manner baffled him. "I will see him before he dies, and no man alive shall say me nay."

Then my Aunt Caroline gathered up her skirt, and made shift to pass the doctor.

"I have come to nurse him," said she, imperiously, and, turning to where I stood near, she added: "Bid a servant fetch from York Street what I shall have need of."

The doctor smiled, but stood firm. He cared little for aught in heaven or earth, did Dr. Leiden, and nothing whatever for Mr. and Mrs. Grafton Carvel.

"I peg you, matam, do not disturp yourself," said he. "Mr. Carvel is aply attended by an excellent voman, Mrs. Villis, and he has no neet of you."

"What," cried my aunt; "this is too much, sir, that I am thrust out of my father-in-law's house, and my place taken by a menial. That woman able!" she fumed, dropping suddenly her cloak of dignity; "Mr. Carvel's charity is all that keeps her here."

Then my uncle drew himself up. "Dr. Leiden," says he, "kindly oblige me by leaving my father's house, and consider your services here at an end. And Richard," he goes on to me, "send my compliments to Dr. Drake, and request him to come at once."

I was stepping forward to say that I would do nothing of the kind, when the doctor stopped me by a signal, as much as to say that the quarrel was wide enough without me. He stood with his back against the great arched window flooded with the yellow light of the setting sun, a little black figure in high relief, with a face of parchment. And he took a pinch of snuff before he spoke.

"I am here py Mr. Carvel's orters, sir," said he, "and py tose alone vill I leaf."

And this is how the Chippendale piece was broke, which you, my children, and especially Bess, admire so extravagantly. It stood that day behind the doctor, and my uncle, making a violent move to get by, struck it, and so it fell with a great crash lengthwise on the landing; and the wonderful vases Mr. Carroll had given my grandfather rolled down the stairs and lay crushed at the bottom. Withal he had spoken so quietly, Dr. Leiden possessed a temper drawn from his Teutonic ancestors. With his little face all puckered, he swore so roundly at my uncle in some lingo he had got from his father, — High German or Low German, — I know not what, that Grafton and his wife were glad enough to pick their way amongst the broken bits of glass and china, to the hall again. Dr. Leiden shook his fist at their retreating persons, saying that the Sabbath was no day to do murder.

I followed them with the pretence of picking up what was left of the ornaments. What between anger against the doctor and Mrs. Willis, and fright and chagrin at the fall of the Chippendale piece, my aunt was in such a state of nervous flurry that she bade the ashy Scipio call her chairmen, and vowed, in a trembling voice, she would never again enter a house where that low-bred German was to be found. But my Uncle Grafton was of a different nature. He deemed defeat but a postponement of the object he wished to gain, and settled himself in the library with a copy of "Miller on the Distinction of Ranks in Society." He appeared at supper suave as ever, gravely concerned as to his father's health, which formed the chief topic between us. He gave me to understand that he would take the green room until the old gentleman was past danger. Not a word, mind you, of Dr. Leiden, nor did my uncle express a wish to go into the sick-room, from which even I was forbid. Nay, the next morning he met the doctor in the hall and conversed with him at some length over the case as though nothing had occurred between them.

While my Uncle Grafton was in the house I had opportunity of marking the intimacy which existed between him and the rector of St. Anne's. The latter swung each evening the muffled knocker, and was ushered on tiptoe across the polished floor to the library where my uncle sat in state. It was often after supper before the rector left, and coming in upon them

F

once I found wine between them and empty decanters on the board, and they fell silent as I passed the doorway.

Our dear friend Captain Clapsaddle was away when my grandfather fell sick, having been North for three months or more on some business known to few. 'Twas generally supposed he went to Massachusetts to confer with the patriots of that colony. Hearing the news as he rode into town, he came booted and spurred to Marlboro' Street before going to his lodgings. I ran out to meet him, and he threw his arms about me on the street so that those who were passing smiled, for all knew the captain. And Harvey, who always came to take the captain's horse, swore that he was glad to see a friend of the family once again. I told the captain very freely of my doings, and showed him the clipping from the *Gazette*, which made him laugh heartily. But a shade came upon his face when I rehearsed the scene we had with my uncle and Mr. Allen in the garden.

"What," says he, "Mr. Carvel hath sent you to Mr. Allen on your uncle's advice?"

"No," I answered, "to do my uncle justice, he said not a word to Mr. Carvel about it."

The captain turned the subject. He asked me much concerning the rector and what he taught me, and appeared but ill-pleased at that I had to tell him. But he left me without so much as a word of comment or counsel. For it was a principle with Captain Clapsaddle not to influence in any way the minds of the young, and he would have deemed it unfair to Mr. Carvel had he attempted to win my sympathies to his. Captain Daniel was the first the old gentleman asked to see when visitors were permitted him, and you may be sure the faithful soldier was below stairs waiting for the summons.

I was some three weeks with my new tutor, the rector, before my grandfather's illness, and went back again as soon as he began to mend. I was not altogether unhappy, owing to a certain grim pleasure I had in debating with him, which I shall presently relate. There was much to annoy and anger me, too. My cousin Philip was forever carping and criticising my Greek and Latin, and it was impossible not to feel his sneer at my back when I construed. He had pat replies ready to correct me when called upon, and 'twas only out of consideration for Mr. Carvel that I kept my hands from him when we were dismissed.

I think the rector disliked Philip in his way as much as did I in mine. The Reverend Bennett Allen, indeed, might have been a very good fellow had Providence placed him in a different setting; he was one of those whom his Excellency dubbed "fools from necessity." He should have been born with a fortune, though I can think of none he would not have run through in a year or so. But nature had given him aristocratic tastes, with no other means toward their gratification than good looks, convincing ways, and a certain bold, half-defiant manner, which went far with his Lordship and those like him, who thought Mr. Allen excellent good company. With the rector, as with too many others, holy orders were but a means to an end. It was a sealed story what he had been before he came to Governor Sharpe with Baltimore's directions to give him the best in the colony. But our rakes and wits, and even our solid men, like my grandfather, received him with open arms. He had ever a tale on his tongue's end tempered to the ear of his listener.

Who had most influenced my way of thinking, Mr. Allen had well demanded. The gentleman was none other than Mr. Henry Swain, Patty's father. Of her I shall speak later. He was a rising barrister and man of note among our patriots, and member of the Lower House; a diffident man in public, with dark, soulful eyes, and a wide, white brow, who had declined a nomination to the Congress of '65. At his fireside, unknown to my grandfather and to Mr. Allen, I had learned the true principles of government. Before the House Mr. Swain spoke only under extraordinary emotion, and then he gained every ear. He had been my friend since childhood, but I never knew the meaning and the fire of oratory until curiosity brought me to the gallery of the Assembly chamber in the Stadt House, where the barrister was on his feet at the time. I well remember the tingle in my chest as I looked and listened. And I went again and again, until the House sat behind closed doors.

And so, when Mr. Allen brought forth for my benefit those arguments of the King's party which were deemed their strength, I would confront him with Mr. Swain's logic. He had in me a tough subject for conversion. I was put to very small pains to rout my instructor out of all his positions, because indolence, and lack of interest in the question, and contempt for the Americans, had made him neglect the study of it. And Philip, who entered at first glibly enough at the rector's side, was soon drawn into depths far beyond him. Many a time was Mr. Allen fain to laugh at his blunders. I doubt not my cousin had the facts straight enough when he rose from the breakfast table at home; but by the time he reached the rectory they were shaken up like so many parts of a puzzle in a bag, and past all straightening.

The rector was especially bitter toward the good people of Boston Town, whom he dubbed Puritan fanatics. To him Mr. Otis was but a meddling fool, and Mr. Adams a traitor whose head only remained on his shoulders by grace of the extreme clemency of his Majesty, which Mr. Allen was at a loss to understand. When beaten in argument, he would laugh out some sneer that would set my blood simmering. One morning he came in late for the lesson, smelling strongly of wine, and bade us bring our books out under the fruit trees in the garden. He threw back his gown and tilted his cap, and lighting his pipe began to speak of that act of Townshend's, passed but the year before, which afterwards proved the King's folly and England's ruin.

"Principle!" exclaimed my fine clergyman at length, blowing a great whiff among the white blossoms. "Oons! your Americans worship his Majesty stamped upon a golden coin. And though he saved their tills from plunder from the French, the miserly rogues are loth to pay for the service."

I rose, and taking a guinea-piece from my pocket, held it up before him.

"They care this much for gold, sir, and less for his Majesty, who cares nothing for them," I said. And walking to the well near by, I dropped the piece carelessly into the clear water. He was beside me before it left my hand, and Philip also, in time to see the yellow coin edging this way and that toward the bottom. The rector turned to me with a smile of cynical amusement playing over his features.

"Such a spirit has brought more than one brave fellow to Tyburn, Master Carvel," he said. And then he added reflectively, "But if there were more like you, we might well have cause for alarm."

CHAPTER VIII

OVER THE WALL

Dorothy treated me ill enough that spring. Since the minx had tasted power at Carvel Hall, there was no accounting for her. On returning to town Dr. Courtenay had begged her mother to allow her at the assemblies, a request which Mrs. Manners most sensibly refused. Mr. Marmaduke had given his consent, I believe, for he was more impatient than Dolly for the days when she would become the toast of the province. But the doctor contrived to see her in spite of difficulties, and Will Fotheringay was forever at her house, and half a dozen other lads. And many gentlemen of fashion like the doctor called ostensibly to visit Mrs. Manners, but in reality to see Miss Dorothy. And my lady knew it. She would be lingering in the drawing-room in her best bib and tucker, or strolling in the garden as Dr. Courtenay passed, and I got but scant attention indeed. I was but an awkward lad, and an old playmate, with no novelty about me.

"Why, Richard," she would say to me as I rode or walked beside her, or sat at dinner in Prince George Street, "I know every twist and turn of your nature. There is nothing you could do to surprise me. And so, sir, you are very tiresome."

"You once found me useful enough to fetch and carry, and amusing when I walked the *Oriole's* bowsprit," I replied ruefully.

"Why don't you make me jealous?" says she, stamping her foot. "A score of pretty girls are languishing for a glimpse of you, — Jennie and Bess Fotheringay, and Betty Tayloe, and Heaven knows how many others. They are actually accusing me of keeping you trailing. 'La, girls!' said I, 'if you will but rid me of him for a day, you shall have my lasting gratitude.'"

And she turned to the spinet and began a lively air. But the taunt struck deeper than she had any notion of. That spring arrived out from London on the *Belle of the Wye* a box of fine clothes my grandfather had commanded for me from his own tailor; and a word from a maid of fifteen did more to make me wear them than any amount of coaxing from Mr. Allen and my Uncle Grafton. My uncle seemed in particular anxious that I should make a good appearance, and reminded me that I should dress as became the heir of the Carvel house. I took counsel with Patty Swain, and then went to see Betty Tayloe, and the Fotheringay girls, and the Dulany girls, near the Governor's. And (fie upon me!) I was not ill-pleased with the brave appearance I made. I would show my mistress how little I cared. But the worst of it was, the baggage seemed to trouble less than I, and had the effrontery to tell me how happy she was I had come out of my shell, and broken loose from her apron-strings.

"Indeed, they would soon begin to think I meant to marry you, Richard," says she at supper one Sunday before a tableful, and laughed with the rest.

"They do not credit you with such good sense, my dear," says her mother, smiling kindly at me.

And Dolly bit her lip, and did not join in that part of the merriment.

I fled to Patty Swain for counsel, nor was it the first time in my life I had done so. Some good women seem to have been put into this selfish world to comfort and advise. After Prince George Street with its gilt and marbles and stately hedged gardens, the low-beamed, vine-covered house in the Duke of Gloucester Street was a home and a rest. In my eyes there was not its equal in Annapolis for beauty within and without. Mr. Swain had bought the dwelling from an aged man with a history, dead some nine years back. Its furniture, for the most part, was of the Restoration, of simple and massive oak blackened by age, which I ever fancied better than the Frenchy baubles of tables and chairs with spindle legs, and cabinets of glass and gold lacquer which were then making their way into the fine mansions of our town. The house was full of twists and turns, and steps up and down, and nooks and passages and queer hiding-places which we children knew, and in parts queer leaded windows of bulging glass set high in the wall, and older than the reign of Hanover. Here was the shrine of cleanliness, whose high-priestess was Patty herself. Her floors were like satin-wood, and her brasses lights in themselves. She had come honestly enough by her gifts, her father having married the daughter of an able townsman of Salem, in the Massachusetts colony, when he had gone north after his first great success in court. Now the poor lady sat in a padded armchair from morning to night, beside the hearth in winter, and under the trees in summer, by reason of a fall she had had. There she knitted all the day long. Her placid face and quiet way come before me as I write.

My friendship with Patty had begun early. One autumn day when I was a little lad of eight or nine, my grandfather and I were driving back from Whitehall in the big coach, when we spied a little maid of six by the Severn's bank, with her apron full of chestnuts. She was trudging bravely through the dead leaves toward the town. Mr. Carvel pulled the cord to stop, and asked her name. "Patty Swain, and it please your honour," the child answered, without fear. "So you are the young barrister's daughter?" says he, smiling at something I did not understand. She nodded. "And how is it you are so far from home, and alone, my little one?" asked Mr. Carvel again. For some time he could get nothing out of her; but at length she explained, with much coaxing, that her big brother Tom had deserted her. My grandfather wished that Tom were his brother, that he might be punished as he deserved. He commanded young Harvey to lift the child into the coach, chestnuts and all, and there she sat primly between us. She was not as pretty as Dorothy, so I thought, but her clear gray eyes and simple ways impressed me by their very honesty, as they did Mr. Carvel. What must he do but drive her home to Green Street, where Mr. Swain then lived in a little cottage. Mr. Carvel himself lifted her out and kissed her, and handed her to her mother at the gate, who was vastly overcome by the circumstance. The good lady had not then received that fall which made her a cripple for life. "And will you not have my chestnuts, sir, for your kindness?" says little Patty. Whereat my grandfather laughed and kissed her again, for he loved children, and wished to know if she would not be his daughter, and come to live in Marlboro' Street; and told the story of Tom, for fear she would not. He was silent as we drove away, and I knew he was thinking of my own mother at that age.

Not long after this Mr. Swain bought the house in the Duke of Gloucester Street. This, as you know, is back to back with Marlboro'. To reach Patty's garden I had but to climb the brick wall at the rear of our grounds, and to make my way along the narrow green lane left there for perhaps a hundred paces of a lad, to come to the gate in the wooden paling. In return I used to hoist Patty over the wall, and we would play at children's games under the fruit trees that skirted it. Some instinct kept her away from the house. I often caught her gazing wistfully at its wings and gables. She was not born to a mansion, so she said.

"But your father is now rich," I objected. I had heard Captain Daniel say so. "He may have a mansion of his own and he chooses. He can better afford it than many who are in debt for the fine show they make." I was but repeating gossip.

"I should like to see the grand company come in, when your grandfather has them to dine," said the girl. "Sometimes we have grand gentlemen come to see father in their coaches, but they talk of nothing but politics. We never have any fine ladies like—like your Aunt Caroline."

I startled her by laughing derisively.

"And I pray you never may, Patty," was all I said.

I never told Dolly of my intimacy with the barrister's little girl over the wall. This was not because I was ashamed of the friendship, but arose from a fear—well-founded enough—that she would make sport of it. At twelve Dolly had notions concerning the walks of life that most other children never dream of. They were derived, of course, from Mr. **Marmaduke. But the day** of reckoning arrived. Patty and I were romping beside the back wall when suddenly a stiff little figure in a starched frock appeared through the trees in the direction of the house, followed by Master Will Fotheringay in his visiting clothes. I laugh now when I think of that formal meeting between the two **little ladies. There** was no time to hoist Miss Swain **over the wall, or to drive Miss** Manners back upon the house. Patty stood blushing as though caught in a guilty act, while she of the Generations came proudly on, Will sniggering behind her.

"Who is this, Richard?" asks **Miss Manners, pointing a** small forefinger.

"Patty **Swain, if you** must **know!"** I cried, and **added boy-like: "**And **she is just as good as you or me, and better."** I was **quite red in the face, and angry because of it. "This is** Dorothy Manners, Patty, and Will Fotheringay."

The moment was a pregnant one. But I was resolved to carry the matter out with a bold front. **"Will** you join us at catch and swing?" I asked.

Will promptly declared that he would join, for Patty was good to look upon. Dolly glanced at her dress, tossed her head, and marched back alone.

"Oh, Richard!" cried Patty; "I shall never forgive myself! I have made you quarrel with —"

"His sweetheart," said Will, wickedly.

"I don't care," said I. Which was not so.

Patty felt no **resentment for my miss's** haughty conduct, but only a tearful **penitence for having been the cause** of **a strife between us. Will's** arguments and mine availed nothing. I **must lift her over the wall** again, and she **went home.** When **we reached the garden** we found Dolly seated beside her mother **on my grandfather's bench, from** which stronghold **our combined tactics** were powerless to **drag her.**

When Dolly was gone, I asked my grandfather **in great indignation** why Patty did not play with the children I knew, with Dorothy and the Fotheringays. **He** shook his head dubiously. "When **you are older,** Richard, you will understand **that our social ranks are cropped close.** Mr. Swain is an honest and an able man, though he believes in things I do not. I hear he is becoming wealthy. And I have no doubt," the shrewd old gentleman added, "that when Patty grows up she will be going to the assemblies, though it was not so in my time." So liberal was he that he used to laugh at my lifting her across the wall, and in his leisure delight to listen to my accounts of her childish housekeeping. Her life was indeed a contrast to Dorothy's. She had all the solid qualities that my lady lacked in early years. And yet I never wavered in my liking to the more brilliant and wayward of the two. The week before my next birthday, when Mr. Carvel drew me to him and asked me what I wished for a present that year, as was his custom, I said promptly: —

"I should like to have Patty Swain at my party, sir."

"So you shall, my lad," he cried, taking his snuff and eying me with pleasure. "I am glad to see, Richard, that you have none of Mr. Marmaduke's nonsense about you. She is a good girl, i' faith, and more of a lady now than many who call themselves such. And you shall have your present to boot. Hark'ee, Daniel," said he to the captain; "if the child comes to my house, the poll-parrots and follow-me-ups will be wanting her, too."

But the getting her to go was a matter of five days. For Patty was sensitive, like her father, and dreaded a slight. Not so with Master Tom, who must needs be invited, too. He arrived half an hour ahead of time, arrayed like Solomon, and without his sister! I had to go for Patty, indeed, after the party had begun, and to get the key to the wicket in the wall to take her in that way, so shy was she. My dear grandfather showed her particular attention. And Miss Dolly herself, being in the humour, taught her a minuet.

After that she came to all my birthdays, and lost some of her shyness. And was invited to other great houses, even as Mr. Carvel had predicted. But her chief pleasure seemed ever her duty. Whether or no such characters make them one and the same, who can tell? She became the light of her father's house, and used even to copy out his briefs, at which task I often found her of an evening.

As for Tom, that graceless scamp, I never could stomach him. I wondered then, as I have since, how he was the brother of such a sister. He could scarce bide his time until Mr. Swain should have a coach and a seat in the country with the gentry. "A barrister," quoth he, "is as good as any one else. And if my father came out a redemptioner, and worked his way, so had old Mr. Dulany. Our family at home was the equal of his." All of which was true, and more. He would deride Patty for sewing and baking, vowing that they had servants enough now to do the work twice over. She bore with him with a patience to be marvelled at; and I could never get it through my head why Mr. Swain indulged him, though he was the elder, and his mother's favourite. Tom began to dress early. His open admiration was Dr. Courtenay, his confessed hope to wear five-pound ruffles and gold sword knots. He clung to Will Fotheringay with a tenacity that became proverbial among us boys, and his boasts at King William's School were his father's growing wealth and intimacy with the great men of the province.

As I grew older, I took the cue of political knowledge, as I have said, from Mr. Swain rather than Captain Daniel, who would tell me nothing. I fell into the habit of taking supper in Gloucester Street. The meal was early there. And when the dishes were cleared away, and the barrister's pipe lit, and Patty and her mother had got their sewing, he would talk by the hour on the legality of our resistance to the King, and discuss the march of affairs in England and the other colonies. He found me a ready listener, and took pains to teach me clearly the right and wrong of the situation. 'Twas his religion, even as loyalty to the King was my grandfather's, and he did not think it wrong to spread it. He likewise instilled into me in that way more of history than Mr. Allen had ever taught me, using it to throw light upon this point or that. But I never knew his true power and eloquence until I followed him to the Stadt House.

Patty was grown a girl of fifteen then, glowing with health, and had ample good looks of her own. 'Tis odd enough that I did not fall in love with her when Dolly began to use me so outrageously. But a lad of eighteen is scarce a rational creature. I went and sat before my oracle upon the vine-covered porch under the eaves, and poured out my complaint. She laid down her needlework and laughed.

"You silly boy," said she, "can't you see that she herself has prescribed for you? She was right when she told you to show attention to Jenny. And if you dangle about Miss Dolly now, you are in danger of losing her. She knows it better than you."

I had Jenny to ride the very next day. Result: my lady smiled on me more sweetly than ever when I went to Prince George Street, and vowed Jenny had never looked prettier than when she went past the house. This left my victory in such considerable doubt that I climbed the back wall forthwith in my new top-boots.

"So you looked for her to be angry?" said Patty.

"Most certainly," said I.

"Unreasoning vanity!" she cried, for she knew how to speak plain. "By your confession to me you have done this to please her, for she warned you at the beginning it would please her. And now you complain of it. I believe I know your Dorothy better than you."

And so I got but little comfort out of Patty that time.

CHAPTER IX

UNDER FALSE COLOURS

AND now I come to a circumstance in my life I would rather pass over quickly. Had I steered the straight course of my impulse I need never have deceived that dear gentleman whom I loved and honoured above any in this world, and with whom I had always lived and dealt openly. After my grandfather was pronounced to be mending, I went back to Mr. Allen until such time as we should be able to go to the country. Philip no longer shared my studies, his hours having been changed from morning to afternoon. I thought nothing of this, being content with the rector's explanation that my uncle had a task for Philip in the morning, now that Mr. Carvel was better. And I was well content to be rid of Philip's company. But as the days passed I began to mark an absence still stranger. I had my Horace and my Ovid still: but the two hours from eleven to one, which he was wont to give up to history and what he was pleased to call instruction in loyalty, were filled with other matter. Not a word now of politics from Mr. Allen. Not even a comment from him concerning the spirited doings of our Assembly, with which the town was ringing. That body had met but a while before, primed to act on the circular drawn up by Mr. Adams of Massachusetts. The Governor's message had not been so prompt as to forestall them, and I am occupied scarce the time in the writing of this that it took our brave members to adopt the petition to his Majesty and to pass resolutions of support to our sister colony of the North. This being done, and a most tart reply penned to his Excellency, they ended that sitting and passed in procession to the Governor's mansion to deliver it, Mr. Speaker Lloyd at their head, and a vast concourse of cheering people at their heels. Shutters were barred on the Tory houses we passed. And though Mr. Allen spied me in the crowd, he never mentioned the circumstance. More than once I essayed to draw from him an opinion of Mr. Adams's petition, which was deemed a work of great moderation and merit, and got nothing but evasion from my tutor. That he had become suddenly an American in principle I could not believe. At length I made bold to ask him why our discussions were now omitted. He looked up from the new play he was reading on the study lounge, with a glance of dark meaning I could not fathom.

"You are learning more than I can teach you in Gloucester Street, and at the Stadt House," he said.

In truth I was at a loss to understand his attitude until the day in June my grandfather and I went to Carvel Hall.

The old gentleman was weak still, so feeble that he had to be carried to his barge in a chair, a vehicle he had ever held in scorn. But he was cheerful, and his spirit remained the same as of old: but for that spirit I believe he had never again risen from his bed in Marlboro' Street. My uncle and the rector were among those who walked by his side to the dock, and would have gone to the Hall with him had he permitted them. He was kind enough to say that my arm was sufficient to lean on.

What peace there was sitting once again under the rustling trees on the lawn with the green river and the blue bay spread out before us, and Scipio standing by with my grandfather's punch. Mr. Carvel would have me rehearse again all that had passed in town and colony since his illness, which I did with as much moderation as I was able. And as we talked he reached out and took my hand, for I sat near him, and said : —

"Richard, I have heard tidings of you that gladden my heart, and they have done more than Dr. Leiden's physic for this old frame of mine. I well knew a Carvel could never go a wrong course, lad, and you least of any."

"Tidings, sir?" I said.

"Ay, tidings," answered Mr. Carvel. Such a note of relief and gladness there was in the words as I had not heard for months from him, and a vague fear came upon me.

"Scipio," he said merrily, "a punch for Mr. Richard." And when the glass was brought my grandfather added: "May it be ever thus!"

I drained the toast, not falling into his humour or comprehending his reference, but dreading that aught I might say would disturb him, held my peace. And yet my apprehension increased. He set down his glass and continued:—

"I had no hope of this yet, Richard, for you were ever slow to change. Your conversion does credit to Mr. Allen as well as to you. In short, sir, the rector gives me an excellent good account of your studies, and adds that the King hath gained another loyal servant, for which I thank God."

I have no words to write of my feelings then. My head swam and my hand trembled on my grandfather's, and I saw dimly the old gentleman's face aglow with joy and pride, and knew not what to say or do. The answer I framed, alas, remained unspoken. From his own lips I had heard how much the news had mended him, and for once I lacked the heart, nay, the courage, to speak the truth. But Mr. Carvel took no heed of my silence, setting it down to another cause.

"And so, my son," he said, "there is no need of sending you to Eton next fall. I am not much longer for this earth, and can ill spare you: and Mr. Allen kindly consents to prepare you for Oxford."

"Mr. Allen *consents* to that, sir?" I gasped. I think, could I have laid hands on the rector then, I would have thrashed him, cloth and all, within an inch of his life.

And as if to crown my misery Mr. Carvel rose, and bearing heavily on my shoulder led me to the stable where Harvey and one of the black grooms stood in livery to receive us. Harvey held by the bridle a blooded bay hunter, and her like could scarce be found in the colony. As she stood arching her neck and pawing the ground, I all confusion and shame, my grandfather said simply:—

"Richard, this is Firefly. I have got her for you from Mr. Randolph, of Virginia, for you are now old enough to have a good mount of your own."

All that night I lay awake, trying to sift some motive **for**

Mr. Allen's deceit. For the life of me I could see no farther than a desire to keep me as his pupil, since he was well paid for his tuition. Still, the game did not seem worth the candle. However, he was safe in his lie. Shrewd rogue that he was, he well knew that I would not risk the attack a disappointment might bring my grandfather.

What troubled me most of all was the fear that Grafton had reaped the advantage of the opportunity the illness gave him, and by his insidious arts had worked himself back into the good graces of his father. You must not draw from this, my dears, that I feared for the inheritance. Praised be God, I never thought of that! But I came by nature to hate and to fear my uncle, as I hated and feared the devil. I saw him with my father's eyes, and with my mother's, and as my grandfather had seen him in the old days when he was strong. Instinct and reason alike made me loathe him. As the months passed, and letters in Grafton's scroll hand came from the Kent estate or from Annapolis, my misgivings were confirmed by odd remarks that dropped from Mr. Carvel's lips. At length arrived the revelation itself.

"I fear, Richard," he had said querulously, "I fear that all these years I have done your uncle an injustice. Dear Elizabeth was wont to plead for him before she died, but I would never listen to her. I was hearty and strong then, and my heart was hard. And a remembrance of many things was fresh in my mind." He paused for breath, as was his habit now. And I said nothing. "But Grafton has striven to wipe out the past. Sickness teaches us that we must condone, and not condemn. He has lived a reputable life, and made the most of the little start I gave him. He has supported his Majesty and my Lord in most trying times. And his Excellency tells me that the coming governor, Eden, will surely reward him with a seat in the Council."

I thought of Governor Sharpe's biting words to Grafton. The Governor knew my uncle well, and I was sure he had never sat at his Council.

"A son is a son, Richard," continued Mr. Carvel. "You will one day find that out. Your uncle has atoned. He hath been faithful during my illness, despite my cold treatment. And he hath convinced me that your welfare is at his heart. I believe he is fond of you, my lad."

No greater sign of breaking health did I need than this, that Mr. Carvel should become blind to Grafton's hypocrisy; forget his attempts to prevent my father's marriage, and to throw doubt upon my mother's birth. The agony it gave me, coming as it did on top of the cruel deception, I shall not dwell upon. And the thought bursting within me remained unspoken.

I saw less of Dorothy then than I had in any summer of my life before. In spite of Mrs. Manners, the chrysalis had burst into the butterfly, and Wilmot House had never been so gay. It must be remembered that there were times when young ladies made their entrance into the world at sixteen, and for a beauty to be unmarried at twenty-two was rare indeed. When I went to Wilmot House to dine, the table would be always full, and Mr. Marmaduke simpering at the head of it, his air of importance doubled by his reflected glory.

"We see nothing of you, my lad," he would say; "you must not let these young gallants get ahead of you. How does your grandfather? I must pay my compliments to-morrow."

Of gallants there were enough, to be sure. Dr. Courtenay, of course, with a nosegay on his coat, striving to catch the beauty's eye. And Mr. Worthington and Mr. Dulany, and Mr. Fitzhugh and Mr. Paca, and I know not how many other young bachelors of birth and means. And Will Fotheringay, who spent some of his time with me at the Hall. Silver and China, with the Manners coat-of-arms, were laid out that had not seen the light for many a long day. And there were picnics, and sailing parties, and dances galore, some of which I attended, but heard of more. It seemed to me that my lady was tiring of the doctor's compliments, and had transferred her fickle favour to young Mr. Fitzhugh, who was much more worthy, by the way. As for me, I had troubles enough then, and had become used in some sort to being shelved.

One night in July,—'twas the very day Mr. Carvel had spoken to me of Grafton,—I had ridden over to Wilmot House to supper. I had little heart for going, but good Mrs.

"WHY DO YOU NOT COME OVER, AS YOU USED TO?"

Manners herself had made me promise, and I could not break my word. I must have sat very silent and preoccupied at the table, where all was wit and merriment. And more than once I saw the laughter leave Dorothy's face, and caught her eyes upon me with such a look as set my heart throbbing. They would not meet my own, but would turn away instantly. I was heavy indeed that night, and did not follow the company into the ball-room, but made my excuses to Mrs. Manners.

The lawn lay bathed in moonlight; and as I picked my way over it toward the stables for Firefly, I paused to look back at the house aglow with light, the music of the fiddles and the sound of laughter floating out of the open windows. Even as I gazed a white figure was framed in the doorway, paused a moment on the low stone step, and then came on until it stood beside me.

"Are you not well, Richard?"

"Yes, I am well," I answered. I scarcely knew my own voice.

"Is your grandfather worse?"

"No, Dorothy; he seems better to-day."

She stood, seemingly irresolute, her eyes now lifted, now falling before mine. Her slender arms bare, save for the little puff at the shoulders; her simple dress drawn a little above the waist, then falling straight to the white slippers. How real the ecstasy of that moment, and the pain of it!

"Why do you not come over, as you used to?" she asked, in a low tone.

"I am very busy," I replied evasively; "Mr. Carvel cannot attend to his affairs." I longed to tell her the whole truth, but the words would not come.

"I hear you are managing the estate all alone," she said.

"There is no one else to do it."

"Richard," she cried, drawing closer, "you are in trouble. I — I have seen it. You are so silent, and — and you seem to have become older. Tell me, is it your Uncle Grafton?"

So astonished was I at the question, and because she had divined so surely, that I did not answer.

"Is it?" she asked again.

"Yes," I said; "yes, in part."

And then came voices calling from the house. They had missed her.

"I am so sorry, Richard. I shall tell no one."

She laid her hand ever so lightly upon mine and was gone. I stood staring after her until she disappeared in the door. All the way home I marvelled, my thoughts tumultuous, my hopes rising and falling.

But when next I saw her, I thought she had forgotten.

We had little company at the Hall that year, on account of Mr. Carvel. And I had been busy indeed. I sought with all my might to master a business for which I had but little taste, and my grandfather complimented me, before the season was done, upon my management. I was wont to ride that summer at four of a morning to canter beside Mr. Starkie afield, and I came to know the yield of every patch to a hogshead and the pound price to a farthing. I grew to understand as well as another the methods of curing the leaf. And the wheat pest appearing that year, I had the good fortune to discover some of the clusters in the sheaves, and ground our oyster-shells in time to save the crop. Many a long evening I spent on the wharves with old Stanwix, now toothless and living on his pension, with my eye on the glow of his pipe and my ear bent to his stories of the sea. It was his fancy that the gift of prophecy had come to him with the years; and at times, when his look would wander to the black rigging in the twilight, he would speak strangely enough.

"Faith, Mr. Richard," he would say; "tho' your father was a soldier afore ye, ye were born to the deck of a ship-o'-war. Mark an old man's words, sir."

"Can you see the frigate, Stanwix?" I laughed once, when he had repeated this with more than common solemnity.

His reply rose above the singing of the locusts.

"Ay, sir, that I can. But she's no frigate, sir. Devil knows what she is. She looks like a big merchantman to me, such as I've seed in the Injy trade, with a high poop in the old style. And her piercin's be not like a frigate." He said this with a readiness to startle me, and little enough superstition I had. A light was on his seared face, and his pipe lay neglected on the boards. "Ay, sir, and there be a flag astern of her never yet seed on earth, nor on the waters under the earth. The tide is settin' in, the tide is settin' in."

These were words to set me thinking. And many a time they came back to me when the old man was laid away in the spot reserved for those who sailed the seas for Mr. Carvel.

Every week I drew up a report for my grandfather, and thus I strove by shouldering labour and responsibility to ease my conscience of that load which troubled it. For often, as we walked together through the yellow fields of an evening, it had been on my tongue to confess the lie Mr. Allen had led me into. But the sight of the old man, trembling and tremulous, aged by a single stroke, his childlike trust in my strength and beliefs, and above all his faith in a political creed which he nigh deemed needful for the soul's salvation,—these things still held me back. Was it worth while now, I asked myself, to disturb the peace of that mind?

Thus the summer wore on to early autumn. And one day I was standing booted and spurred in the stables, Harvey putting the bridle upon Firefly, when my boy Hugo comes running in.

"Marse Dick!" he cries, "Marse Satan he come in he pinnace, and young Marse Satan and Missis Satan, and Marse Satan's pastor!"

"What the devil do you mean, Hugo?"

"Young ebony's right, sir," chuckled Harvey; "'tis the devil and his following."

"Do you mean Mr. Grafton, fellow?" I demanded, the unwelcome truth coming over me.

"That he does," remarked Harvey, laconically. "You won't be wanting her now, your honour?"

"Hold my stirrup," I cried, for the news had put me in anger. "Hold my stirrup, sirrah!"

I believe I took Firefly the best of thirty miles that afternoon and brought her back in the half-light, my saddle discoloured with her sweat. I clanked into the hall like a captain of horse. The night was sharp with the first touch of autumn, and a huge backlog lay on the irons. Around it, in a comfortable half-circle, sat our guests, Grafton and Mr. Allen and Philip smoking and drinking for a whet against supper, and Mrs. Grafton in my grandfather's chair. There was an easy air of possession about the party of them that they had never before assumed, and the sight made me rattle again the big door behind me.

"A surprise for you, my dear nephew," Grafton said gayly. "I'll lay a puncheon you did not expect us."

Mr. Carvel woke with a start at the sound of the door and said querulously, "Guests, my lad, and I have done my poor best to make them welcome in your absence."

The sense of change in him stung me. How different would his tone have been a year ago!

He tattooed with his cane, which was the sign he generally made when he was ready for bed. Toward night his speech would hurt him. I assisted him up the stairs, my uncle taking his arm on the other side. And together, with Diomedes's help, we undressed him, Grafton talking in low tones the while. Since this was an office I was wont to perform, my temper was now overwhelming me. But I kept my mouth closed. At last he had had the simple meal Dr. Leiden allowed him, his candles were snuffed, and my uncle and I made our way to the hall together. There my aunt and Mr. Allen were at picquet.

"Supper is insupportably late," says she, with a yawn, and rings the hand-bell. "Scipio," she cries, "why are we not served?"

I took a stride forward. But my uncle raised a restraining hand.

"Caroline, remember that this is not our house," says he, reprovingly.

There fell a deep silence, the log cracking; and just then the door swung on its hinges, and Mr. Starkie entered with the great bunch of keys in his hand.

"The buildings are all secure, Mr. Richard," he said.

"Very good, Starkie," I replied. I turned to Scipio, standing by the low-boy, his teeth going like a castanet.

"You may serve at the usual hour, Scipio," said I.

Supper began stiff as a state banquet. My uncle was conciliatory, with the manners of a Crichton. My aunt, not having come from generations of silver and self-control, flatly in a bad humour. Mr. Allen talked from force of habit, being used to pay in such kind for his meals. But presently the madeira warmed these two into a better spirit. I felt that I had victory on my side, and was nothing loth to join them at whist, Philip and I against the rector and my aunt, and won something like two pounds apiece from them. Grafton made it a rule never to play.

The next morning, when I returned from my inspection, I found the rector and Philip had decamped with two of our choice horses, and that my uncle and aunt had commanded the barge, and gone to Mr. Lloyd's. I sent for Scipio.

"Fore de Lawd, Marse Richard," he wailed, "'twan't Scipio's fault. Marse Grafton is de fambly!" This was Scipio's strongest argument. "I jes' can't refuse one of de fambly, Marse Dick; and old Marse he say he too old now for quarrellin'."

I saw that resistance was useless. There was nothing for it but to bide my time. And I busied myself with bills of cargo until I heard the horses on the drive. Mr. Allen and Philip came swaggering in, flushed with the exercise, and calling for punch, and I met them in the hall.

"A word with you, Mr. Allen!" I called out.

"A thousand, Mr. Richard, if you like," he said gayly, "as soon as this thirst of mine be quenched."

I waited while he drained two glasses, when he followed me into the library, closing the door behind him.

"Now, sir," I began, "though by a chance you are my mental and spiritual adviser, I intend speaking plain. For I know you to be one of the greatest rogues in the colony."

I watched him narrowly the while, for I had some notion he might run me through. But I had misjudged him.

"Speak plain, by all means," he replied; "but first let me ask for some tobacco."

He filled the bowl of his pipe, and sat him down by the window. For the moment I was silent with sheer surprise.

"You know I can't call you out," he went on, surrounding himself with clouds of smoke, "a lad of eighteen or so. And even if I could, I doubt whether I should. I like you, Richard," said he. "You are straight-spoken and commanding. In brief, sir, you are the kind of lad I should have been had not fate pushed me into a corner, and made me squirm for life's luxuries. I hate squirming as much as another. This is prime tobacco, Richard."

He had come near disarming me; I was on the edge of a dangerous admiration for this man of the world, and for the life of me, I could not help liking him then. He had a fine presence, was undeniably handsome, and his riding clothes were of the latest London cut.

"Are there not better methods for obtaining what you wish than those you practise?" I asked curiously.

"No doubt," he answered carelessly; "but these are well enough, and shorter. You were about to do me the honour of a communication?"

This brought me to my senses. I had, however, lost much of my heat in the interval.

"I should like to know why you lied to Mr. Carvel about my convictions, Mr. Allen," I said. "I am not of the King's party now, and never shall be. And you know this better than another."

"Those are strong words, Richard, my lad," said he, bringing his eyebrows together.

"They are true words," I retorted. "Why did you lie, I say?"

He said nothing for a while, but his breath came heavily.

"I will pass it, I will pass it," he said at length, "but, by God! it is more than I have had to swallow in all my life before. Look at your grandfather, sir!" he cried; "behold him on the very brink of the grave, and ask me again why I lied to him! His hope of heaven is scarce less sacred to him than his love of the King, and both are so tightly wrapped about his heart that this knowledge of you would break it. Yes, break his heart, I say" (and he got to his legs), "and you would kill him for the sake of a boyish fancy!"

I knew he was acting, as well as though he had climbed upon the table and said it. And yet he had struck the very note of my own fears, and hit upon the one reason why I had not confessed long ago.

"There is more you might have said, Mr. Allen," I remarked presently; "you have a cause for keeping me under your instruction, and that is behind all."

He gave me a strange look.

"You are too acute by far," said he; "your imagination runs with you. I have said I like you, and I can teach you classics as well as another. Is it not enough to admit that the money I get for your instruction keeps me in champagne?"

"No, it is not enough," I said stoutly.

"Then you must guess again, my lad," he answered with a laugh, and left the room with the easy grace that distinguished him.

There was armed peace the rest of my uncle's visit. They departed on the third day. My Aunt Caroline, when she was not at picquet with Mr. Allen or quarrelling with Mrs. Willis or with Grafton himself, yawned without cessation. She declared in one of her altercations with her lord and master that she would lose her wits were they to remain another day, a threat that did not seem to move Grafton greatly. Philip ever maintained the right to pitch it on the side of his own convenience, and he chose in this instance to come to the rescue of his dear mamma, and turned the scales in her favour. He was pleased to characterize the Hall as insupportable, and vowed that his clothes would be out of fashion before they reached Rousby Hall, their next stopping-place. To do Philip justice, he was more honest a rascal than his father, tho' I am of the opinion that he had not the brain for great craft. And he had drawn from his mother a love of baubles which kept his mind from scheming. He had little to say to me, and I less to him.

Grafton, as may be supposed, made me distinct advances before his departure, perceiving the unwisdom of antagonizing me unnecessarily. He had the imprudence once to ask of me the facts and figures of the estate; and tho' 'twas skilfully done by contrasting his own crops in Kent, you may be sure I was on my guard, and that he got nothing.

I was near forgetting an incident of their visit which I afterwards had good cause to remember. The morning of my talk with Mr. Allen I went to the stables to see how he had used Cynthia, and found old Harvey wiping her down, and rumbling the while like a crater.

"What think you of the rector as a representative of heaven, Harvey?" I asked.

"Him a representative of heaven!" he snorted; "I've heard tell of rotten boroughs, and I'm thinking Mr. Allen will be standing for one. What be him and Mr. Grafton adoing here, sir, plotting all kinds o' crime while the old gentleman's nigh on his back?"

"Plotting?" I said, catching at the word.

"Ay, plotting," repeated Harvey, casting his cloth away; "murder and all the crimes in the calendar, I take it. I hear him and Mr. Grafton among the stalls this morning, and when they sees me they look like Knipe, here, caught with a fowl."

"And what were they saying?" I demanded.

"Saying! God only knows their wickedness. I got the words 'Upper Marlboro'' and 'South River' and 'next voyage,' and that profligate rector wanted to know as to how 'Griggs was reliable.'"

I thought no more of it at the time, believing it to be some of the small rascalities they were forever at. But that name of Griggs (why, the powers only know) stuck in my mind to turn up again.

CHAPTER X

THE RED IN THE CARVEL BLOOD

AFTER that, when we went back to Annapolis for the winter, there was no longer any disguise between my tutor and myself. I was not of a mind to feign a situation that did not exist, nor to permit him to do so. I gave him to understand that tho' I went to him for instruction, 'twas through no fault of mine. That I would learn what I pleased and do what pleased me. And the rector, a curse upon him, seemed well content with that; nor could I come at his devil's reason for wanting me, save for the money, as he had declared. There were days when he and I never touched a book, both being out of humour for study, when he told me yarns of Frederick of Prussia and his giant guard, of Florence and of Venice, and of the court of his Holiness of Rome. For he had drifted about the earth like a log-end in the Atlantic, before his Lordship gave him his present berth. We passed, too, whole mornings at picquet, I learning enough of Horace to quote at the routs we both attended, but a deal more of kings and deuces. And this I may add, that he got no more of my money than did I of his.

The wonder of it was that we never became friends. He was two men, this rector of St. Anne's, half of him as lovable as any I ever encountered. But trust him I never would, always meeting him on the middle ground; and there were times, after his talks with Grafton, when his eyes were like a cat's, and I was conscious of a sinister note in his dealing which put me on my guard.

You will say, my dears, that some change had come over me, that I was no longer the same lad I have been telling you of.

Those days were not these, yet I make no show of hiding or of palliation. Was it Dorothy's conduct that drove me? Not wholly. A wild red was ever in the Carvel blood, in Captain Jack, in Lionel, in the ancestor of King Charles's day, who fought and bled and even gambled for his king. And my grandfather knew this; he warned me, but he paid my debts. And I thank Heaven he felt that my heart was right.

I was grown now, certainly in stature. And having managed one of the largest plantations in the province, I felt the man, as lads are wont after their first responsibilities. I commanded my wine at the Coffee House with the best of the bucks, and was made a member of the South River and Jockey clubs. I wore the clothes that came out to me from London, and vied in fashion with Dr. Courtenay and other macaronies. And I drove a carriage of mine own, the Carvel arms emblazoned thereon, and Hugo in the family livery.

After a deal of thought upon the subject, I decided, for a while at least, to show no political leanings at all. And this was easier of accomplishment than you may believe, for at that time in Maryland Tory and Whig were amiable enough, and the young gentlemen of the first families dressed alike and talked alike at the parties they both attended. The non-importation association had scarce made itself felt in the dress of society. Gentlemen of degree discussed differences amicably over their decanters. And only on such occasions as Mr. Hood's return, and the procession of the Lower House through the streets, and the arrival of the *Good Intent*, did high words arise among the quality. And it was because class distinctions were so strongly marked that it took so long to bring loyalists and patriots of high rank to the sword's point.

I found time to manage such business affairs of Mr. Carvel's as he could not attend to himself. Grafton and his family dined in Marlboro' Street twice in the week; my uncle's conduct toward me was the very soul of consideration, and he compelled that likewise from his wife and his son. So circumspect was he that he would have fooled one who knew him a whit less than I. He questioned me closely upon my studies, and in my grandfather's presence I was forced to answer. And when the rector came to dine and read to Mr. Carvel, my uncle catechised him so searchingly on my progress that he was pushed to the last source of his ingenuity for replies. More than once was I tempted to blurt out the whole wretched business, for I well understood there was some deep game between him and Grafton. In my uncle's absence, my aunt never lost a chance for an ill-natured remark upon Patty, whom she had seen that winter at the assemblies and elsewhere. And she deplored the state our people of fashion were coming to, that they allowed young girls without family to attend their balls.

"But we can expect little else, father," she would say to Mr. Carvel nodding in his chair, "when some of our best families openly espouse the pernicious doctrines of republicanism. They are gone half mad over that Wilkes, who should have been hung before this. Philip, dear, pour the wine for your grandfather."

Miss Patty had been well received. I took her to her first assembly, where her simple and unassuming ways had made her an instant favourite; and her face, which had the beauty of dignity and repose even so early in life, gained her ample attention. I think she would have gone but little had not her father laughed her out of some of her domesticity. No longer at Sunday night supper in Gloucester Street was the guest seat empty. There was more than one guest seat now, and the honest barrister himself was the most pleased at the change. As I took my accustomed place on the settle cushion, — Patty's first embroidery, — he would cry : —

"Heigho, Richard, our little Miss Prim hath become a belle. And I must have another clerk now to copy out my briefs, and a housekeeper soon, i' faith."

Patty would never fail to flush up at the words, and run to perch on her father's knee and put her hand over his mouth.

"How can you, Mr. Swain?" says she; "how can you, when 'tis you and mother, and Richard here, who make me go into the world? You know I would a thousand times rather bake your cakes and clean your silver! But you will not hear of it."

"Fie!" says the barrister. "Listen to her, Richard! And yet she will fly up the stairs to don a fine gown at the first rap of the knocker. Oh, the wenches, the wenches! Are they not all alike, mother?"

"They have changed none since I was a lass," replies the quiet invalid, with a smile. "And you should know what I was, Henry."

"Know!" cries he; "none better. Well I recall the salmon and white your mother gave you before I came to Salem." He sighed and then laughed at the recollection. "And when this strapping young Singleton comes, Richard, 'twould do you good to be hiding there in that cupboard, — and it would hold you, — and count the seconds until Miss Prim has her skirt in her hand and her foot on the lower step. And yet how innocent is she now before you and me."

Here he would invariably be smothered.

"Percy Singleton!" says Patty, with a fine scorn; "'twill be Mr. Eglinton, the curate, next."

"This I know," says her father, slapping me on the shoulder, "this I know, that you are content to see Richard without primping."

"But I have known Richard since I was six," says she. "Richard is one of the family. There is no need of disguise from him."

I thought, ruefully enough, that it seemed my fate to be one of the family everywhere I went.

And just then, as if in judgment, the gate snapped and the knocker sounded, and Patty leaped down with a blush. "What did I say?" cries the barrister. "I have not seen human nature in court for naught. Run, now," says he, pinching her cheek as she stood hesitating whether to fly or stay; "run and put on the new dress I have bought you. And Richard and I will have a cup of ale in the study."

The visitor chanced to be Will Fotheringay that time. He was not the only one worn out with the mad chase in Prince George Street, and preferred a quiet evening with a quiet beauty to the crowded lists of Miss Manners. Will declared that the other gallants were fools over the rare touch of blue in the black hair: give him Miss Swain's, quoth he, lifting his glass,—hers was the colour of a new sovereign. Will was not the only one. But I think Percy Singleton was the best of them all, tho' Patty ridiculed him every chance she got, and even to his face. So will the best-hearted and soberest of women play the coquette. Singleton was rather a reserved young Englishman of four and twenty, who owned a large estate in Talbot, which he was laying out with great success. Of a Whig family in the old country, he had been drawn to that party in the new, and so had made Mr. Swain's acquaintance. The next step in his fortunes was to fall in love with Patty, which was natural enough. Many a night that winter I walked with him from Gloucester Street to the Coffee House, to sit an hour over a bottle. And there Master Tom and Dr. Hamilton, and other gay macaronies would sometimes join us. Singleton had a greater contempt for Tom than I, but bore with him for his sister's sake. For Tom, in addition to his other follies, was become an open loyalist, and never missed his Majesty's health, though he knew no better than my Hugo the question at issue. 'Twas not zeal for King George, however, that made him drunk at one of the assemblies, and forced his sister to leave in the midst of a dance for very shame.

"Oh, Richard, is there not something you can do?" she cried, when I had got her back in the little parlour in Gloucester Street; "father has argued and pleaded and threatened in vain. I thought,—I thought perhaps you might help him."

"I think I am not one to preach, or to boast," I replied soberly.

"Yes," said she, looking grave; "I know you are wilder than you used to be; that you play more than you ought, and higher than you ought."

I was silent.

"And I suspect at whose door it lies," said she.

"'Tis in the blood, Patty," I answered.

She glanced at me quickly.

"I know you better than you think," she said. "But Tom has not your excuse. And if he had only your faults I would say nothing. He does not care for those he should, and he is forever in the green-room of the theatre."

I made haste to change the subject, and to give her what comfort I might; for she was sobbing before she finished. And the next day I gave Tom a round talking-to for having so little regard for his sister, the hem of whose skirt he was not worthy to touch. He took it meekly enough, with a barrel of pat excuses to come after. And he asked me to lend him my phaeton, that he might go a-driving with Miss Crane, of the theatrical company, to Round Bay!

Meanwhile I saw Miss Manners more frequently than was good for my peace of mind, and had my turn as her partner at the balls. But I could not bring myself to take third or fourth rank in the army that attended her. I, who had been her playmate, would not become her courtier. Besides, I had not the wit.

Was it strange that Dr. Courtenay should pride himself upon the discovery of a new beauty? And in the Coffee House, and in every drawing-room in town, prophesy for her a career of conquest such as few could boast? She was already launched upon that career. And rumour had it that Mr. Marmaduke was even then considering taking her home to London, where the stage was larger and the triumph greater. Was it surprising that the *Gazette* should contain a poem with the doctor's well-known ear-marks upon it? It set the town a-wagging, and left no room for doubt as to who had inspired it.

> "Sweet Pandora, tho' formed of Clay,
> Was fairer than the Light of Day.
> By Venus learned in Beauty's Arts,
> And destined thus to conquer Hearts.
> A Goddess of this Town, I ween,
> Fair as Pandora, scarce Sixteen,
> Is destined, e'en by Jove's Command,
> To conquer all of Maryland.
> Oh, Bachelors, pray have a Care,
> For She will all your Hearts ensnare."

So it ran. I think, if dear Mrs. Manners could have had her way, Dolly would have passed that year at a certain young ladies' school in New York. But Mr. Marmaduke's pride in his daughter's beauty got the better of her. The strut in his gait became more marked the day that poem appeared, and he went to the Coffee House both morning and evening, taking snuff to hide his emotions when Miss Manners was spoken of; and he was perceived by many in Church Street arm in arm with Dr. Courtenay himself.

As you may have imagined before now, the doctor's profession was leisure, not medicine. He had known ambition once, it was said, and with reason, for he had studied surgery in Germany for the mere love of the science. After which, making the grand tour in France and Italy, he had taken up that art of being a gentleman in which men became so proficient in my young days. He had learned to speak French like a Parisian, had hobnobbed with wit and wickedness from Versailles to Rome, and then had come back to Annapolis to set the fashions and to spend the fortune his uncle lately had left him. He was our censor of beauty, and passed judgment upon all young ladies as they stepped into the arena. To be noticed by him meant success; to be honoured in the *Gazette* was to be crowned at once a reigning belle. The chord of his approval once set a-vibrating, all minor chords sang in harmony. And it was the doctor who raised the first public toast to Miss Manners. Alas! I might have known it would be so!

But Miss Dorothy was not of a nature to remain dependent upon a censor's favour. The minx deported herself like any London belle of experience, as tho' she had known the world from her cradle. She was not to be deceived by the face value of the ladies' praises, nor rebuffed unmercifully by my Aunt Caroline, who had held the sceptre in the absence of a younger aspirant. The first time these ladies clashed, which was not long in coming, my aunt met with a wit as sharp again as her own, and never afterwards essayed an open tilt. The homage of men Dolly took as Cæsar received tribute, as a matter of course. The doctor himself rode to the races beside the Manners coach, leaning gallantly over the door. My lady held court in her father's box, received and dismissed, smiled and frowned, with Courtenay as her master of ceremonies. Mr. Dulany was one of the presidents of the Jockey Club that year, and his horse winning the honours he presented her with his colours, scarlet and white, which she graciously wore. The doctor swore he would import a horse the next season on the chance of the privilege. My aunt was furious. I have never mentioned her beauty because I never could see it. 'Twas a coarser type than attracted me. She was then not greatly above six and thirty, appearing young for that age, and she knew the value of lead in judicious quantity. At that meet gentlemen came to her box only to talk of Miss Manners, to marvel that one so young could have the *bel air*, to praise her beauty and *addresse*, or to remark how well Mr. Dulany's red and white became her. With all of which Mrs. Grafton was fain to agree, and must even excel, until her small stock of patience was exhausted. To add to her chagrin my aunt lost a pretty sum to the rector by Mr. Dulany's horse. I came upon her after the race trying to coax her head-dress through her coach door, Mr. Allen having tight hold of her hand the while.

"And so he thinks he has found a divinity, does he?" I overheard her saying. "I, for one, am heartily sick of Dr. Courtenay's notions. Were he to choose a wench out of the King's passengers I'd warrant our macaronies to compose odes to her eyebrows." And at that moment perceiving me she added, "Why so disconsolate, my dear nephew? Miss Dolly is the craze now, and will last about as long as another of the doctor's whims. And then you shall have her to yourself."

"A pretty woman is ever the fashion, Aunt Caroline," I said.

"Hoity-toity," returned my aunt, who had by then succeeded in getting her head-gear safe within; "the fashion, yes, until a prettier comes along."

"There is small danger of that for the present," I said, smiling. "Surely you can find no fault with this choice!"

"Gadzooks! If I were blind, sir, I think I might!" she cried unguardedly.

"I will not dispute that, Aunt Caroline," I answered.

And as I rode off I heard her giving directions in no mild tone to the coachman through Mr. Allen.

Perchance you did not know, my dears, that Annapolis had the first theatre in all the colonies. And if you care to search through the heap of Maryland *Gazettes* in the garret, I make no doubt you will come across this announcement for a certain night in the spring of the year 1769:—

> By Permission of his Excellency, the Governor,
> at the New Theatre in Annapolis,
> by the American Company of Comedians, on Monday next, being the 22nd of this Instant, will be performed
>
> ROMEO AND JULIET.
>
> (Romeo by a young Gentleman for his Diversion.)
> Likewise the Farce called
>
> MISS IN HER TEENS.
>
> To begin precisely at Seven of the Clock. Tickets to be had at the Printing Office. Box 10s. Pit 1s 6d.
> No Person to be admitted behind the Scenes.

The gentleman to perform Romeo was none other than Dr. Courtenay himself. He had a gentlemanly passion for the stage, as was the fashion in those days, and had organized many private theatricals. The town was in a ferment over the event, boxes being taken a week ahead. The doctor himself writ the epilogue, to be recited by the beautiful Mrs. Hallam, who had inspired him the year before to compose that famous poem beginning:—

> "Around her see the Graces play,
>   See Venus' Wanton doves,
> And in her Eye's Pellucid Ray
>   See little Laughing Loves.
> Ye gods! 'Tis Cytherea's Face."

You may find that likewise in Mr. Green's newspaper.

The new theatre was finished in West Street that spring, the old one having proven too small for our gay capital. 'Twas then the best in the New World, the censor having pronounced it far above any provincial playhouse he had seen abroad. The scenes were very fine, the boxes carved and gilded in excellent good taste, and both pit and gallery commodious. And we, too, had our "Fops' Alley," where our macaronies ogled the fair and passed from box to box.

For that night of nights when the doctor acted I received an invitation from Dolly to Mr. Marmaduke's box, and to supper afterward in Prince George Street. When I arrived, the playhouse was lit with myriad candles, — to be snuffed save the footlights presently, — and the tiers were all brilliant with the costumes of ladies and gentlemen. Miss Tayloe and Miss Dulany were of our party, with Fitzhugh and Worthington, and Mr. Manners for propriety. The little fop spent his evening, by the way, in a box opposite, where my Aunt Caroline gabbled to him and Mr. Allen during the whole performance. My lady got more looks than any in the house. She always drew admiration, indeed, but there had been much speculation of late whether she favoured Dr. Courtenay or Fitzhugh, and some had it that the doctor's acting would decide between the two.

When Romeo came upon the stage he was received with loud applause. But my lady showed no interest, — not she, — while the doctor fervently recited, "Out of her favour, where I am in love." In the first orchard scene, with the boldness of a practised lover, he almost ignored Mrs. Hallam in the balcony. It seemed as though he cast his burning words and languishing glances at my lady in the box, whereupon there was a deal of nudging round about. Miss asked for her smelling salts, and declared the place was stifling. But I think if the doctor had cherished a hope of her affections he lost it when he arrived at the lines, "She speaks, yet she says nothing." At that unhappy moment Miss Dorothy was deep in conversation with Fitzhugh, the audible titter in the audience arousing her. How she reddened when she perceived the faces turned her way!

"What was it, Betty?" she demanded quickly.

But Betty was not spiteful, and would not tell. Fitzhugh himself explained, and to his sorrow, for during the rest of the evening she would have nothing to do with him. Presently she turned to me. Glancing upward to where Patty leaned on the rail between Will Fotheringay and Singleton, she whispered: —

"I wonder you can sit here so quiet, Richard. You are showing a deal of self-denial."

"I am happy enough," I answered, surprised.

"I hear you have a rival," says she.

"I know I have a dozen," I answered.

"I saw Percy Singleton walking with her in Mr. Galloway's fields but yesterday," said Dolly, "and as they came out upon the road they looked as guilty as if I had surprised them arm in arm."

Now that she should think I cared for Patty never entered my head. . I was thrown all in a heap.

"You need not be so disturbed," whispers my lady. "Singleton has a crooked mouth, and I credit Patty with ample sense to choose between you. I adore her, Richard. I wish I had her sweet ways."

"But," I interrupted, when I was somewhat recovered, "why should you think me in love with Patty? I have never been accused of that before."

"Oh, fie! You deny her?" says Dolly. "I did not think that of you, Richard."

"You should know better," I replied, with some bitterness.

We were talking in low tones, Dolly with her head turned from the stage, whence the doctor was flinging his impassioned speeches in vain. And though the light fell not upon her face, I seemed to feel her looking me through and through.

"You do not care for Patty?" she whispered. And I thought a quiver of earnestness was in her voice. Her face was so close to mine that her breath fanned my cheek.

"No," I said. "Why do you ask me? Have I ever been one to make pretences?"

She turned away.

"But you," I said, bending to her ear, "is it Fitzhugh, Dorothy?"

I heard her laugh softly.

"No," said she, "I thought you might divine, sir."

Was it possible? And yet she had played so much with me that I dared not risk the fire. She had too many accomplished gallants at her feet to think of Richard, who had no novelty and no wit. I sat still, barely conscious of the rising and falling voices beyond the footlights, feeling only her living presence at my side. She spoke not another word until the playhouse servants had relighted the chandeliers, and Dr. Courtenay came in, flushed with triumph, for his mead of praise.

"And how went it, Miss Manners?" says he, very confident.

"Why, you fell over the orchard wall, doctor," retorts my lady. "La! I believe I could have climbed it better myself."

And all he got was a hearty laugh for his pains, Mr. Marmaduke joining in from the back of the box. And the story was at the Coffee House early on the morrow.

CHAPTER XI

A FESTIVAL AND A PARTING

My grandfather and I were seated at table together. It was early June, the birds were singing in the garden, and the sweet odours of the flowers were wafted into the room.

"Richard," says he, when Scipio had poured his claret, "my illness cheated you out of your festival last year. I dare swear you deem yourself too old for birthdays now."

I laughed.

"So it is with lads," said Mr. Carvel; "they will rush into manhood as heedless as you please. Take my counsel, boy, and remain young. Do not cross the bridge before you have to. And I have been thinking that we shall have your fête this year, albeit you are grown, and Miss Dolly is the belle of the province. 'Tis like sunshine into my old heart to see the lads and lasses again, and to hear the merry, merry fiddling. I will have his new Excellency, who seems a good and a kindly man, and Lloyd and Tilghman and Dulany and the rest, with their ladies, to sit with me. And there will be plenty of punch and syllabub and sangaree, I warrant; and tarts and jellies and custards, too, for the misses. Ring for Mrs. Willis, my son."

Willis came with her curtsey to the old gentleman, who gave his order then and there. He never waited for a fancy of this kind to grow cold.

"We shall all be children again, on that day, Mrs. Willis," says he. "And I catch any old people about, they shall be thrust straight in the town stocks, i' faith."

Willis made another curtsey.

"We missed it sorely, last year, please your honour," says she, and departs smiling.

"And you shall have your Patty Swain, Richard," Mr. Carvel continued. " Do you mind how you once asked the favour of inviting her in the place of a present? Oons! I loved you for that, boy. 'Twas like a Carvel. And I love that lass, Whig or no Whig. 'Pon my soul, I do. She hath demureness and dignity, and suits me better than you whimsical baggage you are all mad over. I'll have Mr. Swain beside me, too. I'll warrant I'd teach his daughter loyalty in a day, and I had again your years and your spirit!"

I have but to close my eyes, and my fancy takes me back to that birthday festival. Think of it, my dears! Near three-score years are gone since then, when this old man you call grandfather, and some — bless me! — great-grandfather, was a lusty lad like Comyn here. But his hand is steady as he writes these words and his head clear, because he hath not greatly disabused that life which God has given him.

How can I, tho' her face and form are painted on my memory, tell you what fair, pert Miss Dorothy was at that time? Ay, I know what you would say: that Sir Joshua's portrait hangs above, executed but the year after, and hung at the second exhibition of the Royal Academy. As I look upon it now, I say that no whit of its colour is overcharged. And there is likewise Mr. Peale's portrait, done much later. I answer that these great masters have accomplished what poor, human art can do. But Nature hath given us a better picture. "Come hither, Bess! Yes, truly, you have Dolly's hair, with the very gloss upon it. But fashions have changed, my child, and that is not as Dolly wore it." Whereupon Bess goes to the portrait, and presently comes back to give me a start. And then we go hand in hand up the stairs of Calvert House even to the garret, where an old cedar chest is laid away under the eaves. Bess, the minx, well knows it, and takes out a prim little gown with the white fading yellow, and white silk mits without fingers, and white stockings with clocks, and a gauze cap, with wings and streamers, that sits saucily on the black locks; and the lawn-embroidered apron; and such dainty, high-heeled slippers with the pearls still aglisten upon the buckles. Away she flies to put them on. And then my heart gives a leap to see my Dorothy back again,—back again as she was that June afternoon we went together to my last birthday party, her girlish arms bare to the elbow, and the lace about her slender throat. Yes, Bess hath the very tilt of her chin, the regal grace of that slim figure, and the deep blue eyes.

"Grandfather, dear, you are crushing the gown!"

And so the fire is not yet gone out of this old frame.

Ah, yes, there they are again, those unpaved streets of old Annapolis arched with great trees on either side. And here is Dolly, holding her skirt in one hand and her fan in the other, and I in a brave blue coat, and pumps with gold buttons, and a cocked hat of the newest fashion. I had met her leaning over the gate in Prince George Street. And, what was strange for her, so deep in thought that she jumped when I spoke her name.

"Dorothy, I have come for you to walk to the party, as we used when we were children."

"As we used when we were children!" cried she. And flinging wide the gate, stretched out her hand for me to take. "And you are eighteen years to-day! It seems but last year when we skipped hand in hand to Marlboro' Street with Mammy Lucy behind us. Are you coming, mammy?" she called.

"Yes, mistis, I'se comin'," said a voice from behind the golden-rose bushes, and out stepped Aunt Lucy in a new turban, making a curtsey to me. "La, Marse Richard!" said she, "to think you'se growed to be a fine gemman! 'Taint but t'other day you was kissin' Miss Dolly on de plantation."

"It seems longer than that to me, Aunt Lucy," I answered, laughing at Dolly's blushes.

"You have too good a memory, mammy," said my lady, withdrawing her fingers from mine.

"Bress you, honey! De ole woman doan't forgit some things."

And she fell back to a respectful six paces.

"Those were happy times," said Dorothy. Then the little sigh became a laugh. "I mean to enjoy myself to-day, Richard. But I fear I shall not see as much of you as I used. You are old enough to play the host, now."

"You shall see as much as you will."

"Where have you been of late, sir? In Gloucester Street?"

"'Tis your own fault, Dolly. You are changeable as the sky,— to-day sunny, and to-morrow cold. I am sure of my welcome in Gloucester Street."

She tripped a step as we turned the corner, and came closer to my side.

"You must learn to take me as you find me, dear Richard. To-day I am in a holiday humour."

Some odd note in her tone troubled me, and I glanced at her quickly. She was a constant wonder and puzzle to me. After that night at the theatre my hopes had risen for the hundredth time, but I had gone to Prince George Street on the morrow to meet another rebuff — and Fitzhugh. So I had learned to interpret her by other means than words, and now her mood seemed reckless rather than merry.

"Are you not happy, Dolly?" I asked abruptly.

She laughed. "What a silly question!" she said. "Why do you ask?"

"Because I believe you are not."

In surprise she looked up at me, and then down at the pearls upon her satin slippers.

"I am going with you to your birthday festival, Richard. Could we wish for more? I am as happy as you."

"That may well be, for I might be happier."

Again her eyes met mine, and she hummed an air. So we came to the gate, beside which stood Diomedes and Hugo in the family claret-red. A coach was drawn up, and another behind it, and we went down the leafy walk in the midst of a bevy of guests.

We have no such places nowadays, my dears, as was my grandfather's. The ground between the street and the brick wall in the rear was a great stretch, as ample in acreage as many a small country-place we have in these times. The house was on the high land in front, hedged in by old trees, and thence you descended by stately tiers until you came to the level which held the dancers. Beyond that, and lower still, a lilied pond widened out of the sluggish brook with a cool and rustic spring-house at one end. The spring-house was thatched, with windows looking out upon the water. Long after, when I went to France, I was reminded of the shy beauty of this part of my old home by the secluded pond of the Little Trianon. So was it that King Louis's Versailles had spread its influence a thousand leagues to our youthful continent.

My grandfather sat in his great chair on the sward beside the fiddlers, his old friends gathering around him, as in former years.

"And this is the miss that hath already broken half the bachelor hearts in town!" said he, gayly. "What was my prediction, Miss Dolly, when you stepped your first dance at Carvel Hall?"

"Indeed, you do me wrong, Mr. Carvel!"

"And I were a buck, you would not break mine, I warrant, unless it were tit for tat," said my grandfather; thereby putting me to more confusion than Dolly, who laughed with the rest.

"'Tis well to boast, Mr. Carvel, when we are out of the battle," cried Mr. Lloyd.

Dolly was carried off immediately, as I expected. The doctor and Worthington and Fitzhugh were already there, and waiting. I stood by Mr. Carvel's chair, receiving the guests, and presently came Mr. Swain and Patty.

"Heigho!" called Mr. Carvel, when he saw her; "here is the young lady that hath my old affections. You are right welcome, Mr. Swain. Scipio, another chair! 'Tis not over the wall any more, Miss Patty, with our flowered India silk. But I vow I love you best with your étui."

Patty, too, was carried off, for you may be sure that Will Fotheringay and Singleton were standing on one foot and then the other, waiting for Mr. Carvel to have done. Next arrived my aunt, in a wide calash and a wider hoop, her stays laced so that she limped, and her hair wonderfully and fearfully arranged by her Frenchman. Neither she nor Grafton was slow to shower congratulations upon my grandfather and

myself. Mr. Marmaduke went through the ceremony after
them. Dorothy's mother drew me aside. As long as I could
remember her face had been one that revealed a life's disappointment. But to-day I thought it bore a trace of a deeper
anxiety.

"How well I recall this day, eighteen years ago, Richard,"
she said. "And how proud your dear mother was that she
had given a son to Captain Jack. She had prayed for a son.
I hope you will always do your parents credit, my dear boy.
They were both dear, dear friends of mine."

My Aunt Caroline's harsher voice interrupted her.

"Gadzooks, ma'am!" she cried, as she approached us, "I
have never in my life laid eyes upon such beauty as your
daughter's. You will have to take her home, Mrs. Manners,
to do her justice. You owe it her, ma'am. Come, nephew, off
with you, and head the minuet with Miss Dolly!"

My grandfather was giving the word to the fiddlers. But
whether a desire to cross my aunt held me back, or a sense of
duty to greet the guests not already come, or a vague intuition
of some impending news drawn from Mrs. Manners and
Dorothy, I know not. Mr. Fitzhugh was easily persuaded
to take my place, and presently I slipped unnoticed into a
shaded seat on the side of the upper terrace, whence I could
see the changing figures on the green. And I thought of the
birthday festivals Dolly and I had spent here, almost since we
were of an age to walk. Wet June days, when the broad
wings of the house rang with the sound of silver laughter and
pattering feet, and echoed with music from the hall; and
merry June days, when the laughter rippled among the lilacs,
and pansies and poppies and sweet peas were outshone by
bright gowns and brighter faces. And then, as if to complete
the picture of the past, my eye fell upon our mammies modestly seated behind the group of older people, Aunt Hester
and Aunt Lucy, their honest, black faces aglow with such
unselfish enjoyment as they alone could feel.

How easily I marked Dorothy among the throng!

Other girls found it hard to compress the spirits of youth
within the dignity of a minuet, and thought of the childish

romp of former years. Not so my lady. Long afterwards I saw her lead a ball with the first soldier and gentleman of the land, but on that Tuesday she carried herself full as well,— so well that his Excellency and the gentlemen about him applauded heartily. As the strains died away and the couples moved off among the privet-lined paths, I went slowly down the terrace. Dorothy had come up to speak to her mother, Dr. Courtenay lingering impatient at her side. And though her colour glowed deeper, and the wind had loosed a wisp of her hair, she took his Excellency's compliments undisturbed. Colonel Sharpe, our former governor, who now made his home in the province, sat beside him.

"Now where a-deuce were you, Richard?" said he. "You have missed as pleasing a sight as comes to a man in a lifetime. Why were you not here to see Miss Manners tread a minuet? My word! Terpsichore herself could scarce have made it go better."

"I saw the dance, sir, from a safe distance," I replied.

"I'll warrant!" said he, laughing, while Dolly shot me a wayward glance from under her long lashes. "I'll warrant your eyes were fast on her from beginning to end. Come, sir, confess!"

His big frame shook with the fun of it, for none in the colony could be jollier than he on holiday occasions: and the group of ladies and gentlemen beside him caught the infection, so that I was sore put to it.

"Will your Excellency confess likewise?" I demanded.

"So I will, Richard, and make patent to all the world that she hath the remains of that shuttlecock, my heart."

Up gets his Excellency (for so we still called him) and makes Dolly a low reverence, kissing the tips of her white fingers. My lady drops a mock curtsey in return.

"Your Excellency can do no less than sue for a dance," drawled Dr. Courtenay.

"And no more, I fear, sir, not being so nimble as I once was. I resign in your favour, doctor," said Colonel Sharpe.

Dr. Courtenay made his bow, his hat tucked under his arm. But he had much to learn of Miss Manners if he thought that even one who had been governor of the province could command her. The music was just begun again, and I making off in the direction of Patty Swain, when I was brought up as suddenly as by a rope. A curl was upon Dorothy's lips.

"The dance belongs to Richard, doctor," she said.

"Egad, Courtenay, there you have a buffer!" cried Colonel Sharpe, as the much-discomfited doctor bowed with a very ill grace; while I, in no small bewilderment, walked off with Dorothy. And a parting shot of the delighted colonel brought the crimson to my face. Like the wind or April weather was my lady, and her ways far beyond such a great simpleton as I.

"So I am ever forced to ask you to dance!" said Dolly. "What were you about, moping off alone, with a party in your honour, sir?"

"I was watching you, as I told his Excellency."

"Oh, fie!" she cried. "Why don't you assert yourself, Richard? There was a time when you gave me no peace."

"And then you rebuked me for dangling," I retorted.

Up started the music, the fiddlers bending over their bows with flushed faces, having dipped into the cool punch in the interval. Away flung my lady to meet Singleton, while I swung Patty, who squeezed my hand in return. And soon we were in the heat of it, — sober minuet no longer, but romp and riot, the screams of the lasses a-mingle with our own laughter, as we spun them until they were dizzy. My brain was a-whirl as well, and presently I awoke to find Dolly pinching my arm.

"Have you forgotten me, Richard?" she whispered. "My other hand, sir. It is 'down the middle.'"

Down we flew between the laughing lines, Dolly tripping with her head high, and then back under the clasped hands in the midst of a fire of raillery. Then the music stopped. Some strange exhilaration was in Dorothy.

"Do you remember the place where I used to play fairy godmother, and wind the flowers into my hair?" said she.

What need to ask?

"Come!" she commanded decisively.

A FESTIVAL AND A PARTING

"With all my heart!" I exclaimed, wondering at this new caprice.

"If we can but slip away unnoticed, they will never find us there," she said. And led the way herself, silent. At length we came to the damp shade where the brook dived under the corner of the wall. I stooped to gather the lilies of the valley, and she wove them into her hair as of old. Suddenly she stopped, the bunch poised in her hand.

"Would you miss me if I went away, Richard?" she asked, in a low voice.

"What do you mean, Dolly?" I cried, my voice failing.

"Just that," said she.

"I would miss you, and sorely, tho' you give me trouble enough."

"Soon I shall not be here to trouble you, Richard. Papa has decided that we sail next week, on the *Annapolis*, for home."

"Home!" I gasped. "England?"

"I am going to make my bow to royalty," replied she, dropping a deep curtsey. "'Your Majesty, this is Miss Manners, of the province of Maryland!'"

"But next week!" I repeated, with a blank face. "Surely you cannot be ready for the *Annapolis!*"

"McAndrews has instructions to send our things after," said she. "There! You are the first person I have told. You should feel honoured, sir."

I sat down upon the grass by the brook, and for the moment the sap of life seemed to have left me. Dolly continued to twine the flowers. Through the trees sifted the voices and the music, sounds of happiness far away. When I looked up again, she was gazing into the water.

"Are you glad to go?" I asked.

"Of course," answered the minx, readily. "I shall see the world, and meet people of consequence."

"So you are going to England to meet people of consequence!" I cried bitterly.

"How provincial you are, Richard! What people of consequence have we here? The Governor and the honourable members of his Council, forsooth! There is not a title save his Excellency's in our whole colony, and Virginia is scarce better provided."

In spite of my feeling I was fain to laugh at this, knowing well that she had culled it all from little Mr. Marmaduke himself.

"All in good time," said I. "We shall have no lack of noted men presently."

"Mere twopenny heroes," she retorted. "I know your great men, such as Mr. Henry and Dr. Franklin and Mr. Adams."

I began pulling up the grass savagely by the roots.

"I'll lay a hundred guineas you have no regrets at leaving any of us, my fine miss!" I cried, getting to my feet. "You would rather be a lady of fashion than have the love of an honest man,—you who have the hearts of too many as it is."

Her eyes lighted, but with mirth. Laughing, she chose a little bunch of the lilies and worked them into my coat.

"Richard, you silly goose!" she said; "I dote upon seeing you in a temper."

I stood between anger and God knows what other feelings, now starting away, now coming back to her. But I always came back.

"You have ever said you would marry an earl, Dolly," I said sadly. "I believe you do not care for any of us one little bit."

She turned away, so that for the moment I could not see her face, then looked at me with exquisite archness over her shoulder. The low tones of her voice were of a richness indescribable. 'Twas seldom she made use of them.

"You will be coming to Oxford, Richard."

"I fear not, Dolly," I replied soberly. "I fear not, now. Mr. Carvel is too feeble for me to leave him."

At that she turned to me, another mood coming like a gust of wind on the Chesapeake.

"Oh, how I wish they were all like you!" she cried, with a stamp of her foot. "Sometimes I despise gallantry. I hate the smooth compliments of your macaronies. I thank Heaven you are big and honest and clumsy and—"

"And what, Dorothy?" I asked, bewildered.

"And stupid," said she. "Now take me back, sir."

We had not gone thirty paces before we heard a hearty bass voice singing:—

> "'It was a lover and his lass,
> With a hey, with a ho, with a hey nonino.'"

And there was Colonel Sharpe, straying along among the privet hedges.

And so the morning of her sailing came, so full of sadness for me. Why not confess, after nigh threescore years, that break of day found me pacing the deserted dock. At my back, across the open space, was the irregular line of quaint, top-heavy shops since passed away, their sightless windows barred by solid shutters of oak. The good ship *Annapolis*, which was to carry my playmate to broader scenes, lay among the shipping, in the gray roads just quickening with returning light. How my heart ached that morning none shall ever know. But, as the sun shot a burning line across the water, a new salt breeze sprang up and fanned a hope into flame. 'Twas the very breeze that was to blow Dorothy down the bay. Sleepy apprentices took down the shutters, and polished the windows until they shone again; and chipper Mr. Denton Jacques, who did such a thriving business opposite, presently appeared to wish me a bright good morning.

I knew that Captain Waring proposed to sail at ten of the clock; but after breakfasting, I was of two minds whether to see the last of Miss Dorothy, foreseeing a levee in her honour upon the ship. And so it proved. I had scarce set out in a pungy from the dock, when I perceived a dozen boats about the packet; and when I thrust my shoulders through the gangway, there was the company gathered at the mainmast. They made a gay bit of colour,—Dr. Courtenay in a green coat laced with fine Mechlin, Fitzhugh in claret and silk stockings of a Quaker gray, and the other gentlemen as smartly drest. The Dulany girls and the Fotheringay girls, and I know not how many others, were there to see their friend off for home.

In the midst of them was Dorothy, in a crimson silk capuchin, for we had had one of our changes of weather. It was she who spied me as I was drawing down the ladder again.

"It is Richard!" I heard her cry. "He has come at last."

I gripped the rope tightly, sprang to the deck, and faced her as she came out of the group, her lips parted, and the red of her cheeks vying with the hood she wore. I took her hand silently.

"I had given you over, Richard," she said, her eyes looking reproachfully into mine. "Another ten minutes, and I should not have seen you."

Indeed, the topsails were already off the caps, the captain on deck, and the men gathered at the capstan.

"Have you not enough to wish you good-by, Dolly?" I asked.

"There must be a score of them," said my lady, making a face. "But I wish to talk to you."

Mr. Marmaduke, however, had no notion of allowing a gathering in his daughter's honour to be broken up. It had been wickedly said of him, when the news of his coming departure got around, that he feared Dorothy would fall in love with some provincial beau before he could get her within reach of a title. When he observed me talking to her, he hurried away from the friends come to see his wife (he had none himself), and seizing me by the arm implored me to take good care of my dear grandfather, and to write them occasionally of the state of his health, and likewise how I fared.

"I think Dorothy will miss you more than any of them, Richard," said he. "Will you not, my dear?"

But she was gone. I, too, left him without ceremony, to speak to Mrs. Manners, who was standing apart, looking shoreward. She started when I spoke, and I saw that tears were in her eyes.

"Are you coming back soon, Mrs. Manners?" I asked.

"Oh, Richard! I don't know," she answered, with a little choke in her voice. "I hope it will be no longer than a year, for we are leaving all we hold dear for a very doubtful pleasure."

A FESTIVAL AND A PARTING 115

She bade me write to them, as Mr. Marmaduke had, only she was sincere. Then the mate came, with his hand to his cap, respectfully to inform visitors that the anchor was up and down. Albeit my spirits were low, 'twas no small entertainment to watch the doctor and his rivals at their adieus. Courtenay had at his command an hundred subterfuges to outwit his fellows, and so manœuvred that he was the last of them over the side. As for me, luckily, I was not worth a thought. But as the doctor leaned over her hand, I vowed in my heart that if Dorothy was to be gained only in such a way I would not stoop to it. And in my heart I doubted it. I heard Dr. Courtenay hint, looking meaningly at her cloak, that some of his flowers would not have appeared amiss there.

"Why, doctor," says my lady aloud, with a side glance at me, "the wisdom of Solomon might not choose out of twenty baskets."

And this was all the thanks he got for near a boat-load of roses! When at length the impatient mate had hurried him off, Dolly turned to me. It was not in me to say more than:—

"Good-by, Dorothy. And do not forget your old playmate. He will never forget you."

We stood within the gangway. With a quick movement she threw open her cloak, and pinned to her gown I saw a faded bunch of lilies of the valley.

I had but the time to press her hand. The boatswain's pipe whistled, and the big ship was already sliding in the water as I leaped into my pungy, which Hugo was holding to the ladder. We pulled off to where the others waited.

But the *Annapolis* sailed away down the bay, and never another glimpse we caught of my lady.

CHAPTER XII

NEWS FROM A FAR COUNTRY

If perchance, my dears, there creeps into this chronicle too much of an old man's heart, I know he will be forgiven. What life ever worth living has been without its tender attachment? Because, forsooth, my hair is white now, does Bess flatter herself I do not know her secret? Or does Comyn believe that these old eyes can see no farther than the spectacles before them? Were it not for the lovers, my son, satins and broadcloths had never been invented. And were it not for the lovers, what joys and sorrows would we lack in our lives!

That was a long summer indeed. And tho' Wilmot House was closed, I often rode over of a morning when the dew was on the grass. It cheered me to smoke a pipe with old McAndrews, Mr. Manners's factor, who loved to talk of Miss Dorothy near as much as I. He had served her grandfather, and people said that had it not been for McAndrews, the Manners fortune had long since been scattered, since Mr. Marmaduke knew nothing of anything that he should. I could not hear from my lady until near the first of October, and so I was fain to be content with memories — memories and hard work. For I had complete charge of the plantation now.

My Uncle Grafton came twice or thrice, but without his family, Aunt Caroline and Philip having declared their independence. My uncle's manner to me was now of studied kindness, and he was at greater pains than before to give me no excuse for offence. I had little to say to him. He spent his visits reading to Mr. Carvel, who sat in his chair all the day long. Mr. Allen came likewise, to perform the same office.

My contempt for the rector was grown more than ever. On my grandfather's account, however, I refrained from quarrelling with him. And, when we were alone, my plain speaking did not seem to anger him, or affect him in any way. Others came, too. Such was the affection Mr. Carvel's friends bore him that they did not desert him when he was no longer the companion he had been in former years. We had more company than the summer before.

In the autumn a strange thing happened. When we had taken my grandfather to the Hall in June, his dotage seemed to settle upon him. He became a trembling old man, at times so peevish that we were obliged to summon with an effort what he had been. He was suspicious and fault-finding with Scipio and the other servants, though they were never so busy for his wants. Mrs. Willis's dainties were often untouched, and he would frequently sit for hours between slumber and waking, or mumble to himself as I read the prints. But about the time of the equinoctial a great gale came out of the south so strongly that the water rose in the river over the boat landing; and the roof was torn from one of the curing-sheds. The next morning dawned clear, and brittle, and blue. To my great surprise, Mr. Carvel sent for me to walk with him about the place, that he might see the damage with his own eyes. A huge walnut had fallen across the drive, and when he came upon it he stopped abruptly.

"Old friend!" he cried, "have you succumbed? After all these years have you dropped from the weight of a blow?" He passed his hand caressingly along the trunk, and scarce ever had I seen him so affected. In truth, for the instant I thought him deranged. He raised his cane above his shoulder and struck the bark so heavily that the silver head sunk deep into the wood. "Look you, Richard," he said, the water coming into his eyes, "look you, the heart of it is gone, lad; and when the heart is rotten 'tis time for us to go. That walnut was a life friend, my son. We have grown together," he continued, turning from me to the giant and brushing his cheeks, "but by God's good will we shall not die so, for my heart is still as young as the days when you were sprouting."

And he walked back to the house more briskly than he had come, refusing, for the first time, my arm. And from that day, I say, he began to mend. The lacing of red came again to his cheeks, and before we went back to town he had walked with me to Master Dingley's tavern on the highroad, and back.

We moved into Marlboro' Street the first part of November. I had seen my lady off for England, wearing my faded flowers, the panniers of the fine gentleman in a neglected pile at her cabin door. But not once had she deigned to write me. It was McAndrews who told me of her safe arrival. In Annapolis rumours were a-flying of conquests she had already made. I found Betty Tayloe had had a letter, filled with the fashion in caps and gowns, and the mention of more than one noble name. All of this being, for unknown reasons, sacred, I was read only part of the postscript, in which I figured: "The London Season was done almost before we arrived," so it ran. "We had but the Opportunity to pay our Humble Respects to their Majesties, and appear at a few Drum-Majors and Garden Fêtes. Now we are off to Brighthelmstone, and thence, so Papa says, to Spa and the Continent until the end of January. I am pining for news of Maryland, dearest Betty. Address me in care of Mr. Ripley, Barrister, of Lincoln's Inn, and bid Richard Carvel write me."

"Which does not look as if she were coming back within the year," said Betty, as she poured me a dish of tea.

Alas, no! But I did not write. I tried and failed. And then I tried to forget. I was constant at all the gayeties, gave every miss in town a share of my attention, rode to hounds once a week at Whitehall or the South River Club with a dozen young beauties. But cantering through the winter mists 'twas Dolly, in her red riding-cloak and white beaver, I saw beside me. None of them had her seat in the saddle, and none of them her light hand on the reins. And tho' they lacked not fire and skill, they had not my lady's dash and daring to follow over field and fallow, stream and searing, and be in at the death with heightened colour, but never a lock awry.

Then came the first assembly of the year. I got back from

Bentley Manor, where I had been a-visiting the Fotheringays, just in time to call for Patty in Gloucester Street.

"Have you heard the news from abroad, Richard?" she asked, as I handed her into my chariot.

"Never a line," I replied.

"Pho!" exclaimed Patty; "you tell me that! Where have you been hiding? Then you shall not have it from me."

I had little trouble, however, in persuading her. For news was a rare luxury in those days, and Patty was plainly uncomfortable until she should have it out.

"I would not give you the vapours to-night for all the world, Richard," she exclaimed. "But if you must, — Dr. Courtenay has had a letter from Mr. Manners, who says that Dolly is to marry his Grace of Chartersea. There now!"

"And I am not greatly disturbed," I answered, with a fine, careless air.

The lanthorn on the chariot was burning bright. And I saw Patty look at me, and laugh.

"Indeed!" says she; "what a sex is that to which you belong. How ready are men to deny us at the first whisper! And I thought you the most constant of all. For my part, I credit not a word of it. 'Tis one of Mr. Marmaduke's lies and vanities."

"And for my part, I think it true as gospel," I cried. "Dolly always held a coronet above her colony, and all her life has dreamed of a duke."

"Nay," answered Patty, more soberly; "nay, you do her wrong. You will discover one day that she is loyal to the core, tho' she has a fop of a father who would serve his Grace's chocolate. We are all apt to talk, my dear, and to say what we do not mean, as you are doing."

"Were I to die to-morrow, I would repeat it," I exclaimed. But I liked Patty the better for what she had said.

"And there is more news, of less import," she continued, as I was silent. "The *Thunderer* dropped anchor in the roads to-day, and her officers will be at the assembly. And Betty tells me there is a young lord among them, — la! I have clean forgot the string of adjectives she used, — but she would have had me know he was as handsome as Apollo, and so dashing and diverting as to put Courtenay and all our wits to shame. She dined with him at the Governor's."

I barely heard her, tho' I had seen the man-o'-war in the harbour as I sailed in that afternoon.

The assembly hall was filled when we arrived, aglow with candles and a-tremble with music, the powder already flying, and the tables in the recesses at either end surrounded by those at the cards. A lively scene, those dances at the old Stadt House, but one I love best to recall with a presence that endeared it to me. The ladies in flowered aprons and caps and brocades and trains, and the gentlemen in brilliant coats, trimmed with lace and stiffened with buckram. That night, as Patty had predicted, there was a smart sprinkling of uniforms from the *Thunderer*. One of those officers held my eye. He was as well-formed a lad, or man (for he was both), as it had ever been my lot to see. He was neither tall nor short, but of a good breadth. His fair skin was tanned by the weather, and he wore his own wavy hair powdered, as was just become the fashion, and tied with a ribbon behind.

"Mercy, Richard, that must be his Lordship. Why, his good looks are all Betty claimed for them!" exclaimed Patty. Mr. Lloyd, who was standing by, overheard her, and was vastly amused at her downright way.

"I will fetch him directly, Miss Swain," said he, "as I have done for a dozen ladies before you." And fetch him he did.

"Miss Swain, this is my Lord Comyn," said he. "Your Lordship, one of the boasts of our province."

Patty grew red as the scarlet with which his Lordship's coat was lined. She curtseyed, while he made a profound bow.

"What! Another boast, Mr. Lloyd!" he cried. "Miss Swain is the tenth I have met. But I vow they excel as they proceed."

"Then you must meet no more, my Lord," said Patty, laughing at Mr. Lloyd's predicament.

"Egad, then, I will not," declared Comyn. "I protest I am satisfied."

Then I was presented. He had won me on the instant with his open smile and frank, boyish manner.

"And this is young Mr. Carvel, whom I hear wins every hunt in the colony?" said he.

"I fear you have been misinformed, my Lord," I replied, flushing with pleasure nevertheless.

"Nay, my Lord," Mr. Lloyd struck in; "Richard could ride down the devil himself, and he were a fox. You will see for yourself to-morrow."

"I pray we may not start the devil," said his Lordship; "or I shall be content to let Mr. Carvel run him down."

This Comyn was a man after my own fancy, as, indeed, he took the fancy of every one at the ball. Though a viscount in his own right, he gave himself not half the airs over us provincials as did many of his messmates. Even Mr. Jacques, who was sour as last year's cider over the doings of Parliament, lost his heart, and asked why we were not favoured in America with more of his sort.

By a great mischance Lord Comyn had fallen into the tender clutches of my Aunt Caroline. It seemed she had known his uncle, the Honourable Arthur Comyn, in New York; and now she undertook to be responsible for his Lordship's pleasure at Annapolis, that he might meet only those of the first fashion. Seeing him talking to Patty, my aunt rose abruptly from her loo and made toward us, all paint and powder and patches, her chin in the air, which barely enabled her to look over Miss Swain's head.

"My Lord," she cries, "I will show you our colonial reel. which is about to begin, and I warrant you is gayer than any dance you have at home."

"Your very devoted, Mrs. Carvel," says his Lordship, with a bow, "but Miss Swain has done me the honour."

"O Lud!" cries my aunt, sweeping the room, "I vow I cannot keep pace with the misses nowadays. Is she here?"

"She was but a moment since, ma'am," replied Comyn, instantly, with a mischievous look at me, while poor Patty stood blushing not a yard distant.

There were many who overheard, and who used their fans

and their napkins to hide their laughter at the very just snub
Mrs. Grafton had received. And I wondered at the readiness
with which he had read her character, liking him all the
better. But my aunt was not to be disabled by this, — not she.
After the dance she got hold of him, keeping him until certain
designing ladies with daughters took him away; their names
charity forbids me to mention. But in spite of them all he
contrived to get Patty for supper, when I took Betty Tayloe,
and we were very merry at table together. His Lordship
proved more than able to take care of himself, and contrived to send Philip about his business when he pulled up a
chair beside us. He drank a health to Miss Swain, and another to Miss Tayloe, and was on the point of filling a third
glass to the ladies of Maryland, when he caught himself and
brought his hand down on the table.

"Gad's life!" cried he, "but I think she's from Maryland,
too!"

"Who?" demanded the young ladies, in a breath.

But I knew.

"Who!" exclaimed Comyn. "Who but Miss Dorothy Manners! Isn't she from Maryland?" And marking our astonished nods, he continued: "Why, she descended upon Mayfair
when they were so weary for something to worship, and they
went mad over her in a s'ennight. I give you Miss Manners!"

"And you know her!" exclaimed Patty, her voice quivering
with excitement.

"Faith!" said his Lordship, laughing. "For a whole month
I was her most devoted, as were we all at Almack's. I stayed
until the last minute for a word with her, — which I never got,
by the way, — and paid near a guinea a mile for a chaise to
Portsmouth as a consequence. Already she has had her choice
from a thousand a year up, and I tell you our English ladies
are green with envy."

I was stunned, you may be sure. And yet, I might have
expected it.

"If your Lordship has left your heart in England," said
Betty, with a smile, "I give you warning you must not tell
our ladies here of it."

"I care not who knows it, Miss Tayloe," he cried. That fustian, insincerity, was certainly not one of his faults. "I care not who knows it. To pass her chariot is to have your heart stolen, and you must needs run after and beg mercy. But, ladies," he added, his eye twinkling; "having seen the women of your colony, I marvel no longer at Miss Manners's beauty."

He set us all a-laughing.

"I fear you were not born a diplomat, sir," says Patty. "You agree that we are beautiful, yet to hear that one of us is more so is small consolation."

"We men turn as naturally to Miss Manners as plants to the sun, ma'am," he replied impulsively. "Yet none of us dare hope for alliance with so brilliant and distant an object. I make small doubt those are Mr. Carvel's sentiments, and still he seems popular enough with the ladies. How now, sir? How now, Mr. Carvel? You have yet to speak on so tender a subject."

My eyes met Patty's.

"I will be no more politic than you, my Lord," I said boldly, "nor will I make a secret of it that I adore Miss Manners full as much."

"Bravo, Richard!" cries Patty; and "Good!" cries his Lordship, while Betty claps her hands. And then Comyn swung suddenly round in his chair.

"Richard Carvel!" says he. "By the seven chimes I have heard her mention your name. The devil fetch my memory!"

"My name!" I exclaimed, in surprise, and prodigiously upset.

"Yes," he answered, with his hand to his head; "some such thought was in my mind this afternoon when I heard of your riding. Stay! I have it! I was at Ampthill, Ossory's place, just before I left. Some insupportable coxcomb was boasting a marvellous run with the hounds nigh across Hertfordshire, and Miss Manners brought him up with a round turn and a half hitch by relating one of your exploits, Richard Carvel. And take my word on't she got no small applause. She told how you had followed a fox over one of your rough provincial counties, which means three of Hertfordshire, *with your arm broken*, by Heaven! and how they lifted you off at the death. And, Mr. Carvel," said my Lord, generously, looking at my flushed face, "you must give me your hand for that."

So Dorothy in England had thought of me at least. But what booted it if she were to marry a duke! My thoughts began to whirl over all Comyn had said of her so that I scarce heard a question Miss Tayloe had put.

"Marry Chartersea! That profligate pig!" Comyn was saying. "She would as soon marry a chairman or a chimney-sweep, I'm thinking. Why, Miss Tayloe, Sir Charles Grandison himself would scarce suit her!"

"Good lack!" said Betty, "I think Sir Charles would be the very last for Dorothy."

CHAPTER XIII

MR. ALLEN SHOWS HIS HAND

So Dorothy's beauty had taken London by storm, even as it had conquered Annapolis! However, 'twas small consolation to me to hear his Grace of Chartersea called a pig and a profligate while better men danced her attendance in Mayfair. Nor, in spite of what his Lordship had said, was I quite easy on the score of the duke. It was in truth no small honour to become a duchess. If Mr. Marmaduke had aught to say, there was an end to hope. She would have her coronet. But in that hour of darkness I counted upon my lady's spirit.

Dr. Courtenay came to the assembly very late, with a new fashion of pinchbeck buckles on his pumps and a new manner of taking snuff. (I caught Fotheringay practising this by the stairs shortly after.) Always an important man, the doctor's prominence had been increased that day by the letter he had received. He was too thorough a courtier to profess any grief over Miss Manners's match, and went about avowing that he had always predicted a duke for Miss Dorothy. And he drew a deal of pleasure from the curiosity of those who begged but one look at the letter. Show it, indeed! For no consideration. A private communication from one gentleman to another must be respected. Will Fotheringay swore the doctor was a sly dog, and had his own reasons for keeping it to himself.

The doctor paid his compliment to the captain of the *Thunderer*, and to his Lordship; hoped that he would see them at the meet on the morrow, tho' his gout forbade his riding to hounds. He saluted me in the most friendly way, for I played billiards with him at the Coffee House now, and he won my money. He had pronounced my phaeton to be as well appointed as any equipage in town, and had done me the honour to drive out with me on several occasions. It was Betty that brought him humiliation that evening.

"What do you think of the soar our Pandora hath taken, Miss Betty?" says he. "From a Maryland manor to a ducal palace. 'Tis a fable, egad! No less!"

"Indeed, I think it is," retorted Betty. "Mark me, doctor, Dorothy will not put up an instant with a *roué* and a brute."

"A *roué!*" cries he, "and a brute! What the plague, Miss Tayloe! I vow I do not understand you."

"Then ask my Lord Comyn, who knows your Duke of Chartersea," said Betty.

Dr. Courtenay's expression was worth a pistole.

"Comyn know him!" he repeated.

"That he does," replied Betty, laughing. "His Lordship says Chartersea is a pig and a profligate, and I remember not what else. And that Dolly will not look at him. And so little Mr. Marmaduke may go a-hunting for another title."

No wonder I had little desire for dancing that night! I wandered out of the assembly-room and through the silent corridors of the Stadt House, turning over and over again what I had heard, and picturing Dorothy reigning over the macaronies of St. James's Street. She had said nothing of this in her letter to Betty, and had asked me to write to her. But now, with a duke to refuse or accept, could she care to hear from her old playmate? I took no thought of the time, until suddenly my conscience told me I had neglected Patty.

As I entered the hall I saw her at the far end of it talking to Mr. Allen. This I thought strange, for I knew she disliked him. Lord Comyn and Mr. Carroll, the barrister, and Singleton, were standing by, listening. By the time I was halfway across to them the rector turned away. I remember thinking afterwards that he changed colour when he said: "Your servant, Mr. Richard." But I thought nothing of it at the time, and went on to Patty.

"I have come for a country dance, before we go, Patty," I said.

Then something in her mien struck me. Her eyes expressed a pain I had remarked in them before only when she spoke to me of Tom, and her lips were closed tightly. She flushed, and paled, and looked from Singleton to Mr. Carroll. They and his Lordship remained silent.

"I — I cannot, Richard. I am going home," she said, in a low voice.

"I will see if the chariot is here," I answered, surprised, but thinking of Tom.

She stopped me.

"I am going with Mr. Carroll," she said.

I hope a Carvel never has to be rebuffed twice, nor to be humbled by craving an explanation before a company. I was confounded that Patty should treat me thus, when I had done nothing to deserve it. As I made for the door, burning and indignant, I felt as tho' every eye in the room was upon me. Young Harvey drove me that night.

"Marlboro' Street, Mr. Richard?" said he.

"Coffee House," replied I, that place coming first into my head.

Young Harvey seldom took liberties; but he looked down from the box.

"Better home, sir; your pardon, sir."

"D—n it!" I cried, "drive where I bid you!"

I pulled down the fore-glass, though the night was cold, and began to cast about for the cause of Patty's action. And then it was the rector came to my mind. Yes, he had been with her just before I came up, and I made sure on the instant that my worthy instructor was responsible for the trouble. I remembered that I had quarrelled with him the morning before I had gone to Bentley Manor, and threatened to confess his villany and my deceit to Mr. Carvel. He had answered me with a sneer and a dare. I knew that Patty put honour and honesty before all else in the world, and that she would not have suffered my friendship for a day had she believed me to lack either. But she, who knew me so well, was not likely to believe anything he might say without giving me the chance to clear myself. And what could he have told her?

I felt my anger growing big within me, until I grew afraid of what I would do if I were tempted. I had a long score and a heavy score against this rector of St. Anne's,—a score that had been gathering these years. And I felt that my uncle was somewhere behind him; that the two of them were plotters against me, even as Harvey had declared; albeit my Uncle Grafton was little seen in his company now. And finally, in a sinister flash of revelation, came the thought that Grafton himself was at the back of this deception of my grandfather, as to my principles. Fool that I was, it had never occurred to me before. But how was he to gain by it? Did he hope that Mr. Carvel, in a fit of anger, would disinherit me when he found I had deceived him? Yes. And so had left the matter in abeyance near these two years, that the shock might be the greater when it came. I recalled now, with a shudder, that never since the spring of my grandfather's illness had my uncle questioned me upon my politics. I was seized with a fit of fury. I suspected that Mr. Allen would be at the Coffee House after the assembly. And I determined to seize the chance at once and have it out with him then and there.

The inn was ablaze, but as yet deserted; Mr. Claude expectant. He bowed me from my chariot door, and would know what took me from the ball. I threw him some short answer, bade Harvey go home, saying that I would have some fellow light me to Marlboro' Street when I thought proper. And coming into the long room I flung aside my greatcoat and commanded a flask of Mr. Stephen Bordley's old sherry, some of which Mr. Claude had obtained at that bachelor's demise.

The wine was scarce opened before I heard some sort of stir at the front, and two servants in a riding livery of scarlet and white hurried in to seek Mr. Claude. The sight of them sufficed mine host, for he went out as fast as his legs would go, giving the bell a sharp pull as he passed the door; and presently I heard him complimenting two gentlemen into the house. The voice of one I knew,—being no other than Captain Clapsaddle's; and him I had not seen for the past six months. I was just risen to my feet when they came in at the door beside me.

MR. ALLEN SHOWS HIS HAND

"Richard!" cried the captain, and grasped my hand in both his own. I returned his pressure, too much pleased to speak. Then his eye was caught by my finery.

"So ho!" says he, shaking his head at me for a sad rogue. "Wine and women and fine clothes, and not nineteen, or I mistake me. It was so with Captain Jack, who blossomed in a week; and few could vie with him, I warrant you, after he made his decision. But bless me!" he went on, drawing back, "the lad looks mature, and a fair two inches broader than last spring. But why are you not at the assembly, Richard?"

"I have but now come from there, sir," I replied, not caring in the presence of a stranger to enter into reasons.

At my answer the captain turned from me to the gentleman behind him, who had been regarding us both as we talked. There are some few men in the world, I thank God for it, who bear their value on their countenance; who stand unmistakably for qualities which command respect and admiration and love! We seem to recognize such men, and to wonder where we have seen them before. In reality we recognize the virtues they represent. So it was with him I saw in front of me, and by his air and carriage I marked him then and there as a man born to great things. You all know his face, my dears, and I pray God it may live in the sight of those who come after you, for generation upon generation!

"Colonel Washington," said the captain, "this is Mr. Richard Carvel, the son of Captain Carvel."

Mr. Washington did not speak at once. He stood regarding me a full minute, his eye seeming to penetrate the secrets of my life. And I take pride in saying it was an eye I could meet without flinching.

"Your father was a brave man, sir," he said soberly, "and it seems you favour him. I am happy in knowing the son."

For a moment he stood debating whether he would go to the house of one of his many friends in Annapolis, knowing that they would be offended when they learned he had stopped at the inn. He often came to town, indeed, but seldom tarried long; and it had never been my fortune to see him. Being arrived unexpectedly, and obliged to be away early on the morrow, he decided to order rooms of Mr. Claude, sat down with me at the table, and commenced supper. They had ridden from Alexandria. I gathered from their conversation that they were on their way to Philadelphia upon some private business, the nature of which, knowing Captain Daniel's sentiments and those of Colonel Washington, I went not far to guess. The country was in a stir about the Townshend duties; and there being some rumour that all these were to be discharged save only that on tea, anxiety prevailed in our middle colonies that the merchants of New York would abandon the association formed and begin importation. It was of some mission to these merchants that I suspected them.

As I sat beside Colonel Washington, I found myself growing calmer, and ashamed of my lack of self-control. Unconsciously, when we come in contact with the great of character, we mould our minds to their qualities. His very person seemed to exhale, not sanctity, but virility. I felt that this man could command himself and others. In his presence self-command came to me, as a virtue gone out of him. 'Twas not his speech, I would have you know, that took hold of me. He was by no means a brilliant talker, and I had the good fortune to see him at his ease, since he and the captain were old friends. As they argued upon the questions of the day, the colonel did not seek to impress by words, or to fascinate by manner. His opinions were calm and moderate, and appeared to me so just as to admit of no appeal. He scrupled not to use a forceful word when occasion demanded. And yet, now and then, he had a lively way about him with all his dignity. When he had finished his supper he bade Mr. Claude bring another bottle of Mr. Bordley's sherry, having tested mine, and addressed himself to me.

He would know what my pursuits had been; for my father's sake, what were my ambitions? He questioned me about Mr. Carvel's plantation, of which he had heard, and appeared pleased with the answers I gave as to its management and methods. Captain Daniel was no less so. Mr. Washington had agriculture at his finger ends, and gave me some advice which he had found serviceable at Mount Vernon.

"'Tis a pity, Richard," said he, smiling thoughtfully at the captain, "'tis a pity we have no service afield open to our young men. One of your spirit and bearing should be of that profession. Captain Jack was as brave and dashing an officer as I ever laid eyes on."

I hesitated, tho' tingling at the compliment.

"I begin to think I was born for the sea, sir," I answered, at length.

"What!" cried the captain; "what news is this, Richard? 'Slife! how has this come about?"

My anger subdued by Mr. Washington's presence, a curious mood had taken its place. A foolish mood, I thought it, but one of feeling things to come.

"I believe I shall one day take part in a great sea-fight," I said. And, tho' ashamed to speak of it, I told him of Stanwix's prophecy that I should pace the decks of a man-o'-war.

"A pox on Stanwix!" said the captain, "an artful old sea-dog! I never yet knew one who did not think the sun rises and sets from poop to forecastle, who did not wheedle with all the young blood to get them to follow a bow-legged profession."

Colonel Washington laughed.

"Judge not, Clapsaddle," said he; "here are two of us trying to get the lad for our own bow-legged profession. We are as hot as Methodists to convert."

"Small conversion he needed when I was here to watch him, colonel. And he rides with any trooper I ever laid eyes on. Why, sir, I myself threw him on a saddle before he could well-nigh walk, and 'twere a waste of material to put him in the navy."

"But what this old man said of a flag not yet seen in heaven or earth interests me," said Colonel Washington. "Tell me," he added with a penetration we both remarked, "tell me, does your Captain Stanwix follow the times? Is he a man to read his prints and pamphlets? In other words, is he a man who might predict out of his own heated imagination?"

"Nay, sir," I answered, "he nods over his tobacco the day

long. And I will make bold to swear, he has never heard of the Stamp Act."

"'Tis strange," said the colonel, musing; "I have heard of this second sight — have seen it among my own negroes. But I heartily pray that this may be but the childish fancy of an old mariner. How do you interpret it, sir?" he added, addressing himself to me.

"If a prophecy, I can interpret it in but one way," I began, and there I stopped.

"To be sure," said Mr. Washington. He studied me awhile as though weighing my judgment, and went on: "Needless to say, Richard, that such a service, if it comes, will not be that of his Majesty."

"And it were, colonel, I would not embark in it a step," I cried.

He laughed.

"The lad has his father's impulse," he said to Captain Daniel. "But I thought old Mr. Carvel to be one of the warmest loyalists in the colonies."

I bit my lip; for, since that unhappy deception of Mr. Carvel, I had not meant to be drawn into an avowal of my sentiments. But I had, alas, inherited a hasty tongue.

"Mr. Washington," said the captain, "old Mr. Carvel has ever been a good friend to me. And, though I could not but perceive which way the lad was tending, I had held it but a poor return for friendship had I sought by word or deed to bring him to my way of thinking. Nor have I ever suffered his views in my presence."

"My dear sir, I honour you for it," put in the colonel, warmly.

"It is naught to my credit," returned the captain. "I would not, for the sake of my party and beliefs, embitter what remains of my old friend's life."

I drew a long breath and drained the full glass before me.

"Captain Daniel!" I cried, "you must hear me now. I have been waiting your coming these months. And if Colonel Washington gives me leave, I will speak before him."

The colonel bade me proceed, avowing that Captain Carvel's son should have his best assistance.

With that I told them the whole story of Mr. Allen's villany. How I had been sent to him because of my Whig sentiments, and for thrashing a Tory schoolmaster and his flock. This made the gentlemen laugh, tho' Captain Daniel had heard it before. I went on to explain how Mr. Carvel had fallen ill, and was like to die; and how Mr. Allen, taking advantage of his weakness when he rose from his bed, had gone to him with the lie of having converted me. But when I told of the scene between my grandfather and me at Carvel Hall, of the tears of joy that the old gentleman shed, and of how he had given me Firefly as a reward, the captain rose from his chair and looked out of the window into the blackness, and swore a great oath all to himself. And the expression I saw come into the colonel's eyes I shall never forget.

"And you feared the consequences upon your grandfather's health?" he asked gravely.

"So help me God!" I answered, "I truly believe that to have undeceived him would have proved fatal."

"And so, for the sake of the sum he receives for teaching you," cried the captain, with another oath, "this scoundrelly clergyman has betrayed you into a lie. A scheme, by God's life! worthy of a Machiavelli!"

"I have seen too many of his type in our parishes," said Mr. Washington; "and yet the bishop of London seems powerless. And so used have we become in these Southern colonies to tippling and gaming parsons, that I warrant his people accept him as nothing out of the common."

"He is more discreet than the run of them, sir. His parishioners dislike him, not because of his irregularities, but because he is attempting to obtain All Saints from his Lordship, in addition to St. Anne's. He is thought too greedy."

He was silent, his brow a little furrowed, and drummed with his fingers upon the table.

"But this I cannot reconcile," said he, presently, "that the reward is out of all proportion to the risk. Such a clever rascal must play for higher stakes."

I was amazed at his insight. And for the moment was impelled to make a clean breast of my suspicions, — nay, of my convictions of the whole devil's plot. But I had no proofs. I remembered that to the colonel my uncle was a gentleman of respectability and of wealth, and a member of his Excellency's Council. That to accuse him of scheming for my inheritance would gain me nothing in Mr. Washington's esteem. And I caught myself before I had said aught of Mr. Allen's conduct that evening.

"Have you confronted this rector with his perfidy, Richard?" he asked.

"I have, colonel, at my first opportunity." And I related how Mr. Allen had come to the Hall, and what I had said to him, and how he had behaved. And finally told of the picquet we now had during lessons, not caring to shield myself. Both listened intently, until the captain broke out. Mr. Washington's indignation was the stronger for being repressed.

"I will call him out!" cried Captain Daniel, fingering his sword, as was his wont when angered; "I will call him out despite his gown, or else horse him publicly!"

"No, my dear sir, you will do nothing of the kind," said the colonel. "You would gain nothing by it for the lad, and lose much. Such rascals walk in water, and are not to be tracked. He cannot be approached save through Mr. Lionel Carvel himself, and that channel, for Mr. Carvel's sake, must be closed."

"But he must be shown up!" cried the captain.

"What good will you accomplish?" said Mr. Washington; "Lord Baltimore is notorious, and will not remove him. Nay, sir, you must find a way to get the lad from his influence." And he asked me how was my grandfather's health at present.

I said that he had mended beyond my hopes.

"And does he seem to rejoice that you are of the King's party?"

"Nay, sir. Concerning politics he seems strangely apathetic, which makes me fear he is not so well as he appears. All his life he has felt strongly."

"Then I beg you, Richard, take pains to keep neutral. Nor let any passing event, however great, move you to speech or action."

The captain shook his head doubtfully, as tho' questioning the ability of one of my temper to do this.

"I do not trust myself, sir," I answered.

He rose, declaring it was past his hour for bed, and added some kind things which I shall cherish in my memory. As he was leaving he laid his hand on my shoulder.

"One word of advice, my lad," he said. "If by any chance your convictions are to come to your grandfather's ears, let him have them from your own lips." And he bade me good night.

The captain tarried but a moment longer.

"I have a notion who is to blame for this, Richard," he said. "When I come back from New York, we shall see what we shall see."

"I fear he is too slippery for a soldier to catch," I answered.

He went away to bed, telling me to be prudent, and mind the colonel's counsel until he returned from the North.

CHAPTER XIV

THE VOLTE COUPE

I WAS of a serious mind to take the advice. To prove this I called for my wrap-rascal and cane, and for a fellow with a flambeau to light me. But just then the party arrived from the assembly. I was tempted, and I sat down again in a corner of the room, resolved to keep a check upon myself, but to stay awhile.

The rector was the first in, humming a song, and spied me.

"Ho!" he cried, "will you drink, Richard? Or do I drink with you?"

He was already purple with wine.

"God save me from you and your kind!" I replied.

"'Sblood! what a devil's nest of fireworks!" he exclaimed, as he went off down the room, still humming, to where the rest were gathered. And they were soon between bottle and stopper, and quips a-coursing. There was the captain of the *Thunderer*, Collinson by name, Lord Comyn and two brother officers, Will Fotheringay, my cousin Philip, openly pleased to be found in such a company, and some dozen other toadeaters who had followed my Lord a-chair and afoot from the ball, and would have tracked him to perdition had he chosen to go; and lastly Tom Swain, leering and hiccoughing at the jokes, in such a beastly state of drunkenness as I had rarely seen him. His Lordship recognized me and smiled, and was pushing his chair back, when something Collinson said seemed to restrain him.

I believe I was the butt of more than one jest for my aloofness, though I could not hear distinctly for the noise they made. I commanded some French cognac, and kept my eye on the rector, and the sight of him was making me dangerous.

I forgot the advice I had received, and remembered only the months he had goaded me. And I was even beginning to speculate how I could best pick a quarrel with him on any issue but politics, when an unexpected incident diverted me. Of a sudden the tall, ungainly form of Percy Singleton filled the doorway, wrapped in a greatcoat. He swept the room at a glance, and then strode rapidly toward the corner where I sat.

"I had thought to find you here," he said, and dropped into a chair beside me. I offered him wine, but he refused.

"Now," he went on, "what has Patty done?"

"What have I done that I should be publicly insulted?" I cried.

"Insulted!" says he, "and did she insult you? She said nothing of that."

"What brings you here, then?" I demanded.

"Not to talk, Richard," he said quietly, "'tis no time tonight. I came to fetch you home. Patty sent me."

Patty sent him! Why had Patty sent him? But this I did not ask, for I felt the devil within me.

"We must first finish this bottle," said I, offhand, "and then I have a little something to be done which I have set my heart upon. After that I will go with you."

"Richard, Richard, will you never learn prudence? What is it you speak of?"

I drew my sword and laid it upon the table.

"I mean to spit that eel of a rector," said I, "or he will bear a slap in the face. And you must see fair play."

Singleton seized my coat, at the same time grasping the hilt of my sword with the other hand. But neither my words nor my action had gone unnoticed by the other end of the room. The company there fell silent awhile, and then we heard Captain Collinson talking in even, drawling tones.

"'Tis strange," said he, "what hot sparks a man meets in these colonies. They should be stamped out. His Majesty pampers these d——d Americans, is too lenient by far. Gentlemen, this is how I would indulge them!" He raised a closed fist and brought it down on the board.

He spoke to Tories, but he forgot that Tories were Americans. In those days only the meanest of the King's party would listen to such without protest from an Englishman. But some of the meaner sort were there: Philip and Tom laughed, and Mr. Allen, and my Lord's sycophants. Fotheringay and some others of sense shook their heads one to another, comprehending that Captain Collinson was somewhat gone in wine. For, indeed, he had not strayed far from the sideboard at the assembly. Comyn made a motion to rise.

"It is already past three bells, sir, and a hunt to-morrow," he said.

"From bottle to saddle, and from saddle to bottle, my Lord. We must have our pleasure ashore, and sleep at sea," and the captain tipped his flask with a leer. He turned his eye uncertainly first on me, then on my Lord. "We are lately from Boston, gentlemen, that charnel-house of treason, and before we leave, my Lord, I must tell them how Mr. Robinson of the customs served that dog Otis, in the British Coffee House. God's word, 'twas as good as a play."

I know not how many got to their feet at that, for the story of the cowardly beating of Mr. Otis by Robinson and the army officers had swept over the colonies, burning like a flame all true-hearted men, Tory and Whig alike. I wrested my sword from Singleton's hold, and in a trice I had reached the captain over chairs and table, tearing myself from Fotheringay on the way. I struck a blow that measured a man on the floor. Then I drew back, amazed.

I had hit Lord Comyn instead! The captain stood a yard beyond me.

The thing had been so deftly done by the rector of St. Anne's — Comyn jostled at the proper moment between me and Collinson — that none save me guessed beyond an accident; least of all my Lord Comyn himself. He was up again directly and his sword drawn, addressing me.

"Bear witness, my Lord, that I have no desire to fight with you," said I, with what coolness I could muster. "But there is one here I would give much for a chance to run through."

And I made a step toward Mr. Allen with such a purpose

in my face and movements that he could not mistake. I saw the blood go from his face; yet he was no coward to physical violence. But he (or I?) was saved by the Satan's luck that followed him, for my Lord stepped in between us with a bow, his cheek red where I had struck him.

"It is my quarrel now, Mr. Carvel," he cried.

"As you please, my Lord," said I.

"It boots not who crosses with him," Captain Collinson put in. "His Lordship uses the sword better than any here. But it boots not so that he is opposed by a loyal servant of the King."

I wheeled on him for this.

"I would have you know that loyalty does not consist in outrage and murder, sir," I answered, "nor in the ridiculing of them. And brutes cannot be loyal save through interest."

He was angered, as I had desired. I had hopes then of shouldering the quarrel on to him, for I had near as soon drawn against my own brother as against Comyn. I protest I loved him then as one with whom I had been reared.

"Let me deal with this young gamecock, Comyn," cried the captain, with an oath. "He seems to think his importance sufficient."

But Comyn would brook no interference. He swore that no man should strike him with impunity, and in this I could not but allow he was right.

"You shall hear from me, Mr. Carvel," he said.

"Nay," I answered, "and fighting is to be done, sir, let us be through with it at once. A large room upstairs is at our disposal; and there is a hunt to-morrow which one of us may like to attend."

There was a laugh at this, in which his Lordship joined.

"I would to God, Mr. Carvel," he said, "that I had no quarrel with you!"

"Amen to that, my Lord," I replied; "there are others here I would rather fight." And I gave a meaning look at Mr. Allen. I was of two minds to announce the scurvy trick he had played, but saw that I would lose rather than gain by the attempt. Up to that time the wretch had not spoken a word; now he pushed himself forward, though well clear of me.

"I think it my duty as Mr. Carvel's tutor, gentlemen, to protest against this matter proceeding," he said, a sneer creeping into his voice. "Nor can I be present at it. Mr. Carvel is young and, besides, is not himself with liquor. And, in the choice of politics, he knows not which leg he stands upon. My Lord and gentlemen, your most humble and devoted."

He made a bow and, before the retort on my lips could be spoken, left the tavern. My cousin Philip left with him. Tom Swain had fallen asleep in his chair.

Captain Collinson and Mr. Furness, of the *Thunderer*, offered to serve his Lordship, which made me bethink that I, too, would have need of some one. 'Twas then I remembered Singleton, who had passed from my mind.

He was standing close behind me, and nodded simply when I asked him. And Will Fotheringay came forward.

"I will act, Richard, if you allow me," he said. "I would have you know I am in no wise hostile to you, my Lord, and I am of the King's party. But I admire Mr. Carvel, and I may say I am not wholly out of sympathy with that which prompted his act."

It was a noble speech, and changed Will in my eyes; and I thanked him with warmth. He of all that company had the courage to oppose his Lordship!

Mr. Claude was called in and, as is the custom in such cases, was told that some of us would play awhile above. He was asked for his private room. The good man had his suspicions, but could not refuse a party of such distinction, and sent a drawer thither with wine and cards. Presently we followed, leaving the pack of toadies in sad disappointment below.

We gathered about the table and made shift at loo until the fellow had retired, when the seconds proceeded to clear the room of furniture, and Lord Comyn and I stripped off our coats and waistcoats. I had lost my anger, but felt no fear, only a kind of pity that blood should be shed between two so united in spirit as we. Yes, my dears, I thought of Dorothy. If I died, she would hear that it was like a man — like a Carvel. But the thought of my old grandfather tightened my heart. Then the clock on the inn stairs struck two, and the noise of harsh laughter floated up to us from below.

And Comyn,—of what was he thinking? Of some fair home set upon the downs across the sea, of some heroic English mother who had kept her tears until he was gone? Her image rose in dumb entreaty, invoked by the lad before me. What a picture was he in his spotless shirt with the ruffles, his handsome boyish face all that was good and honest!

I had scarce felt his Lordship's wrist than I knew I had to deal with a pupil of Angelo. At first his attacks were all simple, without feint or trickery, as were mine. Collinson cursed and cried out that it was buffoonery, and called on my Lord not to let me off so easily; swore that I fenced like a mercer, that he could have stuck me like a pin-cushion twenty and twenty times. Often have I seen two animals thrust into a pit with nothing but good-will between them, and those without force them into anger and a deadly battle. And so it was, unconsciously, between Comyn and me. I forgot presently that I was not dealing with Captain Collinson, and my feelings went into my sword. Comyn began to press me, nor did I give back. And then, before it came over me that we had to do with life and death, he was upon me with a *volte coupe*, feinting in high *carte* and thrusting in low *tierce*, his point passing through a fold in my shirt. And I were not alive to write these words had I not leaped out of his measure.

"Bravo, Richard!" cried Fotheringay.

"Well made, gad's life!" from Mr. Furness.

We engaged again, our faces hot. Now I knew that if I did not carry the matter against him I should be killed out of hand, and Heaven knows I was not used to play a passive part. I began to go carefully, but fiercely; tried one attack after another that my grandfather and Captain Daniel had taught me,—flanconnades, beats, and lunges. Comyn held me even, and in truth I had much to do to defend myself. Once I thought I had him in the sword-arm, after a circular parry, but he was too quick for me. We were sweating freely by now, and by reason of the buzzing in my ears I could scarce hear the applause of the seconds.

What unlucky chance it was I know not that impelled Comyn to essay again the trick by which he had come so near to spitting me; but try it he did, this time in *prime* and *seconde*. I had come by nature to that intuition which a true swordsman must have, gleaned from the eyes of his adversary. Long ago Captain Daniel had taught me the remedy for this *coupe*. I parried, circled, and straightened, my body in swift motion and my point at Comyn's heart, when Heaven brought me recollection in the space of a second. My sword rang clattering on the floor.

His Lordship understood, but too late. Despairing his life, he made one wild lunge at me that had never gone home had I held to my hilt. But the rattle of the blade had scarce reached my ears when there came a sharp pain at my throat, and the room faded before me. I heard the clock striking the half-hour.

I was blessed with a sturdy health such as few men enjoy, and came to myself sooner than had been looked for, with a dash of cold water. And the first face I beheld was that of Colonel Washington. I heard him speaking in a voice that was calm, yet urgent and commanding.

"I pray you, gentlemen, give back. He is coming to, and must have air. Fetch some linen!"

"Now God be praised!" I heard Captain Daniel cry.

With that his Lordship began to tear his own shirt into strips, and the captain bringing a bowl and napkin, the colonel himself washed the wound and bound it deftly, Singleton and Captain Daniel assisting. When Mr. Washington had finished, he turned to Comyn, who stood, anxious and dishevelled, at my feet.

"You may be thankful that you missed the artery, my Lord," he said.

"With all my heart, Colonel Washington!" cried his Lordship. "I owe my life to his generosity."

"What's that, sir?"

"Mr. Carvel dropped his sword, rather than run me through."

"I'll warrant!" Captain Daniel put in; "'Od's heart! The

lad has skill to point the eye of a button. I taught him myself."

Colonel Washington stood up and laid his hand on the captain's arm.

"He is Jack Carvel over again," I heard him say, in a low voice.

I tried to struggle to my feet, to speak, but he restrained me. And sending for his servants, he ordered them to have his baggage removed from the Roebuck, which was the best bed in the house. At this moment the door opened, and Mr. Swain came in hurriedly.

"I pray you, gentlemen," he cried, "and he is fit to be moved, you will let me take him to Marlboro' Street. I have a chariot at the door."

CHAPTER XV

OF WHICH THE RECTOR HAS THE WORST

'Twas late when I awoke the next day with something of a dull ache in my neck, and a prodigious stiffness, studying the pleatings of the bed canopy over my head. And I know not how long I lay idly thus when I perceived Mrs. Willis moving quietly about, and my grandfather sitting in the armchair by the window, looking into Freshwater Lane. As my eyes fell upon him my memory came surging back, — first of the duel, then of its cause. And finally, like a leaden weight, the thought of the deception I had practised upon him, of which he must have learned ere this. Nay, I was sure from the troubled look of his face that he knew of it.

"Mr. Carvel," I said.

At the sound of my voice he got hastily from his chair and hurried to my side.

"Richard," he answered, taking my hand, "Richard!"

I opened my mouth to speak, to confess. But he prevented me, the tears filling the wrinkles around his eyes.

"Nay, lad, nay. We will not talk of it. I know all."

"Mr. Allen has been here — " I began.

"And be d—d to him! Be d—d to him for a wolf in sheep's clothing!" shouted my grandfather, his manner shifting so suddenly to anger that I was taken back. "So help me God I will never set foot in St. Anne's while he is rector. Nor shall he come to this house!"

And he took three or four disorderly turns about the room.

"Ah!" he continued more quietly, with something of a sigh, "I might have known how stubborn your mind should be. That you was never one to blow from the north one day and from the south the next. I deny not that there be good men and able of your way of thinking: Colonel Washington, for one, whom I admire and honour; and our friend Captain Daniel. They have been here to-day, Richard, and I promise you were good advocates."

Then I knew that I was forgiven. And I could have thrown myself at Mr. Carvel's feet for happiness.

"Has Colonel Washington spoken in my favour, sir?"

"That he has. He is upon some urgent business for the North, I believe, which he delayed for your sake. Both he and the captain were in my dressing-room before I was up, ahead of that scurrilous clergyman, who was for pushing his way to my bed-curtains. Ay, the two of them were here at nigh dawn this morning, and Mr. Allen close after them. And I own that Captain Daniel can swear with such a consuming violence as to put any rogue out of countenance. 'Twas all Mr. Washington could do to restrain Clapsaddle from booting his Reverence over the balustrade and down two runs of the stairs, the captain declaring he would do for every cur's son of the whelps. 'Diomedes,' says I, waking up, 'what's this damnable racket on the landing? Is Mr. Richard home?' For I had some notion it was you, sir, after an over-night brawl. And I profess I would have caned you soundly. The fellow answered that Captain Clapsaddle's honour was killing Mr. Allen, and went out; and came back presently to say that some tall gentleman had the captain by the neck, and that Mr. Allen was picking his way down the ice on the steps outside. With that I went in to them in my dressing-gown.

"'What's all this to-do, gentlemen?' said I.

"'I'd have finished that son of a dog,' says the captain, 'and Colonel Washington had let me.'

"'What, what!' said I. 'How now? What! Drive a clergyman from my house! What's Richard been at now, gentlemen?'

"Mr. Washington asked me to dress, saying that they had something very particular to speak about; that they would stay to breakfast with me, tho' they were in haste to be gone to New York. I made my compliments to the colonel and had them shown to the library fire, and hurried down after them. Then they told me of this affair last night, and they cleared you, sir. 'Faith,' cried I, 'and I would have fought, too. The lad was in the right of it, though I would have him a little less hasty.' D—n me if I don't wish you had knocked that seacaptain's teeth into his throat, and his brains with them. I like your spirit, sir. A pox on such men as he, who disgrace his Majesty's name and set better men against him."

"And they told you nothing else, sir?" I asked, with misgiving.

"That they did. Mr. Washington repeated the confession you made to them, sir, in a manner that did you credit. He made me compliments on you, — said that you were a man, sir, though a trifle hasty: in the which I agreed. Yes, d—n me, a trifle hasty like your father. I rejoice that you did not kill his Lordship, my son."

The twilight was beginning; and the old gentleman going back to his chair was set a-musing, gazing out across the bare trees and gables falling gray after the sunset.

What amazed me was that he did not seem to be shocked by the revelation near as much as I had feared. So this matter had brought me happiness where I looked for nothing but sorrow.

"And the gentlemen are gone north, sir?" said I, after a while.

"Yes, Richard, these four hours. I commanded an early dinner for them, since the colonel was pleased to tarry long enough for a little politics and to spin a glass. And I profess, was I to live neighbours with such a man, I might come to his way of thinking, despite myself. Though I say it that shouldn't, some of his Majesty's ministers are d—d rascals."

I laughed. As I live, I never hoped to hear such words from my grandfather's lips.

"He did not seek to convince, like so many of your hotheaded know-it-alls," said Mr. Carvel; "he leaves a man to convince himself. He has great parts, Richard, and few can stand before him." He paused. And then his smooth-shaven face became creased in a roguish smile which I had often seen upon it. "What baggage is this I hear of that you quarrelled over at the assembly? Ah, sir, I fear you are become but a sad rake!" says he.

But by great good fortune Dr. Leiden was shown in at this instant. And the candles being lighted, he examined my neck, haranguing the while in his vile English against the practice of duelling. He bade me keep my bed for two days, thereby giving me no great pleasure.

"As I hope to live," said Mr. Carvel when the doctor was gone, "one would have thought his Excellency himself had been pinked instead of a whip of a lad, for the people who have been here. His Lordship and Dr. Courtenay came before the hunt, and young Mr. Fotheringay, and half a score of others. Mr. Swain is but now left to go to Baltimore on some barrister's business."

I was burning to learn what the rector had said to Patty, but it was plain Mr. Carvel knew nothing of this part of the story. He had not mentioned Grafton among the callers. I wondered what course my uncle would now pursue, that his plans to alienate me from my grandfather had failed. And I began debating whether or not to lay the whole plot before Mr. Carvel. Prudence bade me wait, since Grafton had not consorted with the rector — openly, at least — for more than a year. And yet I spoke.

"Mr. Carvel!"

He stirred in his chair.

"Yes, my son."

He had to repeat, and still I held my tongue. Even as I hesitated there came a knock at the door, and Scipio entered, bearing candles.

"Massa Grafton, suh," he said.

My uncle was close at his heels. He was soberly dressed in dark brown silk, and his face wore that expression of sorrow and concern he knew how to assume at will. After greeting his father with his usual ceremony, he came to my bedside and asked gravely how I did.

"How now, Grafton!" cried Mr. Carvel; "this is no funeral. The lad has only a scratch, thank God!"

My uncle looked at me and forced a smile.

"Indeed I am rejoiced to find you are not worried over this matter, father," said he. "I am but just back from Kent to learn of it, and looked to find you in bed."

"Why, no, sir, I am not worried. I fought a duel in my own day,—over a lass, it was."

This time Grafton's smile was not forced.

"Over a lass, was it?" he asked, and added in a tone of relief, "and how do you, nephew?"

Mr. Carvel saved me from replying.

"'Od's life!" he cried; "no, I did not say this was over a lass. I have heard the whole matter; how Captain Collinson, who is a disgrace to the service, brought shame upon his Majesty's supporters, and how Richard felled the young lord instead. I'll be sworn, and I had been there, I myself would have run the brute through."

My uncle did not ask for further particulars, but took a chair, and a dish of tea from Scipio. His smug look told me plainer than words that he thought my grandfather still ignorant of my Whig sentiments.

"I often wish that this deplorable practice of duelling might be legislated against," he remarked. "Was there no one at the Coffee House with character enough to stop the lads?"

Here was my chance.

"Mr. Allen was there," I said.

"A devil's plague upon him!" shouted my grandfather, beating the floor with his stick. "And the lying hypocrite ever crosses my path, by gad's life! I'll tear his gown from his back!"

I watched Grafton narrowly. Such as he never turn pale, but he set down his tea so hastily as to spill the most of it on the dresser.

"Why, you astound me, my dear father!" he faltered; "Mr. Allen a lying hypocrite? What can he have done?"

"Done!" cried my grandfather, sputtering and red as a cherry with indignation. "He is as rotten within as a pricked pear, I tell you, sir! For the sake of retaining the lad in his tuition he came to me and lied, sir, just after I had escaped death, and said that by his influence Richard had become loyal, and set dependence upon Richard's fear of the shock 'twould give me if he confessed — Richard, who never told me a falsehood in his life! And instead of teaching him, he has gamed with the lad at the rectory. I dare make oath he has treated your son to a like instruction. 'Slife, sir, and he had his deserts, he would hang from a gibbet at the Town Gate."

I raised up in bed to see the effect of this on my uncle. But however the wind veered, Grafton could steer a course. He got up and began pacing the room, and his agitation my grandfather took for indignation such as his own.

"The dog!" he cried fiercely. "The villain! Philip shall leave him to-morrow. And to think that it was I who moved you to put Richard to him!"

His distress seemed so real that Mr. Carvel replied: —

"No, Grafton, 'twas not your fault. You were deceived as much as I. You have put your own son to him. But if I live another twelve hours I shall write his Lordship to remove him. What! You shake your head, sir!"

"It will not do," said my uncle. "Lord Baltimore has had his reasons for sending such a scoundrel — he knew what he was, you may be sure, father. His Lordship, sir, is the most abandoned rake in London, and that unmentionable crime of his but lately in the magazines —"

"Yes, yes," my grandfather interrupted; "I have seen it. But I will publish him in Annapolis."

My uncle's answer startled me, so like was it to the argument Colonel Washington himself had used.

"What would you publish, sir? Mr. Allen will reply that what he did was for the lad's good, and your own. He may swear that since Richard mentioned politics no more he had taken his conversion for granted."

My grandfather groaned, and did not speak, and I saw the futility of attempting to bring Grafton to earth for a while yet.

My uncle had recovered his confidence. He had hoped, so he said, that I had become a good loyalist: perchance as I grew older I would see the folly of those who called themselves Patriots. But my grandfather cried out to him not to bother me then. And when at last he was gone, of my own volition I proposed to promise Mr. Carvel that, while he lived, I would take no active part in any troubles that might come. He stopped me with some vehemence.

"I pray God there may be no troubles, lad," he answered; "but you need give me no promise. I would rather see you in the Whig ranks than a trimmer, for the Carvels have ever been partisans."

I tried to express my gratitude. But he sighed and wished me good night, bidding me get some rest.

I had scarce finished my breakfast the next morning when I heard a loud rat-tat-tat upon the street door — surely the footman of some person of consequence. And Scipio was in the act of announcing the names when, greatly to his disgust, the visitors themselves rushed into my bedroom and curtailed the ceremony. They were none other than Dr. Courtenay and my Lord Comyn himself. His Lordship had no sooner seen me than he ran to the bed, grasped both my hands and asked me how I did, declaring he would not have gone to yesterday's hunt had he been permitted to visit me.

"Richard," cried the doctor, "your fame has sprung up like Jonah's gourd. The *Gazette* is but just distributed. Here's for you! 'Twill set the wags a-going, I'll warrant."

He drew the newspaper from his pocket and began to read, stopping now and anon to laugh:—

"Rumour hath it that a Young Gentleman of Quality of this Town, who is possessed of more Valour than Discretion, and whose Skill at Fence and in the Field is beyond his Years, crossed Swords on Wednesday Night with a Young Nobleman from the Thunderer. The Cause of this Deplorable Quarrel, which had its Origin at the Ball, is purported to have been a Young Lady of Wit and Beauty. (& we doubt it not; for, alas! the Sex hath Much to answer for of this Kind.)

"The Gentlemen, with their Seconds, repaired after the Assembly to the Coffee House. 'Tis said upon Authority that H-s L—dsh-p owes his Life to the Noble Spirit of our Young American, who cast down his Blade rather than sheathe it in his Adversary's Body, thereby himself receiving a Grievous, the' happily not Mortal, Wound. Our Young Gentleman is become the Hero of the Town, and the Subject of Prodigious Anxiety of all the Ladies thereof."

"There's for you, my lad!" says he; "Mr. Green has done for you both cleverly."

"Upon my soul," I cried, raising up in bed, "he should be put in the gatehouse for his impudence! My Lord,—"

"Don't 'My Lord' me," says Comyn; "plain 'Jack' will do."

There was no resisting such a man: and I said as much. And took his hand and called him 'Jack,' the doctor posing before the mirror the while, stroking his ruffles. "Out upon you both," says he, "for a brace of sentimental fools!"

"Richard," said Comyn, presently, with a roguish glance at the doctor, "there were some reason in our fighting had it been over a favour of Miss Manners. Eh? Come, doctor," he cried, "you will break your neck looking for the reflection of wrinkles. Come, now, we must have little Finery's letter. I give you my word Chartersea is as ugly as all three heads of Cerberus, and as foul as a ship's barrel of grease. I tell you Miss Dorothy would sooner marry you."

"And she might do worse, my Lord," the doctor flung back, with a strut.

"Ay, and better. But I promise you Richard and I are not such fools as to think she will marry his Grace. We must have the little coxcomb's letter."

"Well, have it you must, I suppose," returns the doctor. And with that he draws it from his pocket, where he has it buttoned in. Then he took a pinch of Holland and began.

The first two pages had to deal with Miss Dorothy's triumph, to which her father made full justice. Mr. Manners would have the doctor (and all the province) to know that peers of the realm, soldiers, and statesmen were at her feet. Orders were as plentiful in his drawing-room as the candles. And he had taken a house in Arlington Street, where Horry Walpole lived when not at Strawberry, and their entrance was crowded night and day with the footmen and chairmen of the *grand monde*. Lord Comyn broke in more than once upon the reading, crying,—"Hear, hear!" and,—"My word, Mr. Manners has not perjured himself thus far. He has not done her justice by half." And I smiled at the thought that I had aspired to such a beauty!

"'*Entre nous, mon cher* Courtenay,' Mr. Manners writes, '*entre nous*, our Dorothy hath had many offers of great advantage since she hath been here. And but yesterday comes a chariot with a ducal coronet to our door. His Grace of Chartersea, if you please, to request a private talk with me. And I rode with him straightway to his house in Hanover Square.'"

"'Egad! And would gladly have ridden straightway to Newgate, in a ducal chariot!" cried his Lordship, in a fit of laughter.

"'I rode to Hanover Square,' the doctor continued, 'where we discussed the matter over a bottle. His Grace's generosity was such that I could not but cry out at it, for he left me to name any settlement I pleased. He must have Dorothy at any price, said he. And I give you my honour, *mon cher* Courtenay, that I lost no time in getting back to Arlington Street, and called Dorothy down to tell her.'"

"Now may I be flayed," said Comyn, "if ever there was such another ass!"

The doctor took more snuff and fell a-laughing.

"But hark to this," said he, "here's the cream of it all: 'You will scarce believe me when I say that the baggage was near beside herself with anger at what I had to tell her. "Marry that misshapen duke!" cries she, "I would quicker marry Doctor Johnson!" And truly, I begin to fear she hath formed an affection for some like, foul-linened beggar. That his Grace is misshapen I cannot deny; but I tried reason upon her. "Think of the coronet, my dear, and of the ancient name to which it belongs." She only stamps her foot and cries out: "Coronet fiddlesticks! And are you not content with the name you bear, sir?" "Our name is good as any in the three kingdoms," said I, with truth. "Then you would have me, for the sake of the coronet, joined to a wretch who is steeped in debauchery. Yes, debauchery, sir! You might then talk, forsooth, to the macaronies of Maryland, of your daughter the Duchess."'"

"There's spirit for you, my lad!" Comyn shouted; "I give you Miss Dorothy." And he drained a glass of punch Scipio had brought in, Doctor Courtenay and I joining him with a will.

"I pray you go on, sir," I said to the doctor.

"A pest on your impatience!" replied he; "I begin to think you are in love with her yourself."

"To be sure he is," said Comyn; "he had lost my esteem and he were not."

The doctor gave me an odd look. I was red enough, indeed.

"'I could say naught, my dear Courtenay, to induce her to believe that his Grace's indiscretions arose from the wildness of youth. And I pass over the injustice she hath unwittingly done me, whose only efforts are for her bettering. The end of it all was that I must needs post back to the duke, who was stamping with impatience up and down, and drinking Burgundy. I am sure I meant him no offence, but told him in as many words, that my daughter had refused him. And, will you believe me, sir? He took occasion to insult me (I cannot with propriety repeat his speech), and he flung a bottle after me as I passed out the door. Was he not far gone in wine at the time, I assure you I had called him out for it.'"

"And, gentlemen," said the doctor, when our merriment was somewhat spent, "I'll lay a pipe of the best Madeira, that our little fool never knows the figure he has cut with his Grace."

CHAPTER XVI

IN WHICH SOME THINGS ARE MADE CLEAR

THE *Thunderer* weighed the next day, Saturday, while I was still upon my back, and Comyn sailed with her. Not, however, before I had seen him again. Our affection was such as comes not often to those who drift together to part. And he left me that sword with the jewelled hilt, that hangs above my study fire, which he had bought in Toledo. He told me that he was heartily sick of the navy; that he had entered only in respect for a wish of his father's, the late Admiral Lord Comyn, and that the *Thunderer* was to sail for New York, where he looked for a release from his commission, and whence he would return to England. He would carry any messages to Miss Manners that I chose to send. But I could think of none, save to beg him to remind her that she was constantly in my thoughts. He promised me, roguishly enough, that he would have thought of a better than that by the time he sighted Cape Clear. And were I ever to come to London he would put me up at Brooks's Club, and warrant me a better time and more friends than ever had a Caribbee who came home on a visit.

My grandfather kept his word in regard to Mr. Allen, and on Sunday commanded the coach at eight. We drove over bad roads to the church at South River. And he afterwards declined the voluntary aid he hitherto had been used to give to St. Anne's. In the meantime, good Mr. Swain had called again, bringing some jelly and cake of Patty's own making; and a letter writ out of the sincerity of her heart, full of tender concern and of penitence. She would never cease to blame herself for the wrong she now knew she had done me.

Though still somewhat weak from my wound and confinement, after dinner that Sunday I repaired to Gloucester Street. From the window she saw me coming, and, bare-headed, ran out in the cold to meet me. Her eyes rested first on the linen around my throat, and she seemed all in a fire of anxiety.

"I had thought you would come to-day, when I heard you had been to South River," she said.

I was struck all of a sudden with her looks. Her face was pale, and I saw that she had suffered as much again as I. Troubled, I followed her into the little library. The day was fading fast, and the leaping flames behind the andirons threw fantastic shadows across the beams of the ceiling. We sat together in the deep window.

"And you have forgiven me, Richard?" she asked.

"An hundred times," I replied. "I deserved all I got, and more."

"If I had not wronged and insulted you —"

"You did neither, Patty," I broke in; "I have played a double part for the first and last time in my life, and I have been justly punished for it."

"'Twas I sent you to the Coffee House," she cried, "where you might have been killed. How I despise myself for listening to Mr. Allen's tales!"

"Then it was Mr. Allen!" I exclaimed, fetching a long breath.

"Yes, yes; I will tell you all."

"No," said I, alarmed at her agitation; "another time."

"I must," she answered more calmly; "it has burned me enough. You recall that we were at supper together, with Betty Tayloe and Lord Comyn, and how merry we were, altho' 'twas nothing but 'Dorothy' with you gentlemen. Then you left me. Afterwards, as I was talking with Mr. Singleton, the rector came up. I never have liked the man, Richard, but I little knew his character. He began by twitting me for a Whig, and presently he said: 'But we have gained one convert, Miss Swain, who sees the error of his ways. Scarce a year since young Richard Carvel promised to be one of those with whom his Majesty will have to reckon. And he is now become,' — laughing, — 'the King's most loyal and devoted.'

I was beside myself. 'That is no subject for jest, Mr. Allen,' I cried; 'I will never believe it of him!' 'Jest!' said he; 'I give you my word I was never soberer in my life.' Then it all came to me of a sudden that you sat no longer by the hour with my father, as you used, and you denounced the King's measures and ministers no more. My father had spoken of it. 'Tell me why he has changed?' I asked, faltering with doubt of you, which I never before had felt. 'Indeed, I know not,' replied the rector, with his most cynical smile; 'unless it is because old Mr. Carvel might disinherit a Whig. But I see you doubt my word, Miss Swain. Here is Mr. Carroll, and you may ask him.' God forgive me, Richard! I stopped Mr. Carroll, who seemed mightily surprised. And he told me yes, that your grandfather had said but a few days before, and with joy, that you were now of his Majesty's party."

"Alas! I might have foreseen this consequence," I exclaimed. "Nor do I blame you, Patty."

"But my father has explained all," Patty continued, brightening. "His admiration for you is increased tenfold, Richard. Your grandfather told him of the rector's treachery, which he says is sufficient to make him turn Methodist or Lutheran. We went to the curate's service to-day. And — will you hear more, sir? Or do your ears burn? That patriots and loyalists are singing your praises from Town Gate to the dock, and regretting that you did not kill that detestable Captain Collinson — but I have something else, and of more importance, to tell you, Richard," she continued, lowering her voice.

"What Mr. Carroll had told me stunned me like a blow, such had been my faith in you. And when Mr. Allen moved off, I stood talking to Percy Singleton and his Lordship without understanding a word of the conversation. I could scarce have been in my right mind. It was not your going over to the other side that pained me so, for all your people are Tories. But I had rather seen you dead than a pretender and a hypocrite, selling yourself for an inheritance. Then you came. My natural impulse should have been to draw you aside and there accuse you. But this was beyond my strength. And when I saw you go away without a word I knew that I had been unjust. I could have wept before them all. Mr. Carroll went for his coach, and was a full half an hour in getting it. But this is what I would tell you in particular, Richard. I have not spoken of it to a soul, and it troubles me above all else: While Maria was getting my cardinal I heard voices on the other side of the dressing-room door. The supper-room is next, you know. I listened, and recognized the rector's deep tones: 'He has gone to the Coffee House,' he was saying; 'Collinson declares that his Lordship is our man, if we can but contrive it. He is the best foil in the service, and was taught by'—there! I have forgot the name."

"Angelo!" I cried.

"Yes, yes, Angelo it was. How did you know?" she demanded, rising in her excitement.

"Angelo is the great fencing-master of London," I replied.

"When I heard that," she said, "I had no doubt of your innocence. I ran out into the assembly room as I was, in my hood, and tried to find Tom. But he —" She paused, ashamed.

"Yes, I know," I said hurriedly; "you could not find him."

She glanced at me in gratitude.

"How everybody stared at me! But little I cared! 'Twas that gave rise to Mr. Green's report. I thought of Percy Singleton, and stopped him in the midst of a dance to bid him run as fast as his legs would carry him to the Coffee House, and to see that no harm befell you. 'I shall hold you responsible for Richard,' I whispered. 'You must get him away from Mr. Claude's, or I shall never speak to you again.' He did not wait to ask questions, but went at once, like the good fellow he is. Then I rode home with Maria. I would not have Mr. Carroll come with me, though he begged hard. Father was in here, writing his brief. But I was all in pieces, Richard, and so shaken with sobbing that I could tell him no more than that you had gone to the Coffee House, where they meant to draw you into a duel. He took me up to my own room, and I heard him going out to wake Limbo to harness, and at last heard him driving away in our coach. I hope I may never in my life spend such another hour as I passed then."

The light in the sky had gone out. I looked up at the girl before me as she stood gazing into the flame, her features in strong relief, her lips parted, her hair red-gold, and the rounded outlines of her figure softened. I wondered why I had never before known her beauty. Perchance it was because, until that night, I had never seen her heart.

I leaped to my feet and seized her hands. For a second she looked at me, startled. Then she tore them away and ran behind the dipping chair in the corner.

"Richard, Richard!" she exclaimed. "Did Dorothy but know!"

"Dorothy is occupied with titles," I said.

Patty's lip quivered. And I knew, blundering fool that I was, that I had hurt her.

"Oh, you wrong her!" she cried; "believe me when I say that she loves you, and you only, Richard."

"Loves me!" I retorted bitterly, — brutally, I fear. "No. She may have once, long ago. But now her head is turned."

"She loves you now," answered Patty, earnestly; "and I think ever will, if you but deserve her."

And with that she went away, leaving me to stare after her in perplexity and consternation.

CHAPTER XVII

SOUTH RIVER

My grandfather's defection from St. Anne's called forth a deal of comment in Annapolis. His Excellency came to remonstrate, but to no avail, and Mr. Carvel denounced the rector in such terms that the Governor was glad to turn the subject. My Uncle Grafton acted with such quickness and force as would have served to lull the sharpest suspicions. He forbid the rector his house, attended the curate's service, and took Philip from his care. It was decided that both my cousin and I were to go to King's College after Christmas. Grafton's conduct greatly pleased my grandfather. "He has behaved very loyally in this matter, Richard," he said to me. "I grow to reproach myself more every day for the injustice I once did him. He is heaping coals of fire upon my old head. But, faith! I cannot stomach your Aunt Caroline. You do not seem to like your uncle, lad."

I answered that I did not.

"It was ever the Carvel way not to forget," he went on. "Nevertheless, Grafton hath your welfare at heart, I think. His affection for you as his brother's son is great."

O that I had spoken the words that burned my tongue!

Christmas fell upon Monday of that year, 1769. There was to be a ball at Upper Marlboro' on the Friday before, to which many of us were invited. Though the morning came in with a blinding snowstorm from the north, the first of that winter, about ten of the clock we set out from Annapolis an exceeding merry party, the ladies in four coaches-and-six, the gentlemen and their servants riding at the wheels. We laughed and joked despite the storm, and exchanged signals with the fair ones behind the glasses.

But we had scarce got two miles beyond the town gate when a messenger overtook us with a note for Mr. Carvel, writ upon an odd slip of paper, and with great apparent hurry: —

"Honoured Sir,

"I have but just come to Annapolis from New York, with Instructions to put into your Hands, & no Others, a Message of the greatest Import. Hearing you are but now set out for Upper Marlboro I beg of you to return for half an Hour to the Coffee House. By so doing you will be of service to a Friend, and confer a Favour upon y'r most ob'd't Humble Servant,

"Silas Ridgeway."

Our cavalcade had halted while I read, the ladies letting down the glasses and leaning out in their concern lest some trouble had befallen me or my grandfather. I answered them and bade them ride on, vowing that I would overtake the coaches before they reached the Patuxent. Then I turned Cynthia's head for town, with Hugo at my heels.

Patty, leaning from the window of the last coach, called out to me as I passed. I waved my hand in return, and did not remember until long after the anxiety in her eyes.

As I rode, and I rode hard, I pondered over the words of this letter. I knew not this Mr. Ridgeway from the Lord Mayor of London; but I came to the conclusion before I had repassed the gate that his message was from Captain Daniel. And I greatly feared that some evil had befallen my good friend. So I came to the Coffee House, and throwing my bridle to Hugo, I ran in.

I found Mr. Ridgeway neither in the long room nor in the billiard room nor the bar. Mr. Claude told me that indeed a man had arrived that morning from the North, a spare person with a hooked nose and scant hair, in a brown greatcoat with a torn cape. He had gone forth afoot half an hour since. His messenger, a negro lad whose face I knew, was in the stables with Hugo. He had never seen the stranger till he met him that morning in State House Circle inquiring for Mr.

Carvel, and had been given a shilling to gallop after me. Impatient as I was to be gone, I sat me down in the coffee room, thinking every minute the man must return, and strongly apprehensive that Captain Daniel must be in some grave predicament. That the favour he asked was of such a nature as I, and not my grandfather, could best fulfil.

At length, about a quarter after noon, my man comes in with Mr. Claude close behind him. I liked his looks less than his description, and the moment I clapped eyes on him I knew that Captain Daniel had never chose such a messenger.

"This is Mr. Richard Carvel," said Mr. Claude.

The fellow made me a low bow, which I scarcely returned.

"I am sure, sir," he began in a whining voice, "that I crave your forbearance for this prodigious, stupid mistake I have made."

"Mistake!" I exclaimed hotly; "you mean to say, sir, that you have brought me back for nothing?"

The man's eye shifted, and he made me another bow.

"I scarce know what to say, Mr. Carvel," he answered with much humility; "to speak truth, 'twas zeal to my employers, and methought to you, that caused you to retrace your steps in this pestiferous storm. I travel," he proceeded with some importance, "I travel for Messrs. Rinnell and Runn, Barristers of the town of New York, and carry letters to men of mark all over these middle and southern colonies. And my instructions, sir, were to come to Annapolis with all reasonable speed with this double-sealed enclosure for Mr. Carvel: and to deliver it to him, and him only, the very moment I arrived. As I came through your town I made inquiries, and was told by a black fellow in the Circle that Mr. Carvel was but just left for Upper Marlboro' with a cavalcade of four coaches-and-six and some dozen gentlemen with their servants. I am sure my mistake was pardonable, Mr. Carvel," he concluded with a smirk; "this gentleman was plainly of the first quality, as was he to whom I was directed. And as he was about to leave town for I knew not how long, I hope I was in the right in bidding the black ride after him, for I give you my word the business was most pressing for him. I crave your forgiveness, and the pleasure of drinking your honour's health."

I barely heard the fellow through, and was turning on my heel in disgust, when it struck me to ask him what Mr. Carvel he sought, for I feared lest my grandfather had got into some lawsuit.

"And it please your honour, Mr. Grafton Carvel," said he; "your uncle, I understand. Unfortunately he has gone to his estate in Kent County, whither I must now follow him."

I bade Mr. Claude summon my servant, not stopping to question the man further, such was my resentment against him. And in ten minutes we were out of the town again, galloping between the nearly filled tracks of the coaches, now three hours ahead of us. The storm was increasing, and the wind cutting, but I dug into Cynthia so that poor Hugo was put to it to hold the pace, and, tho' he had a pint of rum in him, was near perished with the cold. As my anger cooled somewhat I began to wonder how Mr. Silas Ridgeway, whoever he was, could have been such a simpleton as his story made him out. Indeed, he looked more the rogue than the ass; nor could I conceive how reliable barristers could hire such a one. I wished heartily that I had exhausted him further, and a suspicion crossed my brain that he might have come to Mr. Allen, who had persuaded him to deliver a letter to Grafton intended for me. Some foreboding beset me, and I was once close to a full mind for going back, and slacked Cynthia's pace to a trot. But the thought of the pleasures at Upper Marlboro' and the hope of overtaking the party at Mr. Dorsey's place, over the Patuxent, where they looked to dine, decided me in pushing on. And thus we came to South River, with the snow so thick that we could scarce see ten yards in front of us.

Beyond, the road winds up the hill around the end of Mr. Wiley's plantation and plunges shortly into the woods, gray and cold indeed to-day. At their skirt a trail branches off which leads to Mr. Wiley's warehouses, on the water's edge a mile or so below. And I marked that this path was freshly trodden. I recall a small shock of surprise at this, for the way was used only in the early autumn to connect with some fields beyond the hill. And then I heard a sharp cry from Hugo and pulled Cynthia short. He was some ten paces behind me.

"Marse Dick!" he shouted, the whites of his eyes rolled up. "We'se gwine to be robbed, Marse Dick." And he pointed to the footprints in the snow; "somefin done tole Hugo not come to-day."

"Nonsense!" I cried; "Mr. Wiley is making his lazy beggars cut wood against Christmas."

When in this temper the poor fellow had more fear of me than of aught else, and he closed up to my horse's flank, glancing apprehensively to the right and left, his teeth rattling. We went at a brisk trot. We know not, indeed, how to account for many things in this world, for with each beat of Cynthia's feet I found myself repeating the words *South River* and *Marlboro'*, and seeking in my mind a connection to something gone before. Then, like a sudden gust of wind, comes to me that strange talk between Grafton and the rector, overheard by old Harvey in the stables at Carvel Hall. And Cynthia's ears were pointing forward.

With a quick impulse I loosed the lower frogs of my coat, for my sword was buckled beneath, and was reaching for one of the brace of pistols in my saddle-bags. I had but released them when Hugo cried out: "Gawd, Marse Dick, run for yo' life!" and I caught a glimpse of him flying down the road. As I turned a shot rang out, Cynthia reared high with a rough brute of a fellow clinging to her bridle. I sent my charge full into his chest, and as he tumbled in the snow I dug my spurs to the rowels.

What happened then is still a blurred picture in my brain. I know that Cynthia was shot from under me before she had taken her leap, and we fell heavily together. And I was scarcely up again and my sword drawn, when the villains were pressing me from all sides. I remember spitting but one, and then I heard a great seafaring oath, the first word out of their mouths, and I was felled from behind with a mighty blow.

CHAPTER XVIII

THE "BLACK MOLL"

I HAVE no intention, my dears, of dwelling upon that part of my adventures which must be as painful to you as to me, the very recollection of which, after all these years, suffices to cause the blood within me to run cold. In my youth men whose natures shrank not from encounter with their enemies lacked not, I warrant you, a checkered experience. Those of us who are wound the tightest go the farthest and strike the hardest. Nor is it difficult for one, the last of whose life is being recorded, to review the outspread roll of it, and trace the unerring forces which have drawn for themselves.

Some, indeed, traverse this world weighing, before they partake, pleasure and business alike. But I am not sure, my children, that they better themselves; or that God, in His all-wise judgment, prefers them to such as are guided by the divine impulse with which He has endowed them. Far be it from me to advise rashness or imprudence, as such; nor do I believe you will take me so. But I say unto you: do that which is right, and let God, not man, be your interpreter.

My narrative awaits me.

I came to my wits with an immoderate feeling of faintness and sickness, with no more remembrance of things past than has a man bereft of reason. And for some time I swung between sense and oblivion before an overpowering stench forced itself upon my nostrils, accompanied by a creaking, straining sound and sweeping motion. I could see nothing for the pitchy blackness. Then I recalled what had befallen me, and cried aloud to God in my anguish, for I well knew

I had been carried aboard ship, and was at sea. I had oftentimes heard of the notorious press-gang which supplied the need of the King's navy, and my first thought was that I had fallen in their clutches. But I wondered that they had dared attack a person of my consequence.

I had no pain. I lay in a bunk that felt gritty and greasy to the touch, and my hair was matted behind by a clot of blood. I had been stripped of my clothes, and put into some coarse and rough material, the colour and condition of which I could not see for want of light. I began to cast about me, to examine the size of the bunk, which I found to be narrow, and plainly at some distance from the deck, for I laid hold upon one of the rough beams above me. By its curvature I knew it to be a knee, and thus I came to the caulked sides of the vessel, and for the first time heard the rattling thud and swish of water on the far side of it. I had no sooner made this discovery, which drew from me an involuntary groan, when a ship's lanthorn was of a sudden thrust over me, and I perceived behind it a head covered with shaggy hair and beard, and beetling brows. Never had I been in such a terrifying presence.

"Damn my blood and bones, life signals at last! Another three bells gone, my silks and laces, and we had given you to the sharks."

The man hung his lanthorn to a hook on the beam, and thrust a case-bottle of rum toward me, at the same time biting off a great quid of tobacco. For all my alarm I saw that his manner was not unkindly, and as I was conscious of a consuming thirst I seized and tipped it eagerly.

"'Tis no fine Madeira, my blood," said he, "such as I fancy your palate is acquainted with. Yet 'tis as fair a Jamaica as ever Griggs put ashore i' the dark."

"Griggs!" I cried, the whole affair coming to me: *Griggs*, *Upper Marlboro'*, *South River*, Grafton and the rector plotting in the stalls, and Mr. Silas Ridgeway the accomplice.

"Ay, Griggs," replied he; "ye may well repeat it, the ——. I'll lay a puncheon he'll be hailing you shortly. Guinea Griggs, Gold-Coast Griggs, Smuggler Griggs, Skull-and-Bones

Griggs. Damn his soul and eyes, he hath sent to damnation many a ship's company."

He drained what remained of the bottle, took down the lanthorn, and left me sufficiently terrified to reflect upon my situation, which I found desperate enough, my dears. I have no words to describe what I went through in that vile, foul-smelling place. My tears flowed fast when I thought of my grandfather and of the dear friends I had left behind, and of Dorothy, whom I never hoped to see again. And then, perchance 'twas the rum put heart into me, I vowed I would face the matter: show this cut-throat of a Griggs a bold front. Had he meant to murder me, I reflected, he had done the business long since. Then I fell asleep.

I awoke, I know not how soon, to discover the same shaggy countenance, and the lanthorn.

"Canst walk, Mechlin?" says he.

"I can try, at least," I answered.

He seemed pleased at this.

"You have courage a-plenty, and, by G—, you will have need of it all with that —— of a Griggs!" He gave me his bottle again, and assisted me down, and I found that my legs, save for the rocking of the ship, were steady enough. I followed him out of the hole in which I had lain on to a deck, which, in the half light, I saw covered with slush and filth. It was small, and but dimly illuminated by a hatchway, up the which I pushed after him, and then another. And so we came to the light of day, which near blinded me: so that I was fain to clap my hand to mine eyes, and stood for a space looking about me like a man dazed. The wind, tho' blowing stiff, was mild, and league after league of the green sea danced and foamed in the morning sunlight, and I perceived that I was on a large schooner under full sail, the crew of which were littered about at different occupations. Some gaming and some drinking, while on the forecastle two men were settling a dispute at fisticuffs. And they gave me no more notice, nor as much, than I had been a baboon thrust among them. From this indifference to a captive I augured no good. Then my conductor, whom I rightly judged to be the mate of this devil's crew, took me roughly by the shoulder and bade me accompany him to the cabin.

As we drew near the topgallant poop there sounded in my ears a noise like a tempest, which I soon became aware was a man swearing with a prodigious vehemence in a fog-horn of a voice. "'Sdeath and wounds! Where is that dog-fish of a Cockle? Damn his entrails, and he is not come soon, I'll mast-head him naked, by the seven holy spritsails!" And much more and worse to the same tune until we passed the door and stood before him, when he let out an oath like the death-cry of a monster.

He was a short, lean man with a leathery face and long, black ropy hair, and beady black eyes that caught the light like a cat's. His looks, indeed, would have scared a timid person into a fit; but I resolved I would die rather than show the fear with which he inspired me. He was dressed in an old navy uniform with dirty lace. His cabin was bare enough, being scattered about with pistols and muskets and cutlasses, with a ragged pallet in one corner, and he sat behind an oaken table covered with greasy charts and spilled liquor and tobacco.

"So ho, you are risen from the dead, are you, my fine buck? Mr. What-do-they-call-you?" cried the captain, with a word as foul as any he had yet uttered. "By the Lord, you shall pay for running my bo'sun through!"

"And by the Lord, Captain What's-your-name," I cried back, for the rum I had taken had heated me, "you and your fellow-rascals shall pay in blood for this villanous injury!"

Griggs got to his feet and seized his hanger, his face like livid marble seamed with blue. And from force of habit I made motion for my sword, to make the shameful discovery that I was clothed from head to foot in linsey-woolsey.

"G— d— my soul," he roared, "if I don't slit you like a herring! The devil burn me to a cinder if I don't give your guts to the sharks!" And he made at me in such a fury that I would certainly have been cut to pieces had I not grasped a cutlass and parried his blow, Cockle looking on with his jaw dropped like a peak without haulyards. With a stroke of my weapon I disarmed Captain Griggs, his sword flying through the cabin window. For I made up my mind I would better die fighting than expire at a hideous torture, which I doubted not he would inflict, and so I took up a posture of defence, with one eye on the mate; despite the kind offices of the latter below I knew not whether he were disposed to befriend me before the captain. What was my astonishment, therefore, to behold Griggs's truculent manner change.

"Avast, my man-o-war," he cried; "blood and wounds! I had more than an eye when they brought thee aboard, else I would have killed thee like a sucking-pig under the forecastle, as I have given oath to do. By the Ghost, you are worth seven of that Roger Spratt whom you sent to hell in his boots."

Wherewith Cockle, who for all his terrible appearance stood in a mighty awe of his captain, set up a loud laugh, and vowed that Griggs knew a man when he spared me, and was cursed for his pains.

"So you were contracted to murder me, Captain Griggs?" said I.

"Ay," he replied, a devilish gleam coming into his eye, "but I have now got you and the money to boot. But harkye, I'll stand by my half of the bargain, by G—. If ever you reach Maryland alive, they may hang me to the yardarm of a ship-of-the-line."

And I live long enough, my dears, I hope some day to write for you the account of all that befell me on this slaver, *Black Moll*, for so she was called. 'Twould but delay my story now. Suffice it to say that we sailed for a fortnight or so in the West India seas. From some observations that fell from the mouth of Griggs I gathered that he was searching for an island which evaded him; and each day added to his vexation at not finding it. At times he was drunk for forty hours at a stretch, when he would shut himself in his cabin and leave his ship to the care of Cockle, who navigated with the sober portion of the crew. And such a lousy, brawling lot of convicts I had never clapped eyes upon. As for me, I was treated indifferently well, though 'twas in truth punishment enough to live in that filthy ship, to eat their shins of beef and briny pork and wormy biscuit, to wear rough clothes that chafed my skin. I shared Cockle's cabin, in every way as dirty a place as the den I had left, but with the advantage of air, for which I fervently thanked God.

I think the mate had some little friendship for me, though he was too hardened by the life he had led to care a deal what became of me. He encouraged me secretly to continue to beard Griggs as I had begun, saying that it was my sole chance of a whole skin, and vowing that if he had had the courage to pursue the same course his own back had not been checkered like a grating. He told me stories of the captain's cruelty which I dare not repeat for their very horror, and indeed I lacked not for instances to substantiate what he said; men with their backs beaten to a pulp, and others with ears cut off, and mouths slit, and toes missing. So that I lived in hourly fear lest in some drunken fit Griggs might command me to be tortured. But, fortunately, he held small converse with me, and when sober busied himself in trying to find the island and in cursing the fate by which it eluded him.

So I existed, and prayed daily for deliverance. I plied Cockle with questions as to what they purposed doing with me, but he was wont to turn sulky, and would answer me not a word. But once, when he was deeper in his cups than common, he let me know that Griggs was to sell me to a certain planter. You may well believe that this did not serve to liven my spirits.

At length, one morning, Captain Griggs came out of his cabin and climbed upon the poop, calling all hands aft to the quarterdeck. Whereupon he proceeded to make them a speech that for vileness exceeded aught I have ever heard before or since. He finished by reminding them that this was the anniversary of the scuttling of the sloop *Jane*, which had made them all rich a year before, off the Canaries; the day that he had sent three and twenty men over the plank to hell. Wherefore he decreed a holiday, as the weather was bright and the trades light, and would serve quadruple portions of rum to every man jack aboard; and they set up a cheer that started the Mother Careys astern.

I have no language to depict the bestiality of that day; and if I had I would think it sin to write of it. The helm was lashed on the port tack, the haulyards set taut, and all hands down to the lad who was the cook's scullion proceeded to get drunk. I took the precaution to have a hanger at my side and to slip one of Cockle's pistols within the band of my breeches. I was in an exquisite agony of indecision as to what manner to act and how to defend myself from their drunken brutality, for I well knew that if I refused to imbibe with them I should probably be murdered for my abstemiousness; and, if I drank, the stuff was so near to alcohol that I could not hope to keep my senses. While in this predicament I received a polite invitation to partake in the captain's company, which I did not see my way clear to refuse, and repaired to the cabin accordingly.

There I found Griggs and Cockle seated, and a fair-sized barrel of rum between them that the captain had just moved thither. By way of welcome he shot at me a volley of curses and bade me to fill up, and through fear of offending him I took down my first mug with a fair good grace. Then, in his own particular language, he began the account of the capture of the *Jane*, taking care in the pauses to see that my mug was full. But, as luck would have it, he got no farther than the boarding by the *Black Moll's* crew, when he fell to squabbling with Cockle as to who had been the first man over the side; and while they were settling this difference I grasped the opportunity to escape.

The maudlin scene that met my eyes on deck defies description; some were fighting, others grinning with a hideous laughter, and still others shouting tavern jokes unspeakable. And suddenly, whilst I was observing these things from a niche behind the cabin door, I heard the captain cry from within, "The ensign, the ensign!" Forgetting his dispute with Cockle, he bumped past me and made his way with some trouble to the poop. I climbed the ladder after him, and to my horror beheld him in a drunken frenzy drag a black flag with a rudely painted skull and cross-bones from the signal-chest, and with uncertain fingers toggle it to the ensign haulyards and hoist to the peak, where it fluttered grimly in the light wind like an evil augur on a fair day. At sight of it the wretches on deck fell to shouting and huzzaing, Griggs standing leering up at it. Then he gravely pulled off his hat and made it a bow, and turned upon me.

"Salute it, ye lubberly ——! Ye are no first-rate here," he thundered. "Salute the flag!"

Unless fear had kept me sober, 'tis past my understanding why I was not as drunk as he. Be that as it may, I was near as quarrelsome, and would as soon have worshipped the golden calf as saluted that rag. I flung back some reply, and he lugged out and came at me with a spring like a wild beast; and his men below, seeing us fall out, made a rush for the poop with knives and cutlasses drawn. Betwixt them all I should soon have been in slivers had not the main shrouds offered themselves handy. And up them I sprung, the captain cutting at my legs as I left the sheer-pole, and I stopped not until I reached the schooner's cross-trees, where I drew my cutlass. They pranced around the mast and showered me with oaths, for all the world like a lot of howling dogs which had treed a cat.

I began to feel somewhat easier, and cried aloud that the first of them who came up after me would go down again in two pieces. Despite my warning a brace essayed to climb the ratlines, as pitiable an attempt as ever I witnessed, and fell to the deck again. 'Twas a miracle that they missed falling into the sea. And after a while, becoming convinced that they could not get at me, and being too far gone to shoot with any accuracy, they tumbled off the poop swearing to serve me in a hundred horrible ways when they caught me, and fell again to drinking and quarrelling amongst themselves. I was indeed in an unenviable plight, by no means sure that I would not be slain out of hand when they became sufficiently sober to capture me. As I marked the progress of their damnable orgy I cast about for some plan to take advantage of their condition. I observed that a stupor was already beginning to overcome a few of them. Then suddenly an incident happened to drive all else from my mind.

Nothing less, my dears, than a white speck of sail gleaming on the southern horizon!

For an hour I watched it, now in a shiver of apprehension lest it pass us by, now weeping in an ecstasy of joy over a possible deliverance. But it grew steadily larger, and when about three miles on our port bow I saw that the ship was a brigantine. Though she had long been in sight from our deck, 'twas not until now that she was made out by a man on the forecastle, who set up a cry that brought about him all who could reel thither, Griggs staggering out of his cabin and to the nettings. The sight sobered him somewhat, for he immediately shouted orders to cast loose the guns, himself tearing the breeching from the nine-pounder next him and taking out the tompion. About half the crew were in a liquorish stupor from which the trump itself could scarce have aroused them; the rest responded with savage oaths, swore that they would boil their suppers in the blood of the brigantine's men and give their corpses to the sea. They fell to work on the port battery in so ludicrous a manner that I was fain to laugh despite the gravity of the situation. But when they came to rig the powder-hoist and a couple of them descended into the magazine with pipes lighted, I was in imminent expectation of being blown as high as a kite.

So absorbed had I been in these preparations that I neglected to watch the brigantine, which I discovered to be standing on and off in a very undecided manner, as though hesitating to attack. My spirits fell again at this, for with all my inexperience I knew her to be a better sailer than the *Black Moll*. Her master, as Griggs remarked, "was no d—d slouching lubber, and knew a yardarm from a rattan cane."

Finally, about six bells of the watch, the stranger wore ship and bore down across our bows, hoisting English colours, at sight of which I could scarce forbear a cheer. At this instant, Captain Griggs woke to the fact that his helm was still lashed, and bestowing a hearty kick on his prostrate quartermaster stuck fast to the pitchy seams of the deck, took the wheel himself, and easing off before the wind to bring the vessels broadside to broadside, commanded that the guns be shotted to the muzzle, an order that was barely executed before the brigantine came within close range. Aboard her was all order and readiness; the men at her guns fuse in hand, an erect and pompous figure of a man, in a cocked hat, on the break of her poop. He raised his hand, two puffs of white smoke darted out, and I heard first the shrieking of shot, the broadside came crashing round us, one tearing through the mainsail below me, another mangling two men in the waist of our schooner, and Griggs gave the order to touch off. But two of his guns answered, one of which had been so gorged with shot that it burst in a hundred pieces and sent the fellow with the swab to perdition, and such a hell of blood and confusion as resulted is indescribable. I saw Griggs in a wild fit of rage force the helm down, the schooner flying into the wind. And by this time, the brigantine having got round and presented her port battery, raked us at a bare hundred yards, and I was the first to guess by the tilting forward of the mast that our hull was hit between wind and water, and was fast settling by the bow.

The schooner was sinking like a gallipot.

That day, with the sea flashing blue and white in the sun, I saw men go to death with a curse upon their lips and a fever in their eyes, with murder and defiance of God's holy will in their hearts. Overtaken in bestiality, like the judgment of Nineveh, five and twenty disappeared from beneath me, and I had scarce the time to throw off my cutlass before I, too, was engulfed. So expired the *Black Moll*.

CHAPTER XIX

A MAN OF DESTINY

I WAS picked up and thrown into the brigantine's long-boat with a head and stomach full of salt water, and a heart as light as spray with the joy of it all. A big, red-bearded man lifted my heels to drain me.

"The mon's deid," said he.

"Dead!" cried I, from the bottom-board. "No more dead than you!"

I turned over so lustily that he dropped my feet, and I sat up, something to his consternation. And they had scarce hooked the ship's side when I sprang up the sea-ladder, to the great gaping of the boat's crew, and stood with the water running off me in rivulets before the captain himself. I shall never forget the look of his face as he regarded my sorry figure.

"Now by Saint Andrew," exclaimed he, "are ye kelpie or pirate?"

"Neither, captain," I replied, smiling as the comical end of it came up to me, "but a young gentleman in misfortune."

"Hoots!" says he, frowning at the grinning half-circle about us, "it's daft ye are—"

But there he paused, and took of me a second sizing. How he got at my birth behind my tangled mat of hair and wringing linsey-woolsey I know not to this day. But he dropped his Scotch and merchant-captain's manner, and was suddenly a French courtier, making me a bow that had done credit to a Richelieu.

"Your servant, Mr. —"

"Richard Carvel, of Carvel Hall, in his Majesty's province of Maryland."

"ARE YE KELPIE OR PIRATE?"

in my throat and flowed out of my eyes. For the thought of the horrors from which he had saved me for the first time swept over me; his own kind treatment overcame me, and I blubbered like a child. With that he turned his back.

"Hoots," says he, again, "dinna ye thank me. 'Tis naething to scuttle a nest of vermin, but the duty of ilka man who sails the seas." By this, having got the better of his emotion, he added: "And if it has been my good fortune to save a gentleman, Mr. Carvel, I thank God for it, as you must."

Save for a slackness inside the leg and in the hips, MacMuir's clothes fitted me well enough, and presently I reappeared in the captain's cabin rigged out in the mate's shore suit of purplish drab, and brass-buckled shoes that came high over the instep, with my hair combed clear and tied with a ribbon behind. I felt at last that I might lay some claim to respectability. And what was my surprise to find Captain Paul buried to his middle in a great chest, and the place strewn about with laced and broidered coats and waistcoats, frocks and Newmarkets, like any tailor's shop in Church Street. So strange they looked in those tropical seas that he was near to catching me in a laugh as he straightened up. 'Twas then I noted that he was a younger man than I had taken him for.

"You gentlemen from the southern colonies are too well nourished, by far," says he; "you are apt to be large of chest and limb. 'Odds bods, Mr. Carvel, it grieves me to see you apparelled like a barber surgeon. If the good Lord had but made you smaller, now," and he sighed, "how well this sky-blue frock had set you off."

"Indeed, I am content, and more, captain," I replied with a smile, "and thankful to be safe amongst friends. Never, I assure you, have I had less desire for finery."

"Ay," said he, "you may well say that, you who have worn silk all your life, and will the rest of it, and we get safe to port. But believe me, sir, the pleasure of seeing one of your face and figure in such a coat as that would not be a small one."

And disregarding my blushes and protests, he held up the watchet blue frock against me, and it was near fitting me but for my breadth,—the skirts being prodigiously long. I wondered mightily what tailor had thrust this garment upon him; its fashion was of the old king's time, the cuffs slashed like a sea-officer's uniform, and the shoulders made carefully round. But other thoughts were running within me then.

"Captain," I cut in, "you are sailing eastward."

"Yes, yes," he answered absently, fingering some Point d'Espagne.

"There is no chance of touching in the colonies?" I persisted.

"Colonies! No," said he, in the same abstraction; "I am making for the Solway, being long overdue. But what think you of this, Mr. Carvel?"

And he held up a wondrous vellum-hole waistcoat of a gone-by vintage, and I saw how futile it were to attempt to lead him, while in that state of absorption, to topics which touched my affair. Of a sudden the significance of what he had said crept over me, the word *Solway* repeating itself in my mind. That firth bordered England itself, and Dorothy was in London! I became reconciled. I had no particle of objection to the Solway save the uneasiness my grandfather would come through, which was beyond helping. Fate had ordered things well.

Then I fell to applauding, while the captain tried on (for he was not content with holding up) another frock of white drab, which, cuffs and pockets, I'll take my oath mounted no less than twenty-four: another plain one of pink cut-velvet; tail-coats of silk, heavily broidered with flowers, and satin waistcoats with narrow lace. He took an inconceivable enjoyment out of this parade, discoursing the while, like a nobleman with nothing but dress in his head, or, perhaps, like a mastercutter, about the turn of this or that lapel, the length from armpit to fold, and the number of button-holes that was proper. And finally he exhibited with evident pride a pair of doeskins that buttoned over the calf to be worn with high shoes, which I make sure he would have tried on likewise had he been offered the slightest encouragement. So he exploited the whole of his wardrobe, such an unlucky assortment of finery as I never wish to see again; all of which, however, became him marvellously, though I think he had looked well in anything. I hope I may be forgiven the perjury I did that day. I wondered greatly that such a foible should crop out in a man of otherwise sound sense and plain ability.

At length, when the last chest was shut again and locked, and I had exhausted my ingenuity at commendation, and my patience also, he turned to me as a man come out of a trance.

"Od's fish, Mr. Carvel," he cried, "you will be starved. I had forgot your state."

I owned that hunger had nigh overcome me, whereupon he became very solicitous, bade the boy bring in supper at once, and in a short time we sat down together to the best meal I had seen for a month. It seemed like a year. Porridge, and bacon nicely done, and duff and ale, with the sea rushing past the cabin windows as we ate, touched into colour by the setting sun. Captain Paul did not mess with his mates, not he, and he gave me to understand that I was to share his cabin, apologizing profusely for what he was pleased to call poor fare. He would have it that he, and not I, were receiving favour.

"My dear sir," he said once, "you cannot know what a bit of finery is to me, who has so little chance for the wearing of it. To discuss with a gentleman, a *connoisseur* (I know a bit of French, Mr. Carvel), is a pleasure I do not often come at."

His simplicity in this touched me; it was pathetic.

"How know you I am a gentleman, Captain Paul?" I asked curiously.

"I should lack discernment, sir," he retorted, with some heat, "if I could not see as much. Breeding shines through sack-cloth, sir. Besides," he continued, in a milder tone, "the look of you is candour itself. Though I have not greatly the advantage of you in age, I have seen many men, and I know that such a face as yours cannot lie."

Here Mr. Lowrie, the second mate, came in with a report; and I remarked that he stood up hat in hand whilst making it, very much as if Captain Paul commanded a frigate. The captain went to a locker and brought forth some mellow Madeira, and after the mate had taken a glass of it standing, he withdrew. Then we lighted pipes and sat very cosey with a lanthorn swung between us, and Captain Paul expressed a wish to hear my story.

I gave him my early history briefly, dwelling but casually upon the position enjoyed in Maryland by my family; but I spoke of my grandfather, now turning seventy, gray-haired in the service of King and province. The captain was indeed a most sympathetic listener, now throwing in a question showing keen Scotch penetration, and anon making a most ludicrous inquiry as to the dress livery our footmen wore, and whether Mr. Carvel used outriders when he travelled abroad. This was the other side of the man. As the wine warmed and the pipe soothed, I spoke at length of Grafton and the rector; and when I came to the wretched contrivance by which they got me aboard the *Black Moll*, he was stalking hither and thither about the cabin, his fists clenched and his voice thick, breaking into Scotch again and vowing that hell were too good for such as they.

His indignation, which seemed real and generous, transformed him into another man. He showered question after question upon me concerning my uncle and Mr. Allen; declared that he had known many villains, but had yet to hear of their equals; and finally, cooling a little, gave it as his judgment that the crime could never be brought home to them. This was my own opinion. He advised me, before we turned in, to "gie the parson a crunt" as soon as ever I could lay hands upon him.

The *John* made a good voyage for that season, with fair winds and clear skies for the most part. 'Twas a stout ship and a steady, with generous breadth of beam, and kept by the master as clean and bright as his porringer. He was Emperor aboard her. He spelt Command with a large C, and when he inspected, his jacks stood to attention like man-o'-war's men. The *John* mounting only four guns, and but two of them nine-pounders, I expressed my astonishment that he had dared attack a pirate craft like the *Black Moll*, without knowing her condition and armament.

"Richard," says he, impressively, for we had become very friendly, "I would close with a thirty-two and she flew that flag. Why, sir, a bold front is half the battle, using circumspection, of a course. A pretty woman, whatever her airs and quality, is to be carried the same way, and a man ought never to be frightened by appearances."

Sometimes, at our meals, we discussed politics. But he seemed lukewarm upon this subject. He had told me that he had a brother William in Virginia, who was a hot Patriot. The American quarrel seemed to interest him very little. I should like to underscore this last sentence, my dears, in view of what comes after. What he said on the topic leaned perhaps to the King's side, tho' he was careful to say nothing that would give me offence. I was not surprised, for I had made a fair guess of his ambitions. It is only honest to declare that in my soberer moments my estimate of his character suffered. But he was a strange man, — a genius, as I soon discovered, to rouse the most sluggish nature to enthusiasm.

The joy of sailing is born into some men, and those who are marked for the sea go down thither like the very streams, to be salted. Whatever the sign, old Stanwix was not far wrong when he read it upon me, and 'twas no great while before I was part and parcel of the ship beneath my feet, breathing deep with her every motion. What feeling can compare with that I tasted when the brigantine lay on her side, the silver spray hurling over the bulwarks and stinging me to life! Or, in the watches, to hear the sea lashing along her strakes in never ending music! I gave MacMuir his shore suit again, and hugely delighted and astonished Captain Paul by donning a jacket of Scotch wool and a pair of seaman's boots, and so became a sailor myself. I had no mind to sit idle the passage, and the love of it, as I have said, was in me. In a fortnight I went aloft with the best of the watch to reef topsails, and trod a foot-rope without losing head or balance, bent an earing, and could lay hand on any lift, brace, sheet, or haulyards in the racks. John Paul himself taught me to tack and wear ship, and MacMuir to stow a headsail. The craft came to me, as it were, in a hand-gallop.

At first I could make nothing of the crew, not being able to understand a word of their Scotch; but I remarked, from the first, that they were sour and sulky, and given to gathering in knots when the captain or MacMuir had not the deck. For Mr. Lowrie, poor man, they had little respect. But they plainly feared the first mate, and John Paul most of all. Of me their suspicion knew no bounds, and they would give me gruff answers, or none, when I spoke to them. These things roused both curiosity and foreboding within me.

Many a watch I paced thro' with MacMuir, big and red and kindly, and I was not long in letting him know of the interest which Captain Paul had inspired within me. His own feeling for him was little short of idolatry. I had surmised much as to the rank of life from which the captain had sprung, but my astonishment was great when I was told that John Paul was the son of a poor gardener.

"A gardener's son, Mr. MacMuir!" I repeated.

"Just that," said he, solemnly, "a guid man an' haly was auld Paul. Unco puir, by reason o' seven bairns. I kennt the daddie weel. I mak sma' doubt the captain'll tak ye hame wi' him, syne the mither an' sisters still be i' the cot i' Mr. Craik's croft."

"Tell me, MacMuir," said I, "is not the captain in some trouble?"

For I knew that something, whatever it was, hung heavy on John Paul's mind as we drew nearer Scotland. At times his brow would cloud and he would fall silent in the midst of a jest. And that night, with the stars jumping and the air biting cold (for we were up in the 40's), and the *John* wish-washing through the seas at three leagues the hour, MacMuir told me the story of Mungo Maxwell. You may read it for yourselves, my dears, in the life of John Paul Jones.

"Wae's me!" he said, with a heave of his big chest, "I reca' as yestreen the night Maxwell cam aboord. The sun gaed doon a' bluidy, an' belyve the morn rose unco mirk an' dreary, wi' bullers[1] frae the west like muckle sowthers[2] wi' white plumes. I tauld the captain 'twas a' the faut o' Maxwell. I

---

[1] Rollers.   [2] Soldiers.

ne'er cad bide the blellum.¹ Dour an' din² he was, wi' ae girn like th' auld hornie.³ But the captain wadna hark to my rede when I tauld him naught but dool⁴ wad coom o' taking Mungo."

It seemed that John Paul, contrary to MacMuir's advice, had shipped as carpenter on the voyage out — near seven months since — a man by the name of Mungo Maxwell. The captain's motive had nothing in it but kindness, and a laudable desire to do a good turn to a playmate of his boyhood. As MacMuir said, "they had gaed barefit thegither amang the braes." The man hailed from Kirkbean, John Paul's own parish. But he had within him little of the milk of kindness, being in truth a sour and mutinous devil; and instead of the gratitude he might have shown, he cursed the fate that had placed him under the gardener's son, whom he deemed no better than himself. The *John* had scarce cleared the Solway before Maxwell showed signs of impudence and rebellion.

The crew was three-fourths made of Kirkcudbright men who had known the master from childhood, many of them, indeed, being older than he; they were mostly jealous of Paul, envious of the command he had attained to over them, and impatient under the discipline he was ever ready to inflict. 'Tis no light task to enforce obedience from those with whom one has bird-nested. But, having more than once felt the weight of his hand, they feared him.

Dissatisfaction among such spreads apace, if a leader is but given; and Maxwell was such a one. His hatred for John Paul knew no bounds, and, having once tasted of his displeasure, he lay awake o' nights scheming to ruin him. And this was the plot: when the Azores should be in the wake, Captain Paul was to be murdered as he paced his quarterdeck in the morning, the two mates clapt into irons, and so brought to submission. And Maxwell, who had no more notion of navigation than a carpenter should, was to take the *John* to God knows where, — the Guinea coast, most probably. He would have no more navy regulations on a merchant brigantine, he promised them, nor banyan days, for the matter o' that.

¹ I never could put up with the villain. ³ Devil.
² Sour and sullen. ⁴ Sorrow.

Happily, MacMuir himself discovered the affair on the eve of its perpetration, overhearing two men talking in the bread-room, and he ran to the cabin with the sweat standing out on his forehead. But the captain would have none of the precautions he urged; declared he would walk the deck as usual, and vowed he could cope single-handed with a dozen cowards like Maxwell. Sure enough, at crowdie-time, the men were seen coming aft, with Maxwell in the van carrying a bowl, on the pretext of a complaint against the cook.

"John Paul," said MacMuir, with admiration in his voice and gesture, "John Paul wasna feart a pickle,[1] but gaed to the mast, whyles I stannt chittering i' my claes,[2] fearfu' for his life. He teuk the horn[3] from Mungo, priet[4] a soup o' the crowdie, an' wi' that he seiz't haut o' the man by baith shouthers ere the blastie[5] raught[6] for 's knife. My aith upo 't, sir, the lave[7] o' the batch cowert frae his e'e for a' the warld like thumpit tykes.[8]"

So ended that mutiny, by the brave act of a brave man. The carpenter was clapt into irons himself, and given no less of the cat-o'-nine-tails than was good for him, and properly discharged at Tobago with such as had supported him. But he brought Captain Paul before the vice-admiralty court of that place, charging him with gross cruelty, and this proceeding had delayed the brigantine six months from her homeward voyage, to the great loss of her owners. And tho' at length the captain was handsomely acquitted, his character suffered unjustly, for there lacked not those who put their own interpretation upon the affair. He would most probably lose the brigantine. "He expected as much," said MacMuir.

"There be mony aboord," he concluded, with a sigh, "as'll muckle gash[9] when we win to Kirkcudbright."

[1] Little bit.
[2] Shivering in my clothes.
[3] Spoon.
[4] Tasted.
[5] Scoundrel.
[6] Reached.
[7] Rest.
[8] Cowered from his eye for all the world like whipt dogs.
[9] Gossip.

CHAPTER XX

A SAD HOME-COMING

Mr. Lowrie and Auctherlonnie, the Dumfries bo'sun, both of whom would have died for the captain, assured me of the truth of MacMuir's story, and shook their heads gravely as to the probable outcome. The peculiar water-mark of greatness that is woven into some men is often enough to set their own community bitter against them. Sandie, the plodding peasant, finds it a hard matter to forgive Jamie, who is taken from the plough next to his, and ends in Parliament. The affair of Mungo Maxwell, altered to suit, had already made its way on more than one vessel to Scotland. For according to Lowrie, there was scarce a man or woman in Kirkcudbrightshire who did not know that John Paul was master of the *John*, and (in their hearts) that he would be master of more in days to come. Human nature is such that they resented it, and cried out aloud against his cruelty.

On the voyage I had many sober thoughts of my own to occupy me: of the terrible fate, from which, by Divine interposition, I had been rescued; of the home I had left behind. I was all that remained to Mr. Carvel in the world, and I was sure that he had given me up for dead. How had he sustained the shock? I saw him heavily mounting the stairs upon Scipio's arm when first the news was brought to him. Next Grafton would come hurrying in from Kent to Marlboro' Street, disavowing all knowledge of the messenger from New York, and intent only upon comforting his father. And when I pictured my uncle soothing him to his face, and grinning behind his bed-curtains, my anger would scald me, and the realization of my helplessness bring tears of very bitterness.

What would I not have given then for one word with that honest and faithful friend of our family, Captain Daniel! I knew that he suspected Grafton: he had told me as much that night at the Coffee House. Perhaps the greatest of my fears was that my uncle would deny him access to Mr. Carvel when he returned from the North.

In the evening, when the sun settled red upon the horizon, I would think of Patty and my friends in Gloucester Street. For I knew they missed me sadly of a Sunday at the supper-table. But it has ever been my nature to turn forward instead of back, and to accept the twists and flings of fortune with hope rather than with discouragement. And so, as we left league after league of the blue ocean behind us, I would set my face to the forecastle. For Dorothy was in England.

On a dazzling morning in March, with the brigantine running like a beagle in full cry before a heaping sea that swayed her body,—so I beheld for the first time the misty green of the high shores of Ireland. Ah! of what heroes' deeds was I capable as I watched the lines come out in bold relief from a wonderland of cloud! With what eternal life I seemed to tingle! 'Twas as though I, Richard Carvel, had discovered all this colour; and when a tiny white speck of a cottage came out on the edge of the cliff, I thought irresistibly of the joy to live there the year round with Dorothy, with the wind whistling about our gables, and the sea thundering on the rocks far below. Youth is in truth a mystery.

How long I was gazing at the shifting coast I know not, for a strange wildness was within me that made me forget all else, until suddenly I became conscious of a presence at my side, and turned to behold the captain.

"'Tis a braw sight, Richard," said he, "but no sae bonnie as auld Scotland. An' the wind hauds, we shall see her shores the morn."

His voice broke, and I looked again to see two great tears rolling upon his cheeks.

"Ah, Scotland!" he pressed on, heedless of them, "God aboon kens what she is to me! But she hasna' been ower guid to me, laddie." And he walked to the taffrail, and stood looking astern that two men who had come aft to splice a haulyard might not perceive his disorder. I followed him, emboldened to speak at last what was in me.

"Captain Paul," said I, "MacMuir has told me of your trouble. My grandfather is rich, and not lacking in gratitude,"— here I paused for suitable words, as I could not solve his expression,— "you, sir, whose bravery and charity will have restored me to him, shall not want for friends and money."

He heard me through.

"Mr. Carvel," he replied with an impressiveness that took me aback, "reward is a thing that should not be spoken of between gentlemen."

And thus he left me, upbraiding myself that I should have mentioned money. And yet, I reflected secondly, why not? He was no more nor less than a master of a merchantman, and surely nothing was out of the common in such a one accepting what he had honestly come by. Had my affection for him been less sincere, had I not been racked with sympathy, I had laughed over his notions of gentility. I resolved, however, that when I had reached London and seen Mr. Dix, Mr. Carvel's agent, he should be rewarded despite his scruples. And if he lost his ship, he should have one of my grandfather's.

But at dinner he had plainly forgot any offence, and I had more cause than ever to be puzzled over his odd mixture of confidence and aloofness. He talked gayly on a score of subjects,— on dress, of which he was never tired, and described ports in the Indies and South America, in a fashion that betrayed prodigious powers of acute observation; nor did he lack for wit when he spoke of the rich planters who had wined him, and had me much in laughter. We fell into a merry mood, in sooth, jingling the glasses in many toasts, for he had a list of healths to make me gasp, near as long as the brigantine's articles,— Inez in Havana and Maraquita in Cartagena, and Clotilde, the Creole, of Martinico, each had her separate charm. Then there was Bess, in Kingston, the relict of a customs official, Captain Paul relating with ingenuous gusto a midnight brush with a lieutenant of his Majesty, in which the fair widow figured, and showed her preference, too. But his adoration for the ladies of the more northern colonies, he would have me to understand, was unbounded. For example, Miss Arabella Pope of Norfolk, in Virginia,—and did I know her? No, I had not that pleasure, though I assured him the Popes of Virginia were famed. Miss Pope danced divinely as any sylph, and the very memory of her tripping at the Norfolk Assembly roused the captain to such a pitch of enthusiasm as I had never seen in him. Marvellous to say, his own words failed him, and he had recourse to the poets:—

> "Her feet beneath her petticoat
> Like little mice stole in and out,
> As if they feared the light;
> But, oh, she dances such a way!
> No sun upon an Easter-day
> Is half so fine a sight."

The lines, he told me, were Sir John Suckling's; and he gave them standing, in excellent voice and elegant gesture.

He was in particular partial to the poets, could quote at will from Gay and Thomson and Goldsmith and Gray, and even from Shakespeare, much to my own astonishment and humiliation. Saving only Dr. Courtenay of Annapolis I had never met his equal for versatility of speech and command of fine language; and, having heard that he had been at sea since the age of twelve, I made bold to ask him at what school he had got his knowledge.

"At none, Richard," he answered with pride, "saving the rudiments at the Parish School at Kirkbean. Why, sir, I hold it to be within every man's province to make himself what he will, and I early recognized in Learning the only guide for such as me. I may say that I married her for the furtherance of my fortunes, and have come to love her for her own sake. Many and many the 'tween-watch have I passed in a coil of rope in the tops, a volume of the classics in my hand. And my happiest days, when not at sea, have been spent in my brother William's little library. He hath a modest estate near Fredericksburg, in Virginia, and none holds higher than he the worth of an education. Ah, Richard," he added, with a certain sadness, "I fear you little know the value of that which hath been so lavishly bestowed upon you. There is no creation in the world to equal your fine gentleman!"

It struck me indeed as strange that a man of his powers should set store by such trumpery, and, too, that these notions had not impaired his ability as a seaman. I did not reply. He gave no heed, however, but drew from a case a number of odes and compositions, which he told me were his own. They were addressed to various of his enamouritas, abounded in orrery, and were all, I make no doubt, incredibly fine, tho' not so much as one sticks in my mind. To speak truth I listened with a very ill grace, longing the while to be on deck, for we were about to sight the Isle of Man. The wine and the air of the cabin had made my eyes heavy. But presently, when he had run through with some dozen or more, he put them by, and with a quick motion got from his chair, a light coming into his dark eyes that startled me to attention. And I forgot the merchant captain, and seemed to be looking forward into the years.

"Mark you, Richard," said he, "mark well when I say that my time will come, and a day when the best of them will bow to me. And every ell of that triumph shall be mine, sir, — ay, every inch!"

Such was his force, which sprang from some hidden fire within him, that I believed his words as firmly as they had been writ down in the Book of Isaiah. Brimming over with enthusiasm, I pledged his coming greatness in a reaming glass of Malaga.

"Alack," he cried, "an' they all had your faith, laddie, a fig for the prophecy! Ye maun ken th' incentive's the maist o' the battle."

There was more of wisdom in this than I dreamed of then. Here lay hid the very keynote of that ambitious character: he stooped to nothing less than greatness for a triumph over his slanderers.

I rose betimes the next morning to find the sun peeping above the wavy line of the Scottish hills far up the Solway, and the brigantine sliding smoothly along in the lee of the Galloway Rhinns. And, though the month was March, the slopes of Burrow Head were green as the lawn of Carvel Hall in May, and the slanting rays danced on the ruffed water. By eight of the clock we had crept into Kirkcudbright Bay and anchored off St. Mary's Isle, the tide running ebb, and leaving a wide brown belt of sand behind it.

St. Mary's Isle! As we looked upon it that day, John Paul and I, and it lay low against the bright water with its bare oaks and chestnuts against the dark pines, 'twas perhaps as well that the future was sealed to us.

Captain Paul had conned the brigantine hither with a master's hand; but now that the anchor was on the ground, he became palpably nervous. I had donned again good MacMuir's shore suit, and was standing by the gangway when the captain approached me.

"What'll ye be doing now, Dickie lad?" he asked kindly.

What indeed! I was without money in a foreign port, still dependent upon my benefactor. And since he had declared his unwillingness to accept any return I was of no mind to go farther into his debt. I thanked him again for his goodness in what sincere terms I could choose, and told him I should be obliged if he would put me in the way of working my passage to London upon some coasting vessel. But my voice was thick, my affection for him having grown past my understanding.

"Hoots!" he replied, moved in his turn, "whyles I hae siller ye shallna lack. Ye maun gae post-chaise to London, as befits yere station."

And scouting my expostulations, he commanded the longboat, bidding me be ready to go ashore with him. I had nothing to do but to say farewell to MacMuir and Lowrie and Auctherlonnie, which was hard enough. For the honest first mate I had a great liking, and was touched beyond speech when he enjoined me to keep his shore suit as long as I had want of it.

"But you will be needing it, MacMuir," I said, suspecting he had no other.

"Haith! I am but a plain man, Mr. Carvel, and ye can sen' back the claes frae London, wi' this geordie."

He slipped a guinea into my hand, but this I positively refused to take; and to hide my feelings I climbed quickly over the side and into the stern of the boat, beside the captain, and was rowed away through the little fleet of cobles gathering about the ship. Twisting my neck for a parting look at the *John*, I caught a glimpse of MacMuir's ungainly shoulders over the fokesle rail, and I was near to tears as he shouted a hearty "God speed" after me.

As we drew near the town of Kirkcudbright, which lies very low at the mouth of the river Dee, I made out a group of men and women on the wharves. The captain was silent, regarding them. When we had got within twenty feet or so of the landing, a dame in a red woollen kerchief called out: —

"What hae ye done wi' Mungo, John Paul?"

"*Captain* John Paul, Mither Birkie," spoke up a coarse fellow with a rough beard. And a laugh went round.

"Ay, captain! I'll *captain* him!" screamed the carlin, pushing to the front as the oars were tossed, "I'll tak aith Mr. Currie'll be *captaining* him for his towmond voyage o' piratin'. He be leukin' for ye noo, John Paul." With that some of the men on the thwarts, perceiving that matters were likely to go ill with the captain, began to chaff with their friends above. The respect with which he had inspired them, however, prevented any overt insult on their part. As for me, my temper had flared up like the burning of a loose charge of powder, and by instinct my right hand sought the handle of the mate's hanger. The beldame saw the motion.

"An' hae ye murder't MacMuir, John Paul, an' gien's claes to a Buckskin gowk?"

The knot stirred with an angry murmur: in truth they meant violence, — nothing less. But they had counted without their man, for Paul was born to ride greater crises. With his lips set in a line he stepped lightly out of the boat into their very midst, and they looked into his eyes to forget time and place. MacMuir had told me how those eyes could conquer mutiny, but I had not believed had I not been there to see the pack of them give back in sullen wonder. And so we walked through and on to the little street beyond, and never a word from the captain until we came opposite the sign of the "Hurcheon."

"Do you await me here, Richard," he said quite calmly; "I must seek Mr. Currie, and make my report."

I have still the remembrance of that pitiful day in the clean little village. I went into the inn and sat down upon an oak settle in a corner of the bar, under the high lattice, and thought of the bitterness of this home-coming. If I was amongst strangers, he was amongst worse: verily, to have one's own people set against one is heaviness of heart to a man whose love of Scotland was great as John Paul's. After a while the place began to fill, Willie and Robbie and Jamie arriving to discuss Paul's return over their nappy. The little I could make of their talk was not to my liking, but for the captain's sake I kept my anger under as best I could, for I had the sense to know that brawling with a lot of alehouse frequenters would not advance his cause. At length, however, came in the same sneering fellow I had marked on the wharf, calling loudly for swats. "Ay, *Captain* Paul was noo at Mr. Currie's, syne banie Alan see'd him gang forbye the kirk." The speaker's name, I learned, was Davie, and he had been talking with each and every man in the long-boat. Yes, Mungo Maxwell had been cat-o'-nine-tailed within an inch of his life; and that was the truth; for a trifling offence, too; and cruelly discharged at some outlandish port because, forsooth, he would not accept the gospel of the divinity of *Captain* Paul. He would as soon sign papers with the devil.

This Davie was gifted with a dangerous kind of humour which I have heard called innuendo, and he soon had the bar packed with listeners who laughed and cursed turn about, filling the room to a closeness scarce supportable. And what between the foul air and my resentment, and apprehension lest John Paul would come hither after me, I was in prodigious discomfort of body and mind. But there was no pushing my way through them unnoticed, wedged as I was in a far corner; so I sat still until unfortunately, or fortunately, the eye of Davie chanced to fall upon me, and immediately his yellow face lighted malignantly.

"Oh! here be the *gentleman* the *captain's* brocht hame!" he cried, emphasizing the two words; "as braw a *gentleman* as eer taen frae pirates, an' nae doubt sin to ae bien Buckskin bonnet-laird."

I saw through his game of getting satisfaction out of John Paul thro' goading me, and determined he should have his fill of it. For, all in all, he had me mad enough to fight three times over.

"Set aside the *gentleman*," said I, standing up and taking off MacMuir's coat, "and call me a lubberly clout like yourself, and we will see which is the better clout." I put off the long-sleeved jacket, and faced him with my fists doubled, crying: "I'll teach you, you spawn of a dunghill, to speak ill of a good man!"

A clamour of "Fecht! fecht!" arose, and some of them applauded me, calling me a "swankie," which I believe is a compliment. A certain sense of fairness is often to be found where least expected. They capsized the fat, protesting browster-wife o r her own stool, and were pulling Jamie's coat from his back, when I began to suspect that a fight was not to the sniveller's liking. Indeed, the very look of him made me laugh out — 'twas now as mild as a summer's morn.

"Wow," says Jamie, "ye maun fecht wi' a man o' yere ain size."

"I'll lay a guinea that we weigh even," said I; and suddenly remembered that I had not so much as tuppence to bless me.

Happily he did not accept the wager. In huge disgust they hustled him from the inn and put forward the blacksmith, who was standing at the door in his leather apron. Now I had not bargained with the smith, who seemed a well-natured enough man, and grinned broadly at the prospect. But they made a ring on the floor, I going over it at one end, and he at the other, when a cry came from the street, those about the entrance parted, and in walked John Paul himself. At sight of him my new adversary, who was preparing to deal me out a blow to fell an ox, dropped his arms in surprise, and held out his big hand.

"Haith! John Paul," he shouted heartily, forgetting me, "'tis blythe I am to see yere bonnie face ance mair!"

IN WALKED JOHN PAUL HIMSELF

"An' wha are ye, Jamie Darrell," said the captain, "to be bangin' yere betters? Dinna ye ken gentry when ye see't?"

A puzzled look spread over the smith's grimy face.

"Gentry!" says he; "nae gentry that I ken, John Paul. Th' fecht be but a bit o' fun, an' nane o' my seekin'."

"What quarrel is this, Richard?" says John Paul to me.

"In truth I have no quarrel with this honest man," I replied; "I desired but the pleasure of beating a certain evil-tongued Davie, who seems to have no stomach for blows, and hath taken his lies elsewhere."

So quiet was the place that the tinkle of the guidwife's needle, which she had dropped to the flags, sounded clear to all. John Paul stood in the middle of the ring, erect, like a man inspired, and the same strange sense of prophecy that had stirred my blood crept over him and awed the rest, as tho' 'twere suddenly given to see him, not as he was, but as he would be. Then he spoke.

"You, who are my countrymen, who should be my oldest and best friends, are become my enemies. You who were companions of my childhood are revilers of my manhood; you have robbed me of my good name and my honour, of my ship, of my very means of livelihood, and you are not content; you would rob me of my country, which I hold dearer than all. And I have never done you evil, nor spoken aught against you. As for the man Maxwell, whose part you take, his child is starving in your very midst, and you have not lifted your hands. 'Twas for her sake I shipped him, and none other. May God forgive you! He alone sees the bitterness in my heart this day. He alone knows my love for Scotland, and what it costs me to renounce her."

He had said so much with an infinite sadness, and I read a response in the eyes of more than one of his listeners, the guidwife weeping aloud. But now his voice rose, and he ended with a fiery vigour.

"Renounce her I do," he cried, "now and forevermore! Henceforth I am no countryman of yours. *And if a day of repentance should come for this evil, remember well what I have said to you.*"

o

They stood for a moment when he had finished, shifting uneasily, their tongues gone, like lads caught in a lie. I think they felt his greatness then, and had any one of them possessed the nobility to come forward with an honest word, John Paul might yet have been saved to Scotland. As it was, they slunk away in twos and threes, leaving at last only the good smith with us. He was not a man of talk, and the tears had washed the soot from his face in two white furrows.

"Ye'll hae a waught wi' me afore ye gang, John," he said clumsily, "for th' morns we've paddl' 't thegither i' th' Nith."

The ale was brought by the guidwife, who paused, as she put it down, to wipe her eyes with her apron. She gave John Paul one furtive glance and betook herself again to her knitting with a sigh, speech having failed her likewise. The captain grasped up his mug.

"May God bless you, Jamie," he said.

"Ye'll be gaen noo to see the mither," said Jamie, after a long space.

"Ay, for the last time. An', Jamie, ye'll see that nae harm cams to her when I'm far awa'?"

The smith promised, and also agreed to have John Paul's chests sent by wagon, that very day, to Dumfries. And we left him at his forge, his honest breast torn with emotion, looking after us.

CHAPTER XXI

THE GARDENER'S COTTAGE

So we walked out of the village, with many a head craned after us and many an eye peeping from behind a shutter, and on into the open highway. The day was heavenly bright, the wind humming around us and playing mad pranks with the white cotton clouds, and I forgot awhile the pity within me to wonder at the orderly look of the country, the hedges with never a stone out of place, and the bars always up. The ground was parcelled off in such bits as to make me smile when I remembered our own wide tracts in the New World. Here waste was sin: with us part and parcel of a creed. I marvelled, too, at the primness and solidity of the houses along the road, and remarked how their lines belonged rather to the landscape than to themselves. But I was conscious ever of a strange wish to expand, for I felt as tho' I were in the land of the Liliputians, and the thought of a gallop of forty miles or so over these honeycombed fields brought me to a laugh. But I was yet to see some estates of the gentry.

I had it on my tongue's tip to ask the captain whither he was taking me, yet dared not intrude on the sorrow that still gripped him. Time and time we met people plodding along, some of them nodding uncertainly, others abruptly taking the far side of the pike, and every encounter drove the poison deeper into his soul. But after we had travelled some way, up hill and down dale, he vouchsafed the intelligence that we were making for Arbigland, Mr. Craik's seat near Dumfries, which lies on the Nith twenty miles or so up the Solway from Kirkcudbright. On that estate stood the cottage where John Paul was born, and where his mother and sisters still dwelt.

"I'll juist be saying guidbye, Richard," he said; "and leave them a bit siller I hae saved, an' syne we'll be aff to London thegither, for Scotland's no but a cauld kintra."

"You are going to London with me?" I cried.

"Ay," answered he; "this is hame nae mair for John Paul." I made bold to ask how the *John's* owners had treated him.

"I have naught to complain of, laddie," he answered; "both Mr. Beck and Mr. Currie bore the matter of the admiralty court and the delay like the gentlemen they are. They well know that I am hard driven when I resort to the lash. They were both sore at losing me, and says Mr. Beck: 'We'll not soon get another to keep the brigantine like a man-o'-war, as did you, John Paul.' I thanked him, and told him I had sworn never to take another merchantman out of the Solway. And I will keep that oath."

He sighed, and added that he never hoped for better owners. In token of which he drew a certificate of service from his pocket, signed by Messrs. Currie and Beck, proclaiming him the best master and supercargo they had ever had in their service. I perceived that talk lightened him, and led him on. I inquired how he had got the *John*.

"I took passage on her from Kingston, laddie. On the trip both Captain Macadam and the chief mate died of the fever. And it was I, the passenger, who sailed her into Kirkcudbright, tho' I had never been more than a chief mate before. That is scarce three years gone, when I was just turned one and twenty. And old Mr. Currie, who had known my father, was so pleased that he gave me the ship. I had been chief mate of the *Two Friends*, a slaver out of Kingston."

"And so you were in that trade!" I exclaimed.

He seemed to hesitate.

"Yes," he replied, "and sorry I am to say it. But a man must live. It was no place for a gentleman, and I left of my own accord. Before that, I was on a slaver out of Whitehaven."

"You must know Whitehaven, then."

I said it only to keep the talk going, but I remembered the remark long after.

THE GARDENER'S COTTAGE 197

"I do," said he. "'Tis a fair sample of an English coast town. And I have often thought, in the event of war with France, how easy 'twould be for Louis's cruisers to harry the place, and an hundred like it, and raise such a terror as to keep the British navy at home."

I did not know at the time that this was the inspiration of an admiral and of a genius. The subject waned. And as familiar scenes jogged his memory, he launched into Scotch and reminiscence. Every barn he knew, and cairn and croft and steeple recalled stories of his boyhood.

We had long been in sight of Criffel, towering ahead of us, whose summit had beckoned for cycles to Helvellyn and Saddleback looming up to the southward, marking the wonderland of the English lakes. And at length, after some five hours of stiff walking, we saw the brown Nith below us going down to meet the Solway, and so came to the entrance of Mr. Craik's place. The old porter recognized Paul by a mere shake of the head and the words, "Yere back, are ye?" and a lowering of his bushy white eyebrows. We took a by-way to avoid the manor-house, which stood on the rising ground twixt us and the mountain, I walking close to John Paul's shoulder and feeling for him at every step. Presently, at a turn of the path, we were brought face to face with an elderly gentleman in black, and John Paul stopped.

"Mr. Craik!" he said, removing his hat.

But the gentleman only whistled to his dogs and went on.

"My God, even he!" exclaimed the captain, bitterly; "even he, who thought so highly of my father!"

A hundred yards more and we came to the little cottage nigh hid among the trees. John Paul paused a moment, his hand upon the latch of the gate, his eyes drinking in the familiar picture. The light of day was dying behind Criffel, and the tiny panes of the cottage windows pulsed with the rosy flame on the hearth within, now flaring, and again deepening. He sighed. He walked with unsteady step to the door and pushed it open. I followed, scarce knowing what I did, halted at the threshold and drew back, for I had been upon holy ground.

John Paul was kneeling upon the flags by the ingleside, his face buried on the open Bible in his mother's lap. Her snowy-white head was bent upon his, her tears running fast, and her lips moving in silent prayer to Him who giveth and taketh away. Verily, here in this humble place dwelt a love that defied the hard usage of a hard world!

After a space he came to the door and called, and took me by the hand, and I went in with him. Though his eyes were wet, he bore himself like a cavalier.

"Mother, this is Mr. Richard Carvel, heir to Carvel Hall in Maryland,—a young gentleman whom I have had the honour to rescue from a slaver."

I bowed low, such was my respect for Dame Paul, and she rose and curtseyed. She wore a widow's cap and a black gown, and I saw in her deep-lined face a resemblance to her son.

"Madam," I said, the title coming naturally, "I owe Captain Paul a debt I can never repay."

"An' him but a laddie!" she cried. "I'm thankfu', John, I'm thankfu' for his mither that ye saved him."

"I have no mother, Madam Paul," said I, "and my father was killed in the French war. But I have a grandfather who loves me dearly as I love him."

Some impulse brought her forward, and she took both my hands in her own.

"Ye'll forgive an auld woman, sir," she said, with a dignity that matched her son's, "but ye're sae young, an' ye hae sic a leuk in yere bonny gray e'e that I ken ye'll aye be a true friend o' John's. He's been a guid sin to me, an' ye maunna reck what they say o' him."

When now I think of the triumph John Paul has achieved, of the scoffing world he has brought to his feet, I cannot but recall that sorrowful evening in the gardener's cottage, when a son was restored but to be torn away. The sisters came in from their day's work,—both well-favoured lasses, with John's eyes and hair,—and cooked the simple meal of broth and porridge, and the fowl they had kept so long against the captain's home-coming. He carved with many a light word that cost him dear. Did Janet reca' the simmer nights they had supped here, wi' the bumclocks bizzin' ower the candles? And was Nancy, the cow, still i' the byre? And did the bees still give the same bonnie hiney, and were the red apples still in the far orchard? Ay, Meg had thocht o' him that autumn, and ran to fetch them with her apron to her face, to come back smiling through her tears. So it went; and often a lump would rise in my throat that I could not eat, famished as I was, and the mother and sisters scarce touched a morsel of the feast.

The one never failing test of a son, my dears, lies in his treatment of his mother, and from that hour forth I had not a doubt of John Paul. He was a man who had seen the world and become, in more than one meaning of the word, a gentleman. Whatever foibles he may have had, he brought no conscious airs and graces to this lowly place, but was again the humble gardener's boy.

But time pressed, as it ever does. The hour came for us to leave, John Paul firmly refusing to remain the night in a house that belonged to Mr. Craik. Of the tenderness, nay, of the pity and cruelty of that parting, I have no power to write. We knelt with bowed heads while the mother prayed for the son, expatriated, whom she never hoped to see again on this earth. She gave us bannocks of her own baking, and her last words were to implore me always to be a friend to John Paul.

Then we went out into the night and walked all the way to Dumfries in silence.

We lay that night at the sign of the "Twa Naigs,"[1] where Bonnie Prince Charlie had rested in the Mars year.[2] Before I went to bed I called for pen and paper, and by the light of a tallow dip sat down to compose a letter to my grandfather, telling him that I was alive and well, and recounting as much of my adventures as I could. I said that I was going to London, where I would see Mr. Dix, and would take passage

---

[1] I have not been able to discover why Mr. Carvel disguised the name of this hostelry. It is probable that he forgot it. He kept no journal. — D. C. C.
[2] The year 1715.

thence for America. I prayed that he had been able to bear up against the ordeal of my disappearance. I dwelt upon the obligations I was under to John Paul, relating the misfortunes of that worthy seaman (which he so little deserved!). And said that it was my purpose to bring him to Maryland with me, where I knew Mr. Carvel would reward him with one of his ships, explaining that he would accept no money. But when it came to accusing Grafton and the rector, I thought twice, and bit the end of the feather. The chances were so great that my grandfather would be in bed and under the guardianship of my uncle that I forbore, and resolved instead to write it to Captain Daniel at my first opportunity.

I arose early to discover a morning gray and drear, with a mist falling to chill the bones. News travels apace the world over, and that of John Paul's home-coming and of his public renunciation of Scotland at the "Hurcheon" had reached Dumfries in good time, substantiated by the arrival of the teamster with the chests the night before. I descended into the courtyard in time to catch the captain in his watchet-blue frock haggling with the landlord for a chaise, the two of them surrounded by a muttering crowd anxious for a glimpse of Mr. Craik's gardener's son, for he had become a nine-day sensation to the country round about. But John Paul minded them not so much as a swarm of flies, and the teamster's account of the happenings at Kirkcudbright had given them so wholesome a fear of his speech and presence as to cause them to misdoubt their own wit, which is saying a deal of Scotchmen. But when the bargain had been struck and John Paul gone with the 'ostler to see to his chests, mine host thought it a pity not to have a fall out of me.

"So ye be the Buckskin laird," he said, with a wink at a leering group of farmers; "ye hae braw gentles in America."

He was a man of sixty or thereabout, with a shrewd but not unkindly face that had something familiar in it.

"You have discernment indeed to recognize a gentleman in Scotch clothes," I replied, turning the laugh on him.

"Dinna raise ae Buckskin, Mr. Rawlinson," said a man in corduroy.

"Rawlinson!" I exclaimed at random, "there is one of your name in the colonies who knows his station better."

"Trowkt!" cried mine host, "ye ken Ivie o' Maryland,— Ivie my brither?"

"He is my grandfather's miller at Carvel Hall," I said.

"Syne ye maun be nane ither than Mr. Richard Carvel. Yere servan', Mr. Carvel," and he made me a low bow, to the great dropping of jaws round about, and led me into the inn. With trembling hands he took a packet from his cabinet and showed me the letters, twenty-three in all, which Ivie had written home since he had gone out as the King's passenger in '45. The sight of them brought tears to my eyes and carried me out of the Scotch mist back to dear old Maryland. I had no trouble in convincing mine host that I was the lad eulogized in the scrawls, and he put hand on the very sheet which announced my birth, nineteen years since, — the fourth generation of Carvels Ivie had known.

So it came that the captain and I got the best chaise and pair in place of the worst, and sat down to a breakfast such as was prepared only for my Lord Selkirk when he passed that way, while I told the landlord of his brother; and as I talked I remembered the day I had caught the arm of the mill and gone the round, to find that Ivie had written of that, too!

After that our landlord would not hear of a reckoning. I might stay a month, a year, at the "Twa Naigs" if I wished. As for John Paul, who seemed my friend, he would say nothing, only to advise me privately that the man was queer company, shaking his head when I defended him. He came to me with ten guineas, which he pressed me to take for Ivie's sake, and repay when occasion offered. I thanked him, but was of no mind to accept money from one who thought ill of my benefactor.

The refusal of these recalled the chaise, and I took the trouble to expostulate with the captain on that score, pointing out as delicately as I might that, as he had brought me to Scotland, I held it within my right to incur the expense of the trip to London, and that I intended to reimburse him when I saw Mr. Dix. For I knew that his wallet was not over full, since he had left the half of his savings with his mother. Much to my secret delight, he agreed to this as within the compass of a gentleman's acceptance. Had he not, I had the full intention of leaving him to post it alone, and of offering myself to the master of the first schooner.

Despite the rain, and the painful scenes gone through but yesterday, and the sour-looking ring of men and women gathered to see the start, I was in high spirits as we went spinning down the Carlisle road, with my heart leaping to the crack of the postilion's whip.

I was going to London and to Dorothy!

CHAPTER XXII

ON THE ROAD

MANY were the ludicrous incidents we encountered on our journey to London. As long as I live, I shall never forget John Paul's alighting upon the bridge of the Sark to rid himself of a mighty farewell address to Scotland he had been composing upon the road. And this he delivered with such appalling voice and gesture as to frighten to a standstill a chaise on the English side of the stream, containing a young gentleman in a scarlet coat and a laced hat, and a young lady who sobbed as we passed them. They were, no doubt, running to Gretna Green to be married.

Captain Paul, as I have said, was a man of moods, and strangely affected by ridicule. And this we had in plenty upon the road. Landlords, grooms, and 'ostlers, and even our own post-boys, laughed and jested coarsely at his sky-blue frock, and their sallies angered him beyond all reason, while they afforded me so great an amusement that more than once I was on the edge of a serious falling-out with him as a consequence of my merriment. Usually, when we alighted from our vehicle, the expression of mine host would sour, and his *sir* would shift to a *master;* while his servants would go trooping in again, with many a coarse fling that they would get no vails from such as we. And once we were invited into the kitchen. He would be sour for half a day at a spell after a piece of insolence out of the common, and then deliver me a solemn lecture upon the advantages of birth in a manor. Then his natural buoyancy would lift him again, and he would be in childish ecstasies at the prospect of getting to London, and seeing the great world; and I began to think that he secretly cherished the hope of meeting some of its votaries. For I had told him, casually as possible, that I had friends in Arlington Street, where I remembered the Manners were established.

"Arlington Street!" he repeated, rolling the words over his tongue; "it has a fine sound, laddie, a fine sound. That street must be the very acme of fashion."

I laughed, and replied that I did not know. And at the ordinary of the next inn we came to, he took occasion to mention to me, in a louder voice than was necessary, that I would do well to call in Arlington Street as we went into town. So far as I could see, the remark did not compel any increase of respect from our fellow-diners.

Upon more than one point I was worried. Often and often I reflected that some hitch might occur to prevent my getting money promptly from Mr. Dix. Days would perchance elapse before I could find the man in such a great city as London; he might be out of town at this season, Easter being less than a se'nnight away. For I had heard my grandfather say that the elder Mr. Dix had a house in some merchant's suburb, and loved to play at being a squire before he died. Again (my heart stood at the thought), the Manners might be gone back to America. I cursed the stubborn pride which had led the captain to hire a post-chaise, when the wagon had served us so much better, and besides relieved him of the fusillade of ridicule he got travelling as a gentleman. But such reflections always ended in my upbraiding myself for blaming him whose generosity had rescued me from perhaps a life-long misery.

But, on the whole, we rolled southward happily, between high walls and hedges, past trim gardens and fields and meadows, and I marvelled at the regular, park-like look of the country, as though stamped from one design continually recurring, like our butter at Carvel Hall. The roads were sometimes good, and sometimes as execrable as a colonial byway in winter, with mud up to the axles. And yet, my heart went out to this country, the home of my ancestors. Spring was at hand; the ploughboys whistled between the furrows, the larks circled overhead, and the lilacs were cautiously pushing forth their noses. The air was heavy with the perfume of living things.

The welcome we got at our various stopping-places was often scanty indeed, and more than once we were told to go farther down the street, that the inn was full. And I may as well confess that my mind was troubled about John Paul. Despite all I could say, he would go to the best hotels in the larger towns, declaring that there we should meet the people of fashion. Nor was his eagerness damped when he discovered that such people never came to the ordinary, but were served in their own rooms by their own servants.

"I shall know them yet," he would vow, as we started off of a morning, after having seen no more of my Lord than his liveries below stairs. "Am I not a gentleman in all but birth, Richard? And that is a difficulty many before me have overcome. I have the classics, and the history, and the poets. And the French language, though I have never made the grand tour. I flatter myself that my tone might be worse. By the help of your friends, I shall have a title or two for acquaintances before I leave London; and when my money is gone, there is a shipowner I know of who will give me employment, if I have not obtained preferment."

The desire to meet persons of birth was near to a mania with him. And I had not the courage to dampen his hopes. But, inexperienced as I was, I knew the kind better than he, and understood that it was easier for a camel to enter the eye of a needle, than for John Paul to cross the thresholds of the great houses of London. The way of adventurers is hard, and he could scarce lay claim then to a better name.

"We shall go to Maryland together, Captain Paul," I said, "and waste no time upon London save to see Vauxhall, and the opera, and St. James's and the Queen's House and the Tower, and Parliament, and perchance his Majesty himself," I added, attempting merriment, for the notion of seeing Dolly only to leave her gave me a pang. And the captain knew nothing of Dolly.

"So, Richard, you fear I shall disgrace you," he said reproachfully. "Know, sir, that I have pride enough and to spare. That I can make friends without going to Arlington Street."

I was ready to cry with vexation at this childish speech.

"And a time will come when they shall know me," he went on. "If they insult me now they shall pay dearly for it."

"My dear captain," I cried; "nobody will insult you, and least of all my friends, the Manners." I had my misgivings about little Mr. Marmaduke. "But we are, neither of us, equipped for a London season. I am but an unknown provincial, and you —" I paused for words.

For a sudden realization had come upon me that our positions were now reversed. It seemed strange that I should be interpreting the world to this man of power.

"And I?" he repeated bitterly.

"You have first to become an admiral," I replied, with inspiration; "Drake was once a common seaman."

He did not answer. But that evening as we came into Windsor, I perceived that he had not abandoned his intentions. The long light flashed on the peaceful Thames, and the great, grim castle was gilded all over its western side.

The captain leaned out of the window.

"Postilion," he called, "which inn here is most favoured by gentlemen?"

"The 'Castle,'" said the boy, turning in his saddle to grin at me. "But if I might be so bold as to advise your honour, the 'Swan' is a comfortable house, and well attended."

"Know your place, sirrah," shouted the captain, angrily, "and drive us to the 'Castle.'"

The boy snapped his whip disdainfully, and presently pulled us up at the inn, our chaise covered with the mud of three particular showers we had run through that day. And, as usual, the landlord, thinking he was about to receive quality, came scraping to the chaise door, only to turn with a gesture of disgust when he perceived John Paul's sea-boxes tied on behind, and the costume of that hero, as well as my own.

The captain demanded a room. But mine host had turned his back, when suddenly a thought must have struck him, for he wheeled again.

"Stay," he cried, glancing suspiciously at the sky-blue frock; "if you are Mr. Dyson's courier, I have reserved a suite."

This same John Paul, who was like iron with mob and mutiny, was pitiably helpless before such a prop of the aristocracy. He flew into a rage, and rated the landlord in Scotch and English, and I was fain to put my tongue in my cheek and turn my back that my laughter might not anger him the more.

And so I came face to face with another smile, behind a spying-glass,—a smile so cynical and unpleasant withal that my own was smothered. A tall and thin gentleman, who had come out of the inn without a hat, was surveying the dispute with a keen delight. He was past the middle age. His clothes bore that mark which distinguishes his world from the other, but his features were so striking as to hold my attention unwittingly.

After a while he withdrew his glass, cast one look at me which might have meant anything, and spoke up.

"Pray, my good Goble, why all this fol-de-rol about admitting a gentleman to your house?"

I scarce know which was the more astonished, the landlord, John Paul, or I. Goble bowed at the speaker.

"A gentleman, your honour!" he gasped. "Your honour is joking again. Surely this trumpery Scotchman in Jews' finery is no gentleman, nor the 'longshore lout he has got with him. They may go to the 'Swan.'"

"Jews' finery!" shouted the captain, with his fingers on his sword.

But the stranger held up a hand deprecatingly.

"'Pon my oath, Goble, I gave you credit for more penetration," he drawled; "you may be right about the Scotchman, but your 'longshore lout has had both birth and breeding, or I know nothing."

John Paul, who was in the act of bowing to the speaker, remained petrified with his hand upon his heart, entirely discomfited. The landlord forsook him instantly for me, then stole a glance at his guest to test his seriousness, and looked at my face to see how greatly it were at variance with my clothes. The temptation to lay hands on the cringing little toadeater grew too strong for me, and I picked him up by the scruff of the collar, — he was all skin and bones, — and spun him round like a corpse upon a gibbet, while he cried mercy in a voice to wake the dead. The slim gentleman under the sign laughed until he held his sides, with a heartiness that jarred upon me. It did not seem to fit him.

"By Hercules and Vulcan," he cried, when at last I had set the landlord down, "what an arm and back the lad has! He must have the best in the house, Goble, and sup with me."

Goble pulled himself together.

"And he is your honour's friend," he began, with a scowl.

"Ay, he is my friend, I tell you," retorted the important personage, impatiently.

The innkeeper, sulky, half-satisfied, yet fearing to offend, welcomed us with what grace he could muster, and we were shown to "The Fox and the Grapes," a large room in the rear of the house.

John Paul had not spoken since the slim gentleman had drawn the distinction between us, and I knew that the affront was rankling in his breast. He cast himself into a chair with such an air of dejection as made me pity him from my heart. But I had no consolation to offer. His first words, far from being the torrent of protest I looked for, almost startled me into laughter.

"He can be nothing less than a duke," said the captain. "Ah, Richard, see what it is to be a gentleman!"

"Fiddlesticks! I had rather own your powers than the best title in England," I retorted sharply.

He shook his head sorrowfully, which made me wonder the more that a man of his ability should be unhappy without this one bauble attainment.

"I shall begin to believe the philosophers have the right of it," he remarked presently. "Have you ever read anything of Monsieur Rousseau's, Richard?"

The words were scarce out of his mouth when we heard a loud rap on the door, which I opened to discover a Swiss fellow in a private livery, come to say that his master begged the young gentleman would sup with him. The man stood immovable while he delivered this message, and put an impudent emphasis upon the *gentleman*.

"Say to your master, whoever he may be," I replied, in some heat at the man's sneer, "that I am travelling with Captain Paul. That any invitation to me must include him."

The lackey stood astounded at my answer, as though he had not heard aright. Then he retired with less assurance than he had come, and John Paul sprang to his feet and laid his hands upon my shoulders, as was his wont when affected. He reproached himself for having misjudged me, and added a deal more that I have forgotten.

"And to think," he cried, "that you have forgone supping with a nobleman on my account!"

"Pish, captain, 'tis no great denial. His Lordship — if Lordship he is — is stranded in an inn, overcome with *ennui*, and must be amused. That is all."

Nevertheless I think the good captain was distinctly disappointed, not alone because I gave up what in his opinion was a great advantage, but likewise because I could have regaled him on my return with an account of the meal. For it must be borne in mind, my dears, that those days are not these, nor that country this one. And in judging Captain Paul it must be remembered that rank inspired a vast respect when King George came to the throne. It can never be said of John Paul that he lacked either independence or spirit. But a nobleman was a nobleman then.

So when presently the gentleman himself appeared smiling at our door, which his servant had left open, we both of us rose up in astonishment and bowed very respectfully, and my face burned at the thought of the message I had sent him. For, after all, the captain was but twenty-one and I nineteen, and the distinguished unknown at least fifty. He took a pinch of snuff and brushed his waistcoat before he spoke.

"Egad," said he, with good nature, looking up at me, "Mohammed was a philosopher, and so am I, and come to the mountain. 'Tis worth crossing an inn in these times to see a young man whose strength has not been wasted upon foppery. May I ask your name, sir?"

P

"Richard Carvel," I answered, much put aback.

"Ah, Carvel," he repeated; "I know three or four of that name. Perhaps you are Robert Carvel's son, of Yorkshire. But what the devil do you do in such clothes? I was resolved to have you though I am forced to take a dozen watchet-blue mountebanks in the bargain."

"Sir, I warn you not to insult my friend," I cried, in a temper again.

"There, there, not so loud, I beg you," said he, with a gesture. "Hot as pounded pepper,— but all things are the better for a touch of it. I had no intention of insulting the worthy man, I give my word. I must have my joke, sir. No harm meant." And he nodded at John Paul, who looked as if he would sink through the floor. "Robert Carvel is as testy as the devil with the gout, and you are not unlike him in feature."

"He is no relation of mine," I replied, undecided whether to laugh or be angry. And then I added, for I was very young, "I am an American, and heir to Carvel Hall in Maryland."

"Lord, lord, I might have known," exclaimed he. "Once I had the honour of dining with your Dr. Franklin, from Pennsylvania. He dresses for all the world like you, only worse, and wears a hat I would not be caught under at Bagnigge Wells, were I so imprudent as to go there."

"Dr. Franklin has weightier matters than hats to occupy him, sir," I retorted. For I was determined to hold my own.

He made a French gesture, a shrug of his thin shoulders, which caused me to suspect he was not always so good-natured.

"Dr. Franklin would better have stuck to his newspaper, my young friend," said he. "But I like your appearance too well to quarrel with you, and we'll have no politics before eating. Come, gentlemen, come! Let us see what Goble has left after his shaking."

He struck off with something of a painful gait, which he explained was from the gout. And presently we arrived at his parlour, where supper was set out for us. I had not tasted its equal since I left Maryland. We sat down to a capon stuffed with eggs, and dainty sausages, and hot rolls, such as we had at home; and a wine which had cobwebbed and mellowed under the Castle Inn for better than twenty years. The personage did not drink wine. He sent his servant to quarrel with Goble because he had not been given iced water. While he was tapping on the table I took occasion to observe him. His was a physiognomy to strike the stranger, not by reason of its nobility, but because of its oddity. He had a prodigious length of face, the nose long in proportion, but not prominent. The eyes were dark, very bright, and wide apart, with little eyebrows dabbed over them at a slanting angle. The thin-lipped mouth rather pursed up, which made his smile the contradiction it was. In short, my dears, while I do not lay claim to the reading of character, it required no great astuteness to perceive the scholar, the man of the world, and the ascetic — and all affected. His conversation bore out the summary. It astonished us. It encircled the earth, embraced history and letters since the world began. And added to all this, he had a thousand anecdotes on his tongue's tip. His words he chose with too great a nicety; his sentences were of a foreign formation, twisted around; and his stories were illustrated with French gesticulations. He threw in quotations galore, in Latin, and French, and English, until the captain began casting me odd, uncomfortable looks, as though he wished himself well out of the entertainment. Indeed, poor John Paul's perturbation amused me more than the gentleman's anecdotes. To be ill at ease is discouraging to any one, but it was peculiarly fatal with the captain. This arch-aristocrat dazzled him. When he attempted to follow in the same vein he would get lost. And his really considerable learning counted for nothing. He reached the height of his mortification when the slim gentleman dropped his eyelids and began to yawn. I was wickedly delighted. He could not have been better met. Another such encounter, and I would warrant the captain's illusions concerning the gentry to go up in smoke. Then he might come to some notion of his own true powers. As for me, I enjoyed the supper which our host had insisted upon our partaking, drank his wine, and paid him very little attention.

"May I make so bold as to ask, sir, whether you are a patron of literature?" said the captain, at length.

"A very poor patron, my dear man," was the answer. "Merely a humble worshipper at the shrine. And I might say that I partake of its benefits as much as a gentleman may. And yet," he added, with a laugh and a cough, "those silly newspapers and magazines insist on calling me a literary man."

"And now that you have indulged in a question, and the claret is coming on," said he, "perhaps you will tell me something of yourself, Mr. Carvel, and of your friend, Captain Paul. And how you come to be so far from home." And he settled himself comfortably to listen, as a man who has bought his right to an opera box.

Here was my chance. And I resolved that if I did not further enlighten John Paul, it would be no fault of mine.

"Sir," I replied, in as dry a monotone as I could assume, "I was kidnapped by the connivance of some unscrupulous persons in my colony, who had designs upon my grandfather's fortune. I was taken abroad in a slaver and carried down to the Caribbean seas, when I soon discovered that the captain and his crew were nothing less than pirates. For one day all hands got into a beastly state of drunkenness, and the captain raised the skull and cross-bones, which he had handy in his chest. I was forced to climb the main rigging in order to escape being hacked to pieces."

He sat bolt upright, those little eyebrows of his gone up full half an inch, and he raised his thin hands with an air of incredulity. John Paul was no less astonished at my little ruse.

"Holy Saint Clement!" exclaimed our host; "pirates! This begins to have a flavour indeed. And yet you do not seem to be a lad with an imagination. Egad, Mr. Carvel, I had put you down for one who might say, with Alceste: '*Etre franc et sincère est mon plus grand talent.*' But pray go on, sir. You have but to call for pen and ink to rival Mr. Fielding."

With that I pushed back my chair, got up from the table, and made him a bow. And the captain, at last seeing my drift, did the same.

"I am not used at home to have my word doubted, sir," I said. "Sir, your humble servant. I wish you a very good evening." He rose precipitately, crying out from his gout, and laid a hand upon my arm.

"Pray, Mr. Carvel, pray, sir, be seated," he said, in some agitation. "Remember that the story is unusual, and that I have never clapped eyes on you until to-night. Are all young gentlemen from Maryland so fiery? But I should have known from your face that you are incapable of deceit. Pray be seated, captain."

I was persuaded to go on, not a little delighted that I had scored my point, and broken down his mask of affectation and careless cynicism. I told my story, leaving out the family history involved, and he listened with every mark of attention and interest. Indeed, to my surprise, he began to show some enthusiasm, of which sensation I had not believed him capable.

"What a find! what a find!" he continued to exclaim, when I had finished. "And true. You say it is true, Mr. Carvel?"

"Sir!" I replied, "I thought we had thrashed that out."

"Yes, yes, to be sure. I beg pardon," said he. And then to his servant: "Colomb, is my writing-tablet unpacked?"

I was more mystified than ever as to his identity. Was he going to put the story in a magazine?

After that he seemed plainly anxious to be rid of us. I bade him good night, and he grasped my hand warmly enough. Then he turned to the captain in his most condescending manner. But a great change had come over John Paul. He was ever quick to see and to learn, and I rejoiced to remark that he did not bow over the hand, as he might have done two hours since. He was again Captain Paul, the man, who fought his way on his own merits. He held himself as tho' he was once more pacing the deck of the *John*.

The slim gentleman poured the width of a finger of claret in his glass, soused it with water, and held it up.

"Here's to your future, my good captain," he said, "and to Mr. Carvel's safe arrival home again. When you get to town, Mr. Carvel, don't fail to go to Davenport, who makes clothes for most of us at Almack's, and let him remodel you. I wish to

God he might get hold of your doctor. And put up at the Star and Garter in Pall Mall. I take it that you have friends in London."

I replied that I had. But he did not push the inquiry.

"You should write out this history for your grandchildren, Mr. Carvel," he added, as he bade his Swiss light us to our room. "A strange yarn indeed, captain."

"And therefore," said the captain, coolly, "as a stranger give it welcome.

> "'There are more things in heaven and earth, Horatio,
> Than are dreamt of in your philosophy.'"

Had a meteor struck at the gentleman's feet, he could not have been more taken aback.

"What! What's this?" he cried. "You quote Hamlet! And who the devil are you, sir, that you know my name?"

"Your name, sir!" exclaims the captain, in astonishment.

"Well, well," he said, stepping back and eying us closely, "'tis no matter. Good night, gentlemen, good night."

And we went to bed with many a laugh over the incident.

"His name must be Horatio. We'll discover it in the morning," said John Paul.

CHAPTER XXIII

LONDON TOWN

But he had not risen when we set out, nor would the ill-natured landlord reveal his name. It mattered little to me, since I desired to forget him as quickly as possible. For here was one of my own people of quality, a gentleman who professed to believe what I told him, and yet would do no more for me than recommend me an inn and a tailor; while a poor sea-captain, driven from his employment and his home, with no better reason to put faith in my story, was sharing with me his last penny. Goble, in truth, had made us pay dearly for our fun with him, and the hum of the vast unknown fell upon our ears with the question of lodging still unsettled. The captain was for going to the Star and Garter, the inn the gentleman had mentioned. I was in favour of seeking a more modest and less fashionable hostelry.

"Remember that you must keep up your condition, Richard," said John Paul.

"And if all English gentlemen are like our late friend," I said, "I would rather stay in a city coffee-house. Remember that you have only two guineas left after paying for the chaise, and that Mr. Dix may be out of town."

"And your friends in Arlington Street?" said he.

"May be back in Maryland," said I; and added inwardly, "God forbid!"

"We shall have twice the chance at the Star and Garter. They will want a show of gold at a humbler place, and at the Star we may carry matters with a high hand. Pick out the biggest frigate," he cried, for the tenth time, at least, "or the most beautiful lady, and it will surprise you, my lad, to find out how many times you will win."

I know of no feeling of awe to equal that of a stranger approaching for the first time a huge city. The thought of a human multitude is ever appalling as that of infinity itself,— a human multitude with its infinity of despairs and joys, disgraces and honours, each small unit with all the world in its own brain, and all the world out of it! Each intent upon his own business or pleasure, and striving the while by hook or crook to keep the ground from slipping beneath his feet. For, if he falls, God help him!

Yes, here was London, great and pitiless, and the fear of it was upon our souls as we rode into it that day.

Holland House with its shaded gardens, Kensington Palace with the broad green acres of parks in front of it stitched by the silver Serpentine, and Buckingham House, which lay to the south over the hill,—all were one to us in wonder as they loomed through the glittering mist that softened all. We met with a stream of countless wagons that spoke of a trade beyond knowledge, sprinkled with the equipages of the gentry floating upon it; coach and chaise, cabriolet and chariot, gorgeously bedecked with heraldry and wreaths; their numbers astonished me, for to my mind the best of them were no better than we could boast in Annapolis. One matter, which brings a laugh as I recall it, was the oddity to me of seeing white coachmen and footmen.

We clattered down St. James's Street, of which I had often heard my grandfather speak, and at length we drew up before the Star and Garter in Pall Mall, over against the palace. The servants came hurrying out, headed by a chamberlain clad in magnificent livery, a functionary we had not before encountered. John Paul alighted to face this personage, who, the moment he perceived us, shifted his welcoming look to one of such withering scorn as would have daunted a more timid man than the captain. Without the formality of a *sir* he demanded our business, which started the inn people and our own boy to snickering, and made the passers-by pause and stare. Dandies who were taking the air stopped to ogle us with their spying-glasses and to offer quips, and behind them gathered the flunkies and chairmen awaiting their masters at the clubs and coffee-houses near by. What was my astonishment, therefore, to see a change in the captain's demeanour. Truly for quick learning and the application of it I have never known his equal. His air became the one of careless ease habitual to the little gentleman we had met at Windsor, and he drew from his pocket one of his guineas, which he tossed in the man's palm.

"Here, my man," said he, snapping his fingers; "an apartment at once, or you shall pay for this nonsense, I promise you." And walked in with his chin in the air, so grandly as to dissolve ridicule into speculation.

For an instant the chamberlain wavered, and I trembled, for I dreaded a disgrace in Pall Mall, where the Manners might hear of it. Then fear, or hope of gain, or something else got the better of him, for he led us to a snug, well-furnished suite of a parlour and bedroom on the first floor, and stood bowing in the doorway for his honour's further commands. They were of a sort to bring the sweat to my forehead.

"Have a fellow run to bid Davenport, the tailor, come hither as fast as his legs will carry him. And you may make it known that this young gentleman desires a servant, a good man, mind you, with references, who knows a gentleman's wants. He will be well paid."

That name of Davenport was a charm,—the mention of a servant was its finishing touch. The chamberlain bent almost double, and retired, closing the door softly behind him. And so great had been my surprise over these last acquirements of the captain that until now I had had no breath to expostulate.

"I must have my fling, Richard," he answered, laughing; "I shall not be a gentleman long. I must know how it feels to take your ease, and stroke your velvet, and order lackeys about. And when my money is gone I shall be content to go to sea again, and think about it o' stormy nights."

This feeling was so far beyond my intelligence that I made no comment. And I could not for the life of me chide him, but prayed that all would come right in the end.

In less than an hour Davenport himself arrived, bristling with importance, followed by his man carrying such a variety of silks and satins, flowered and plain, and broadcloths and velvets, to fill the furniture. And close behind the tailor came a tall haberdasher from Bond Street, who had got wind of a customer, with a bewildering lot of ruffles and handkerchiefs and neckerchiefs, and bows of lawn and lace which (so he informed us) gentlemen now wore in the place of solitaires. Then came a hosier and a bootmaker and a hatter; nay, I was forgetting a jeweller from Temple Bar. And so imposing a front did the captain wear as he picked this and recommended the other that he got credit for me for all he chose, and might have had more besides. For himself he ordered merely a modest street suit of purple, the sword to be thrust through the pocket, Davenport promising it with mine for the next afternoon. For so much discredit had been cast upon his taste on the road to London that he was resolved to remain indoors until he could appear with decency. He learned quickly, as I have said.

By the time we had done with these matters, which I wished to perdition, some score of applicants was in waiting for me. And out of them I hired one who had been valet to the young Lord Rereby, and whose recommendation was excellent. His name was Banks, his face open and ingenuous, his stature a little above the ordinary, and his manner respectful. I had Davenport measure him at once for a suit of the Carvel livery, and bade him report on the morrow.

All this while, my dears, I was aching to be off to Arlington Street, but a foolish pride held me back. I had heard so much of the fashion in which the Manners moved that I feared to bring ridicule upon them in poor MacMuir's clothes. But presently the desire to see Dolly took such hold upon me that I set out before dinner, fought my way past the chairmen and chaisemen at the door, and asked my way of the first civil person I encountered. 'Twas only a little rise up the steps of St. James's Street, Arlington Street being but a small pocket of Piccadilly, but it seemed a dull English mile; and my heart thumped when I reached the corner, and the houses danced before my eyes. I steadied myself by a post and looked again. At last, after a thousand leagues of wandering,

I was near her! But how to choose between fifty severe and imposing mansions? I walked on toward that endless race of affairs and fashion, Piccadilly, scanning every door, nay, every window, in the hope that I might behold my lady's face framed therein. Here a chair was set down, there a chariot or a coach pulled up, and a clocked flunky bowing a lady in. But no Dorothy. Finally, when I had near made the round of each side, I summoned courage and asked a butcher's lad, whistling as he passed me, whether he could point out the residence of Mr. Manners.

"Ay," he replied, looking me over out of the corner of his eye, "that I can. But ye'll not get a glimpse o' the beauty this day, for she's but just off to Kensington with a coachful o' quality."

And he led me, all in a tremble over his answer, to a large stone dwelling with arched windows, and pillared portico with lanthorns and link extinguishers, an area and railing beside it. The flavour of generations of aristocracy hung about the place, and the big knocker on the carved door seemed to regard with such a forbidding frown my shabby clothes that I took but the one glance (enough to fix it forever in my memory), and hurried on. Alas, what hope had I of Dorothy now!

"What cheer, Richard?" cried the captain when I returned; "have you seen your friends?"

I told him that I had feared to disgrace them, and so refrained from knocking — a decision which he commended as the very essence of wisdom. Though a desire to meet and talk with quality pushed him hard, he would not go a step to the ordinary, and gave orders to be served in our room, thus fostering the mystery which had enveloped us since our arrival. Dinner at the Star and Garter being at the fashionable hour of half after four, I was forced to give over for that day the task of finding Mr. Dix.

That evening — shall I confess it? — I spent between the Green Park and Arlington Street, hoping for a glimpse of Miss Dolly returning from Kensington.

The next morning I proclaimed my intention of going to Mr. Dix.

"Send for him," said the captain. "Gentlemen never seek their men of affairs."

"No," I cried; "I can contain myself in this place no longer. I must be moving."

"As you will, Richard," he replied, and giving me a queer, puzzled look he settled himself between the *Morning Post* and the *Chronicle*.

As I passed the servants in the lower hall, I could not but remark an altered treatment. My friend the chamberlain, more pompous than ever, stood erect in the door with a stony stare, which melted the moment he perceived a young gentleman who descended behind me. I heard him cry out "A chaise for his Lordship!" at which command two of his assistants ran out together. Suspicion had plainly gripped his soul overnight, and this, added to mortified vanity at having been duped, was sufficient for him to allow me to leave the inn unattended. Nor could I greatly blame him, for you must know, my dears, that at that time London was filled with adventurers of all types.

I felt a deal like an impostor, in truth, as I stepped into the street, disdaining to inquire of any of the people of the Star and Garter where an American agent might be found. The day was gray and cheerless, the colour of my own spirits as I walked toward the east, knowing that the city lay that way. But I soon found plenty to distract me.

To a lad such as I, bred in a quiet tho' prosperous colonial town, a walk through London was a revelation. Here in the Pall Mall the day was not yet begun, tho' for some scarce ended. I had not gone fifty paces from the hotel before I came upon a stout gentleman with twelve hours of claret inside him, brought out of a coffee-house and put with vast difficulty into his chair; and I stopped to watch the men stagger off with their load to St. James's Street. Next I met a squad of red-coated guards going to the palace, and after them a grand coach and six rattled over the Scotch granite, swaying to a degree that threatened to shake off the footmen clinging behind. Within, a man with an eagle nose sat impassive, and I set him down for one of the King's ministers.

Presently I came out into a wide space, which I knew to be Charing Cross by the statue of Charles the First which stood in the centre of it, and the throat of a street which was just in front of me must be the Strand. Here all was life and bustle. On one hand was Golden's Hotel, and a crowded mail-coach was dashing out from the arch beneath it, the horn blowing merrily; on the other hand, so I was told by a friendly man in brown, was Northumberland House, the gloomy grandeur whereof held my eyes for a time. And I made bold to ask in what district were those who had dealings with the colonies. He scanned me with a puzzling look of commiseration.

"Ye're not a-going to sell yereself for seven year, my lad?" said he. "I was near that myself when I was young, and I thank God to this day that I talked first to an honest man, even as you are doing. They'll give ye a pretty tale, — the factors, — of a land of milk and honey, when it's naught but stripes and curses ye'll get."

And he was about to rebuke me hotly, when I told him I had come from Maryland, where I was born.

"Why, ye speak like a gentleman!" he exclaimed. "I was informed that all talk like naygurs over there. And is it not so of your redemptioners?"

I said that depended upon the master they got.

"Then I take it ye are looking for the lawyers, who mostly represent the planters. And ye'll find them at the Temple or Lincoln's Inn."

I replied that he I sought was not an attorney, but a man of business. Whereupon he said that I should find all those in a batch about the North and South American Coffee House, in Threadneedle Street. And he pointed me into the Strand, adding that I had but to follow my nose to St. Paul's, and there inquire.

I would I might give you some notion of the great artery of London in those days, for it has changed much since I went down it that heavy morning in April, 1770, fighting my way. Ay, truly, fighting my way, for the street then was no place for the weak and timid, when bullocks ran through it in droves on the way to market, when it was often jammed from wall to wall with wagons, and carmen and truckmen and coachmen swung their whips and cursed one another to the extent of their lungs. Near St. Clement Danes I was packed in a crowd for ten minutes while two of these fellows formed a ring and fought for the right of way, stopping the traffic as far as I could see. Dustmen, and sweeps, and even beggars, jostled you on the corners, bullies tried to push you against the posts or into the kennels; and once, in Butchers' Row, I was stopped by a flashy, soft-tongued fellow who would have lured me into a tavern near by.

The noises were bedlam ten times over. Shopmen stood at their doors and cried, "Rally up, rally up, buy, buy, buy!" venders shouted saloop and barley, furmity, Shrewsbury cakes and hot peascods, rosemary and lavender, small coal and sealing-wax, and others bawled "Pots to solder!" and "Knives to grind!" Then there was the incessant roar of the heavy wheels over the rough stones, and the rasp and shriek of the brewers' sledges as they moved clumsily along. As for the odours, from that of the roasted coffee and food of the taverns, to the stale fish on the stalls, and worse, I can say nothing. They surpassed imagination.

At length, upon emerging from Butchers' Row, I came upon some stocks standing in the street, and beheld ahead of me a great gateway stretching across the Strand from house to house. Its stone was stained with age, and the stern front of it seemed to mock the unseemly and impetuous haste of the tide rushing through its arches. I stood and gazed, nor needed one to tell me that those two grinning skulls above it, swinging to the wind on the pikes, were rebel heads. Bare and bleached now, and exposed to a cruel view, but once caressed by loving hands, was the last of those whose devotion to the house of Stuart had brought from their homes to Temple Bar.

I halted by the Fleet Market, nor could I resist the desire to go into St. Paul's, to feel like a pebble in a bell under its mighty dome; and it lacked but half an hour of noon when I had come out at the Poultry and finished gaping at the Mansion House. I missed Threadneedle Street and went down Cornhill, in my ignorance mistaking the Royal Exchange, with its long piazza and high tower, for the coffeehouse I sought: in the great hall I begged a gentleman to direct me to Mr. Dix, if he knew such a person. He shrugged his shoulders, which mystified me somewhat, but answered with a ready good-nature that he was likely to be found at that time at Tom's Coffee House, in Birchin Lane near by, whither I went with him. He climbed the stairs ahead of me and directed me, puffing, to the news room, which I found filled with men, some writing, some talking eagerly, and others turning over newspapers. The servant there looked me over with no great favour, but on telling him my business he went off, and returned with a young man of a pink and white complexion, in a green riding-frock, leather breeches, and top boots, who said:—

"Well, my man, I am Mr. Dix."

There was a look about him, added to his tone and manner, set me strong against him. I knew his father had not been of this stamp.

"And I am Mr. Richard Carvel, grandson to Mr. Lionel Carvel, of Carvel Hall, in Maryland," I replied, much in the same way.

He thrust his hands into his breeches and stared very hard.

"You?" he said finally, with something very near a laugh.

"Sir, a gentleman's word usually suffices!" I cried.

He changed his tone a little.

"Your pardon, Mr. Carvel," he said, "but we men of business have need to be careful. Let us sit, and I will examine your letters. Your determination must have been suddenly taken," he added, "for I have nothing from Mr. Carvel on the subject of your coming."

"Letters! You have heard nothing!" I gasped, and there stopped short and clinched the table. "Has not my grandfather written of my disappearance?"

Immediately his expression went back to the one he had met me with. "Pardon me," he said again.

I composed myself as best I could in the face of his incredulity, swallowing with an effort the aversion I felt to giving him my story.

"I think it strange he has not informed you," I said; "I was kidnapped near Annapolis last Christmas-time, and put on board of a slaver, from which I was rescued by great good fortune, and brought to Scotland. And I have but just made my way to London."

"The thing is not likely, Mr. —, Mr. —," he said, drumming impatiently on the board.

Then I lost control of myself.

"As sure as I am heir to Carvel Hall, Mr. Dix," I cried, rising, "you shall pay for your insolence by forfeiting your agency!"

Now the man was a natural coward, with a sneer for some and a smirk for others. He went to the smirk.

"I am but looking to Mr. Carvel's interests the best I know how," he replied; "and if indeed you be Mr. Richard Carvel, then you must applaud my caution, sir, in seeking proofs."

"Proofs I have none," I cried; "the very clothes on my back are borrowed from a Scotch seaman. My God, Mr. Dix, do I look like a rogue?"

"Were I to advance money upon appearances, sir, I should be insolvent in a fortnight. But stay," he cried uneasily, as I flung back my chair, "stay, sir. Is there no one of your province in the town to attest your identity?"

"Ay, that there is," I said bitterly; "you shall hear from Mr. Manners soon, I promise you."

"Pray, Mr. Carvel," he said, overtaking me on the stairs, "you will surely allow the situation to be — extraordinary, you will surely commend my discretion. Permit me, sir, to go with you to Arlington Street." And he sent a lad in haste to the Exchange for a hackney-chaise, which was soon brought around.

I got in, somewhat mollified, and ashamed of my heat: still disliking the man, but acknowledging he had the better right on his side. True to his kind he gave me every mark of politeness now, asked particularly after Mr. Carvel's health, and encouraged me to give him as much of my adventure as I thought proper. But what with the rattle of the carriage and the street noises and my disgust, I did not care to talk, and presently told him as much very curtly. He persisted, however, in pointing out the sights, the Fleet prison, and where the Ludgate stood six years gone; and the Devil's Tavern, of old Ben Jonson's time, and the Mitre and the Cheshire Cheese and the Cock, where Dr. Johnson might be found near the end of the week at his dinner. He showed me the King's Mews above Charing Cross, and the famous theatre in the Haymarket, and we had but turned the corner into Piccadilly when he cried excitedly at a passing chariot:—

"There, Mr. Carvel, there go my Lord North and Mr. Rigby!"

"The devil take them, Mr. Dix!" I exclaimed.

He was silent after that, glancing at me covertly from while to while until we swung into Arlington Street. Before I knew we were stopped in front of the house, but as I set foot on the step I found myself confronted by a footman in the Manners livery, who cried out angrily to our man: "Make way, make way for his Grace of Chartersea!" Turning, I saw a coach behind, the horses dancing at the rear wheels of the chaise. We alighted hastily, and I stood motionless, my heart jumping quick and hard in the hope and fear that Dorothy was within, my eye fixed on the coach door. But when the footman pulled it open and lowered the step, out lolled a very broad man with a bloated face and little, beady eyes without a spark of meaning, and something very like a hump was on the top of his back. He wore a yellow top-coat, and red-heeled shoes of the latest fashion, and I settled at once he was the Duke of Chartersea.

Next came little Mr. Manners, stepping daintily as ever; and then, as the door closed with a bang, I remembered my errand. They had got halfway to the portico.

"Mr. Manners!" I cried.

He faced about, and his Grace also, and both stared in well-bred surprise. As I live, Mr. Manners looked into my face,— into my very eyes, and gave no sign of recognition. And what between astonishment and anger, and a contempt that arose within me, I could not speak.

"Give the man a shilling, Manners," said his Grace; "we can't stay here forever."

Q

"Ay, give the man a shilling," lisped Mr. Manners to the footman. And they passed into the house, and the door was shut.

Then I heard Mr. Dix at my elbow, saying in a soft voice:—

"Now, my fine gentleman, is there any good reason why you should not ride to Bow Street with me?"

"As there is a God in heaven, Mr. Dix," I answered, very low, "if you attempt to lay hands on me, you shall answer for it! And you shall hear from me yet, at the Star and Garter hotel."

I spun on my heel and left him, nor did he follow; and a great lump was in my throat and tears welling in my eyes.

What would John Paul say?

CHAPTER XXIV

CASTLE YARD

But I did not go direct to the Star and Garter. No, I lacked the courage to say to John Paul: "You have trusted me, and this is how I have rewarded your faith." And the thought that Dorothy's father, of all men, had served me thus, after what I had gone through, filled me with a bitterness I had never before conceived. And when my brain became clearer I reflected that Mr. Manners had had ample time to learn of my disappearance from Maryland, and that his action had been one of design, and of cold blood. But I gave to Dorothy or her mother no part in it. Mr. Manners never had had cause to hate me, and the only reason I could assign was connected with his Grace of Chartersea, which I dismissed as absurd.

A few drops of rain warned me to seek shelter. I knew not where I was, nor how long I had been walking the streets at a furious pace. But a huckster told me I was in Chelsea, and kindly directed me back to Pall Mall. The usual bunch of chairmen was around the hotel entrance, but I noticed a couple of men at the door, of sharp features and unkempt dress, and heard a laugh as I went in. My head swam as I stumbled up the stairs and fumbled at the knob, when I heard voices raised inside, and the door was suddenly and violently thrown open. Across the sill stood a big, rough-looking man with his hands on his hips.

"Oho! Here be the other fine bird a-homing, I'll warrant," he cried.

The place was full. I caught sight of Davenport, the tailor, with a wry face, talking against the noise; of Banks, the man I had hired, resplendent in my livery. One of the hotel servants was in the corner perspiring over John Paul's chests, and beside him stood a man disdainfully turning over with his foot the contents, as they were thrown on the floor. I saw him kick the precious vellum-hole waistcoat across the room in wrath and disgust, and heard him shout above the rest: —

"The lot of them would not bring a guinea from any Jew in St. Martin's Lane!"

In the other corner, by the writing-desk, stood the hatter and the haberdasher with their heads together. And in the very centre of the confusion was the captain himself. He was drest in his new clothes Davenport had brought, and surprised me by his changed appearance, and looked as fine a gentleman as any I have ever seen. His face lighted with relief at sight of me.

"Now may I tell these rogues begone, Richard?" he cried. And turning to the man confronting me, he added, "This gentleman will settle their beggarly accounts."

Then I knew we had to do with bailiffs, and my heart failed me.

"Likely," laughed the big man; "I'll stake my oath he has not a groat to pay their beggarly accounts, as your honour is pleased to call them."

They ceased jabbering and straightened to attention, awaiting my reply. But I forgot them all, and thought only of the captain, and of the trouble I had brought him. He began to show some consternation as I went up to him.

"My dear friend," I said, vainly trying to steady my voice, "I beg, I pray that you will not lose faith in me, — that you will not think any deceit of mine has brought you to these straits. Mr. Dix did not know me, and has had no word from my grandfather of my disappearance. And Mr. Manners, whom I thought my friend, spurned me in the street before the Duke of Chartersea."

And no longer master of myself, I sat down at the table and hid my face, shaken by great sobs, to think that this was my return for his kindness.

"What," I heard him cry, "Mr. Manners spurned you, Richard! By all the law in Coke and Littleton, he shall answer for it to me. Your fairweather fowl shall have the chance to run me through!"

I sat up in bewilderment, doubting my senses.

"You believe me, captain," I said, overcome by the man's faith; "you believe me when I tell you that one I have known from childhood refused to recognize me to-day?"

He raised me in his arms as tenderly as a woman might.

"And the whole world denied you, lad, I would not. I believe you—" and he repeated it again and again, unable to get farther.

And if his words brought tears to my eyes, my strength came with them.

"Then I care not," I replied; "only to live to reward you."

"Mr. Manners shall answer for it to me!" cried John Paul again, and made a pace toward the door.

"Not so fast, not so fast, captain, or admiral, or whatever you are," said the bailiff, stepping in his way, for he was used to such scenes; "as God reigns, the owners of all these fierce titles be fireeaters, who would spit you if you spilt snuff upon 'em. Come, come, gentlemen, your swords, and we shall see the sights o' London."

This was the signal for another uproar, the tailor shrieking that John Paul must take off the suit, and Banks the livery; asking the man in the corner by the sea-chests (who proved to be the landlord) who was to pay him for his work and his lost cloth. And the landlord shook his fist at us and shouted back, who was to pay him his four pounds odd, which included two ten-shilling dinners and a flask of his best wine? The other tradesmen seized what was theirs and made off with remarks appropriate to the occasion. And when John Paul and my man were divested of their plumes, we were marched downstairs and out through a jeering line of people to a hackney coach.

"Now, sirs, whereaway?" said the bailiff when we were got in beside one of his men, and burning with the shame of it; "to the prison? Or I has a very pleasant hotel for gentlemen in Castle Yard."

The frightful stories my dear grandfather had told me of

the Fleet came flooding into my head, and I shuddered and turned sick. I glanced at John Paul.

"A guinea will not go far in a sponging-house," said he, and the bailiff's man laughed.

The bailiff gave a direction we did not hear, and we drove off. He proved a bluff fellow with a blunt yet not unkindly humour, and despite his calling seemed to have something that was human in him. He passed many a joke on that pitiful journey in an attempt to break our despondency, urging us not to be downcast, and reminding us that the last gentleman he had taken from Pall Mall was in over a thousand pounds, and that our amount was a bagatelle. And when we had gone through Temple Bar, instead of keeping on down Fleet Street, we jolted into Chancery Lane. This roused me.

"My friend has warned you that he has no money," I said, "and no more have I."

The bailiff regarded me shrewdly.

"Ay," he replied, "I know. But I has seen many stripes o' men in my time, my masters, and I know them to trust, and them whose silver I must feel or send to the Fleet."

I told him unreservedly my case, and that he must take his chance of being paid; that I could not hear from America for three months at least. He listened without much show of attention, shaking his head from side to side.

"If you ever cheated a man, or the admiral here either, then I begin over again," he broke in with decision; "it is the fine sparks from the clubs I has to watch. You'll not worry, sir, about me. Take my oath I'll get interest out of you on my money."

Unwilling as we both were to be beholden to a bailiff, the alternative of the Fleet was too terrible to be thought of. And so we alighted after him with a shiver at the sight of the ugly, grimy face of the house, and the dirty windows all barred with double iron. In answer to a knock we were presently admitted by a turnkey to a vestibule as black as a tomb, and the heavy outer door was locked behind us. Then, as the man cursed and groped for the keyhole of the inner door, despair laid hold of me.

Once inside, in the half light of a narrow hallway, a variety of noises greeted our ears,—laughter from above and below, interspersed with oaths; the click of billiard balls, and the occasional hammering of a pack of cards on a bare table before the shuffle. The air was close almost to suffocation, and out of the coffee room, into which I glanced, came a heavy cloud of tobacco smoke.

"Why, my masters, why so glum?" said the bailiff; "my inn is not such a bad place, and you'll find ample good company here, I promise you."

And he led us into a dingy antechamber littered with papers, on every one of which, I daresay, was written a tragedy. Then he inscribed our names, ages, descriptions, and the like in a great book, when we followed him up three flights to a low room under the eaves, having but one small window, and bare of furniture save two narrow cots for beds, a broken chair, and a cracked mirror. He explained that cash boarders got better, and added that we might be happy we were not in the Fleet.

"We dine at two here, gentlemen, and sup at eight. This is not the Star and Garter," said he as he left us.

It was the captain who spoke first, though he swallowed twice before the words came out.

"Come, Richard, come, laddie," he said, "'tis no so bad it micht-na be waur. We'll mak the maist o' it."

"I care not for myself, Captain Paul," I replied, marvelling the more at him, "but to think that I have landed you here, that this is my return for your sacrifice."

"Hoots! How was ye to foresee Mr. Manners was a blellum?" And he broke into threats which, if Mr. Marmaduke had heard and comprehended, would have driven him into the seventh state of fear. "Have you no other friends in London?" he asked, regaining his English.

I shook my head. Then came a question I dreaded.

"And Mr. Manners's family?"

"I would rather remain here for life," I said, "than apply to them now."

For pride is often selfish, my dears, and I did not reflect that if I remained, the captain would remain likewise.

"Are they all like Mr. Manners?"

"That they are not," I returned with more heat than was necessary; "his wife is goodness itself, and his daughter—" Words failed me, and I reddened.

"Ah, he has a daughter, you say," said the captain, casting a significant look at me and beginning to pace the little room. He was keener than I thought, this John Paul.

If it were not so painful a task, my dears, I would give you here some notion of what a London sponging-house was in the last century. Comyn has heard me tell of it, and I have seen Bess cry over the story. Gaming was the king-vice of that age, and it filled these places to overflowing. Heaven help a man who came into the world with that propensity in the early days of King George the Third. Many, alas, acquired it before they were come to years of discretion. Next me, at the long table where we were all thrown in together,—all who could not pay for private meals,—sat a poor fellow who had flung away a patrimony of three thousand a year. Another had even mortgaged to a Jew his prospects on the death of his mother, and had been seized by the bailiffs outside of St. James's palace, coming to Castle Yard direct from his Majesty's levee. Yet another, with such a look of dead hope in his eyes as haunts me yet, would talk to us by the hour of the Devonshire house where he was born, of the green valley and the peaceful stream, and of the old tower-room, caressed by trees, where Queen Bess had once lain under the carved oak rafters. Here he had taken his young wife, and they used to sit together, so he said, in the sunny oriel over the water, and he had sworn to give up the cards. That was but three years since, and then all had gone across the green cloth in one mad night in St. James's Street. Their friends had deserted them, and the poor little woman was lodged in Holborn near by, and came every morning with some little dainty to the bailiff's, for her liege lord who had so used her. He pressed me to share a fowl with him one day, but it would have choked me. God knows where she got the money to buy it. I saw her once hanging on his neck in the hall, he trying to shield her from the impudent gaze of his fellow-lodgers.

But some of them lived like lords in luxury, with never a seeming regret; and had apartments on the first floor, and had their tea and paper in bed, and lounged out the morning in a flowered nightgown, and the rest of the day in a laced coat. These drank the bailiff's best port and champagne, and had nothing better than a frown or haughty look for us, when we passed them at the landing. Whence the piper was paid I knew not, and the bailiff cared not. But the bulk of the poor gentlemen were a merry crew withal, and had their wit and their wine at table, and knew each other's histories (and soon enough ours) by heart. They betted away the week at billiards or whist or picquet or loo, and sometimes measured swords for diversion, tho' this pastime the bailiff was greatly set against, as calculated to deprive him of a lodger.

Although we had no money for gaming, and little for wine or tobacco, the captain and I were received very heartily into the fraternity. After one afternoon of despondency we both voted it the worst of bad policy to remain aloof and nurse our misfortune, and spent our first evening in making acquaintances over a deal of very thin "debtor's claret." I tossed long that night on the hard cot, listening to the scurrying rats among the roof-timbers. They ran like the thoughts in my brain. And before I slept I prayed again and again that God would put it in my power to reward him whom charity for a friendless foundling had brought to a debtor's prison.

Not so much as a single complaint or reproach had passed his lips!

CHAPTER XXV

THE RESCUE

PERCHANCE, my dears, if John Paul and I had not been cast by accident in a debtor's prison, this great man might never have bestowed upon our country those glorious services which contributed so largely to its liberty. And I might never have comprehended that the American Revolution was brought on and fought by a headstrong king, backed by unscrupulous followers who held wealth above patriotism. It is often difficult to lay finger upon the causes which change the drift of a man's opinions, and so I never wholly knew why John Paul abandoned his deep-rooted purpose to obtain advancement in London by grace of the accomplishments he had laboured so hard to attain. But I believe the beginning was at the meeting at Windsor with the slim and cynical gentleman who had treated him to something between patronage and contempt. Then my experience with Mr. Manners had so embedded itself in his mind that he could never speak of it but with impatience and disgust. And, lastly, the bailiff's hotel contained many born gentlemen who had been left here to rot out the rest of their dreary lives by friends who were still in power and opulence. More than once when I climbed to our garret I found the captain seated on the three-legged chair, with his head between his hands, sunk in reflection.

"You were right, Richard," said he; "your great world is a hard world for those in the shadow of it. I see now that it must not be entered from below, but from the cabin window. A man may climb around it, lad, and when he is above may scourge it."

"And you will scourge it, captain!" I had no doubt of his ability one day to do it.

"Ay, and snap my fingers at it. 'Tis a pretty organization, this society, which kicks the man who falls to the dogs. None of your fine gentlemen for me!"

And he would descend to talk politics with our fellow-guests. We should have been unhappy indeed had it not been for this pastime. It seems to me strange that these debtors took such a keen interest in outside affairs, even tho' it was a time of great agitation. We read with eagerness the cast-off newspapers of the first-floor gentlemen. One poor devil who had waddled[1] in Change Alley had collected under his mattress the letters of Junius, then selling the *Public Advertiser* as few publications had ever sold before. John Paul devoured these attacks upon his Majesty and his ministry in a single afternoon, and ere long he had on the tip of his tongue the name and value of every man in Parliament and out of it. He learned, almost by heart, the history of the astonishing fight made by Mr. Wilkes for the liberties of England, and speedily was as good a Whig and a better than the member from Middlesex himself.

The most of our companions were Tories, for, odd as it may appear, they retained their principles even in Castle Yard. And in those days to be a Tory was to be the friend of the King, and to be the friend of the King was to have some hope of advancement and reward at his hand. They had none. The captain joined forces with the speculator from the Alley, who had hitherto contended against mighty odds, and together they bore down upon the enemy — ay, and routed him, too. For John Paul had an air about him and a natural gift of oratory to command attention, and shortly the dining room after dinner became the scene of such contests as to call up in the minds of the old stagers a field night in the good days of Mr. Pitt and the second George. The bailiff often sat by the door, an interested spectator, and the macaroni lodgers condescended to come downstairs and listen. The captain attained to fame in our little world from his maiden address, in which he very

---

[1] Failed.

shrewdly separated the political character of Mr. Wilkes from his character as a private gentleman, and so refuted a charge of profligacy against the people's champion.

Altho' I never had sufficient confidence in my powers to join in these discussions, I followed them zealously, especially when they touched American questions, as they frequently did. This subject of the wrongs of the colonies was the only one I could ever be got to study at King William's School, and I believe that my intimate knowledge of it gave the captain a surprise. He fell into the habit of seating himself on the edge of my bed after we had retired for the night, and would hold me talking until the small hours upon the injustice of taxing a people without their consent, and upon the multitude of measures of coercion which the King had pressed upon us to punish our resistance. He declaimed so loudly against the tyranny of quartering troops upon a peaceable state that our exhausted neighbours were driven to pounding their walls and ceilings for peace. The news of the Boston massacre had not then reached England.

I was not, therefore, wholly taken by surprise when he said to me one night: —

"I am resolved to try my fortune in America, lad. That is the land for such as I, where a man may stand upon his own merits."

"Indeed, we shall go together, captain," I answered heartily, "if we are ever free of this cursed house. And you shall taste of our hospitality at Carvel Hall, and choose that career which pleases you. Faith, I could point you a dozen examples in Annapolis of men who have made their way without influence. But you shall have influence," I cried, glowing at the notion of rewarding him; "you shall experience Mr. Carvel's gratitude and mine. You shall have the best of our ships, and you will."

He was a man to take fire easily, and embraced me. And, strange to say, neither he nor I saw the humour, nor the pity, of the situation. How many another would long before have become sceptical of my promises! And justly. For I had led him to London, spent all his savings, and then got him into a miserable prison, and yet he had faith remaining, and to spare!

It occurred to me to notify Mr. Dix of my residence in Castle Yard, not from any hope that he would turn his hand to my rescue, but that he might know where to find me if he heard from Maryland. And I penned another letter to Mr. Carvel, but a feeling I took no pains to define compelled me to withhold an account of Mr. Manners's conduct. And I refrained from telling him that I was in a debtor's prison. For I believe the thought of a Carvel in a debtor's prison would have killed him. I said only that we were comfortably lodged in a modest part of London; that the Manners were inaccessible (for I could not bring myself to write that they were out of town). Just then a thought struck me with such force that I got up with a cheer and hit the astonished captain between the shoulders.

"How now!" he cried, ruefully rubbing himself. "If these are thy amenities, Richard, Heaven spare me thy blows."

"Why, I have been a fool, and worse," I shouted. "My grandfather's ship, the *Sprightly Bess*, is overhauling this winter in the Severn. And unless she has sailed, which I think unlikely, I have but to despatch a line to Bristol to summon Captain Bell, the master, to London. I think he will bring the worthy Mr. Dix to terms."

"Whether he will or no," said John Paul, hope lighting his face, "Bell must have command of the twenty pounds to free us, and will take us back to America. For I must own, Richard, that I have no great love for London."

No more had I. I composed this letter to Bell in such haste that my hand shook, and sent it off with a shilling to the bailiff's servant, that it might catch the post. And that afternoon we had a two-shilling bottle of port for dinner, which we shared with a broken-down parson who had been chaplain in ordinary to my Lord Wortley, and who had preached us an Easter sermon the day before. For it was Easter Monday. Our talk was broken into by the bailiff, who informed me that a man awaited me in the passage, and my heart leaped into my throat.

There was Banks. Thinking he had come to reproach me, I asked him rather sharply what he wanted. He shifted his hat from one hand to the other and looked sheepish.

"Your pardon, sir," said he, "but your honour must be very ill-served here."

"Better than I should be, Banks, for I have no money," I said, wondering if he thought me a first-floor lodger.

He made no immediate reply to that, either, but seemed more uneasy still. And I took occasion to note his appearance. He was exceeding neat in a livery of his old master, which he had stripped of the trimmings. Then, before I had guessed at his drift, he thrust his hand inside his coat and drew forth a pile of carefully folded bank notes.

"I be a single man, sir, and has small need of this. And — and I knows your honour will pay me when your letter comes from America."

And he handed me five Bank of England notes of ten pounds apiece. I took them mechanically, without knowing what I did. The generosity of the act benumbed my senses, and for the instant I was inclined to accept the offer upon the impulse of it.

"How do you know you would get your money again, Banks?" I asked curiously.

"No fear, sir," he replied promptly, actually brightening at the prospect. "I knows gentlemen, sir, them that are such, sir. And I will go to America with you, and you say the word, sir."

I was more touched than I cared to show over his offer, which I scarce knew how to refuse. In truth it was a difficult task, for he pressed me again and again, and when he saw me firm, turned away to wipe his eyes upon his sleeve. Then he begged me to let him remain and serve me in the sponging-house, saying that he would pay his own way. The very thought of a servant in the bailiff's garret made me laugh, and so I put him off, first getting his address, and promising him employment on the day of my release.

On Wednesday we looked for a reply from Bristol, if not for the appearance of Bell himself, and when neither came apprehension seized us lest he had already sailed for Maryland. The slender bag of Thursday's letters contained none for me. Nevertheless, we both did our best to keep in humour, forbearing to mention to one another the hope that had gone. Friday seemed the beginning of eternity; the day dragged through I know not how, and toward evening we climbed back to our little room, not daring to speak of what we knew in our hearts to be so, — that the *Sprightly Bess* had sailed. We sat silently looking out over the dreary stretch of roofs and down into a dingy court of Bernard's Inn below, when suddenly there arose a commotion on the stairs, as of a man mounting hastily. The door was almost flung from its hinges, some one caught me by the shoulders, gazed eagerly into my face, and drew back. For a space I thought myself dreaming. I searched my memory, and the name came. Had it been Dorothy, or Mr. Carvel himself, I could not have been more astonished, and my knees weakened under me.

"Jack!" I exclaimed; "Lord Comyn!"

He seized my hand. "Yes; Jack, whose life you saved, and no other," he cried, with a sailor's impetuosity. "My God, Richard! it was true, then; and you have been in this place for three weeks!"

"For three weeks," I repeated.

He looked at me, at John Paul, who was standing by in bewilderment, and then about the grimy, cobwebbed walls of the dark garret, and then turned his back to hide his emotion, and so met the bailiff, who was coming in.

"For how much are these gentlemen in your books?" he demanded hotly.

"A small matter, your Lordship, — a mere trifle," said the man, bowing.

"How much, I say?"

"Twenty-two guineas, five shillings, and eight pence, my Lord, counting debts, and board, — and interest," the bailiff glibly replied; for he had no doubt taken off the account when he spied his Lordship's coach. "And I was very good to Mr. Carvel and the captain, as your Lordship will discover—"

"D—n your goodness!" said my Lord, cutting him short.

And he pulled out a wallet and threw some pieces at the bailiff, bidding him get change with all haste. "And now, Richard," he added, with a glance of disgust about him, "pack up, and we'll out of this cursed hole!"

"I have nothing to pack, my Lord," I said.

"My Lord! *Jack*, I have told you, or I leave you here."

"Well, then, *Jack*, and you will," said I, overflowing with thankfulness to God for the friends He had bestowed upon me. "But before we go a step, Jack, you must know the man but for whose bravery I should long ago have been dead of fever and ill-treatment in the Indies, and whose generosity has brought him hither. My Lord Comyn, this is Captain John Paul."

The captain, who had been quite overwhelmed by this sudden arrival of a real lord to our rescue at the very moment when we had sunk to despair, and no less astonished by the intimacy that seemed to exist between the newcomer and myself, had the presence of mind to bend his head, and that was all. Comyn shook his hand heartily.

"You shall not lack reward for this, captain, I promise you," cried he. "What you have done for Mr. Carvel, you have done for me. Captain, I thank you. You shall have my interest."

I flushed, seeing John Paul draw his lips together. But how was his Lordship to know that he was dealing with no common sea-captain?

"I have sought no reward, my Lord," said he. "What I have done was out of friendship for Mr. Carvel, solely."

Comyn was completely taken by surprise by these words, and by the haughty tone in which they were spoken. He had not looked for a gentleman, and no wonder. He took a quizzical sizing of the sky-blue coat. Such a man in such a station was out of his experience.

"Egad, I believe you, captain," he answered, in a voice which said plainly that he did not. "But he shall be rewarded nevertheless, eh, Richard? I'll see Charles Fox in this matter to-morrow. Come, come," he added impatiently, "the bailiff must have his change by now. Come, Richard!" and he led the way down the winding stairs.

"You must not take offence at his ways," I whispered to the captain. For I well knew that a year before I should have taken the same tone with one not of my class. "His Lordship is all kindness."

"I have learned a bit since I came into England, Richard," was his sober reply.

'Twas a pitiful sight to see gathered on the landings the poor fellows we had come to know in Castle Yard, whose horizons were then as gray as ours was bright. But they each had a cheery word of congratulation for us as we passed, and the unhappy gentleman from Devonshire pressed my hand and begged that I would sometime think of him when I was out under the sky. I promised even more, and am happy to be able to say, my dears, that I saw both him and his wife off for America before I left London. Our eyes were wet when we reached the lower hall, and I was making for the door in an agony to leave the place, when the bailiff came out of his little office.

"One moment, sir," he said, getting in front of me; "there is a little form yet to be gone through. The haste of gentlemen to leave us is not flattering."

He glanced slyly at Comyn, and his Lordship laughed a little. I stepped unsuspectingly into the office.

"Richard!"

I stopped across the threshold as tho' I had been struck. The late sunlight filtering through the dirt of the window fell upon the tall figure of a girl and lighted an upturned face, and I saw tears glistening on the long lashes.

It was Dorothy. Her hands were stretched out in welcome, and then I had them pressed in my own. And I could only look and look again, for I was dumb with joy.

"Thank God you are alive!" she cried; "alive and well, when we feared you dead. Oh, Richard, we have been miserable indeed since we had news of your disappearance."

"This is worth it all, Dolly," I said, only brokenly.

She dropped her eyes, which had searched me through in wonder and pity, — those eyes I had so often likened to the deep blue of the sea, — and her breast rose and fell quickly with I knew not what emotions. How the mind runs, and the heart runs, at such a time! Here was the same Dorothy I had known in Maryland, and yet not the same. For she was a woman now, who had seen the great world, who had refused both titles and estates,— and perchance accepted them. She drew her hands from mine.

"And how came you in such a place?" she asked, turning with a shudder. "Did you not know you had friends in London, sir?"

Not for so much again would I have told her of Mr. Manners's conduct. So I stood confused, casting about for a reply with truth in it, when Comyn broke in upon us.

"I'll warrant you did not look for her here, Richard. Faith, but you are a lucky dog," said my Lord, shaking his head in mock dolefulness; "for there is no man in London, in the world, for whom she would descend a flight of steps, save you. And now she has driven the length of the town when she heard you were in a sponging-house, nor all the dowagers in Mayfair could stop her."

"Fie, Comyn," said my lady, blushing and gathering up her skirts; "that tongue of yours had hung you long since had it not been for your peer's privilege. Richard and I were brought up as brother and sister, and you know you were full as keen for his rescue as I."

His Lordship pinched me playfully.

"I vow I would pass a year in the Fleet to have her do as much for me," said he.

"But where is the gallant seaman who saved you, Richard?" asked Dolly, stamping her foot.

"What," I exclaimed; "you know the story?"

"Never mind," said she; "bring him here."

My conscience smote me, for I had not so much as thought of John Paul since I came into that room. I found him waiting in the passage, and took him by the hand.

"A lady wishes to know you, captain," I said.

"A lady!" he cried. "Here? Impossible!" And he looked at his clothes.

"Who cares more for your heart than your appearance," I answered gayly, and led him into the office.

At sight of Dorothy he stopped abruptly, confounded, as a man who sees a diamond in a dust-heap. And a glow came over me as I said: —

"Miss Manners, here is Captain Paul, to whose courage and unselfishness I owe everything."

"Captain," said Dorothy, graciously extending her hand, "Richard has many friends. You have put us all in your debt, and none deeper than his old playmate."

The captain fairly devoured her with his eyes as she made him a curtsey. But he was never lacking in gallantry, and was as brave on such occasions as when all the dangers of the deep threatened him. With an elaborate movement he took Miss Manners's fingers and kissed them, and then swept the floor with a bow.

"To have such a divinity in my debt, madam, is too much happiness for one man," he said. "I have done nothing to merit it. A lifetime were all too short to pay for such a favour."

I had almost forgotten Miss Dolly the wayward, the mischievous. But she was before me now, her eyes sparkling, and biting her lips to keep down her laughter. Comyn turned to fleck the window with his handkerchief, while I was not a little put out at their mirth. But if John Paul observed it, he gave no sign.

"Captain, I vow your manners are worthy of a Frenchman," said my Lord; "and yet I am given to understand you are a Scotchman."

A shadow crossed the captain's face.

"I was, sir," he said.

"You were!" exclaimed Comyn, astonished; "and pray, what are you now, sir?"

"Henceforth, my Lord," John Paul replied with vast ceremony, "I am an American, the compatriot of the beautiful Miss Manners!"

"One thing I'll warrant, captain," said his Lordship, "that you are a wit."

CHAPTER XXVI

THE PART HORATIO PLAYED

THE bailiff's business was quickly settled. I heard the heavy doors close at our backs, and drew a deep draught of the air God has made for all His creatures alike. Both the captain and I turned to the windows to wave a farewell to the sad ones we were leaving behind, who gathered about the bars for a last view of us, for strange as it may seem, the mere sight of happiness is often a pleasure for those who are sad. A coach in private arms and livery was in waiting, surrounded by a crowd. They made a lane for us to pass, and stared at the young lady of queenly beauty coming out of the sponging-house until the coachman snapped his whip in their faces and the footman jostled them back. When we were got in, Dolly and I on the back seat, Comyn told the man to go to Mr. Manners's.

"Oh, no!" I cried, scarce knowing what I said; "no, not there!" For the thought of entering the house in Arlington Street was unbearable.

Both Comyn and Dorothy gazed at me in astonishment.

"And pray, Richard, why not?" she asked. "Have not your old friends the right to receive you?"

It was my Lord who saved me, for I was in agony what to say.

"He is still proud, and won't go to Arlington Street dressed like a bargeman. He must needs plume, Miss Manners."

I glanced anxiously at Dorothy, and saw that she was neither satisfied nor appeased. Well I remembered every turn of her head, and every curve of her lip! In the meantime we were off through Cursitor Street at a gallop, nearly causing the death of a ragged urchin at the corner of Chancery Lane. I had forgotten my eagerness to know whence they had heard of my plight, when some words from Comyn aroused me.

"The carriage is Mr. Horace Walpole's, Richard. He has taken a great fancy to you."

"But I have never so much as clapped eyes upon him!" I exclaimed in perplexity.

"How about his honour with whom you supped at Windsor? how about the landlord you spun by the neck? You should have heard the company laugh when Horry told us that! And Miss Dolly cried out that she was sure it must be Richard, and none other. Is it not so, Miss Manners?"

"Really, my Lord, I can't remember," replied Dolly, looking out of the coach window. "Who put those frightful skulls upon Temple Bar?"

Then the mystery of their coming was clear to me, and the superior gentleman at the Castle Inn had been the fashionable dabbler in arts and letters and architecture of Strawberry Hill, of whom I remembered having heard Dr. Courtenay speak, Horace Walpole. But I was then far too concerned about Dorothy to listen to more. Her face was still turned away from me, and she was silent. I could have cut out my tongue for my blunder. Presently, when we were nearly out of the Strand, she turned upon me abruptly.

"We have not yet heard, Richard," she said, "how you got into such a predicament."

"Indeed, I don't know myself, Dolly. Some scoundrel bribed the captain of the slaver. For I take it Mr. Walpole has told you I was carried off on a slaver, if he recalled that much of the story."

"I don't mean that," answered Dolly, impatiently. "There is something strange about all this. How is it that you were in prison?"

"Mr. Dix, my grandfather's agent, took me for an impostor and would advance me no money," I answered, hard pushed.

But Dorothy had a woman's instinct, which is often the best of understanding. And I was beginning to think that a suspicion was at the bottom of her questions. She gave her head an impatient fling, and, as I feared, appealed to John Paul.

"Perhaps you can tell me, captain, why he did not come to his friends in his trouble."

And despite my signals to him he replied: —

"In truth, my dear lady, he haunted the place for a sight of you, from the moment he set foot in London."

Comyn laughed, and I felt the blood rise to my face, and kicked John Paul viciously. Dolly retained her self-possession.

"Pho!" says she; "for a sight of me! You seamen are all alike. For a sight of me! And had you not strength enough to lift a knocker, sir, — you who can raise a man from the ground with one hand?"

"'Twas before his tailor had prepared him, madam, and he feared to disgrace you," the captain gravely continued, and I perceived how futile it were to attempt to stop him. "And afterward —"

"And afterward?" repeated Dorothy, leaning forward.

"And afterward he went to Arlington Street with Mr. Dix to seek Mr. Manners, that he might be identified before that gentleman. And there he encountered Mr. Manners and his Grace of Something."

"Chartersea," put in Comyn, who had been listening eagerly.

"Getting out of a coach," said the captain.

"When was this?" demanded Dorothy of me, interrupting him. Her voice was steady, but the colour had left her face.

"About three weeks ago."

"Please be exact, Richard."

"Well, if you must," said I, "the day was Tuesday, and the time about half an hour after two."

She said nothing for a while, trying to put down an agitation which was beginning to show itself in spite of her effort. As for me, I was almost wishing myself back in the sponging-house.

"Are you sure my father saw you?" she asked presently.

"As clearly as you do now, Dolly," I said.

"But your clothes? He might have gone by you in such."

"I pray that he did, Dorothy," I replied. But I was wholly convinced that Mr. Manners had recognized me.

"And — and what did he say?" she asked.

For she had the rare courage that never shrinks from the truth. I think I have never admired and pitied her as at that moment.

"He said to the footman," I answered, resolved to go through with it now, "'Give the man a shilling.' That was his Grace's suggestion."

My Lord uttered something very near an oath. And she spoke not a word more until I handed her out in Arlington Street. The rest of us were silent, too, Comyn now and again giving me eloquent glances expressive of what he would say if she were not present; the captain watching her with a furtive praise, and he vowed to me afterward she was never so beautiful as when angry, that he loved her as an avenging Diana. But I was uneasy, and when I stood alone with her before the house I begged her not to speak to her father of the episode.

"Nay, he must be cleared of such an imputation, Richard," she answered proudly. "He may have made mistakes, but I feel sure he would never turn you away when you came to him in trouble — you, the grandson of his old friend, Lionel Carvel."

"Why bother over matters that are past and gone? I would have borne an hundred such trials to have you come to me as you came to-day, Dorothy. And I shall surely see you again," I said, trying to speak lightly; "and your mother, to whom you will present my respects, before I sail for America."

She looked up at me, startled.

"Before you sail for America!" she exclaimed, in a tone that made me thrill at once with joy and sadness. "And are you not, then, to see London now you are here?"

"Are *you* never coming back, Dolly?" I whispered; for I feared Mr. Marmaduke might appear at any moment; "or do you wish to remain in England always?"

For an instant I felt her pressure on my hand, and then she had fled into the house, leaving me standing by the steps looking after her. Comyn's voice aroused me.

"To the Star and Garter!" I heard him command, and on the way to Pall Mall he ceased not to rate Mr. Manners with more vigour than propriety. "I never liked the little cur, d—n him! No one likes him, Richard," he declared. "All the town knows how Chartersea threw a bottle at him, and were it not for his daughter he had long since been put out of White's. Were it not for Miss Dolly I would call him out for this cowardly trick, and then publish him."

"Nay, my Lord, I had held that as my privilege," interrupted the captain, "were it not, as you say, for Miss Manners."

His Lordship shot a glance at John Paul somewhat divided between surprise, resentment, and amusement.

"Now you have seen the daughter, captain, you perceive it is impossible," I hastened to interpose.

"How in the name of lineage did she come to have such a father?" Comyn went on. "I thank Heaven he's not mine. He's not fit to be her lackey. I would sooner twenty times have a profligate like my Lord Sandwich for a parent than a milk and water sop like Manners, who will risk nothing over a crown piece at play or a guinea at Newmarket. By G—, Richard," said his Lordship, bringing his fist against the glass with near force enough to break the pane, "I have a notion why he did not choose to see you that day. Why, he has no more blood than a louse!"

I had come to the guess as soon as he, but I dared not give it voice, nor anything but ridicule. And so we came to the hotel, the red of departing day fading in the sky above the ragged house-line in St. James's Street.

It was a very different reception we got than when we had first come there. You, my dears, who live in this Republic can have no notion of the stir and bustle caused by the arrival of Horace Walpole's carriage at a fashionable hotel, at a time when every innkeeper was versed in the arms of every family of note in the three kingdoms. Our friend the chamberlain was now humility itself, and fairly ran in his eagerness to anticipate Comyn's demands. It was "Yes, my Lord," and "To be sure, your Lordship," every other second, and he seized the first occasion to make me an elaborate apology for his former cold conduct, assuring me that had our honours been pleased to divulge the fact that we had friends in London, such friends as my Lord Comyn and Mr. Walpole, whose great father he had once had the distinction to serve as linkman, all would have been well. And he was desiring me particularly to comprehend that he had been acting under most disagreeable orders when he sent for the bailiff, before I cut him short.

We were soon comfortably installed in our old rooms; Comyn had sent post-haste for Davenport, who chanced to be his own tailor, and for the whole army of auxiliaries indispensable to a gentleman's make-up; and Mr. Dix was notified that his Lordship would receive him at eleven on the following morning, in my rooms. I remembered the faithful Banks with a twinge of gratitude, and sent for him. And John Paul and I, having been duly installed in the clothes made for us, all three of us sat down merrily to such a supper as only the cook of the Star and Garter, who had been *chef* to the Comte de Maurepas, could prepare. Then I begged Comyn to relate the story of our rescue, which I burned to hear.

"Why, Richard," said he, filling his glass, "had you run afoul any other man in London, save perchance Selwyn, you'd have been drinking the bailiff's triple-diluted for a month to come. I never knew such a brace of fools as he and Horry for getting hold of strange yarns and making them stranger; the wonder was that Horry told this as straight as he did. He has written it to all his friends on the Continent, and had he not been in dock with the gout ever since he reached town, he would have told it at the opera, and at a dozen routs and suppers. Beg pardon, captain," said he, turning to John Paul, "but I think 'twas your peacock coat that saved you both, for it caught Horry's eye through the window, as you got out of the chaise, and down he came as fast as he could hobble.

"Horry had a little dinner to-day in Arlington Street, where he lives, and Miss Dorothy was there. I have told you, Richard, there has been no sensation in town equal to that of your Maryland beauty, since Lady Sarah Lennox. You may have some notion of the old beau Horry can be when he tries, and he is over-fond of Miss Dolly — she puts him in mind of some canvas or other of Sir Peter's. He vowed he had been saving this *pièce de résistance*, as he was pleased to call it, expressly for her, since it had to do somewhat with Maryland. 'What d'ye think I met at Windsor, Miss Manners?' he cries, before we had begun the second course.

"'Perhaps a repulse from his Majesty,' says Dolly, promptly.

"'Nay,' says Mr. Walpole, making a face, for he hates a laugh at his cost; 'nothing less than a young American giant, with the attire of Dr. Benjamin Franklin and the manner of the Fauxbourg Saint Germain. But he had a whiff of deer leather about him, and shoulders and back and legs to make his fortune at Hockley in the Hole, had he lived two generations since. And he had with him a strange, Scotch sea-captain, who had rescued him from pirates, bless you, no less. That is, he said he was a sea-captain; but he talked French like a Parisian, and quoted Shakespeare like Mr. Burke or Dr. Johnson. He may have been M. Caron de Beaumarchais, for I never saw him, or a soothsayer, or Cagliostro the magician, for he guessed my name.'

"'Guessed your name!' we cried, for the story was out of the ordinary.

"'Just that,' answered he, and repeated some damned verse I never heard, with *Horatio* in it, and made them all laugh."

John Paul and I looked at each other in astonishment, and we, too, laughed heartily. It was indeed an odd coincidence.

His Lordship continued: —

"'Well, be that as it may,' said Horry, 'he was an able man of sagacity, this sea-captain, and, like many another, had a penchant for being a gentleman. But he was more of an oddity than Hertford's beast of Gevaudan, and was dressed like Salvinio, the monkey my Lord Holland brought back from his last Italian tour.'"

I have laughed over this description since, my dears, and so has John Paul. But at that time I saw nothing funny in it, and winced with him when Comyn repeated it with such brutal unconsciousness. However, young Englishmen of birth and wealth of that day were not apt to consider the feelings of those they deemed below them.

"Come to your story, Comyn," I cut in testily.

But his Lordship missed entirely the cause of my displeasure.

"Listen to him!" he exclaimed good-naturedly. "He will hear of nothing but Miss Dolly. Well, Richard, my lad, you should have seen her as Horry went on to tell that you had been taken from Maryland, with her head forward and her lips parted, and a light in those eyes of hers to make a man fall down and worship. For Mr. Lloyd, or some one in your Colony, had written of your disappearance, and I vow Miss Dorothy has not been the same since. Nor have I been the only one to remark it," said he, waving off my natural protest at such extravagance. "We have talked of you more than once, she and I, and mourned you for dead. But I am off my course again, as we sailors say, captain. Horry was describing how Richard lifted little Goble by one hand and spun all the dignity out of him, when Miss Manners broke in, being able to contain herself no longer.

"'An American, Mr. Walpole, and from Maryland?' she demanded. And the way she said it made them all look at her.

"'*Assurément, mademoiselle*,' replied Horry, in his cursed French; 'and perhaps you know him. He would gladden the heart of Frederick of Prussia, for he stands six and three if an inch. I took such a fancy to the lad that I invited him to sup with me, and he gave me back a message fit for Mr. Wilkes to send to his Majesty, as haughty as you choose, that if I desired him I must have his friend in the bargain. You Americans are the very devil for independence, Miss Manners! 'Ods fish, I liked his spirit so much I had his friend, Captain something or other —' and there he stopped, caught by Miss Manners's appearance, for she was very white.

"'The name is *Richard Carvel!*' she cried.

"'I'll lay a thousand it was!' I shouted, rising in my chair. And the company stared, and Lady Pembroke vowed I had gone mad.

"'Bless me, bless me, here's a romance for certain!' cried Horry; 'it throws my "Castle of Otranto" in the shade' (that's some damned book he has written," Comyn interjected). "You may not believe me, Richard, when I say that Miss Dolly ate but little after that, and her colour came and went like the red of a stormy sunset at sea. 'Here's this dog Richard come to spill all our chances,' I swore to myself. The company had been prodigiously entertained by the tale, and clamoured for more, and when Horry had done I told how you had fought me at Annapolis, and had saved my life. But Miss Manners sat very still, biting her lip, and I knew she was sadly vexed that you had not gone to her in Arlington Street. For a woman will reason thus," said his Lordship, winking wisely. "But I more than suspected something to have happened, so I asked Horry to send his fellow Favre over to the Star and Garter to see if you were there, tho' I was of three minds to let you go to the devil. You should have seen her face when he came back to say that you had been for three weeks in a Castle Yard sponging-house! Then Horry said he would lend me his coach, and when it was brought around Miss Manners took our breaths by walking downstairs and into it, nor would she listen to a word of the objections cried by my Lady Pembroke and the rest. You must know there is no stopping the beauty when she has made her mind. And while they were all chattering on the steps I jumped in, and off we drove, and you will be the most talked-of man in London to-morrow. I give you Miss Manners!" cried his Lordship, as he ended.

We all stood to the toast, I with my blood a-tingle and my brain awhirl, so that I scarce knew what I did.

CHAPTER XXVII

IN WHICH I AM SORE TEMPTED

"Who the devil is this John Paul, and what is to become of him?" asked Comyn, as I escorted him downstairs to a chair. "You must give him two hundred pounds, or a thousand, if you like, and let him get out. He can't be coming to the clubs with you."

And he pulled me into the coffee room after him.

"You don't understand the man, Comyn," said I; "he isn't that kind, I tell you. What he has done for me is out of friendship, as he says, and he wouldn't touch a farthing save what I owe him."

"Cursed if he isn't a rum sea-captain," he answered, shrugging his shoulders; "cursed if I ever ran foul of one yet who would refuse a couple of hundred and call quits. What's he to do? Is he to live like a Lord of the Treasury upon a master's savings?"

"Jack," said I, soberly, resolved not to be angry, "I would willingly be cast back in Castle Yard to-night rather than desert him, who might have deserted me twenty times to his advantage. Mr. Carvel has not wealth enough, nor I gratitude enough, to reward him. But if our family can make his fortune, it shall be made. And I am determined to go with him to America by the first packet I can secure."

He clutched my arm with an earnestness to startle me.

"You must not leave England now," he said.

"And why?"

"Because she will marry Chartersea if you do. And take my oath upon it, you alone can save her from that."

"Nonsense!" I exclaimed, but my breath caught sharply.

"Listen, Richard. Mr. Manners's manœuvres are the talk of the town, and the beast of a duke is forever wining and dining in Arlington Street. At first people ridiculed, now they are giving credit. It is said," he whispered fearfully, "it is said that his Grace has got Mr. Manners in his power, — some question of honour, you understand, which will ruin him, — and that even now the duke is in a position to force the marriage."

He leaned forward and searched me with his keen gray eyes, as tho' watching the effect of the intelligence upon me. I was, indeed, stunned.

"Now, had she refused me fifty times instead of only twice," my Lord continued, "I could not wish her such a fate as that vicious scoundrel. And since she will not have me, I would rather it were you than any man alive. For she loves you, Richard, as surely as the world is turning."

"Oh, no!" I replied passionately; "you are deceived by the old liking she has always had for me since we were children together." I was deeply touched by his friendship. "But tell me how that could affect this marriage with Chartersea. I believe her pride capable of any sacrifice for the family honour."

He made a gesture of impatience that knocked over a candlestick.

"There, curse you, there you are again!" he said, "showing how little you know of women and of their pride. If she were sure that you loved her, she would never marry Chartersea or any one else. She has had near the whole of London at her feet, and toyed with it. Now she has been amusing herself with Charles Fox, but I vow she cares for none of them. Titles, fame, estates, will not move her."

"If she were sure that I loved her!" I repeated, dazed by what he was saying. "How you are talking, Comyn!"

"Just that. Ah, how I know her, Richard! She can be reckless beyond notion. And if it were proved to her that you were in love with Miss Swain, the barrister's daughter, over whom we were said to have fought, she would as soon marry Chartersea, or March, or the devil, to show you how little she cared."

"With Patty Swain!" I exclaimed.

"But if she knew you did not care a rope's end for Patty, Mr. Marmaduke and his reputation might go into exile together," he continued, without heeding. "So much for a woman's pride, I say. The day the news of your disappearance arrived, Richard, she was starting out with a party to visit Lord Carlisle's seat, Castle Howard. Not a step would she stir, though Mr. Marmaduke whined and coaxed and threatened. And I swear to you she has never been the same since, though few but I know why. I might tell you more, my lad, were it not a breach of confidence."

"Then don't," I said; for I would not let my feelings run.

"Egad, then, I will!" he cried impetuously, "for the end justifies it. You must know that after the letter came from Mr. Lloyd, we thought you dead. I could never get her to speak of you until a fortnight ago. We both had gone with a party to see Wanstead and dine at the Spread Eagle upon the Forest, and I stole her away from the company and led her out under the trees. My God, Richard, how beautiful she was in the wood with the red in her cheeks and the wind blowing her black hair! For the second time I begged her to be Lady Comyn. Fool that I was, I thought she wavered, and my heart beat as it never will again. Then, as she turned away, from her hand slipped a little gold-bound purse, and as I picked it up a clipping from a newspaper fluttered out. 'Pon my soul, it was that very scandalous squib of the *Maryland Gazette* about our duel! I handed it back with a bow. I dared not look up at her face, but stood with my eyes on the ground, waiting.

"'Lord Comyn,' says she, presently, with a quiver in her voice, 'before I give you a reply you must first answer, on your word as a gentleman, what I ask you.'

"I bowed again.

"'Is it true that Richard Carvel was in love with Miss Swain?' she asked."

"And you said, Comyn," I broke in, unable longer to contain myself, "you said —"

"I said: 'Dorothy, if I were to die to-morrow, I would swear Richard Carvel loved you, and you only.'"

His Lordship had spoken with that lightness which hides only the deepest emotion.

"And she refused you?" I cried. "Oh, surely not for that!"

"And she did well," said my Lord.

I bowed my head on my arms, for I had gone through a great deal that day, and this final example of Comyn's generosity overwhelmed me. Then I felt his hand laid kindly on my shoulder, and I rose up and seized it. His eyes were dim, as were mine.

"And now, will you go to Maryland and be a fool?" asked his Lordship.

I hesitated, sadly torn between duty and inclination. John Paul could, indeed, go to America without me. Next the thought came over me in a flash that my grandfather might be ill, or even dead, and there would be no one to receive the captain. I knew he would never consent to spend the season at the Star and Garter at my expense. And then the image of the man rose before me, of him who had given me all he owned, and gone with me so cheerfully to prison, though he knew me not from the veriest adventurer and impostor. I was undecided no longer.

"I must go, Jack," I said sadly; "as God judges, I must."

He looked at me queerly, as if I were beyond his comprehension, picked up his hat, called out that he would see me in the morning, and was gone.

I went slowly upstairs, threw off my clothes mechanically, and tumbled into bed. The captain had long been asleep. By the exertion of all the will power I could command, I was able gradually to think more and more soberly, and the more I thought, the more absurd, impossible, it seemed that I, a rough provincial not yet of age, should possess the heart of a beauty who had but to choose from the best of all England. An hundred times I went over the scene of poor Comyn's proposal, nay, saw it vividly, as though the whole of it had been acted before me: and as I became calmer, the plainer I per-

IN WHICH I AM SORE TEMPTED

ceived that Dorothy, thinking me dead, was willing to let Comyn believe that she had loved me, and had so eased the soreness of her refusal. Perhaps, in truth, a sentiment had sprung up in her breast when she heard of my disappearance, which she mistook for love. But surely the impulse that sent her to Castle Yard was not the same as that Comyn had depicted: it was merely the survival of the fancy of a little girl in a grass-stained frock, who had romped on the lawn at Carvel Hall. I sighed as I remembered the sun and the flowers and the blue Chesapeake, and recalled the very toss of her head when she had said she would marry nothing less than a duke.

Alas, Dolly, perchance it was to be nothing more than a duke! The bloated face and beady eyes and the broad crooked back I had seen that day in Arlington Street rose before me, — I should know his Grace of Chartersea again were I to meet him in purgatory. Was it, indeed, possible that I could prevent her marriage with this man? I fell asleep, repeating the query, as the dawn was sifting through the blinds.

I awakened late. Banks was already there to dress me, to congratulate me as discreetly as a well-trained servant should; nor did he remind me of the fact that he had offered to lend me money, for which omission I liked him the better. In the parlour I found the captain sipping his chocolate and reading his morning *Chronicle*, as though all his life he had done nothing else.

"Good morning, captain." And fetching him a lick on the back that nearly upset his bowl, I cried as heartily as I could: "Egad, if our luck holds, we'll be sailing before the week is out."

But he looked troubled. He hemmed and hawed, and finally broke out into Scotch: —

"Indeed, laddie, ye'll no be leaving Miss Dorothy for me."

"What nonsense has Comyn put into your head?" I demanded, with a stitch in my side; "I am no more to Miss Manners than — "

"Than John Paul! Faith, ye'll not make me believe that. Ah, Richard," said he, "ye're a sly dog. You and I have been as thick these twa months as men can well live, and never a word out of you of the most sublime creature that walks. I have seen women in many countries, lad, beauties to set thoughts afire and swords a-play,—and 'tis not her beauty alone. She hath a spirit for a queen to covet, and air and carriage, too."

This eloquent harangue left me purple.

"I grant it all, captain. She has but to choose her title and estate."

"Ay, and I have a notion which she'll be choosing."

"The knowledge is worth a thousand pounds at the least," I replied. "I will lend you the sum, and warrant no lack of takers."

"Now the devil fly off with such temperament! And I had half the encouragement she has given you, I would cast anchor on the spot, and they might hang and quarter me to move me. But I know you well," he exclaimed, his manner changing, "you are making this great sacrifice on my account. And I will not be a drag on your pleasures, Richard, or stand in the way of your prospects."

"Captain Paul," I said, sitting down beside him, "have I deserved this from you? Have I shown a desire to desert you now that my fortunes have changed? I have said that you shall taste of our cheer at Carvel Hall, and have looked forward this long while to the time when I shall take you to my grandfather and say: 'Mr. Carvel, this is he whose courage and charity have restored you to me, and me to you.' And he will have changed mightily if you do not have the best in Maryland. Should you wish to continue on the sea, you shall have the *Belle of the Wye*, launched last year. 'Tis time Captain Elliott took to his pension."

The captain sighed, and a gleam I did not understand came into his dark eyes.

"I would that God had given me your character and your heart, Richard," he said, "in place of this striving thing I have within me. But 'tis written that a leopard cannot change his spots."

"The passage shall be booked this day," I said.

That morning was an eventful one. Comyn arrived first,

IN WHICH I AM SORE TEMPTED

dressed in a suit of mauve French cloth that set off his fine figure to great advantage. He regarded me keenly as he entered, as if to discover whether I had changed my mind over night. And I saw he was not in the best of tempers.

"And when do you sail?" he cried. "I have no doubt you have sent out already to get passage."

"I have been trying to persuade Mr. Carvel to remain in London, my Lord," said the captain. "I tell him he is leaving his best interests behind him."

"I fear that for once you have undertaken a task beyond your ability, Captain Paul," was the rather tart reply.

"The captain has a ridiculous idea that he is the cause of my going," I said quickly.

John Paul rose somewhat abruptly, seized his hat and bowed to his Lordship, and in the face of a rain sallied out, remarking that he had as yet seen nothing of the city.

"Jack, you must do me the favour not to talk of this in John Paul's presence," I said, when the door had closed.

"If he doesn't suspect why you are going, he has more stupidity than I gave him credit for," Comyn answered gruffly.

"I fear he does suspect," I said.

His Lordship went to the table and began to write, leaving me to the *Chronicle*, the pages of which I did not see. Then came Mr. Dix, and such a change I had never beheld in mortal man. In place of the would-be squire I had encountered in Threadneedle Street, here was an unctuous person of business in sober gray; but he still wore the hypocritical smirk with no joy in it. His bow was now all respectful obedience. Comyn acknowledged it with a curt nod.

Mr. Dix began smoothly, where a man of more honesty would have found the going difficult.

"Mr. Carvel," he said, rubbing his hands, "I wish first to express my profound regrets for what has happened."

"Curse your regrets," said Comyn, bluntly. "You come here on business. Mr. Carvel does not stand in need of regrets at present."

"I was but on the safe side of Mr. Carvel's money, my Lord."

"Ay, I'll warrant you are always on the safe side of money," replied Comyn, with a laugh. "What I wish to know, Mr. Dix," he continued, "is whether you are willing to take my word that this is Mr. Richard Carvel, the grandson and heir of Lionel Carvel, Esquire, of Carvel Hall in Maryland?"

"I am your Lordship's most obedient servant," said Mr. Dix.

"Confound you, sir! Can you or can you not answer a simple question?"

Mr. Dix straightened. He may have spoken elsewhere of asserting his dignity.

"I would not presume to doubt your Lordship's word."

"Then, if I were to be personally responsible for such sums as Mr. Carvel may need, I suppose you would be willing to advance them to him."

"Willingly, willingly, my Lord," said Mr. Dix, and added immediately: "Your Lordship will not object to putting that in writing? Merely a matter of form, as your Lordship knows, but we men of affairs are held to a strict accountability."

Comyn made a movement of disgust, took up a pen and wrote out the indorsement.

"There," he said. "You men of affairs will at least never die of starvation."

Mr. Dix took the paper with a low bow, began to shower me with protestations of his fidelity to my grandfather's interests, which were one day to be my own, — he hoped, with me, not soon, — drew from his pocket more than sufficient for my immediate wants, said that I should have more by a trusty messenger, and was going on to clear himself of his former neglect and indifference, when Banks announced: —

"His honour, Mr. Manners!"

Comyn and I exchanged glances, and his Lordship gave a low whistle. Nor was the circumstance without its effect upon Mr. Dix. With my knowledge of the character of Dorothy's father I might have foreseen this visit, which came, nevertheless, as a complete surprise. For a moment I hesitated, and then made a motion to show him up. Comyn voiced my decision.

"Why let the little cur stand in the way?" he said; "he counts for nothing."

IN WHICH I AM SORE TEMPTED

Mr. Marmaduke was not long in ascending, and tripped into the room as Mr. Dix backed out of it, as gayly as tho' he had never sent me about my business in the street. His clothes, of a cherry cut velvet, were as ever a little beyond the fashion, and he carried something I had never before seen, then used by the extreme dandies in London, — an umbrella.

"What! Richard Carvel! Is it possible?" he screamed in his piping voice. "We mourned you for dead, and here you turn up in London alive and well, and bigger and stronger than ever. Oons! one need not go to Scripture for miracles. I shall write my congratulations to Mr. Carvel this day, sir."

And he pushed his fingers into my waistcoat, so that Comyn and I were near to laughing in his face. For it was impossible to be angry with a little coxcomb of such pitiful intelligence.

"Ah, good morning, my Lord. I see your Lordship has risen early in the same good cause, — I myself am up two hours before my time. You will pardon the fuss I am making over the lad, Comyn, but his grandfather is my very dear friend, and Richard was brought up with my daughter Dorothy. They were like brother and sister. What, Richard, you will not take my hand! Surely you are not so unreasonable as to hold against me that unfortunate circumstance in Arlington Street! Yes, Dorothy has shocked me. She has told me of it."

Comyn winked at me as I replied: —

"We shan't mention it, Mr. Manners. I have had my three weeks in prison, and perhaps know the world all the better for them."

He held up his umbrella in mock dismay, and stumbled abruptly into a chair. There he sat looking at me, a whimsical uneasiness on his face.

"We shall indeed mention it, sir. Three weeks in prison, to think of it! And you would not so much as send me a line. Ah, Richard, pride is a good thing, but I sometimes think we from Maryland have too much of it. We shall indeed speak of the matter. Out of justice to me you must understand how it occurred. You must know that I am deucedly absent-minded, and positively lost without my glass. And I had somebody with me, so Dorothy said. Chartersea, I believe. And his Grace made me think you were a cursed beggar. I make a point never to have to do with 'em."

"You are right, Mr. Manners," Comyn cut in dryly; "for I have known them to be so persistently troublesome, when once encouraged, as to interfere seriously with our arrangements."

"Eh!" Mr. Manners ejaculated, and then came to an abrupt pause, while I wondered whether the shot had told. To relieve him I inquired after Mrs. Manners's health.

"Ah, to be sure," he replied, beginning to fumble in his skirts; "London agrees with her remarkably, and she is better than she has been for years. And she is overjoyed at your most wonderful escape, Richard, as are we all."

And he gave me a note. I concealed my eagerness as I took it and broke the seal, to discover that it was not from Dorothy, but from Mrs. Manners herself.

"My dear Richard" (so it ran), "I thank God with your dear Grandfather over y'r Deliverance, & you must bring y'r Deliverer, whom Dorothy describes as Courtly and Gentlemanly despite his Calling, to dine with us this very Day, that we may express to him our Gratitude. I know you are far too Sensible not to come to Arlington Street. I subscribe myself, Richard, y'r sincere Friend,

"MARGARET MANNERS."

There was not so much as a postscript from Dolly, as I had hoped. But the letter was whole-souled, like Mrs. Manners, and breathed the affection she had always had for me. I honoured her the more that she had not attempted to excuse Mr. Manners's conduct.

"You will come, Richard?" cried Mr. Marmaduke, with an attempt at heartiness. "You must come, and the captain, too. For I hear, with regret, that you are not to be long with us."

I caught another significant look from Comyn from between the window curtains. But I accepted for myself, and conditionally for John Paul. Mr. Manners rose to take his leave.

"Dorothy will be glad to see you," he said. "I often think, Richard, that she tires of these generals and King's ministers,

IN WHICH I AM SORE TEMPTED

and longs for a romp at Wilmot House again. Alas," he sighed, offering us a pinch of snuff (which he said was the famous Number 37), "alas, she has had a deal too much of attention, with his Grace of Chartersea and a dozen others wild to marry her. I fear she will go soon," and he sighed again. " Upon my soul I cannot make her out. I'll lay something handsome, my Lord, that the madcap adventure with you after Richard sets the gossips going. One day she is like a schoolgirl, and I blame myself for not taking her mother's advice to send her to Mrs. Terry, at Campden House; and the next, egad, she is as difficult to approach as a crowned head. Well, gentlemen, I give you good day, I have an appointment at White's. I am happy to see you have fallen in good hands, Richard. My Lord, your most obedient!"

"He'll lay something handsome!" said my Lord, when the door had closed behind him.

CHAPTER XXVIII

ARLINGTON STREET

THE sun having come out, and John Paul not returning by two, — being ogling, I supposed, the ladies in Hyde Park, — I left him a message and betook myself with as great trepidation as ever to Dorothy's house. The door was opened by the identical footman who had so insolently offered me money, and I think he recognized me, for he backed away as he told me the ladies were not at home. But I had not gone a dozen paces in my disappointment when I heard him running after me, asking if my honour were Mr. Richard Carvel.

"The ladies will see your honour," he said, and conducted me back into the house and up the wide stairs. I had heard that Arlington Street was known as the street of the King's ministers, and I surmised that Mr. Manners had rented this house, and its furniture, from some great man who had gone out of office, plainly a person of means and taste. The hall, like that of many of the great town-houses, was in semi-darkness, but I remarked that the stair railing was of costly iron-work and polished brass; and, as I went up, that the stone niches in the wall were filled with the busts of statesmen, and I recognized among these, that of the great Walpole. A great copper-gilt chandelier hung above. But the picture of the drawing-room I was led into, with all its colours, remains in the eye of my mind to this day. It was a large room, the like of which I had never seen in any private residence of the New World, situated in the back of the house. Its balcony overlooked the fresh expanse of the Green Park. Upon its high ceiling floated Venus and the graces, by Zucchi; and the mantel, upon which ticked an antique and curious French clock, was carved marble.

On the gilt panels of the walls were wreaths of red roses. At least a half-dozen tall mirrors, framed in rococos, were placed about, the largest taking the space between the two high windows on the park side. And underneath it stood a gold cabinet, lacquered by Martin's inimitable hand, in the centre of which was set a medallion of porcelain, with the head in dark blue of his Majesty, Charles the First. The chairs and lounges were marquetry,— satin-wood and mahogany,— with seats and backs of blue brocade. The floor was polished to the degree of danger, and on the walls hung a portrait by Van Dycke, another, of a young girl, by Richardson, a landscape by the Dutch artist Ruysdael, and a water-colour by Zaccarelli.

I had lived for four months the roughest of lives, and the room brought before me so sharply the contrast between my estate and the grandeur and elegance in which Dorothy lived, that my spirits fell as I looked about me. In front of me was a vase of flowers, and beside them on the table lay a note "To Miss Manners, in Arlington Street," and sealed with a ducal crest. I was unconsciously turning it over, when something impelled me to look around. There, erect in the doorway, stood Dolly, her eyes so earnestly fixed upon me that I dropped the letter with a start. A faint colour mounted to her crown of black hair.

"And so you have come, Richard," she said. Her voice was low, and tho' there was no anger in it, the tone seemed that of reproach. I wondered whether she thought the less of me for coming.

"Can you blame me for wishing to see you before I leave, Dolly?" I cried, and crossed quickly over to her.

But she drew a step backward.

"Then it is true that you are going," said she, this time with a plain note of coldness.

"I must, Dorothy."

"When?"

"As soon as I can get passage."

She passed me and seated herself on the lounge, leaving me to stand like a lout before her, ashamed of my youth and of the clumsiness of my great body.

"Ah, Richard," she laughed, "confess to your old play mate! I should like to know how many young men of wealth and family would give up the pleasures of a London season were there not a strong attraction in Maryland."

How I longed to tell her that I would give ten years of my life to remain in England: that duty to John Paul took me home. But I was dumb.

"We should make a macaroni of you to amaze our colony," said Dolly, lightly, as I sat down a great distance away; "to accept my schooling were to double your chances when you return, Richard. You should have cards to everything, and my Lord Comyn or Mr. Fox or some one would introduce you at the clubs. I vow you would be a sensation, with your height and figure. You should meet all the beauties of England, and perchance," she added mischievously, "perchance you might be taking one home with you."

"Nay, Dolly," I answered; "I am not your match in jesting."

"Jesting!" she exclaimed, "I was never more sober. But where is your captain?"

I said that I hoped that John Paul would be there shortly.

"How fanciful he is! And his conversation,—one might think he had acquired the art at Marly or in the Fauxbourg. In truth, he should have been born on the far side of the Channel. And he has the air of the great man," said she, glancing up at me, covertly. "For my part, I prefer a little more bluntness."

I was nettled at the speech. Dorothy had ever been quick to seize upon and ridicule the vulnerable oddities of a character, and she had all the contempt of the great lady for those who tried to scale by pleasing arts. I perceived with regret that she had taken a prejudice.

"There, Dorothy," I cried, "not even you shall talk so of the captain. For you have seen him at his worst. There are not many, I warrant you, born like him a poor gardener's son who rise by character and ability to be a captain at three and twenty. And he will be higher yet. He has never attended any but a parish school, and still has learning to astonish Mr.

Walpole, learning which he got under vast difficulties. He is a gentleman, I say, far above many I have known, and he is a man. If you would know a master, you should see him on his own ship. If you would know a gentleman, you should have been with me in his mother's cottage." And, warming as I talked, I told her of that saddest of all home-comings to the little cabin under Criffel's height.

Small wonder that I adored Dorothy! Would that I could paint her moods, that I might describe the strange light in her eyes when I had finished, that I might tell how in an instant she was another woman. She rose impulsively and took a chair at my side, and said: —

"'Tis so I love to hear you speak, Richard, when you uphold the absent. For I feel it is so you must champion me when I am far away. My dear old playmate is ever the same, strong to resent, and seeing ever the best in his friends. Forgive me, Richard, I have been worse than silly. And will you tell me that story of your adventures which I long to learn?"

Ay, that I would. I told it her, and she listened silently, save only now and then a cry of wonder or of sympathy that sounded sweet to my ears, — just as I had dreamed of her listening when I used to pace the deck of the brigantine *John*, at sea. And when at length I had finished, she sat looking out over the Green Park, as tho' she had forgot my presence.

And so Mrs. Manners came in and found us.

It had ever pleased me to imagine that Dorothy's mother had been in her youth like Dorothy. She had the same tall figure, grace in its every motion, and the same eyes of deep blue, and the generous but well-formed mouth. A man may pity, but cannot conceive the heroism that a woman of such a mould must have gone through who has been married since early girlhood to a man like Mr. Manners. Some women would have been driven quickly to frivolity, and worse, but this one had struggled year after year to maintain an outward serenity to a critical world, and had succeeded, tho' success had cost her dear. Each trial had deepened a line of that face, had done its share to subdue the voice which had once rung like

Dorothy's; and in the depths of her eyes lingered a sadness indefinable.

She gazed upon me with that kindness and tenderness I had always received since the days when, younger and more beautiful than now, she was the companion of my mother. And the unbidden shadow of a thought came to me that these two sweet women had had some sadness in common. Many a summer's day I remembered them sewing together in the spring-house, talking in subdued voices which were hushed when I came running in. And lo! the same memory was on Dorothy's mother then, half expressed as she laid her hands upon my shoulders.

"Poor Elizabeth!" she said,—not to me, nor yet to Dorothy; "I wish that she might have lived to see you now. It is Captain Jack again."

She sighed, and kissed me. And I felt at last that I had come home after many wanderings. We sat down, mother and daughter on the sofa with their fingers locked. She did not speak of Mr. Manners's conduct, or of my stay in the sponging-house. And for this I was thankful.

"I have had a letter from Mr. Lloyd, Richard," she said.

"And my grandfather?" I faltered, a thickness in my throat.

"My dear boy," answered Mrs. Manners, gently, "he thinks you dead. But you have written him?" she added hurriedly.

I nodded. "From Dumfries."

"He will have the letter soon," she said cheerfully. "I thank Heaven I am able to tell you that his health is remarkable under the circumstances. But he will not quit the house, and sees no one except your uncle, who is with him constantly."

It was what I expected. But the confirmation of it brought me to my feet in a torrent of indignation, exclaiming:—

"The villain! You tell me he will allow Mr. Carvel to see no one?"

She started forward, laying her hand on my arm, and Dorothy gave a little cry.

"What are you saying, Richard? What are you saying?"

"Mrs. Manners," I answered, collecting myself, "I must tell you that I believe it is Grafton Carvel himself that is responsible for my abduction. He meant that I should be murdered."

Then Dorothy rose, her eyes flashing and her head high.

"He would have murdered you — you, Richard?" she cried, in such a storm of anger as I had never seen her. "Oh, he should hang for the thought of it! I have always suspected Grafton Carvel capable of any crime!"

"Hush, Dorothy," said her mother; "it is not seemly for a young girl to talk so."

"Seemly!" said Dorothy. "If I were a man I would bring him to justice, and it took me a lifetime. Nay, if I were a man and could use a sword —"

"Dorothy! Dorothy!" interrupted Mrs. Manners.

Dorothy sat down, the light lingering in her eyes. She had revealed more of herself in that instant than in all her life before.

"It is a grave charge, Richard," said Mrs. Manners, at length. "And your uncle is a man of the best standing in Annapolis."

"You must remember his behaviour before my mother's marriage, Mrs. Manners."

"I do, I do, Richard," she said sadly. "And I have never trusted him since. I suppose you are not making your accusation without cause?"

"I have cause enough," I answered bitterly.

"And proof?" she added. She should have been the man in her family.

I told her how Harvey had overheard the bits of the plot at Carvel Hall near two years gone; and now that I had begun, I was going through with Mr. Allen's part in the conspiracy, when Dorothy startled us both by crying: —

"Oh, there is so much wickedness in the world, I wish I had never been born!"

She flung herself from the room in a passion of tears to shock me. As if in answer to my troubled look, Mrs. Manners said, with a sigh: —

"She has not been at all well, lately, Richard. I fear the

gayety of this place is too much for her. Indeed, I am sorry we ever left Maryland."

I was greatly disturbed, and thought involuntarily of Comyn's words. Could it be that Mr. Manners was forcing her to marry Chartersea?

"And has Mr. Lloyd said nothing of my uncle?" I asked after a while.

"I will not deny that ugly rumours are afloat," she answered. "Grafton, as you know, is not liked in Annapolis, especially by the Patriot party. But there is not the slightest ground for suspicion. The messenger—"

"Yes?"

"Your uncle denies all knowledge of. He was taken to be the tool of the captain of the slaver, and he disappeared so completely that it was supposed he had escaped to the ship. The story goes that you were seized for a ransom, and killed in the struggle. Your black ran all the way to town, crying the news to those he met on the Circle and in West Street, but by the mercy of God he was stopped by Mr. Swain and some others before he had reached your grandfather. In ten minutes a score of men were galloping out of the Town Gate, Mr. Lloyd and Mr. Singleton ahead. They found your horse dead, and the road through the woods all trampled down, and they spurred after the tracks down to the water's edge. Singleton recalled a slaver, the crew of which had been brawling at the Ship tavern a few nights before. But the storm was so thick they could not see the ship's length out into the river. They started two fast sloops from the town wharves in chase, and your uncle has been moving heaven and earth to obtain some clew of you. He has put notices in the newspapers of Charlestown, Philadelphia, New York, and even Boston, and offered a thousand pounds reward."

CHAPTER XXIX

I MEET A VERY GREAT YOUNG MAN

The French clock had struck four, and I was beginning to fear that, despite my note, the captain's pride forbade his coming to Mr. Manners's house, when in he walked, as tho' 'twere no novelty to have his name announced. And so straight and handsome was he, his dark eye flashing with the self-confidence born in the man, that the look of uneasiness I had detected upon Mrs. Manners's face quickly changed to one of surprise and pleasure. Of course the good lady had anticipated a sea-captain of a far different mould. He kissed her hand with a respectful grace, and then her daughter's, for Dorothy had come back to us, calmer. And I was filled with joy over his fine appearance. Even Dorothy was struck by the change the clothes had made in him. Mrs. Manners thanked him very tactfully for restoring me to them, as she was pleased to put it, to which John Paul modestly replied that he had done no more than another would under the same circumstances. And he soon had them both charmed by his address.

"Why, Richard," said Dorothy's mother aside to me, "surely this cannot be your sea-captain!"

I nodded merrily. But John Paul's greatest triumph was yet to come. For presently Mr. Marmaduke arrived from White's, and when he had greeted me with effusion he levelled his glass at the corner of the room.

"Ahem!" he exclaimed. "Pray, my dear, whom have you invited to-day?" And without awaiting her reply, as was frequently his habit, he turned to me and said: "I had hoped we were to have the pleasure of Captain Paul's company,

Richard. For I must have the chance before you go of clasping the hand of your benefactor."

"You shall have the chance, at least, sir," I replied, a fiery exultation in my breast. "Mr. Manners, this is my friend, Captain Paul."

The captain stood up and bowed gravely at the little gentleman's blankly amazed countenance.

"Ahem," said he; "dear me, is it possible!" and advanced a step, but the captain remained immovable. Mr. Marmaduke fumbled for his snuff-box, failed to find it, halted, and began again, for he never was known to lack words for long: "Captain, as one of the oldest friends of Mr. Lionel Carvel I claim the right to thank you in his name for your gallant conduct. I hear that you are soon to see him, and to receive his obligations from him in person. You will not find him lacking, sir, I'll warrant."

Such was Mr. Marmaduke's feline ingenuity! I had a retort ready, and I saw that Mrs. Manners, long tried in such occasions, was about to pour oil on the waters. But it was Dorothy who exclaimed:—

"What, captain! are you, too, going to Maryland?"

John Paul reddened.

"Ay, that he is, Dolly," I cut in hurriedly. "Did you imagine I would let him escape so easily? Henceforth, as he has said, he is to be an American."

She flashed at me such a look as might have had a dozen different meanings, and in a trice it was gone again under her dark lashes.

Dinner was got through I know not how. Mr. Manners led the talk, and spoke more than was needful concerning our approaching voyage. He was at great pains to recommend the *Virginia* packet, which had made the fastest passage from the Capes; and she sailed, as was no doubt most convenient, the Saturday following. I should find her a comfortable vessel, and he would oblige me with a letter to Captain Alsop. Did Captain Paul know him? But the captain was describing West Indian life to Mrs. Manners. Dorothy had little to say; and as for me, I was in no very pleasant humour. I gave a deaf ear to Mr. Marmaduke's sallies, to speculate on the nature of the disgrace which Chartersea was said to hold over his head. And twenty times, as I looked upon Dolly's beauty, I ground my teeth at the notion of returning home. I have ever been slow of suspicion, but suddenly it struck me sharply that Mr. Manners's tactics must have a deeper significance than I had thought. Why was it that he feared my presence in London?

As we made our way back to the drawing-room, I was hoping for a talk with Dolly (alas! I should not have many more), when I heard a voice which sounded strangely familiar.

"You know, Comyn," it was saying, "you know I should be at the Princess's were I not so completely worn out. I was up near all of last night with Rosette."

Mr. Marmaduke, entering before us, cried: —

"The dear creature! I trust you have had medical attendance, Mr. Walpole."

"Egad!" quoth Horry (for it was he), "I sent Favre to Hampstead to fetch Dr. Pratt, where he was attending some mercer's wife. It seems that Rosette had got into the street and eaten something horrible out of the kennel. I discharged the footman, of course."

"A plague on your dog, Horry," said my Lord, yawning, and was about to add something worse, when he caught sight of Dorothy.

Mr. Walpole bowed over her hand.

"And have you forgotten so soon your Windsor acquaintances, Mr. Walpole?" she asked, laughing.

"Bless me," said Horry, looking very hard at me, "so it is, so it is. Your hand, Mr. Carvel. You have only to remain in London, sir, to discover that your reputation is ready-made. I contributed my mite. For you must know that I am a sort of circulating library of odd news which those devils, the printers, contrive to get sooner or later — Heaven knows how! And Miss Manners herself has completed your fame. Yes, the story of your gallant rescue is in all the clubs to-day. Egad, sir, you come down heads up, like a loaded coin. You will soon be a factor in Change Alley." And glancing slyly at the blushing Dolly, he continued: "I have been many things, Miss Manners, but never before an instrument of Providence. And so you discovered your rough diamond yesterday, and have polished him in a day. O that Dr. Franklin had profited as well by our London tailors! The rogue never told me, when he was ordering me about in his swan-skin, that he had a friend in Arlington Street, and a reigning beauty. But I like him the better for it."

"And I the worse," said Dolly.

"I perceive that he still retains his body-guard," said Mr. Walpole; "Captain —"

"Paul," said Dolly, seeing that we would not help him out.

"Ah, yes. These young princes from the New World must have their suites. You must bring them both some day to my little castle at Strawberry Hill."

"Unfortunately, Mr. Walpole, Mr. Carvel finds that he must return to America," Mr. Marmaduke interjected. He had been waiting to get in this word.

Comyn nudged me. And I took the opportunity, in the awkward silence that followed, to thank Mr. Walpole for sending his coach after us.

"And pray where did you get your learning?" he demanded abruptly of the captain, in his most patronizing way. "Your talents are wasted at sea, sir. You should try your fortune in London, where you shall be under my protection, sir. They shall not accuse me again of stifling young genius. Stay," he cried, warming with generous enthusiasm, "stay, I have an opening. 'Twas but yesterday Lady Cretherton told me that she stood in need of a tutor for her youngest son, and you shall have the position."

"Pardon me, sir, but I shall not have the position," said John Paul, coolly. And Horry might have heeded the danger signal. I had seen it more than once on board the brigantine *John*, and knew what was coming.

"Faith, and why not, sir? If I recommend you, why not, sir?"

"Because I shall not take it," he said. "I have my profession, Mr. Walpole, and it is an honourable one. And I would not exchange it, sir, were it in your power to make me a Gibbon or a Hume, or tutor to his Royal Highness, which it is not."

Thus, for the second time, the weapon of the renowned master of Strawberry was knocked from his hand at a single stroke of his strange adversary. I should like to describe John Paul as he made that speech, — for 'twas not so much the speech as the atmosphere of it. Those who heard and saw were stirred with wonder, for Destiny lay bare that instant, just as the powers above are sometimes revealed at a single lightning-bolt. Mr. Walpole made a reply that strove hard to be indifferent; Mr. Marmaduke stuttered, for he was frightened, as little souls are apt to be at such times. But my Lord Comyn, forever natural, forever generous, cried out heartily : —

"Egad, captain, there you are a true sailor! Which would you rather have been, I say, William Shakespeare or Sir Francis?"

"Which would you rather be, Richard," said Dolly to me, under her breath, "Horace Walpole or Captain John Paul? I begin to like your captain better."

Willy nilly, Mr. Walpole was forever doing me a service. Now, in order to ignore the captain more completely, he sat him down to engage Mr. and Mrs. Manners. Comyn was soon hot in an argument with John Paul concerning the sea-going qualities of a certain frigate, every rope and spar of which they seemed to know. And so I stole a few moments with Dorothy.

"You are going to take the captain to Maryland, Richard?" she asked, playing with her fan.

"I intend to get him the *Belle of the Wye*. 'Tis the least I can do. For I am at my wits' end how to reward him, Dolly. And when are you coming back?" I whispered earnestly, seeing her silent.

"I would that I knew, Richard," she replied, with a certain sadness that went to my heart, as tho' the choice lay beyond her. Then she changed. "Richard, there was more in Mr. Lloyd's letter than mamma told you of. There was ill news of one of your friends."

"Ill news!"

She looked at me fixedly, and then continued, her voice so low that I was forced to bend over: —

"Yes. You were not told that Patty Swain fell in a faint when she heard of your disappearance. You were not told that the girl was ill for a week afterwards. Ah, Richard, I fear you are a sad flirt. Nay, you may benefit by the doubt, — perchance you are going home to be married."

You may be sure that this intelligence, from Dorothy's lips, only increased my trouble and perplexity.

"You say that Patty has been ill?"

"Very ill," says she, with her lips tight closed.

"Indeed, I grieve to hear of it," I replied; "but I cannot think that my accident had anything to do with the matter."

"Young ladies do not send their fathers to coffee-houses to prevent duels unless their feelings are engaged," she flung back.

"You have heard the story of that affair, Dorothy. At least enough of it to do me justice."

She was plainly agitated.

"Has Lord Comyn — "

"Lord Comyn has told you the truth," I said; "so much I know."

Alas for the exits and entrances of life! Here comes the footman.

"Mr. Fox," said he, rolling the name, for it was a great one.

Confound Mr. Fox! He might have waited five short minutes.

It was, in truth, none other than that precocious marvel of England who but a year before had taken the breath from the House of Commons, and had sent his fame flying over the Channel and across the wide Atlantic; the talk of London, who set the fashions, cringed not before white hairs, or royalty, or customs, or institutions, and was now, at one and twenty, Junior Lord of the Admiralty — Charles James Fox. His face was dark, forbidding, even harsh — until he smiled. His eyebrows were heavy and shaggy, and his features of a rounded, almost Jewish mould. He put me in mind of the Stuarts, and I was soon to learn that he was descended from them.

As he entered the room I recall remarking that he was possessed of the supremest confidence of any man I had ever met. Mrs. Manners he greeted in one way, Mr. Marmaduke in another, and Mr. Walpole in still another. To Comyn it was "Hello, Jack," as he walked by him. Each, as it were, had been tagged with a particular value.

Chagrined as I was at the interruption, I was struck with admiration. For the smallest actions of these rare men of master passions so compel us. He came to Dorothy, whom he seemed not to have perceived at first, and there passed between them such a look of complete understanding that I suddenly remembered Comyn's speech of the night before, "Now it is Charles Fox." Here, indeed, was the man who might have won her. And yet I did not hate him. Nay, I loved him from the first time he addressed me. It was Dorothy who introduced us.

"I think I have heard of you, Mr. Carvel," he said, making a barely perceptible wink at Comyn.

"And I think I have heard of you, Mr. Fox," I replied.

"The deuce you have, Mr. Carvel!" said he, and laughed. And Comyn laughed, and Dorothy laughed, and I laughed. We were friends from that moment.

"Richard has appeared amongst us like a comet," put in the ubiquitous Mr. Manners, "and, I fear, intends to disappear in like manner."

"And where is the tail of this comet?" demanded Fox, instantly; "for I understood there was a tail."

John Paul was brought up, and the Junior Lord of the Admiralty looked him over from head to toe. And what, my dears, do you think he said to him?

"Have you ever acted, Captain Paul?"

The captain started back in surprise.

"Acted!" he exclaimed; "really, sir, I do not know. I have never been upon the boards."

Mr. Fox vowed that he could act: that he was sure of it, from the captain's appearance.

"And I, too, am sure of it, Mr. Fox," cried Dorothy, clapping her hands. "Persuade him to stay awhile in London, that you may have him at your next theatricals at Holland House. Why, he knows Shakespeare and Pope and — and Chaucer by heart, and Ovid and Horace, — is it not so, Mr. Walpole?"

"Is not what so, my dear young lady?" asked Mr. Walpole, pretending not to have heard.

"There!" exclaimed Dolly, pouting, when the laughter had subsided; "you make believe to care something about me, and yet will not listen to what I say."

I had seen at her feet our own Maryland gallants, the longest of whose reputations stretched barely from the James to the Schuylkill; but here in London men were hanging on her words whose names were familiarly spoken in Paris, and Rome, and Geneva. Not a topic was broached by Mr. Walpole or Mr. Fox, from the remonstrance of the Archbishop against masquerades and the coming marriage of my Lord Albemarle to the rights and wrongs of Mr. Wilkes, but my lady had her say. Mrs. Manners seemed more than content that she should play the hostess, which she did to perfection. She contrived to throw poisoned darts at the owner of Strawberry that started little Mr. Marmaduke to fidgeting in his seat, and he came to the rescue with all the town-talk at his command. He knew little else. Could Mr. Walpole tell him of this club of both sexes just started at Almack's? Mr. Walpole could tell a deal, tho' he took the pains first to explain that he was becoming too old for such frivolous and fashionable society. He could not, for the life of him, say why he was included. But, in spite of Mr. Walpole, John Paul was led out in the paces that best suited him, and finally, to the undisguised delight of Mr. Fox, managed to trip Horry upon an obscure point in Athenian literature. And this broke up the company.

As we took our leave Dorothy and Mr. Fox were talking together with lowered voices.

"I shall see you before I go," I said to her.

She laughed, and glanced at Mr. Fox.

"You are not going, Richard Carvel," said she.

"That you are not, Richard Carvel," said Mr. Fox.

I smiled, rather lamely, I fear, and said good night.

CHAPTER XXX

A CONSPIRACY

"Banks, where is the captain?" I asked, as I entered the parlour the next morning.

"Gone, sir, since seven o'clock," was the reply.

"Gone!" I exclaimed; "gone where?"

"Faith, I did not ask his honour, sir."

I thought it strange, but reflected that John Paul was given to whims. Having so little time before him, he had probably gone to see the sights he had missed yesterday: the Pantheon, which was building, an account of which had appeared in all the colonial papers; or the new Blackfriars Bridge; or the Tower; or perhaps to see his Majesty ride out. The wonders of London might go hang, for all I cared. Who would gaze at the King when he might look upon Dorothy! I sighed. I bade Banks dress me in the new suit Davenport had brought that morning, and then sent him off to seek the shipping agent of the *Virginia* packet to get us a cabin. I would go to Arlington Street as soon as propriety admitted.

But I had scarce finished my chocolate and begun to smoke in a pleasant revery, when I was startled by the arrival of two gentlemen. One was Comyn, and the other none less than Mr. Charles Fox.

"Now where the devil has your captain flown to?" said my Lord, tossing his whip on the table.

"I believe he must be sight-seeing," I said. "I dare swear he has taken a hackney coach to the Tower."

"To see the liberation of the idol of the people, I'll lay ten guineas. But they say the great Mr. Wilkes is to come out quietly, and wishes no demonstration," said Mr. Fox. "I believe the beggar has some sense, if the οἱ πολλοί would only let him have his way. So your captain is a Wilkite, Mr. Carvel?" he demanded.

"I fear you run very fast to conclusions, Mr. Fox," I answered, laughing, tho' I thought his guess was not far from wrong.

"I'll lay you the ten guineas he has been to the Tower," said Mr. Fox, promptly.

"Done, sir," said I.

"Hark ye, Richard," said Comyn, stretching himself in an arm-chair; "we are come to take the wind out of your sails, and leave you without an excuse for going home. And we want your captain, alive or dead. Charles, here, is to give him a commission in his Majesty's Navy."

Then I knew why Dorothy had laughed when I had spoken of seeing her again. Comyn — bless him! — had told her of his little scheme.

"Egad, Charles!" cried his Lordship, "to look at his glum face, one might think we were a couple of Jews who had cornered him."

Alas for the perversity of the heart! Instead of leaping for joy, as no doubt they had both confidently expected, I was both troubled and perplexed by this unlooked-for news. Oak, when bent, is even harder to bend back again. And so it has ever been with me. I had determined, after a bitter struggle, to go to Maryland, and had now become used to that prospect. I was anxious to see my grandfather, and to confront Grafton Carvel with his villany. And there was John Paul. What would he think?

"What ails you, Richard?" Comyn demanded somewhat testily.

"Nothing, Jack," I replied. "I thank you from my heart, and you, Mr. Fox. I know that commissions are not to be had for the asking, and I rejoice with the captain over his good fortune. But, gentlemen," I said soberly, "I had most selfishly hoped that I might be able to do a service to John Paul in return for his charity to me. You offer him something nearer his deserts, something beyond my power to give him."

Fox's eyes kindled.

"You speak like a man, Mr. Carvel," said he. "But you are too modest. Damn it, sir, don't you see that it is you, and no one else, who has procured this commission? Had I not been taken with you, sir, I should scarce have promised it to your friend Comyn, through whose interest you obtain it for your protégé."

I remembered what Mr. Fox's enemies said of him, and smiled at the plausible twist he had given the facts.

"No," I said; "no, Mr. Fox; never that. The captain must not think that I wish to be rid of him. I will not stand in the way, though if it is to be offered him, he must comprehend that I had naught to do with the matter. But, sir," I continued curiously, "what do you know of John Paul's abilities an an officer?"

Mr. Fox and Comyn laughed so immoderately as to bring the blood to my face.

"Damme!" cried the Junior Lord, "but you Americans have odd consciences! Do you suppose Rigby was appointed Paymaster of the Forces because of his fitness? Why was North himself made Prime Minister? For his abilities?" And he broke down again. "Ask Jack, here, how he got into the service, and how much seamanship he knows."

"Faith," answered Jack, unblushingly, "Admiral Lord Comyn, my father, wished me to serve awhile. And so I have taken two cruises, delivered some score of commands, and scarce know a supple jack from a can of flip. Cursed if I see the fun of it in these piping times o' peace, so I have given it up, Richard. For Charles says this Falkland business with Spain will blow out of the touch-hole."

I could see little to laugh over. For the very rottenness of the service was due to the miserable and servile Ministry and Parliament of his Majesty, by means of which instruments he was forcing the colonies to the wall. Verily, that was a time when the greatness of England hung in the balance! How little I suspected that the young man then seated beside me, who had cast so unthinkingly his mighty powers on the side of corruption, was to be one of the chief instruments of her salvation! We were to fight George the Third across the seas. He was to wage no less courageous a battle at home, in the King's own capital. And the cause? Yes, the cause was to be the same as that of the Mr. Wilkes he reviled, who obtained his liberty that day.

At length John Paul came in, calling my name. He broke off abruptly at sight of the visitors.

"Now we shall decide," said Mr. Fox. "Captain, I have bet Mr. Carvel ten guineas you have been to the Tower to see Squinting Jack[1] get his liberty at last."

The captain looked astonished.

"Anan, then, you have lost, Richard," said he. "For I have been just there."

"And helped, no doubt, to carry off the champion on your shoulders," said Mr. Fox, sarcastically, as I paid the debt.

"Mr. Wilkes knows full well the value of moderation, sir," replied the captain, in the same tone.

"Well, damn the odds!" exclaimed the Junior Lord, laughing. "You may have the magic number tattooed all over your back, for all I care. You shall have the commission."

"The commission?"

"Yes," said Fox, carelessly; "I intend making you a lieutenant, sir, in the Royal Navy."

The moment the words were out I was a-tremble as to how he would take the offer. For he had a certain puzzling pride, which flew hither and thither. But there was surely no comparison between the situations of the master of the *Belle of the Wye* and an officer in the Royal Navy. There, his talents would make him an admiral, and doubtless give him the social position he secretly coveted. He confounded us all by his answer.

"I thank you, Mr. Fox. But I cannot accept your kindness."

"'Slife!" said Fox, "you refuse? And you know what you are doing?"

"I know usually, sir."

Comyn swore. My exclamation had something of relief in it.

[1] John Wilkes.

"Captain," I said, "I felt that I could not stand in the way of this. It has been my hope that you will come with me, and I have sent this morning after a cabin on the *Virginia*. You must know that Mr. Fox's offer is his own, and Lord Comyn's."

"I know it well, Richard. I have not lived these three months with you for nothing." His voice seemed to fail him. He drew near me and took my hand. "But did you think I would require of you the sacrifice of leaving London now?"

"It is my pleasure as well as my duty, captain."

"No," he said, "I am not like that. Yesterday I went to the city to see a shipowner whose acquaintance I made when he was a master in the West India trade. He has had some reason to know that I can handle a ship. Never mind what. And he has given me the bark *Betsy*, whose former master is lately dead of the small-pox. Richard, I sail to-morrow."

In Dorothy's coach to Whitehall Stairs, by the grim old palace out of whose window Charles the Martyr had walked to his death. For Dorothy had vowed it was her pleasure to see John Paul off, and who could stand in her way? Surely not Mr. Marmaduke! and Mrs. Manners laughingly acquiesced. Our spirits were such that we might have been some honest mercer's apprentice and his sweetheart away for an outing.

"If we should take a wherry, Richard," said Dolly, "who would know of it? I have longed to be in a wherry ever since I came to London."

The river was smiling as she tripped gayly down to the water, and the red-coated watermen were smiling, too, and nudging one another. But little cared we! Dolly in holiday humour stopped for naught. "Boat, your honour! Boat, boat! To Rotherhithe — Redriff? Two and six apiece, sir." For that intricate puzzle called human nature was solved out of hand by the Thames watermen. Here was a young gentleman who never heard of the Lord Mayor's scale of charges. And what was a shilling to such as he! Intricate puzzle, indeed! Any booby might have read upon the young man's face that secret which is written for all, — high and low, rich and poor alike.

My new lace handkerchief was down upon the seat, lest Dolly soil her bright pink lutestring. She should have worn nothing else but the hue of roses. How the bargemen stared, and the passengers craned their necks, and the 'longshoremen stopped their work as we shot past them! On her account a barrister on the Temple Stairs was near to letting fall his bag in the water. A lady in a wherry! Where were the whims of the quality to lead them next? Past the tall water-tower and York Stairs, the idlers under the straight row of trees leaning over the high river wall; past Adelphi Terrace, where the great Garrick lived; past the white columns of Somerset House, with its courts and fountains and alleys and architecture of all ages, and its river gate where many a gilded royal barge had lain, and many a fine ambassador had arrived in state over the great highway of England; past the ancient trees in the Temple Gardens. And then under the new Blackfriars Bridge to Southwark, dingy with its docks and breweries and huddled houses, but forever famous, — the Southwark of Shakespeare and Jonson and Beaumont and Fletcher. And the shelf upon which they stood in the library at Carvel Hall was before my eyes.

"Yes," said Dolly; "and I recall your mother's name written in faded ink upon the fly-leaves."

Ah, London Town, by what subtleties are you tied to the hearts of those born across the sea? That is one of the mysteries of race.

Under the pointed arches of old London Bridge, with its hooded shelters for the weary, to where the massive Tower had frowned for ages upon the foolish river. And then the forest of ships, and the officious throng of little wherries and lighters that pressed around them, seeming to say, "You clumsy giants, how helpless would you be without us!" Soon our own wherry was dodging among them, ships brought hither by the four winds of the seas; many discharging in the stream, some in the docks then beginning to be built, and hugging the huge warehouses. Hides from frozen Russia were piled high beside barrels of sugar and rum from the moist island cane-fields of the Indies, and pipes of wine from the sunny hillsides of France, and big boxes of tea bearing the hall-mark of the mysterious East. Dolly gazed in wonder. And I was commanded to show her a schooner like the *Black Moll*, and a brigantine like the *John*.

"And Captain Paul told me you climbed the masts, Richard, and worked like a common seaman. Tell me," says she, pointing at the royal yard of a tall East Indiaman, "did you go as high as that when it was rough?"

And, hugely to the boatman's delight, the minx must needs put her fingers on the hard welts on my hands, and vow she would be a sailor and she were a man. But at length we came to a trim-built bark lying off Redriff Stairs, with the words "Betsy, of London," painted across her stern. In no time at all, Captain Paul was down the gangway ladder and at the water-side, to hand Dorothy out.

"This honour overwhelms me, Miss Manners," he said; "but I know whom to thank for it." And he glanced slyly at me.

Dorothy stepped aboard with the air of Queen Elizabeth come to inspect Lord Howard's flagship.

"Then you will thank me," said she. "Why, I could eat my dinner off your deck, captain! Are all merchantmen so clean?"

John Paul smiled.

"Not all, Miss Manners," he said.

"And you are still sailing at the ebb?" I asked.

"In an hour, Richard, if the wind holds good."

With what pride he showed us over his ship, the sailors gaping at the fine young lady. It had taken him just a day to institute his navy discipline. And Dolly went about exclaiming, and asking an hundred questions, and merrily catechising me upon the run of the ropes. All was order and readiness for dropping down the stream when he led us into his cabin, where he had a bottle of wine and some refreshments laid out against my coming.

"Had I presumed to anticipate your visit, Miss Manners, I should have had something more suitable for a lady," he said.

"What, you will not eat, either, Richard?"

I could not, so downcast had I become at the thought of

parting. I had sat up half the night before with him in restless argument and indecision, and even when he had left for Rotherhithe, early that morning, my mind had not been made. My conscience had insisted that I should sail with John Paul; that I might never see my dear grandfather on earth again. I had gone to Arlington Street that morning resolved to say farewell to Dorothy. I will not recount the history of that defeat, my dears. Nay, to this day I know not how she accomplished the matter. Not once had she asked me to remain, or referred to my going. Nor had I spoken of it, weakling that I was. She had come down in the pink lutestring, smiling but pale; and traces of tears in her eyes, I thought. From that moment I knew that I was defeated. It was she herself who had proposed going with me to see the *Betsy* sail.

"I will drink some Madeira to wish you Godspeed, captain," I said.

"What is the matter with you, Richard?" Dolly cried; "you are as sour as my Lord Sandwich after a bad Newmarket. Why, captain," said she, "I really believe he wants to go, too. The swain pines for his provincial beauty."

Poor John Paul! He had not yet learned that good society is seldom literal.

"Upon my soul, Miss Manners, there you do him wrong," he retorted, with ludicrous heat; "you, above all, should know for whom he pines."

"He has misled you by praising me. This Richard, despite his frank exterior, is most secretive."

"There you have hit him, Miss Manners," he declared; "there you have hit him! We were together night and day, on the sea and on the road, and, while I poured out my life to him, the rogue never once let fall a hint of the divine Miss Dorothy. 'Twas not till I got to London that I knew of her existence, and then only by a chance. You astonish me. You speak of a young lady in Maryland?"

Dorothy swept aside my protest.

"Captain," says she, gravely, "I leave you to judge. What is your inference, when he fights a duel about a miss with my Lord Comyn?"

"A duel!" cried the captain, astounded.

"Miss Manners persists in her view of the affair, despite my word to the contrary," I put in rather coldly.

"But a duel!" cried the captain again; "and with Lord Comyn! Miss Manners, I fondly thought I had discovered a constant man, but you make me fear he has had as many flames as I. And yet, Richard," he added meaningly, "I should think shame on my conduct had I had such a subject for constancy as you."

Dorothy's armour was pierced, and my ill-humour broken down, by this characteristic speech. We both laughed, greatly to his discomfiture.

"You had best go home with him, Richard," said Dolly. "I can find my way back to Arlington Street alone."

"Nay; gallantry forbids his going with me now," answered John Paul; "and I have my sailing orders. But had I known of this, I should never have wasted my breath in persuading him to remain."

"And did he stand in need of much persuasion, captain?" asked Dolly, archly.

Time was pressing, and the owner came aboard, puffing,—a round-faced, vociferous, jolly merchant, who had no sooner got his breath than he lost it again upon catching sight of Dolly. While the captain was giving the mate his final orders, Mr. Orchardson, for such was his name, regaled us with a part of his life's history. He had been a master himself, and mangled and clipped King George's English as only a true master might.

"I like your own captain better than ever, Richard," whispered Dolly, while Mr. Orchardson relieved himself of his quid over the other side; "how commanding he is! Were I to take passage in the *Betsy*, I know I should be in love with him long before we got to Norfolk."

I took it upon myself to tell Mr. Orchardson, briefly and clearly as I could, the lamentable story of John Paul's last cruise. For I feared it might sooner or later reach his ears from prejudiced mouths. And I ended by relating how the captain had refused a commission in the navy because he had promised to take the *Betsy*. This appeared vastly to impress him, and he forgot Dorothy's presence.

"Passion o' my 'eart, Mr. Carvel," cried he, excitedly, "John Paul's too big a man, an' too good a seaman, to go into the navy without hinflooence. If flag horfocers I wots of is booted haside to rankle like a lump o' salt butter in a gallipot, 'ow will a poor Scotch lieutenant win hadvancement an' he be not o' the King's friends? 'Wilkes an' Liberty,' say I; 'forever,' say I. An' w'en I see 'im goin' to the Tower to be'old the Champion, 'Captain Paul,' says I, 'yere a man arfter my hown 'eart.' My heye, sir, didn't I see 'im, w'n a mere lad, take the *John* into Kingston 'arbour in the face o' the worst gale I hever seed blowed in the Caribbees? An' I says, 'Bill Horchardson, an' ye hever 'ave ships o' yere own, w'ich I 'ope will be, ye'll know w'ere to look for a marster.' An' I tells 'im that same, Mr. Carvel. I means no disrespect to the dead, sir, but an' John Paul 'ad discharged the *Betsy*, I'd not 'a' been out twenty barrels or more this day by Thames mudlarks an' scuffle hunters. 'Eave me flat, if 'e'll be two blocks wi' liquor an' dischargin' cargo. An' ye may rest heasy, Mr. Carvel, I'll not do wrong by 'im, neither."

He told me that if I would honour him in Maid Lane, Southwark, I should have as many pounds as I liked of the best tobacco ever cured in Cuba. And so he left me to see that the mate had signed all his lighter bills, shouting to the captain not to forget his cockets at Gravesend. Dolly and I stood silent while the men hove short, singing a jolly song to the step. With a friendly wave the round figure of Mr. Orchardson disappeared over the side, and I knew that the time had come to say farewell. I fumbled in my waistcoat for the repeater I had bought that morning over against Temple Bar, in Fleet Street, and I thrust it into John Paul's hand as he came up.

"Take this in remembrance of what you have suffered so unselfishly for my sake, Captain Paul," I said, my voice breaking. "And whatever befalls you, do not forget that Carvel Hall is your home as well as mine."

He seemed as greatly affected as was I. Tears forced themselves to his eyes as he held the watch, which he opened absently to read the simple inscription I had put there.

"Oh, Dickie lad!" he cried, "I'll be missing ye sair three hours hence, and thinking of ye for months to come in the night watches. But something tells me I'll see ye again."

And he took me in his arms, embracing me with such fervour that there was no doubting the sincerity of his feelings.

"Miss Dorothy," said he, when he was calmer, "I give ye Richard for a leal and a true heart. Few men are born with the gift of keeping the affections warm despite absence, and years, and interest. But have no fear of Richard Carvel."

Dorothy stood a little apart, watching us, her eyes that far-away blue of the deepening skies at twilight.

"Indeed, I have no fear of him, captain," she said gently. Then, with a quick movement, impulsive and womanly, she unpinned a little gold brooch at her throat, and gave it to him, saying: "In token of my gratitude for bringing him back to us."

John Paul raised it to his lips.

"I shall treasure it, Miss Manners, as a memento of the greatest joy of my life. And that has been," gracefully taking her hand and mine, "the bringing you two together again."

Dorothy grew scarlet as she curtseyed. As for me, I could speak never a word. He stepped over the side to hand her into the wherry, and embraced me once again. And as we rowed away he waved his hat in a last good-by from the taff-rail. Then the *Betsy* floated down the Thames.

U

CHAPTER XXXI

"UPSTAIRS INTO THE WORLD"

It will be difficult, my dears, without bulging this history out of all proportion, to give you a just notion of the society into which I fell after John Paul left London. It was, above all, a gaming society. From that prying and all-powerful God of Chance none, great or small, escaped. Guineas were staked and won upon frugal King George and his beef and barley-water; Charles Fox and his debts; the intrigues of Choiseul and the Du Barry and the sensational marriage of the Duc d'Orleans with Madame de Montesson (for your macaroni knew his Paris as well as his London); Lord March and his opera singer; and even the doings of Betty, the apple-woman of St. James's Street, and the beautiful barmaid of Nando's in whom my Lord Thurlow was said to be interested. All these, and much more not to be repeated, were duly set down in the betting-books at White's and Brooks's.

Then the luxury of the life was something to startle a provincial, even tho' he came, as did I, from one of the two most luxurious colonies of the thirteen. Annapolis might be said to be London on a small scale,—but on a very small scale. The historian of the future need look no farther than our houses (if any remain), to be satisfied that we had more than the necessities of existence. The Maryland aristocrat with his town place and his country place was indeed a parallel of the patrician at home. He wore his English clothes, drove and rode his English horses, and his coaches were built in Long Acre. His heavy silver service came from Fleet Street, and his claret and Champagne and Lisbon and Madeira were the best that could be bought or smuggled. His sons were often educated at nome, at Eton or Westminster and Oxford or Cambridge. So would I have been if circumstances had permitted. So was James Fotheringay, the eldest of the family, and later the Dulany boys, and half a dozen others I might mention. And then our ladies! 'Tis but necessary to cite my Aunt Caroline as an extreme dame of fashion, who had her French hairdresser, Pitou.

As was my aunt to the Duchess of Kingston, so was Annapolis to London. To depict the life of Mayfair and of St. James's Street during a season about the year of grace 1770 demands a mightier pen than wields the writer of these simple memoirs.

And who was responsible for all this luxury and laxity? Who but the great Mr. Pitt, then the Earl of Chatham, whose wise policy had made Britain the ruler of the world, and rich beyond compare. From all corners of the earth her wealth poured in upon her. Nabob and Caribbee came from East and West to spend their money in the capital. And fortunes near as great were acquired by the City merchants themselves. One by one these were admitted within that charmed circle, whose motto for ages had been "No Trade," to leaven it with their gold. And to keep the pace, — nay, to set it, the nobility and landed gentry were sore pressed. As far back as good Queen Anne, and farther, their ancestors had gamed and tippled away the acres; and now that John and William, whose forebears had been good tenants for centuries, were setting their faces to Liverpool and Birmingham and Leeds, their cottages were empty. So Lord and Squire went to London to recuperate, and to get their share of the game running. St. James's Street and St. Stephen's became their preserves. My Lord wormed himself into a berth in the Treasury, robbed the country systematically for a dozen of years, and sold the places and reversions under him to the highest bidder. Boroughs were to be had somewhat dearer than a pair of colours. And my Lord spent his spare time — he had plenty of it — in fleecing the pigeons at White's and Almack's. Here there was no honour, even amongst thieves. And young gentlemen were hurried through Eton and Oxford, where they learned to drink and swear and to call a main as well as to play tennis and billiards and to write Latin, and were thrust into Brooks's before they knew the difference in value between a farthing and a banknote: at nineteen they were hardened rakes, or accomplished men of the world, or both. Dissipated noblemen of middle age like March and Sandwich, wits and beaus and fine gentlemen like Selwyn and Chesterfield and Walpole, were familiarly called by their first names by youngsters like Fox and Carlisle and Comyn. Difference of age was no difference. Young Lord Carlisle was the intimate of Mr. Selwyn, born thirty years before him.

And whilst I am speaking of intimacies, that short one which sprang up between me and the renowned Charles Fox has always seemed the most unaccountable: not on my part, for I fell a victim to him at once. Pen and paper, brush and canvas, are wholly inadequate to describe the charm of the man. When he desired to please, his conversation and the expression of his face must have moved a temperament of stone itself. None ever had more devoted friends or more ardent admirers. They saw his faults, which he laid bare before them, but they settled his debts again and again, vast sums which he lost at Newmarket and at Brooks's. And not many years after the time of which I now write Lord Carlisle was paying fifteen hundred a year on the sum he had loaned him, cheerfully denying himself the pleasures of London as a consequence.

It was Mr. Fox who discovered for me my lodgings in Dover Street, vowing that I could not be so out of fashion as to live at an inn. The brief history of these rooms, as given by him, was this: "A young cub had owned them, whose mamma had come up from Berkshire on Thursday, beat him soundly on Friday, paid his debts on Saturday, and had taken him back on Sunday to hunt with Sir Henry the rest of his life." Dorothy came one day with her mother and swept through my apartments, commanded all the furniture to be moved about, ordered me to get pictures for the walls, and by one fell decree abolished all the ornaments before the landlady, used as she was to the ways of quality, had time to gasp.

"Why, Richard," says my lady, "you will be wanting no end of pretty things to take back to Maryland when you go. You shall come with me to-morrow to Mr. Josiah Wedgwood's, to choose some of them."

"Dorothy!" says her mother, reprovingly.

"And he must have the Chippendale table I saw yesterday at the exhibition, and chairs to match. And every bachelor should have a punch bowl — Josiah has such a beauty!"

But I am running far ahead. Among the notes with which my table was laden, Banks had found a scrawl. This I made out with difficulty to convey that Mr. Fox was not attending Parliament that day. If Mr. Carvel would do him the honour of calling at his lodging, over Mackie's Italian Warehouse in Piccadilly, at four o'clock, he would take great pleasure in introducing him at Brooks's Club. In those days 'twas far better for a young gentleman of any pretensions to remain at home than go to London and be denied that inner sanctuary, — the younger club at Almack's. Many the rich brewer's son has embittered his life because it was not given him to see more than the front of the house from the far side of Pall Mall. But to be taken there by Charles Fox was an honour falling to few. I made sure that Dolly was at the bottom of it.

Promptly at four I climbed the stairs and knocked at Mr. Fox's door. The Swiss who opened it shook his head dubiously when I asked for his master, and said he had not been at home that day.

"But I had an appointment to meet him," I said, thinking it very strange.

The man's expression changed.

"An appointment, sir! Ah, sir, then you are to step in here." And to my vast astonishment he admitted me into a small room at one side of the entrance. It was bare as poverty, and furnished with benches, and nothing more. On one of these was seated a person with an unmistakable nose and an odour of St. Giles's, who sprang to his feet and then sat down again dejectedly. I also sat down, wondering what it could mean, and debating whether to go or stay.

"Exguse me, your honour," said the person, "but haf you seen Mister Fox?"

I said that I, too, was waiting for him, whereat he cast at me a cunning look beyond my comprehension. Surely, I thought, a man of Fox's inherited wealth and position could not be living in such a place! Before the truth and humour of the situation had dawned upon me, I heard a ringing voice without, swearing in most forcible English, and the door was thrown open, admitting a tall young gentleman, as striking as I have ever seen. He paid not the smallest attention to the Jew, who was bowing and muttering behind me.

"Mr. Richard Carvel?" said he, with a merry twinkle in his eye.

I bowed.

"Gad's life, Mr. Carvel, I'm deuced sorry this should have happened. Will you come with me?"

"Exguse me, your honour!" cried the other visitor.

"Now, what the plague, Aaron!" says he; "you wear out the stairs. Come to-morrow, or the day after."

"Ay, 'tis always 'to-morrow' with you fine gentlemen. But I vill bring the bailiffs, so help me —"

"Damn 'em!" says the tall young gentleman, as he slammed the door and so shut off the wail. "Damn 'em, they worry Charles to death. If he would only stick to quinze and picquet, and keep clear of the hounds,[1] he need never go near a broker. Do you have Jews in America, Mr. Carvel?" Without waiting for an answer, he led me through a parlour, hung with pictures, and bewilderingly furnished with French and Italian things, and Japan and China ware and bronzes, and cups and trophies. "My name is Fitzpatrick, Mr. Carvel, — yours to command, and Charles's. I am his ally for offence and defence. We went to school together," he explained simply.

His manner was so free, and yet so dignified, as to charm me completely. For I heartily despised all that fustian trumpery of the age. Then came a voice from beyond, calling: —

[1] The "hounds," it appears, were the gentlemen of sharp practices at White's and Almack's. — D. C. C.

"That you, Carvel? Damn that fellow Eiffel, and did he thrust you into the Jerusalem Chamber?"

"The Jerusalem Chamber!" I exclaimed.

"Where I keep my Israelites," said he; "but, by Gad's life! I think they are one and all descended from Job, and not father Abraham at all. He must have thought me cursed ascetic, eh, Fitz? Did you find the benches hard? I had 'em made hard as the devil. But if they were of stone, I vow the flock could find their own straw to sit on."

"Curse it, Charles," cut in Mr. Fitzpatrick, in some temper, "can't you be serious for once! He would behave this way, Mr. Carvel, if he were being shriven by the Newgate ordinary before a last carting to Tyburn. Charles, Charles, it was Aaron again, and the dog is like to snap at last. He is talking of bailiffs. Take my advice and settle with him. Hold Cavendish off another fortnight and settle with him."

Mr. Fox's reply was partly a laugh, and the rest of it is not to be printed. He did not seem in the least to mind this wholesale disclosure of his somewhat awkward affairs. And he continued to dress, or to be dressed, alternately swearing at his valet and talking to Fitzpatrick and to me.

"You are both of a name," said he. "Let a man but be called *Richard*, and I seem to take to him. I' faith, I like the hunchback king, and believe our friend Horry Walpole is right in defending him, despite Davie Hume. I vow I shall like you, Mr. Carvel."

I replied that I certainly hoped so.

"Egad, you come well enough recommended," he said, pulling on his breeches. "No, Eiffel, cursed if I go *en petit maître* to-day. How does that strike you for a *demi saison*, Mr. Buckskin? I wore three of 'em through the customs last year, and March's worked olive nightgown tucked under my greatcoat, and near a dozen pairs of shirts and stockings. And each of my servants had on near as much. O Lud, we were amazing — like beef-eaters or blower pigeons. Sorry you won't meet my brother, — he that will have the title. He's out of town."

Going on in this discursory haphazard way while he dressed, he made me feel much at home. For the young dictator — so

Mr. Fitzpatrick informed me afterward — either took to you or else he did not, and stood upon no ceremony. After he had chosen a coat with a small pattern and his feet had been thrust into the little red shoes with the high heels, imported by him from France, he sent for a hackney-chaise. And the three of us drove together to Pall Mall. Mr. Brooks was at the door, and bowed from his hips as we entered.

"A dozen *vin de Graves*, Brooks!" cries Mr. Fox, and ushers me into a dining room, with high curtained windows and painted ceiling, and chandeliers throwing a glitter of light. There, at a long table, surrounded by powdered lackeys, sat a bevy of wits, mostly in blue and silver, with point ruffles, to match Mr. Fox's costume. They greeted my companions uproariously. It was "Here's Charles at last!" "Howdy, Charles!" "Hello, Richard!" and "What have you there? a new Caribbee?" They made way for Mr. Fox at the head of the table, and he took the seat as though it were his right.

"This is Mr. Richard Carvel, gentlemen, of Carvel Hall, in Maryland."

They stirred with interest when my name was called, and most of them turned in their chairs to look at me. I knew well the reason, and felt my face grow hot. Although you may read much of the courtesy of that age, there was a deal of brutal frankness among young men of fashion.

"Egad, Charles, is this he the Beauty rescued from Castle Yard?"

A familiar voice relieved my embarrassment.

"Give the devil his due, Bully. You forget that I had a hand in that."

"Faith, Jack Comyn," retorted the gentleman addressed, "you're already famous for clinging to her skirt."

"But cling to mine, Bully, and we'll all enter the temple together. But I bid you welcome, Richard," said his Lordship; "you come with two of the most delightful vagabonds in the world."

Mr. Fox introduced me in succession to Colonel St. John, known in St. James's Street as *the Baptist*; to my Lord Bolingbroke, Colonel St. John's brother, who was more familiarly called *Bully* ; to Mr. Fitzpatrick's brother, the Earl of Upper Ossory, who had come up to London, so he said, to see a little Italian dance at the Garden; to *Gilly* Williams; to Sir Charles Bunbury, who had married Lady Sarah Lennox, Fox's cousin, the beauty who had come so near to being queen of all England; to Mr. Storer, who was at once a Caribbee and a Crichton; to Mr. Uvedale Price. These I remember, but there are more that escape me. Most good-naturedly they drank my health in Charles's *vin de grave*, at four shillings the bottle; and soon I was astonished to find myself launched upon the story of my adventures, which they had besought me to tell them. When I had done, they pledged me again, and, beginning to feel at home, I pledged them handsomely in return. Then the conversation began. The like of it I have never heard anywhere else in the world. There was a deal that might not be written here, and a deal more that might, to make these pages sparkle. They went through the meetings, of course, and thrashed over the list of horses entered at Ipswich, and York, and Newmarket, and how many were thought to be pulled. Then followed the recent gains and losses of each and every individual of the company. After that there was a roar of merriment over Mr. Storer cracking mottoes with a certain Lady Jane; and how young Lord Stavordale, on a wager, tilted the candles and set fire to the drawing-room at Lady Julia's drum, the day before. Mr. Price told of the rage Topham Beauclerk had got Dr. Johnson into, by setting down a mark for each oyster the sage had eaten, and showing him the count. But Mr. Fox, who was the soul of the club, had the best array of any. He related how he had gone post from Paris to Lyons, to order, among other things, an embroidered canary waistcoat for George Selwyn from Jabot. "'*Et quel dessin, monsieur?*' 'Beetles and frogs, in green.' '*Escarbots! grenouilles!*' he cries, with a shriek; '*Et pour Monsieur Selwyn! Monsieur Fox badine!*' It came yesterday, by Crawford, and I sent it to Chesterfield Street in time for George to wear to the Duchess's. He has been twice to Piccadilly after me, and twice here, and swears he will have my heart. And I believe he is now gone to Matson in a funk."

After that they fell upon politics. I knew that Mr. Fox was already near the head of the King's party, and that he had just received a substantial reward at his Majesty's hands; and I went not far to guess that every one of these easy-going, devil-may-care macaronies was a follower or sympathizer with Lord North's policy. But what I heard was a revelation indeed. I have dignified it by calling it politics. All was frankness here amongst friends. There was no attempt made to gloss over ugly transactions with a veneer of morality. For this much I honoured them. But irresistibly there came into my mind the grand and simple characters of our own public men in America, and it made me shudder to think that, while they strove honestly for our rights, this was the type which opposed them. Motives of personal spite and of personal gain were laid bare, and even the barter and sale of offices of trust took place before my very eyes. I was silent, though my tongue burned me, until one of the gentlemen, thinking me neglected, said:—

"What a-deuce is to be done with those unruly countrymen of yours, Mr. Carvel? Are they likely to be pacified now that we have taken off all except the tea? You who are of our party must lead a sorry life among them. Tell me, do they really mean to go as far as rebellion?"

The blood rushed to my face.

"It is not a question of tea, sir," I answered hotly; "nor yet of tuppence. It is a question of principle, which means more to Englishmen than life itself. And we are Englishmen."

I believe I spoke louder than I intended, for a silence followed my words. Fox glanced at Comyn, who of all of them at the table was not smiling, and said:—

"I thought you came of a loyalist family, Mr. Carvel."

"King George has no more loyal servants than the Americans, Mr. Fox, be they Tory or Whig. And he has but to read our petitions to discover it," I said.

I spoke calmly, but my heart was thumping with excitement

and resentment. The apprehension of the untried is apt to be sharp at such moments, and I looked for them to turn their backs upon me for an impertinent provincial. Indeed, I think they would have, all save Comyn, had it not been for Fox himself. He lighted a pipe, smiled, and began easily, quite dispassionately, to address me.

"I wish you would favour us with your point of view, Mr. Carvel," said he; "for, upon my soul, I know little about the subject."

"You know little about the subject, and you in Parliament!" I cried.

This started them all to laughing. Why, I did not then understand. But I was angry enough.

"Come, let's have it!" said he.

They drew their chairs closer, some wearing that smile of superiority which to us is the Englishman's most maddening trait. I did not stop to think twice, or to remember that I was pitted against the greatest debater in all England. I was to speak that of which I was full, and the heart's argument needs no logic to defend it. If it were my last word, I would pronounce it.

I began by telling them that the Americans had paid their share of the French war, in blood and money, twice over. And I had the figures in my memory. Mr. Fox interrupted. For ten minutes at a space he spoke, and in all my life I have never talked to a man who had the English of King James's Bible, of Shakespeare, and Milton so wholly at his command. And his knowledge of history, his classical citations, confounded me. I forgot myself in wondering how one who had lived so fast had acquired such learning. Afterward, when I tried to recall what he said, I laughed at his surprising ignorance of the question at issue, and wondered where my wits could have gone that I allowed myself to be dazzled and turned aside at every corner. As his speech came faster he twisted fact into fiction and fiction into fact, until I must needs close my mind and bolt the shutters of it, or he had betrayed me into confessing the right of Parliament to quarter troops among us. Though my head swam, I clung doggedly to my text. And that was my salvation. He grew more excited, and they applauded him. In truth, I myself felt near to clapping. And then, as I stared him in the eye, marvelling how a man of such vast power and ability could stand for such rotten practices, the thought came to me (I know not whence) of Saint Paul the Apostle.

"Mr. Fox," I said, when he had paused, "before God, do you believe what you are saying?"

I saw them smiling at my earnestness and simplicity. Fox seemed surprised, and laughed evasively, — not heartily as was his wont.

"My dear Mr. Carvel," he said, glancing around the circle, "political principles are not to be swallowed like religion, but taken rather like medicine, experimentally. If they agree with you, very good. If not, drop them and try others. We are always ready to listen to remedies, here."

"Ay, if they agree with *you*!" I exclaimed. "But food for one is poison for another. Do you know what you are doing? You are pushing home injustice and tyranny to the millions, for the benefit of the thousands. For is it not true, gentlemen, that the great masses of England are against the measures you impose upon us? Their fight is our fight. They are no longer represented in Parliament; we have never been. Taxation without representation is true of your rotten boroughs as well as of your vast colonies. You are helping the King to crush freedom abroad in order that he may the more easily break it at home. You are committing a crime.

"I tell you we would give up all we own were the glory or honour of England at stake. And yet you call us rebels, and accuse us of meanness and of parsimony. If you wish money, leave the matter to our colonial assemblies, and see how readily you will get it. But if you wish war, persist in trying to grind the spirit from a people who have in them the pride of your own ancestors. Yes, you are estranging the colonies, gentlemen. A greater man than I has warned you."

And with that I rose, believing that I had given them all mortal offence. To my astonishment several got to their feet in front of me, huzzaing, and Comyn and Lord Ossory grasped my hands. And Charles Fox reached out over the corner of the table and pulled me back into my chair.

"Bravo, Richard Carvel!" he cried. "Cursed if I don't love a man who will put up a fight against odds. Who will stand bluff to what he believes, and won't be talked out of his boots. We won't quarrel with any such here, my buckskin, I can tell you."

And that is the simple story, my dears, of the beginning of my friendship with one who may rightly be called the Saint Paul of English politics. He had yet some distance to go, alas, ere he was to begin that sturdy battle for the right for which his countrymen and ours will always bless him. I gave him my hand with a better will than I had ever done anything, and we pressed our fingers numb. And his was not the only hand I clasped. And honest Jack Comyn ordered more wine, that they might drink to a speedy reconciliation with America.

"A pint bumper to Richard Carvel!" said Mr. Fitzpatrick.

I pledged Brooks's Club in another pint. Upon which they swore that I was a good fellow, and that if all American Whigs were like me, all cause of quarrel was at an end. Of this I was not so sure, nor could I see that the question had been settled one way or another. And that night I had reason to thank the Reverend Mr. Allen, for the first and last time in my life, that I could stand a deal of liquor, and yet not roll bottom upward.

The dinner was settled on the Baptist, who paid for it without a murmur. And then we adjourned to the business of the evening. The great drawing-room, lighted by an hundred candles, was filled with gayly dressed macaronies, and the sound of their laughter and voices in contention mingled with the pounding of the packs on the mahogany and the rattle of the dice and the ring of the gold pieces. The sight was dazzling, and the noise distracting. Fox had me under his especial care, and I was presented to young gentlemen who bore names that had been the boast of England through the centuries. Lands their forebears had won by lance and sword, they were squandering away as fast as ever they could. I, too, was known. All had heard the romance of the Beauty and

Castle Yard, and some had listened to Horry Walpole tell that foolish story of Goble at Windsor, on which he seemed to set such store. They guessed at my weight. They betted upon it. And they wished to know if I could spin Mr. Brooks, who was scraping his way from table to table. They gave me choice of whist, or picquet, or quinze, or hazard. I was carried away. Nay, I make no excuse. Tho' the times were drinking and gaming ones, I had been brought up that a gentleman should do both in moderation. We mounted, some dozen of us, to the floor above, and passed along to a room of which Fox had the key; and he swung me in on his arm, the others pressing after. And the door was scarce closed and locked again, before they began stripping off their clothes.

To my astonishment, Fox handed me a great frieze coat, which he bade me don, as the others were doing. Some were turning their coats inside out; for luck, said they; and putting on footman's leather guards to save their ruffles. And they gave me a hat with a high crown, and a broad brim to save my eyes from the candle glare. We were as grotesque a set as ever I laid my eyes upon. But I hasten over the scene, which has long become distasteful to me. I mention it only to show to what heights of folly the young men had gone. I recall a gasp when they told me they played for rouleaux of ten pounds each, but I took out my pocket-book as boldly as tho' I had never played for less, and laid my stake upon the board. Fox lost, again and again; but he treated his ill-luck with such a raillery of contemptuous wit, that we must needs laugh with him. Comyn, too, lost, and at supper excused himself, saying that he had promised his mother, the dowager countess, not to lose more than a quarter's income at a sitting. But I won and won, until the fever of it got into my blood, and as the first faint light of that morning crept into the empty streets, we were still at it, Fox vowing that he never waked up until daylight. That the best things he said in the House came to him at dawn.

CHAPTER XXXII

LADY TANKERVILLE'S DRUM-MAJOR

THE rising sun, as he came through the little panes of the windows, etched a picture of that room into my brain. I can see the twisted candles with their wax smearing the sticks, the chairs awry, the tables littered with blackened pipes, and bottles, and spilled wine and tobacco among the dice; and the few that were left of my companions, some with dark lines under their eyes, all pale, but all gay, unconcerned, witty, and cynical; smoothing their ruffles, and brushing the ashes and snuff from the pattern of their waistcoats. As we went downstairs, singing a song Mr. Foote had put upon the stage that week, they were good enough to declare that I should never be permitted to go back to Maryland. That my grandfather should buy me a certain borough, which might be had for six thousand pounds.

The drawing-room made a dismal scene, too, after the riot and disorder of the night. Sleepy servants were cleaning up, but Fox vowed that they should bring us yet another bottle before going home. So down we sat about the famous old round table, Fox fingering the dents the gold had made in the board, and philosophizing; and reciting Orlando Furioso in the Italian, and Herodotus in the original Greek. Suddenly casting his eyes about, they fell upon an ungainly form, stretched on a lounge, that made us all start.

"Bully!" he cried; "I'll lay you fifty guineas that Mr. Carvel gets the Beauty, against Chartersea."

This roused me.

"Nay, Mr. Fox, I beg of you," I protested, with all the

vehemence I could muster. "Miss Manners must not be writ down in such a way."

For answer he snapped his fingers at the drowsy Brooks, who brought the betting book.

"There!" says he; "and there, and there," turning over the pages; "her name adorns a dozen leaves, my fine buckskin. And it will be well to have some truth about her. Enter the wager, Brooks."

"Hold!" shouts Bolingbroke; "I haven't accepted."

You may be sure I was in an agony over this desecration, which I was so powerless to prevent. But as I was thanking my stars that the matter had blown over with Bolingbroke's rejection, there occurred a most singular thing.

The figure on the lounge, with vast difficulty, sat up. To our amazement we beheld the bloated face of the Duke of Chartersea staring stupidly.

"Damme, Bully, you refushe bet like tha'!" he said. "I'll take doshen of 'em — doshen, egad. Gimme the book, Brooksh. Cursh Fox — lay thousand d—d provinshial never getsh 'er — I know —"

I sat very still, seized with a loathing beyond my power to describe to think that this was the man Mr. Manners was forcing her to marry. Fox laughed.

"Help his Grace to his coach," he said to two of the footmen.

"Kill fellow firsht!" cried his Grace, with his hand on his sword, and instantly fell over, and went sound asleep.

"His Grace has sent his coach home, your honour," said one of the men, respectfully. "The duke is very quarrelsome, sir."

"Put him in a chair, then," said Charles.

So they fearfully lifted his Grace, who was too far gone to resist, and carried him to a chair. And Mr. Fox bribed the chairmen with two guineas apiece, which he borrowed from me, to set his Grace down amongst the marketwomen at Covent Garden.

The next morning Banks found in my pockets something over seven hundred pounds more than I had had the day before.

I rose late, my head swimming with *mains* and *nicks*, and combinations of all the numbers under the dozen; debated whether or no I would go to Arlington Street, and decided that I had not the courage. Comyn settled it by coming in his cabriolet, proposed that we should get the air in the park, dine at the Cocoa Tree, and go afterwards to Lady Tankerville's drum-major, where Dolly would undoubtedly be.

"Now you are here, Richard," said his Lordship, with his accustomed bluntness, "and your sea-captain has relieved your Quixotic conscience, what the deuce do you intend to do? Win a thousand pounds every night at Brooks's, or improve your time and do your duty, and get Miss Manners out of his Grace's clutches? I'll warrant something will come of that matter this morning."

"I hope so," I said shortly.

Comyn looked at me sharply.

"Would you fight him?" he asked.

"If he gave me the chance."

His Lordship whistled. "Egad, then," said he, "I shall want to be there to see. In spite of his pudding-bag shape he handles the sword as well as any man in England. I have crossed with him at Angelo's. And he has a devilish tricky record, Richard."

I said nothing to that.

"Hope you do kill him," Comyn continued. "He deserves it richly. But that will be a cursed unpleasant way of settling the business, — unpleasant for you, unpleasant for her, and cursed unpleasant for him, too, I suppose. Can't you think of any other way of getting her? Ask Charles to give you a plan of campaign. You haven't any sense, and neither have I."

"Hang you, Jack, I have no hopes of getting her," I replied, for I was out of humour with myself that day. "In spite of what you say, I know she doesn't care a brass farthing to marry me. So let's drop that."

Comyn made a comic gesture of deprecation. I went on: —

"But I am going to stay here and find out the truth, though it may be a foolish undertaking. And if he is intimidating Mr. Manners —"

x

"You may count on me, and on Charles," said my Lord, generously; "and there are some others I know of. Gad! You made a dozen of friends and admirers by what you said last night, Richard. And his Grace has a few enemies. You will not lack support."

We dined very comfortably at the Cocoa Tree, where Comyn had made an appointment for me with two as diverting gentlemen as had ever been my lot to meet. My Lord Carlisle was the poet and scholar of the little clique which had been to Eton with Charles Fox, any member of which (so 'twas said) would have died for him. His Lordship, be it remarked in passing, was as lively a poet and scholar as can well be imagined. He had been recently *sobered*, so Comyn confided; which I afterwards discovered meant *married*. Charles Fox's word for the same was *fallen*. And I remembered that Jack had told me it was to visit Lady Carlisle at Castle Howard that Dorothy was going when she heard of my disappearance. Comyn's other guest was Mr. Topham Beauclerk, the macaroni friend of Dr. Johnson. He, too, had been recently married, but appeared no more *sobered* than his Lordship. Mr. Beauclerk's wife, by the way, was the beautiful Lady Diana Spencer, who had been divorced from Lord Bolingbroke, the *Bully* I had met the night before. These gentlemen seemed both well acquainted with Miss Manners, and vowed that none but American beauties would ever be the fashion in London more. Then we all drove to Lady Tankerville's drum-major near Chesterfield House.

"You will be wanting a word with her when she comes in," said Comyn, slyly divining. Poor fellow! I fear that I scarcely appreciated his feelings as to Dorothy, or the noble unselfishness of his friendship for me.

We sat aside in a recess of the lower hall, watching the throng as they passed: haughty dowagers, distorted in lead and disfigured in silk and feathers nodding at the ceiling; accomplished beaus of threescore or more, carefully mended for the night by their Frenchmen at home; young ladies in gay brocades with round skirts and stiff, pear-shaped bodices; and youngsters just learning to ogle and to handle their snuff-boxes. One by one their names were sent up and solemnly mouthed by the footman on the landing. At length, when we had all but given her up, Dorothy arrived. A hood of lavender silk heightened the oval of her face, and out from under it crept rebellious wisps of her dark hair. But she was very pale, and I noticed for the first time a worn expression that gave me a twinge of uneasiness. 'Twas then I caught sight of the duke, a surly stamp on his leaden features. And after him danced Mr. Manners. Dolly gave a little cry when she saw me.

"Oh! Richard, I am so glad you are here. I was wondering what had become of you. And Comyn, too." Whispering to me, "Mamma has had a letter from Mrs. Brice; your grandfather has been to walk in the garden."

"And Grafton?"

"She said nothing of your uncle," she replied, with a little shudder at the name; "but wrote that Mr. Carvel was said to be better. So there! your conscience need not trouble you for remaining. I am sure he would wish you to pay a visit home. And I have to scold you, sir. You have not been to Arlington Street for three whole days."

It struck me suddenly that her gayety was the same as that she had worn to my birthday party, scarce a year agone.

"Dolly, you are not well!" I said anxiously.

She flung her head saucily for answer. In the meantime his Grace, talking coldly to Comyn, had been looking unutterable thunders at me. I thought of him awaking in the dew at Covent Garden, and could scarce keep from laughing in his face. Mr. Marmaduke squirmed to the front.

"Morning, Richard," he said, with a marked cordiality. "Have you met the Duke of Chartersea? No! Your Grace, this is Mr. Richard Carvel. His family are dear friends of ours in the colonies."

To my great surprise, the duke saluted me quite civilly. But I had the feeling of facing a treacherous bull which would gore me as soon as ever my back was turned. He was always putting me in mind of a bull, with his short neck and heavy, hunched shoulders, — and with the ugly tinge of red in the whites of his eyes.

"Mr. Manners tells me you are to remain awhile in London, Mr. Carvel," he said, in his thick voice.

I took his meaning instantly, and replied in kind.

"Yes, your Grace, I have some business to attend to here."

"Ah," he answered; "then I shall see you again."

"Probably, sir," said I.

His Lordship watched this thrust and parry with an ill-concealed delight. Dorothy's face was impassive, expressionless. As the duke turned to mount the stairs, he stumbled clumsily across a young man coming to pay his respects to Miss Manners, and his Grace went sprawling against the wall.

"Confound you, sir!" he cried.

For the ducal temper was no respecter of presences. Then a title was a title to those born lower, and the young man plainly had a vast honour for a coronet.

"I beg your Grace's pardon," said he.

"Who the deuce is he?" demanded the duke petulantly of Mr. Manners, thereby setting the poor little man all a-tremble.

"Why, why,—" he replied, searching for his spyglass.

For an instant Dolly's eyes shot scorn. Chartersea had clearly seen and heeded that signal before.

"The gentleman is a friend of mine," she said.

Tho' I were put out of the Garden of Eden as a consequence, I itched to have it out with his Grace then and there. I knew that I was bound to come into collision with him sooner or later. Such, indeed, was my mission in London. But Dorothy led the way upstairs, a spot of colour burning each of her cheeks. The stream of guests had been arrested until the hall was packed, and the curious were peering over the rail above.

"Lord, wasn't she superb!" exclaimed Comyn, exultingly, as we followed. In the drawing-room the buzzing about the card tables was hushed a moment as she went in. But I soon lost sight of her, thanks to Comyn. He drew me on from group to group, and I was duly presented to a score of Lady So-and-sos and honourable misses, most of whom had titles, but little else. Mammas searched their memories, and suddenly discovered that they had heard their parents speak of my grandfather. But, as it was a fair presumption that most colonial gentlemen made a visit home at least once in their lives, I did not allow the dust to get into my eyes. I was invited to dinners, and fairly showered with invitations to balls and drums and garden parties. I was twitted about the Beauty, most often with only a thin coating of amiability covering the spite of the remark. In short, if my head had not been so heavily laden with other matters, it might well have become light under the strain. Had I been ambitious to enter the arena I should have had but little trouble, since eligibility then might be reduced to guineas and another element not moral. I was the only heir of one of the richest men in the colony, vouched for by the Manners and taken up by Mr. Fox and my Lord Comyn. Inquiries are not pushed farther. I could not help seeing the hardness of it all, or refrain from contrasting my situation with that of the penniless outcast I had been but a little time before. The gilded rooms, the hundred yellow candles multiplied by the mirrors, the powder, the perfume, the jewels,—all put me in mind of the poor devils I had left wasting away their lives in Castle Yard. They, too, had had their times of prosperity, their friends who had faded with the first waning of fortune. Some of them had known what it was to be fawned over. And how many of these careless, flitting men of fashion I looked upon could feel the ground firm beneath their feet; or could say with certainty what a change of ministers, or one wild night at White's or Almack's, would bring forth? Verily, one must have seen the under side of life to know the upper!

Presently I was sought out by Mr. Topham Beauclerk, who had heard of the episode below and wished to hear more. He swore at the duke.

"He will be run through some day, and serve him jolly right," said he. "Bet you twenty pounds Charles Fox does it! His Grace knows he has the courage to fight him."

"The courage!" I repeated.

"Yes. Angelo says the duke has diabolical skill. And then he won't fight fair. He killed young Atwater on a foul, you know. Slipped on the wet grass, and Chartersea had him pinned before he caught his guard. But there is Lady Di a-calling, a-calling."

"Do all the women cheat in America too?" asked Topham, as we approached.

I thought of my Aunt Caroline, and laughed.

"Some," I answered.

"They will game, d—n 'em," said Topham, as tho' *he* had never gamed in his life. "And they will cheat, till a man has to close his eyes to keep from seeing their pretty hands. And they will cry, egad, oh so touchingly, if the luck goes against them in spite of it all. Only last week I had to forgive Mrs. Farnham an hundred guineas. She said she'd lost her pin-money twice over, and was like to have wept her eyes out."

Thus primed in Topham's frank terms, I knew what to expect. And I found to my amusement he had not overrun the truth. I lost like a stoic, saw nothing, and discovered the straight road to popularity.

"The dear things expect us to make it up at the clubs," whispered he.

I discovered how he had fallen in love with his wife, Lady Diana, and pitied poor Bolingbroke heartily for having lost her. She was then in her prime,—a beauty, a wit, and a great lady, with a dash of the humanities about her that brought both men and women to her feet.

"You must come to see me, Mr. Carvel," said she. "I wish to talk to you of Dorothy."

"Your Ladyship believes me versed in no other subject?" I asked.

"None other worth the mention," she replied instantly; "Topham tells me you can talk horses, and that mystery of mysteries, American politics. But look at Miss Manners now. I'll warrant she is making Sir Charles see to his laurels, and young Stavordale is struck dumb."

I looked up quickly and beheld Dolly surrounded by a circle of admirers.

"Mark the shot strike!" Lady Di continued, between the deals; "that time Chartersea went down. I fancy he is bowled over rather often," she said slyly. "What a brute it is. And they say that that little woman she has for a father imagines a union with the duke will redound to his glory."

"They say," remarked Mrs. Meynel, sitting next me, "that the duke has thumbscrews of some kind on Mr. Manners."

"Miss Manners is able to take care of herself," said Topham.

"*On dit*, that she has already refused as many dukes as did her Grace of Argyle," said Mrs. Meynel.

I had lost track of the cards, and knew I was losing prodigiously. But my eyes went back again and again to the group by the doorway, where Dolly was holding court and dispensing justice, and perchance injustice. The circle increased. Ribands, generals whose chests were covered with medals of valour, French noblemen, and foreign ambassadors stopped for a word with the Beauty and passed on their way, some smiling, some reflecting, to make room for others. I overheard from the neighbouring tables a spiteful protest that a young upstart from the colonies should turn Lady Tankerville's drum into a levee. My ears tingled as I listened. But not a feathered parrot in the carping lot of them could deny that Miss Manners had beauty and wit enough to keep them all at bay. Hers was not an English beauty: every line of her face and pose of her body proclaimed her of that noble type of Maryland women, distinctly American, over which many Englishmen before and since have lost their heads and hearts.

"Egad!" exclaimed Mr. Storer, who was looking on; "she's already defeated some of the Treasury Bench, and bless me if she isn't rating North himself."

Half the heads in the room were turned toward Miss Manners, who was exchanging jokes with the Prime Minister of Great Britain. I saw a corpulent man, ludicrously like the King's pictures, with bulging gray eyes that seemed to take in nothing. And this was North, upon whose conduct with the King depended the fate of our America. Good-natured he was, and his laziness was painfully apparent. He had the reputation of going to sleep standing, like a horse.

"But the Beauty contrives to keep him awake," said Storer.

"If you stay among us, Mr. Carvel," said Topham, "she will get you a commissionership for the asking."

"Look," cried Lady Di, "there comes Mr. Fox, the precocious, the irresistible. Were he in the Bible, we should read of him passing the time of day with King Solomon."

"Or instructing Daniel in the art of lion-taming," put in Mrs. Meynel.

There was Mr. Fox in truth, and the Beauty's face lighted up at sight of him. And presently, when Lord North had made his bow and passed on, he was seen to lead her out of the room, leaving her circle to go to pieces, like an empire without a head.

CHAPTER XXXIII

DRURY LANE

AFTER a night spent in making resolutions, I set out for Arlington Street, my heart beating a march, as it had when I went thither on my arrival in London. Such was my excitement that I was near to being run over in Piccadilly like many another country gentleman, and roundly cursed by a wagoner for my stupidity. I had a hollow bigness within me, half of joy, half of pain, that sent me onward with ever increasing steps and a whirling storm of contradictions in my head. Now it was: Dolly loved me in spite of all the great men in England. Why, otherwise, had she come to the sponging-house? Berating myself: had her affection been other than that of a life-long friendship she would not have come an inch. But why had she made me stay in London? Why had she spoken so to Comyn? What interpretation might be put upon a score of little acts of hers that came a-flooding to mind, each a sacred treasure of memory? A lover's interpretation, forsooth. Fie, Richard! what presumption to think that you, a raw lad, should have a chance in such a field! You have yet, by dint of hard knocks and buffets, to learn the world.

By this I had come in sight of her house, and suddenly I trembled like a green horse before a cannon. My courage ran out so fast that I was soon left without any, and my legs had carried me as far as St. James's Church before I could bring them up. Then I was sure, for the first time, that she did not love me. In front of the church I halted, reflecting that I had not remained in England with any hope of it, but rather to discover the truth about Chartersea's actions, and to save her, if it were possible. I turned back once more, and now got as far as the knocker, and lifted it as a belfry was striking the hour of noon. I think I would have fled again had not the door been immediately opened.

Once more I found myself in the room looking out over the Park, the French windows open to the balcony, the sunlight flowing in with the spring-scented air. On the table was lying a little leather book, stamped with gold,— her prayer-book. Well I remembered it! I opened it, to read: "Dorothy, from her Mother. Annapolis, Christmas, 1768." The sweet vista of the past stretched before my eyes. I saw her, on such a Mayday as this, walking to St. Anne's under the grand old trees, their budding leaves casting a delicate tracery at her feet. I followed her up the aisle until she disappeared in the high pew, and then I sat beside my grandfather and thought of her, nor listened to a word of Mr. Allen's sermon. Why had they ever taken her to London?

When she came in I sought her face anxiously. She was still pale; and I thought, despite her smile, that a trace of sadness lingered in her eyes.

"At last, sir, you have come," she said severely. "Sit down and give an account of yourself at once. You have been behaving very badly."

"Dorothy—"

"Pray don't 'Dorothy' me, sir. But explain where you have been for this week past."

"But, Dolly—"

"You pretend to have some affection for your old playmate, but you do not trouble yourself to come to see her."

"Indeed, you do me wrong."

"Do you wrong! You prefer to gallivant about town with Comyn and Charles Fox, and with all those wild gentlemen who go to Brooks's. Nay, I have heard of your goings-on. I shall write to Mr. Carvel to-day, and advise him to send for you. And tell him that you won a thousand pounds in one night—"

"It was only seven hundred," I interrupted sheepishly. I thought she smiled faintly.

"And will probably lose twenty thousand before you have

done. And I shall say to him that you have dared to make bold rebel speeches to a Lord of the Admiralty and to some of the King's supporters. I shall tell your grandfather you are disgracing him."

"Rebel speeches!" I cried.

"Yes, rebel speeches at Almack's. Who ever heard of such a thing! No doubt I shall hear next of your going to a drawing-room and instructing his Majesty how to subdue the colonies. And then, sir, you will be sent to the Tower, and I shan't move a finger to get you out."

"Who told you of this, Dolly?" I demanded.

"Mr. Fox, himself, for one. He thought it so good, — or so bad, — that he took me aside last night at Lady Tankerville's, asked me why I had let you out of Castle Yard, and told me I must manage to curb your tongue. I replied that I had about as much influence with you as I have with Dr. Franklin."

I laughed.

"I saw Fox lead you off," I said.

"Oh, you did, did you!" she retorted. "But you never once came near me yourself, save when I chanced to meet you in the hall, tho' I was there a full three hours."

"How could I!" I exclaimed. "You were surrounded by prime ministers and ambassadors, and Heaven knows how many other great people."

"When you wish to do anything, Richard, you usually find a way."

"Nay," I answered, despairing, "I can never explain anything to you, Dolly. Your tongue is too quick for mine."

"Why didn't you go home with your captain?" she asked mockingly.

"Do you know why I stayed?"

"I suppose because you want to be a gay spark and taste of the pleasures of London. That is, what you men are pleased to call pleasures. I can think of no other reason."

"There is another," I said desperately.

"Ah," said Dolly. And in her old aggravating way she got up and stood in the window, looking out over the park. I rose and stood beside her, my very temples throbbing.

"We have no such springs at home," she said. "But oh, I wish I were at Wilmot House to-day!"

"There is another reason," I repeated. My voice sounded far away, like that of another. I saw the colour come into her cheeks again, slowly. The southwest wind, with a whiff of the channel salt in it, blew the curtains at our backs.

"You have a conscience, Richard," she said gently, without turning. "So few of us have."

I was surprised. Nor did I know what to make of that: there were so many meanings.

"You are wild," she continued, "and impulsive, as they say your father was. But he was a man I should have honoured. He stood firm beside his friends. He made his enemies fear him. All strong men must have enemies, I suppose. They must make them."

I looked at her, troubled, puzzled, but burning at her praise of Captain Jack.

"Dolly," I cried, "you are not well. Why won't you come back to Maryland?"

She did not reply to that. Then she faced me suddenly.

"Richard, I know now why you insisted upon going back. It was because you would not desert your sea-captain. Comyn and Mr. Fox have told me, and they admire you for it as much as I."

What language is worthy to describe her as she was then in that pose, with her head high, as she was wont to ride over the field after the hounds. Hers was in truth no beauty of stone, but the beauty of force, — of life itself.

"Dorothy," I cried; "Dorothy, I stayed because I love you. There, I have said it again, what has not passed my lips since we were children. What has been in my heart ever since."

I stopped, awed. For she had stepped back, out on the balcony. She hid her head in her hands, and I saw her breast shaken as with sobs. I waited what seemed a day, — a year. Then she raised her face and looked at me through the tears shining in her eyes.

"Richard," she said sadly, "why, why did you ever tell me? Why can we not always be playmates?"

The words I tried to say choked me. I could not speak for sorrow, for very bitterness. And yet I might have known! I dared not look at her again.

"Dear Richard," I heard her say, "God alone understands how it hurts me to give you pain. Had I only foreseen —"

"Had you only foreseen," I said quickly.

"I should never have let you speak."

Her words came steadily, but painfully. And when I raised my eyes she met them bravely.

"You must have seen," I cried. "These years I have loved you, nor could I have hidden it if I had wished. But I have little to offer you," I went on cruelly, for I knew not what I said; "you who may have English lands and titles for the consenting. I was a fool."

Her tears started again. And at sight of them I was seized with such remorse that I could have bitten my tongue in two.

"Forgive me, Dorothy, if you can," I implored. "I did not mean it. Nor did I presume to think you loved me. I have adored, — I shall be content to adore from far below. And I stayed, — I stayed that I might save you if a danger threatened."

"Danger!" she exclaimed, catching her breath.

"I will come to the point," I said. "I stayed to save you from the Duke of Chartersea."

She grasped the balcony rail, and I think would have fallen but for my arm. Then she straightened, and only the quiver of her lip marked the effort.

"To save me from the Duke of Chartersea?" she said, so coldly that my conviction was shaken. "Explain yourself, sir."

"You cannot love him!" I cried, amazed.

She flashed upon me a glance I shall never forget.

"Richard Carvel," she said, "you have gone too far. Though you have been my friend all my life, there are some things which even you cannot say to me."

And she left me abruptly and went into the house, her head flung back. And I followed in a tumult of mortification and wounded pride, in such a state of dejection that I wished I had never been born. But hers was a nature of surprises, and impulsive, like my own. Beside the cabinet she turned, calm again, all trace of anger vanished from her face. Drawing a hawthorn sprig from a porcelain vase I had given her, she put it in my hand.

"Let us forget this, Richard," said she; "we have both been very foolish."

* * * * * *

Forget, indeed! Unless Heaven had robbed me of reason, had torn the past from me at a single stroke, I could not have forgotten. When I reached my lodgings I sent the anxious Banks about his business and threw myself in a great chair before the window, the chair *she* had chosen. Strange to say, I had no sensation save numbness. The time must have been about two of the clock: I took no account of it. I recall Banks coming timidly back with the news that two gentlemen had called. I bade him send them away. Would my honour not have Mrs. Marble cook my dinner, and be dressed for Lady Pembroke's ball? I sent him off again, harshly.

After a long while the slamming of a coach door roused me, and I was straightway seized with such an agony of mind that I could have cried aloud. 'Twas like the pain of blood flowing back into a frozen limb. Darkness was fast gathering as I reached the street and began to walk madly. Word by word I rehearsed the scene in the drawing-room over the Park, but I could not think calmly, for the pain of it. Little by little I probed, writhing, until far back in my boyhood I was tearing at the dead roots of that cherished plant, which was the Hope of Her Love. It had grown with my own life, and now with its death to-day I felt that I had lost all that was dear to me. Then, in the midst of this abject self-pity, I was stricken with shame. I thought of Comyn, who had borne the same misfortune as a man should. Had his pain been the less because he had not loved her from childhood? Like Comyn, I resolved to labour for her happiness.

What hour of the night it was I know not when a man touched me on the shoulder, and I came to myself with a start. I was in a narrow street lined by hideous houses, their windows glaring with light. Each seemed a skull, with rays darting from its grinning eye-holes. Within I caught glimpses of debauchery that turned me sick. Ten paces away three women and a man were brawling, the low angry tones of his voice mingling with the screeches of their Billingsgate. Muffled figures were passing and repassing unconcernedly, some entering the houses, others coming out, and a handsome coach, without arms and with a footman in plain livery, lumbered along and stopped farther on. All this I remarked before I took notice of him who had intercepted me, and demanded what he wanted.

"Hey, Bill!" he cried with an oath to a man who stood on the steps opposite; "'ere's a soft un as has put 'is gill in."

The man responded, and behind him came two more of the same feather, and suddenly I found myself surrounded by an ill-smelling crowd of flashy men and tawdry women. They jostled me, and I reached for my sword, to make the discovery that I had forgotten it. Regaining my full senses, I struck the man nearest me a blow that sent him sprawling in the dirt. A blade gleamed under the sickly light of the fish-oil lamp overhead, but a man crashed through from behind and caught the ruffian's sword-arm and flung him back in the kennel.

"The watch!" he cried, "the watch!"

They vanished like rats into their holes at the shout, leaving me standing alone with him. The affair had come and gone so quickly that I scarce caught my breath.

"Pardon, sir," he said, knuckling, "but I followed you."

It was Banks. For a second time he had given me an affecting example of his faithfulness. I forgot that he was my servant, and I caught his hand and pressed it.

"You have saved my life at the risk of your own," I said; "I shall not forget it."

But Banks had been too well trained to lose sight of his position. He merely tipped his hat again and said imperturbably:—

"Best get out of here, your honour. They'll be coming again directly."

"Where are we?" I asked.

"Drury Lane, sir," he replied, giving me just the corner of a glance; "shall I fetch a coach, sir?"

No, I preferred to walk. Before we had turned into Long Acre I had seen all of this Sodom of London that it should be given a man to see, if indeed we must behold some of the bestiality of this world. Here alone, in the great city, high and low were met equal. Sin levels rank. The devil makes no choice between my lord and his kitchen wench who has gone astray. Here, in Sodom, painted vice had lain for an hundred years and bred half the crime of a century. How many souls had gone hence in that time to meet their Maker! Some of these brazen creatures who leered at me had known — how long ago! — a peaceful home and a mother's love; had been lured in their innocence to this place of horrors, never to leave it until death mercifully overtakes them. Others, having fallen, had been driven hither by a cruel world that shelters all save the helpless, that forgives all save the truly penitent. I shuddered as I thought of Mr. Hogarth's prints, which, in the library in Marlboro' Street at home, had had so little meaning for me. Verily he had painted no worse than the reality.

As I strode homeward, my own sorrow subdued by the greater sorrow I had looked upon, the craving I had had to be alone was gone, and I would have locked arms with a turnspit. I called to Banks, who was behind at a respectful distance, and bade him come talk to me. His presence of mind in calling on the watch had made even a greater impression upon me than his bravery. I told him that he should have ten pounds, and an increase of wages. And I asked him where I had gone after leaving Dover Street, and why he had followed me. He answered this latter question first. He had seen gentlemen in the same state, or something like it, before: his Lordship, his late master, after he had fought with Mr. Onslow, of the Guards, and Sir Edward Minturn, when he had lost an inheritance and a reversion at Brooks's, and was forced to give over his engagement to marry the Honourable Miss Swift.

"Lord, sir," he said, "but that was a sad case, as set all London agog. And Sir Edward shot hisself at Portsmouth not a se'nnight after."

And he relapsed into silence, no doubt longing to ask the cause of my own affliction. Presently he surprised me by saying: —

"And I might make so bold, Mr. Carvel, I would like to tell your honour something."

I nodded. And he hawed awhile and then burst out: —

"Your honour must know then that I belongs to the footman's club in Berkeley Square, where I meets all the servants o' quality — "

"Yes," I said, wondering what footman's tale he had to tell.

"And Whipple, he's a hintimate o' mine, sir." He stopped again.

"And who may Whipple be?"

"With submission, sir. Whipple's his Grace o' Chartersea's man — and, you'll forgive me, sir — Whipple owns his Grace is prodigious ugly, an' killed young Mr. Atwater unfair, some think. Whipple says he would give notice had he not promised the old duke — "

"Drat Whipple!" I cried.

"Yes, sir. To be sure, sir. His Grace was in a bloody rage when he found hisself in a fruit bin at Covent Garding. An' two redbreasts had carried him to the round house, sir, afore they discovered his title. An' since his Grace ha' said time an' time afore Whipple, that he'll ha' Mr. Carvel's heart for that, and has called you most disgustin' bad names, sir. An' Whipple he says to me: 'Banks, drop your marster a word, an' you get the chance. His Grace'll speak him fair to's face, but let him look behind him.'"

"I thank you again, Banks. I shall bear in mind your devotion," I replied. "But I had nothing to do with sending the duke to Covent Garden."

"Ay, sir, so I tells Whipple."

"Pray, how did you know?" I demanded curiously.

"Lord, sir! All the servants at Almack's is friends o' mine," says he. "But Whipple declares his Grace will be sworn you did it, sir, tho' the Lord Mayor hisself made deposition 'twas not."

"Then mark me, Banks, you are not to talk of this."

Y

"Oh, Lord, no, your honour," he said, as he fell back. But I was not so sure of his discretion as of his loyalty.

And so I was led to perceive that I was not to be the only aggressor in the struggle that was to come. That his Grace did me the honour to look upon me as an obstacle. And that he intended to seize the first opportunity to make way with me, by fair means or foul.

CHAPTER XXXIV

HIS GRACE MAKES ADVANCES

The next morning I began casting about as to what I should do next. There was no longer any chance of getting at the secret from Dorothy, if secret there were. Whilst I am ruminating comes a great battling at the street door, and Jack Comyn blew in like a gust of wind, rating me soundly for being a lout and a blockhead.

"Zooks!" he cried, "I danced the soles off my shoes trying to get in here yesterday, and I hear you were moping all the time, and paid me no more attention than I had been a dog scratching at the door. What! and have you fallen out with my lady?"

I confessed the whole matter to him. He was not to be resisted. He called to Banks for a cogue of Nantsey, and swore amazingly at what he was pleased to term the inscrutability of woman, offering up consolation by the wholesale. The incident, he said, but strengthened his conviction that Mr. Manners had appealed to Dorothy to save him. "And then," added his Lordship, facing me with absolute fierceness, "and then, Richard, why the devil did she weep? There were no tears when I made my avowal. I tell you, man, that the whole thing points but the one way. She loves you. I swear it by the rood."

I could not help laughing, and he stood looking at me with such a whimsical expression that I rose and flung my arms around him.

"Jack, Jack!" I cried, "what a fraud you are! Do you remember the argument you used when you had got me out of the sponging-house? Quoting you, all I had to do was to put

Dorothy to the proof, and she would toss Mr. Marmaduke and his honour broadcast. Now I have confessed myself, and what is the result? Nay, your theory is gone up in vapour."

"Then why," cried his Lordship, hotly, "why before refusing me did she demand to know whether you had been in love with Patty Swain? 'Sdeath! you put me in mind of a woman upon stilts — a man has always to be walking alongside her with encouragement handy. And when a proud creature such as our young lady breaks down as she hath done, 'tis clear as skylight there is something wrong. And as for Mr. Manners, Hare overheard a part of a pow-wow 'twixt him and the duke at the Bedford Arms, — and Chartersea has all but owned in some of his drunken fits that our little fop is in his power."

"Then she is in love with some one else," I said.

"I tell you she is not," said Comyn, still more emphatically; "and you can write that down in red in your table book. Gossip has never been able to connect her name with that of any man save yours, when she went for you in Castle Yard. And, gemini, gossip is like water, and will get in if a crack shows. When the Marquis of Wells was going to Arlington Street once every day, she sent him about his business in a fortnight."

Despite Comyn's most unselfish optimism, I could see no light. And in the recklessness that so often besets youngsters of my temper, on like occasions, I went off to Newmarket next day with Mr. Fox and Lord Ossory, in his Lordship's travelling-chaise and four. I spent a very gay week trying to forget Miss Dolly. I was the loser by some three hundred pounds, in addition to what I expended and loaned to Mr. Fox. This young gentleman was then beginning to accumulate at Newmarket a most execrable stud. He lost prodigiously, but seemed in no wise disturbed thereby. I have never known a man who took his ill-luck with such a stoical nonchalance. Not so while the heat was on. As I write, a most ridiculous recollection rises of Charles dragging his Lordship and me and all who were with him to that part of the course where the race was highest, where he would act like a madman; blowing and perspiring, and whipping and swearing all at a time, and rising up and down as if the horse was throwing him.

At Newmarket I had the good — or ill — fortune to meet that incorrigible rake and profligate, my Lord of March and Ruglen. For him the goddess of Chance had smiled, and he was in the most complaisant humour. I was presented to his Grace, the Duke of Grafton, whose name I had no reason to love, and invited to Wakefield Lodge. We went instead, Mr. Fox and I, to Ampthill, Lord Ossory's seat, with a merry troop. And then we had more racing; and whist and quinze and pharaoh and hazard, until I was obliged to write another draft upon Mr. Dix to settle the vails: and picquet in the travelling-chaise all the way to London. Dining at Brooks's, we encountered Fitzpatrick and Comyn and my Lord Carlisle.

"Now how much has Charles borrowed of you, Mr. Carvel?" demanded Fitzpatrick, as we took our seats.

"I'll lay ten guineas that Charles has him mortgaged this day month, though he owns as much land as William Penn, and is as rich as Fordyce."

Comyn demanded where the devil I had been, though he knew perfectly. He was uncommonly silent during dinner, and then asked me if I had heard the news. I told him I had heard none. He took me by the sleeve, to the quiet amusement of the company, and led me aside.

"Curse you, Richard," says he; "you have put me in such a temper that I vow I'll fling you over. You profess to love her, and yet you go betting to Newmarket and carousing to Ampthill when she is ill."

"Ill!" I said, catching my breath.

"Ay! That hurts, does it? Yes, ill, I say. She was missed at Lady Pembroke's that Friday you had the scene with her, and at Lady Ailesbury's on Saturday. On Monday morning, when I come to you for tidings, you are off watching Charles make an ass of himself at Newmarket."

"And how is she now, Comyn?" I asked, catching him by the arm.

"You may go yourself and see, and be cursed, Richard Carvel. She is in trouble, and you are pleasure-seeking in the country. Damme! you deserve richly to lose her."

Calling for my greatcoat, and paying no heed to the jeers of the company for leaving before the toasts and the play, I fairly ran to Arlington Street. I was in a passion of remorse. Comyn had been but just. Granting, indeed, that she had refused to marry me, was that any reason why I should desert my life-long friend and playmate? A hundred little tokens of her affection for me rose to mind, and last of all that rescue from Castle Yard in the face of all Mayfair. And in that hour of darkness the conviction that something was wrong came back upon me with redoubled force. Her lack of colour, her feverish actions, and the growing slightness of her figure, all gave me a pang, as I connected them with that scene on the balcony over the Park.

The house was darkened, and a coach was in front of it.

"Yessir," said the footman, "Miss Manners has been quite ill. She is now some better, and Dr. James is with her. Mrs. Manners begs company will excuse her."

And Mr. Marmaduke? The man said, with as near a grin as he ever got, that the marster was gone to Mrs. Cornelys's assembly. As I turned away, sick at heart, the physician, in his tie-wig and scarlet cloak, came out, and I stopped him. He was a testy man, and struck the stone an impatient blow with his staff.

"'Od's life, sir. I am besieged day and night by you young gentlemen. I begin to think of sending a daily card to Almack's."

"Sir, I am an old friend of Miss Manners," I replied, "having grown up with her in Maryland—"

"Are you Mr. Carvel?" he demanded abruptly, taking his hat from his arm.

"Yes," I answered, surprised. In the gleam of the portico lanthorn he scrutinized me for several seconds.

"There are some troubles of the mind which are beyond the power of physic to remedy, Mr. Carvel," said he. "She has mentioned your name, sir, and you are to judge of my meaning. Your most obedient, sir. Good night, sir."

And he got into his coach, leaving me standing where I was, bewildered.

That same fear of being alone, which has driven many a man to his cups, sent me back to Brooks's for company. I found Fox and Comyn seated at a table in the corner of the drawing-room, for once not playing, but talking earnestly. Their expressions when they saw me betrayed what my own face must have been.

"What is it?" cried Comyn, half rising; "is she — is she —"

"No, she is better," I said.

He looked relieved.

"You must have frightened him badly, Jack," said Fox.

I flung myself into a chair, and Fox proposed whist, something unusual for him. Comyn called for cards, and was about to go in search of a fourth, when we all three caught sight of the Duke of Chartersea in the door, surveying the room with a cold leisure. His eye paused when in line with us, and we were seized with astonishment to behold him making in our direction.

"Squints!" exclaimed Mr. Fox, "now what the devil can the hound want?"

"To pull your nose for sending him to market," my Lord suggested.

Fox laughed coolly.

"Lay you twenty he doesn't, Jack," he said.

His Grace plainly had some business with us, and I hoped he was coming to force the fighting. The pieces had ceased to rattle on the round mahogany table, and every head in the room seemed turned our way, for the Covent Garden story was well known. Chartersea laid his hand on the back of our fourth chair, greeted us with some ceremony, and said something which, under the circumstances, was almost unheard of in that day: —

"If you stand in need of one, gentlemen, I should deem it an honour."

The situation had in it enough spice for all of us. We welcomed him with alacrity. The cards were cut, and it fell

to his Grace to deal, which he did very prettily, despite his
heavy hands. He drew Charles Fox, and they won steadily.
The conversation between deals was anywhere; on the virtue
of Morello cherries for the gout, to which his Grace was
already subject; on Mr. Fox's *Ariel*, and why he had not
carried Sandwich's cup at Newmarket; on the advisability of
putting three-year-olds on the track; in short, on a dozen
small topics of the kind. At length, when Comyn and I had
lost some fifty pounds between us, Chartersea threw down the
cards.

"My coach waits *to-night*, gentlemen," said he, with some
sort of an accent that did not escape us. "It would give me
the greatest pleasure and you will sup with me in Hanover
Square."

CHAPTER XXXV

IN WHICH MY LORD BALTIMORE APPEARS

His Grace's offer was accepted with a readiness he could scarce have expected, and we all left the room in the midst of a buzz of comment. We knew well that the matter was not so haphazard as it appeared, and on the way to Hanover Square Comyn more than once stepped on my toe, and I answered the pressure. Our coats and canes were taken by the duke's lackeys when we arrived. We were shown over the house. Until now — so his Grace informed us — it had not been changed since the time of the fourth duke, who, as we doubtless knew, had been an ardent supporter of the Hanoverian succession. The rooms were high-panelled and furnished in the German style, as was the fashion when the Square was built. But some were stripped and littered with scaffolding and plaster, new and costly marble mantels were replacing the wood, and an Italian of some renown was decorating the ceilings. His Grace appeared to be at some pains that the significance of these improvements should not be lost upon us; was constantly appealing to Mr. Fox's taste on this or that feature. But those fishy eyes of his were so alert that we had not even opportunity to wink. It was wholly patent, in brief, that the Duke of Chartersea meant to be married, and had brought Charles and Comyn hither with a purpose. For me he would have put himself out not an inch had he not understood that my support came from those quarters.

He tempered off this exhibition by showing us a collection of pottery famous in England, that had belonged to the fifth duke, his father. Every piece of it, by the way, afterwards brought an enormous sum at auction. Supper was served in a warm little room of oak. The game was from Derresley Manor, the duke's Nottinghamshire seat, and the wine, so he told us, was some of fifty bottles of rare Chinon he had inherited. Melted rubies it was indeed, of the sort which had quickened the blood of many a royal gathering at Blois and Amboise and Chenonceaux, — the distilled peasant song of the Loire valley. In it many a careworn crown had tasted the purer happiness of the lowly. Our restraint gave way under its influence. His Grace lost for the moment his deformities, and Mr. Fox made us laugh until our sides ached again. His Lordship told many a capital yarn, and my own wit was afterwards said to be astonishing, though I can recall none of it to support the affirmation.

Not a word or even a hint of Dorothy had been uttered, nor did Chartersea so much as refer to his Covent Garden experience. At length, when some half dozen of the wine was gone, and the big oak clock had struck two, the talk lapsed. It was Charles Fox, of course, who threw the spark into the powder box.

"We were speaking of hunting, Chartersea," he said. "Did you ever know George Wrottlesey, of the Suffolk branch?"

"No," said his Grace, very innocent.

"No! 'Od's whips and spurs, I'll be sworn I never saw a man to beat him for reckless riding. He would take five bars any time, egad, and sit any colt that was ever foaled. The Wrottleseys were poor as weavers then, with the Jews coming down in the wagon from London and hanging round the hall gates. But the old squire had plenty of good hunters in the stables, and haunches on the board, and a cellar that was like the widow's cruse of oil, or barrel of meal — or whatever she had. All the old man had to do to lose a guinea was to lay it on a card. He never nicked in his life, so they say. Well, young George got after a rich tea-merchant's daughter who had come into the country near by. 'Slife! she was a saucy jade, and devilish pretty. Such a face! so Stavordale vowed, and such a neck! and such eyes! so innocent, so ravishingly innocent. But she knew cursed well George was after the bank deposit, and kept him galloping. And when he got a view, halloa, egad! she was stole away again, and no scent.

"One morning George was out after the hounds with Stavordale, who told me the story, and a lot of fellows who had come over from Newmarket. He was upon *Aftermath*, the horse that Foley bought for five hundred pounds and was a colt then. Of course he left the field out of sight behind. He made for a gap in the park wall (faith! there was no lack of 'em), but the colt refused, and over went George and plumped into a cart of winter apples some farmer's sot was taking to Bury Saint Edmunds to market. The fall knocked the sense out of George, for he hasn't much, and Stavordale thinks he must have struck a stake as he went in. Anyway, the apples rolled over on top of him, and the drunkard on the seat never woke up, i' faith. And so they came to town.

"It so chanced, egad, that the devil sent Miss Tea Merchant to Bury to buy apples. She amused herself at playing country gentlewoman while papa worked all week in the city. She saw the cart in the market, and ate three (for she had the health of a barmaid), and bid in the load, and George with it. 'Pon my soul! she did. They found his boots first. And the lady said, before all the grinning Johns and Willums, that since she had bought him she supposed she would have to keep him. And, by Gad's life! she has got him yet, which is a deal stranger."

Even the duke laughed. For, as Fox told it, the story was irresistible. But it came as near to being a wanton insult as a reference to his Grace's own episode might. The red came slowly back into his eye. Fox stared vacantly, as was his habit when he had done or said something especially daring. And Comyn and I waited, straining and expectant, like boys who have prodded a wild beast and stand ready for the spring. There was a metallic ring in the duke's voice as he spoke.

"I have heard, Mr. Carvel, that you can ride any mount offered you."

"'Od's, and so he can!" cried Jack. "I'll take oath on that."

"I will lay you an hundred guineas, my Lord," says his Grace, very off-hand, "that Mr. Carvel does not sit Baltimore's Pollux above twenty minutes."

"Done!" says Jack, before I could draw breath.

"I'll take your Grace for another hundred," added Mr. Fox, calmly.

"It seems to me, your Grace," I cried, angry all at once, "it seems to me that I am the one to whom you should address your wagers. I am not a jockey, to be put up at your whim, and to give you the chance to lose money."

Chartersea swung around my way.

"Your pardon, Mr. Carvel," said he, very coolly, very politely; "yours is the choice of the wager. And you reject it, the others must be called off."

"'Slife! I *double* it!" I said hotly, "provided the horse is alive, and will stand up."

"Devilish well put, Richard!" Mr. Fox exclaimed, casting off his restraint.

"I give you my word the horse is alive, sir," he answered, with a mock bow; "'twas only yesterday that he killed his groom, at Hampstead."

A few moments of silence followed this revelation. It was Charles Fox who spoke first.

"I make no doubt that your Grace, as a man of honour,"— he emphasized the word forcibly,—"will not refuse to ride the horse for another twenty minutes, provided Mr. Carvel is successful. And I will lay your Grace another hundred that you are thrown, or run away with."

Truly, to cope with a wit like Mr. Fox's, the duke had need for a longer head. He grew livid as he perceived how neatly he had been snared in his own trap.

"Done!" he cried loudly; "done, gentlemen. It only remains to hit upon time and place for the contest. I go to York to-morrow, to be back this day fortnight. And if you will do me the favour of arranging with Baltimore for the horse, I shall be obliged. I believe he intends selling it to Astley, the showman."

"And are we to keep it?" asks Mr. Fox.

"I am dealing with men of honour," says the duke, with a bow: "I need have no better assurance that the horse will not be ridden in the interval."

MY LORD BALTIMORE APPEARS 333

"'Od so!" said Comyn, when we were out; "very handsome of him. But I would not say as much for his Grace." And Mr. Fox declared that the duke was no coward, but all other epithets known might be called him. "A very diverting evening, Richard," said he; "let's to your apartments and have a bowl, and talk it over."

And thither we went.

I did not sleep much that night, but 'twas of Dolly I thought rather than of Chartersea. I was abroad early, and over to inquire in Arlington Street, where I found she had passed a good night. And I sent Banks a-hunting for some violets to send her, for I knew she loved that flower.

Between ten and eleven Mr. Fox and Comyn and I set out for Baltimore House. When you go to London, my dears, you will find a vast difference in the neighbourhood of Bloomsbury from what it was that May morning in 1770. Great Russell Street was all a sweet fragrance of gardens, mingling with the smell of the fields from the open country to the north. We drove past red Montagu House with its stone facings and dome, like a French hôtel, and the cluster of buildings at its great gate. It had been then for over a decade the British Museum. The ground behind it was a great resort for Londoners of that day. Many a sad affair was fought there, but on that morning we saw a merry party on their way to play prisoner's base. Then we came to the gardens in front of Bedford House, which are now Bloomsbury Square. For my part I preferred this latter mansion to the French creation by its side, and admired its long and graceful lines. Its windows commanded a sweep from Holburn on the south to Highgate on the north. To the east of it, along Southampton Row, a few great houses had gone up or were building; and at the far end of that was Baltimore House, overlooking her Grace of Bedford's gardens. Beyond, Lamb's Conduit Fields stretched away to the countryside.

I own I had a lively curiosity to see that lordly ruler, the proprietor of our province, whose birthday we celebrated after his Majesty's. Had I not been in a great measure prepared, I should have had a revulsion indeed.

When he heard that Mr. Fox and my Lord Comyn were below stairs he gave orders to show them up to his bedroom, where he received us in a night-gown embroidered with oranges. My Lord Baltimore, alas! was not much to see. He did not make the figure a ruler should as he sat in his easy chair, and whined and cursed his Swiss. He was scarce a year over forty, and he had all but run his race. Dissipation and corrosion had set their seal upon him, had stamped his yellow face with crows'-feet and blotted it with pimples. But then the glimpse of a fine gentleman just out of bed of a morning, before he is made for the day, is unfair.

"Morning, Charles! Howdy, Jack!" said his Lordship, apathetically. "Glad to know you, Mr. Carvel. Heard of your family. 'Slife! Wish there were more like 'em in the province."

This sentiment not sitting very well upon his Lordship, I bowed, and said nothing.

"By the bye," he continued, pouring out his chocolate into the dish, "I sent a damned rake of a parson out there some years gone. Handsome devil, too. Never seen his match with the women, egad. 'Od's fish —" he leered. And then added with an oath and a nod and a vile remark: "Married three times, to my knowledge. Carried off dozen or so more. Some of 'em for me. Many a good night I've had with him. Drank between us one evening at Essex's gallon and half Champagne and Burgundy apiece. He got to know too much, y' know," he concluded, with a wicked wink. "Had to buy him up — pack him off."

"His name, Fred?" said Comyn, with a smile at me.

"'Sdeath! That's it. Trouble to remember. Damned if I can think." And he repeated this remark over and over.

"Allen?" said Comyn.

"Yes," said Baltimore; "Allen. And egad I think he'll find hell a hotter place than me. You know him, Mr. Carvel?"

"Yes," I replied. I said no more. I make no reservations when I avow I was never so disgusted in my life. But as I looked upon him, haggard and worn, with retribution so near at hand, I had no words to protest or condemn.

Baltimore gave a hollow mirthless laugh, stopped short, and looked at Charles Fox.

"Curse you, Charles! I suppose you are after that little matter I owe you for quinze."

"Damn the little matter!" said Fox. "Come, get you perfumed and dressed, and order up some of your Tokay while we wait. I have to go to St. Stephens. Mr. Carvel has come to buy your horse Pollux. He has bet Chartersea two hundred guineas he rides him for twenty minutes."

"The devil he has!" cried his Lordship, jaded no longer. "Why, you must know, Mr. Carvel, there was no groom in my stables who would sit him until Foley made me a present of his man, Miller, who started to ride him to Hyde Park. As he came out of Great Russell Street, by gad's life! the horse broke and ran out the Tottenham Court Road all the way to Hampstead. And the fiend picked out a big stone water trough and tossed Miller against it. Then they gathered up the fragments. Damme if I like to see suicide, Mr. Carvel. If Chartersea wants to kill you, let him try it in the fields behind Montagu House here."

I told his Lordship that I had made the wager, and could not in honour withdraw, though the horse had killed a dozen grooms. But already he seemed to have lost interest. He gave a languid pull at the velvet tassel on his bell-rope, ordered the wine; and, being informed that his anteroom below was full of people, had them all dismissed with the message that he was engaged upon important affairs. He told Mr. Fox he had heard of the Jerusalem Chamber, and vowed he would have a like institution. He told me he wished the colony of Maryland in hell; that he was worn out with the quarrels of Governor Eden and his Assembly, and offered to lay a guinea that the Governor's agent would get to him that day, — will-he, nill-he. I did not think it worth while to argue with such a man.

My Lord took three-quarters of an hour to dress, and swore he had not accomplished the feat so quickly in a year. He washed his hands and face in a silver basin, and the scent of the soap filled the room. He rated his Swiss for putting cinnamon upon his ruffles in place of attar of roses, and attempted to regale us the while with some of his choicest adventures. In more than one of these, by the way, his Grace of Chartersea figured. It was Fox who brought him up.

"See here, Baltimore," he said, "I'm not squeamish. But I'm cursed if I like to hear a man who may die any time between bottles talk so."

His Lordship took the rebuke with an oath, and presently hobbled down the stairs of the great and silent house to the stable court, where two grooms were in waiting with the horse. He was an animal of amazing power, about sixteen hands, and dapple gray in colour. And it required no special knowledge to see that he had a devil inside him. It gleamed wickedly out of his eye.

"'Od's life, Richard!" cried Charles, "he has a Jew nose; by all the seven tribes I bid you 'ware of him."

"You have but to ride him with a gold bit, Richard," said Comyn, "and he is a kitten, I'll warrant."

At that moment Pollux began to rear and kick, so that it took both the 'ostlers to hold him.

"Show him a sovereign," suggested Fox. "How do you feel, Richard?"

"I never feared a horse yet," I said with perfect truth, "nor do I fear this one, though I know he may kill me."

"I'll lay you twenty pounds you have at least one bone broken, and ten that you are killed," Baltimore puts in querulously, from the doorway.

"I'll do this, my Lord," I answered. "If I ride him, he is mine. If he throws me, I give you twenty pounds for him."

The gentlemen laughed, and Baltimore vowed he could sell the horse to Astley for fifty; that Pollux was the son of Renown, of the Duke of Kingston's stud, and much more. But Charles rallied him out by a reference to the debt at quinze, and an appeal to his honour as a sportsman. And swore he was discouraging one of the prettiest encounters that would take place in England for many a long day. And so the horse was sent to the stables of the White Horse Cellar, in Piccadilly, and left there at my order.

CHAPTER XXXVI

A GLIMPSE OF MR. GARRICK

Day after day I went to Arlington Street, each time to be turned away with the same answer: that Miss Manners was a shade better, but still confined to her bed. You will scarce believe me, my dears, when I say that Mr. Marmaduke had gone at this crisis with his Grace to the York races. On the fourth morning, I think, I saw Mrs. Manners. She was much worn with the vigil she had kept, and received me with an apathy to frighten me. Her way with me had hitherto always been one of kindness and warmth. In answer to the dozen questions I showered upon her, she replied that Dorothy's malady was in no wise dangerous, so Dr. James had said, and undoubtedly arose out of the excitement of a London season. As I knew, Dorothy was of the kind that must run and run until she dropped. She had no notion of the measure of her own strength. Mrs. Manners hoped that, in a fortnight, she would be recovered sufficiently to be removed to one of the baths.

"She wishes me to thank you for the flowers, Richard. She has them constantly by her. And bids me tell you how sorry she is that she is compelled to miss so much of your visit to England. Are you enjoying London, Richard? I hear that you are well liked by the best of company."

I left, prodigiously cast down, and went directly to Mr. Wedgwood's, to choose the prettiest set of tea-cups and dishes I could find there. I pitied Mrs. Manners from my heart, and made every allowance for her talk with me, knowing the sorrow of her life. Here was yet another link in the chain of the Chartersea evidence. And I made no doubt that Mr. Manners's brutal desertion at such a time must be hard to bear. I continued my visits of inquiry, nearly always meeting some person of consequence, or the footman of such, come on the same errand as myself. And once I encountered the young man she had championed against his Grace at Lady Tankerville's.

Rather than face the array of anxieties that beset me, I plunged recklessly into the gayeties — nay, the excesses — of Mr. Charles Fox and his associates. I paid, in truth, a very high price for my friendship with Mr. Fox. But, since it did not quite ruin me, I look back upon it as cheaply bought. To know the man well, to be the subject of his regard, was to feel an infatuation in common with the little band of worshippers which had come with him from Eton. They remained faithful to him all his days, nor adversity nor change of opinion could shake their attachment. They knew his faults, deplored them, and paid for them. And this was not beyond my comprehension, tho' many have wondered at it. Did he ask me for five hundred pounds, — which he did, — I gave it freely, and would gladly have given more, tho' I saw it all wasted in a night when the dice rolled against him. For those honoured few of whom I speak likewise knew his virtues, which were quite as large as the faults, albeit so mingled with them that all might not distinguish.

I attended some of the routs and parties, to all of which, as a young colonial gentleman of wealth and family, I was made welcome. I went to a ball at Lord Stanley's, a mixture of French horns and clarionets and coloured glass lanthorns and candles in gilt vases, and young ladies pouring tea in white, and musicians in red, and draperies and flowers *ad libitum*. There I met Mr. Walpole, looking on very critically. He was the essence of friendliness, asked after my *equerry*, and said I had done well to ship him to America. At the opera, with Lord Ossory and Mr. Fitzpatrick, I talked through the round of the boxes, from Lady Pembroke's on the right to Lady Hervey's on the left, where Dolly's illness and Lady Harrington's snuffing gabble were the topics rather than Giardini's fiddling. Mr. Storer took me to Foote's dressing-room at the Haymarket, where we found the Duke of Cumberland lounging. I was presented, and thought his Royal Highness had far less dignity than the monkey-comedian we had come to see.

I must not forget the visit I made to Drury Lane Playhouse with my Lords Carlisle and Grantham and Comyn. The great actor received me graciously in such a company, you may be sure. He appeared much smaller off the boards than on, and his actions and speech were quick and nervous. Gast, his hairdresser, was making him up for the character of Richard III.

"'Ods!" said Mr. Garrick, "your Lordships come five minutes too late. Goldsmith is but just gone hence, fresh from his tailor, Filby, of Water Lane. The most gorgeous creature in London, gentlemen, I'll be sworn. He is even now, so he would have me know, gone by invitation to my Lord Denbigh's box, to ogle the ladies."

"And have you seen your latest lampoon, Mr. Garrick?" asks Comyn, winking at me.

Up leaps Mr. Garrick, so suddenly as to knock the paint-pot from Gast's hand.

"Nay, your Lordship jests, surely!" he cried, his voice shaking.

"Jests!" says my Lord, very serious; "do I jest, Carlisle?" And turning to Mr. Cross, the prompter, who stood by, "Fetch me the *St. James's Evening Post*," says he.

"'Ods my life!" continues poor Garrick, almost in tears; "I have loaned Foote upwards of two thousand pounds. And last year, as your Lordship remembers, took charge of his theatre when his leg was cut off. 'Pon my soul, I cannot account for his ingratitude."

"'Tis not Foote," says Carlisle, biting his lip; "I know Foote's mark."

"Then Johnson," says the actor, "because I would not let him have my fine books in his dirty den to be kicked about the floor, but put my library at his disposal—"

"Nay, nor Johnson. Nor yet Macklin nor Murphy."

"Surely not—" cries Mr. Garrick, turning white under the rouge. The name remained unpronounced.

"Ay, ay, *Junius*, in the *Evening Post*. He has fastened upon you at last," answers Comyn, taking the paper.

"'Sdeath! Garrick," Carlisle puts in, very solemn, "what have you done to offend the Terrible Unknown? Talebearing to his Majesty, I'll warrant! I gave you credit for more discretion."

At these words Mr. Garrick seized the chair for support, and swung heavily into it. Whereat the young lords burst into such a tempest of laughter that I could not refrain from joining them. As for Mr. Garrick, he was so pleased to have escaped that he laughed too, though with a palpable nervousness.[1]

"By the bye, Garrick," Carlisle remarked slyly, when he had recovered, "Mrs. Crewe was vastly taken with the last *vers* you left on her dressing-table."

"Was she, now, my Lord?" said the great actor, delighted, but scarce over his fright. "You must know that I have writ one to my Lady Carlisle, on the occasion of her dropping her fan in Piccadilly." Whereupon he proceeded to recite it, and my Lord Carlisle, being something of a poet himself, pronounced it excellent.

Mr. Garrick asked me many questions concerning American life and manners, having a play in his repertory the scene of which was laid in New York. In the midst of this we were interrupted by a dirty fellow who ran in, crying excitedly:—

"Sir, the Archbishop of York is getting drunk at the Bear, and swears he'll be d—d if he'll act to-night."

"The archbishop may go to the devil!" snapped Mr. Garrick. "I do not know a greater rascal, except yourself."

I was little short of thunderstruck. But presently Mr. Garrick added complainingly:—

"I paid a guinea for the archbishop, but the fellow got me three murderers to-day and the best alderman I ever clapped eyes upon. So we are square."

After the play we supped with him at his new house in Adelphi Terrace, next Topham Beauclerk's. 'Twas hand-

---

[1] Note by the editor. It was not long after this that Mr. Garrick's punishment came, and for the selfsame offence.

somely built in the Italian style, and newly furnished throughout, for Mr. Garrick travelled now with a coach and six and four menservants, forsooth. And amongst other things he took pride in showing us that night was a handsome snuffbox which the King of Denmark had given him the year before, his Majesty's portrait set in jewels thereon.

Presently the news of the trial of Lord Baltimore's horse began to be noised about, and was followed by a deluge of wagers at Brooks's and White's and elsewhere. Comyn and Fox, my chief supporters, laid large sums upon me, despite all my persuasion. But the most unpleasant part of the publicity was the rumour that the match was connected with the struggle for Miss Manners's hand. I was pressed with invitations to go into the country to ride this or that horse. His Grace the Duke of Grafton had a mount he would have me try at Wakefield Lodge, and was far from pleasant over my refusal of his invitation. I was besieged by young noblemen like Lord Derby and Lord Foley, until I was heartily sick of notoriety, and cursed the indiscretion of the person who let out the news, and my own likewise. My Lord March, who did me the honour to lay one hundred pounds upon my skill, insisted that I should make one of a party to the famous amphitheatre near Lambeth. Mr. Astley, the showman, being informed of his Lordship's intention, met us on Westminster Bridge dressed in his uniform as sergeant-major of the Royal Light Dragoons and mounted on a white charger. He escorted us to one of the large boxes under the pent-house reserved for the gentry. And when the show was over and the place cleared, begged, that I would ride his Indian Chief. I refused; but March pressed me, and Comyn declared he had staked his reputation upon my horsemanship. Astley was a large man, about my build, and I donned a pair of his leather breeches and boots, and put Indian Chief to his paces around the ring. I found him no more restive, nor as much so, as Firefly. The gentlemen were good enough to clap me roundly, and Astley vowed (no doubt because of the noble patrons present) that he had never seen a better seat.

We all repaired afterwards for supper to Don Saltero's

Coffee House and Museum in Chelsea. And I remembered having heard my grandfather speak of the place, and tell how he had seen Sir Richard Steele there, listening to the Don scraping away at the "Merry Christ Church Bells" on his fiddle. The Don was since dead, but King James's coronation sword and King Henry VIII.'s coat of mail still hung on the walls.

The remembrance of that fortnight has ever been an appalling one. Mr. Carvel had never attempted to teach me the value of money. My grandfather, indeed, held but four things essential to the conduct of life; namely, to fear God, love the King, pay your debts, and pursue your enemies. There was no one in London to advise me, Comyn being but a wild lad like myself. But my Lord Carlisle gave me a friendly warning:—

"Have a care, Carvel," said he, kindly, "or you will run your grandfather through, and all your relations beside. I little realized the danger of it when I first came up." (He was not above two and twenty then.) "And now I have a wife, am more crippled than I care to be, thanks to this devilish high play. Will you dine with Lady Carlisle in St. James's Place next Friday?"

My heart went out to this young nobleman. Handsome he was, as a picture. And he knew better than most of your fine gentlemen how to put a check on his inclinations. As a friend he had few equals, his purse being ever at the command of those he loved. And his privations on Fox's account were already greater than many knew.

I had a call, too, from Mr. Dix. I found him in my parlour one morning, cringing and smiling, and, as usual, half an hour away from his point.

"I warrant you, Mr. Carvel," says he, "there are few young gentlemen not born among the elect that make the great friends you are blessed with."

"I have been fortunate, Mr. Dix," I replied dryly.

"Fortunate!" he cried; "good Lord, sir! I hear of you everywhere with Mr. Fox, and you have been to Astley's with my Lord March. And I have a draft from you at Ampthill."

"Vastly well manœuvred, Mr. Dix," I said, laughing at the

guilty change in his pink complexion. "And hence you are here."

He fidgeted, and seeing that I paid him no attention, but went on with my chocolate, he drew a paper from his pocket and opened it.

"You have spent a prodigious sum, sir, for so short a time," said he, unsteadily. "'Tis very well for you, Mr. Carvel, but I have to remember that you are heir only. I am advancing you money without advices from his Worship, your grandfather. A most irregular proceeding, sir, and one likely to lead me to trouble. I know not what your allowance may be."

"Nor I, Mr. Dix," I replied, unreasonably enough. "To speak truth, I have never had one. You have my Lord Comyn's signature to protect you," I went on ill-naturedly, for I had not had enough sleep. "And in case Mr. Carvel protests, which is unlikely and preposterous, you shall have ten percentum on your money until I can pay you. That should be no poor investment."

He apologized. But he smoothed out the paper on his knee.

"It is only right to tell you, Mr. Carvel, that you have spent one thousand eight hundred and thirty-seven odd pounds, in home money, which is worth more than your colonial. Your grandfather's balance with me was something less than one thousand five hundred, as I made him a remittance in December last. I have advanced the rest. And yesterday," he went on, resolutely for him, "yesterday I got an order for five hundred more."

And he handed me the paper. I must own that the figures startled me. I laid it down with a fine show of indifference.

"And so you wish me to stop drawing? Very good, Mr. Dix."

He must have seen some threat implied, though I meant none. He was my very humble servant at once, and declared he had called only to let me know where I stood. Then he bowed himself out, wishing me luck with the horse he had heard of, and I lighted my pipe with his accompt.

CHAPTER XXXVII

THE SERPENTINE

WHETHER it was Mr. Dix that started me reflecting, or my Lord Carlisle's warning, or a few discreet words from young Lady Carlisle herself, I know not. At all events, I made a resolution to stop high play, and confine myself to whist and quinze and picquet. For I conceived a notion, enlarged by Mr. Fox, that I had more than once fallen into the tender clutches of the *hounds*. I was so reflecting the morning following Lord Carlisle's dinner, when Banks announced a footman.

"Mr. Manners's man, sir," he added significantly, and handed me a little note. I seized it, and, to hide my emotion, told him to give the man his beer.

The writing was Dorothy's, and some time passed after I had torn off the wrapper before I could compose myself to read it.

"So, Sir, the Moment I am too Ill to watch you you must needs lapse into Wilde & Flity Doings, for thus y'rs are call'd even in London. Never Mind how y'r Extravigancies are come to my Ears Sir. One Matter I have herd that I am Most Concerned about, & I pray you, my Dear Richard do not allow y'r Recklessness & Contemt for Danger to betray you into a Stil more Amazing Follie or I shall be very Miserable Indeed. I have Hopes that the Report is at Best a Rumour & you must sit down & write me that it is Sir that my Minde may be set at Rest. I fear for you Vastly & I beg you not Riske y'r Life Foolishly & this for the Sake of one who subscribs herself y'r Old Plamate & Well Wisher Dolly.

"P.S. I have writ Sir Jon Fielding to put you in the Marshallsee or New Gate until Mr. Carvel can be tolde. I am

Better & hope soon to see you agen & have been informed of y'r Dayly Visitts & y'r Flowers are beside me.   D. M."

In about an hour and a half, Mr. Marmaduke's footman was on his way back to Arlington Street in a condition not to be lightly spoken of. During that period I had committed an hundred silly acts, and incidentally learned the letter by heart. I was much distressed to think that she had heard of the affair of the horse, and more so to surmise that the gossip which clung to it must also have reached her. But I fear I thought most of her anxiety concerning me, which reflection caused my hand to shake from very happiness. "Y'r Flowers are beside me," and "I beg you not Riske y'r Life Foolishly," and "I shall be very Miserable Indeed"! But then: "Y'r Old Plamate & Well Wisher"! Nay, she was inscrutable as ever.

And my reply, — what was that to be? How I composed it in the state of mind I was in, I have no conception to this day. The chimney was clogged with papers ere (in a spelling to vie with Dolly's) I had set down my devotion, my undying devotion, to her interests. I asked forgiveness for my cruelty on that memorable morning I had last seen her. But even to allude to the bet with Chartersea was beyond my powers; and as for renouncing it, though for her sake, — that was not to be thought of. The high play I readily promised to avoid in the future, and I signed myself, — well, it matters not after seventy years.

The same day, Tuesday, I received a letter from his Grace of Chartersea saying that he looked to reach London that night, but very late. He begged that Mr. Fox and Lord Comyn and I would sup with him at the Star and Garter at eleven, to fix matters for the trial on the morrow. Mr. Fox could not go, but Comyn and I went to the inn, having first attended "The Tempest" at Drury Lane with Lady Di and Mr. Beauclerk.

We found his Grace awaiting us in a private room, with Captain Lewis, of the 60th Foot, who had figured as a second in the duel with young Atwater. The captain was a rake and a bully and a toadeater, of course, with a loud and profane tongue, and he had had a bottle too many in the duke's travelling-coach. There was likewise a Sir John Brooke, a country neighbour of his Grace in Nottinghamshire. Sir John apparently had no business in such company. He was a hearty, fox-hunting squire who had seen little of London; a three-bottle man who told a foul story and went asleep immediately afterwards. Much to my disappointment, Mr. Manners had gone to Arlington Street direct. I had longed for a chance to speak a little of my mind to him.

This meeting, which I shall not take the time to recount, was near to ending in an open breach of negotiations. His Grace had lost money at York, and more to Lewis on the way to London. He was in one of his vicious humours. He insisted that Hyde Park should be the place of the contest. In vain did Comyn and I plead for some less public spot on account of the disagreeable advertisement the matter had received. His Grace would be damned before he would yield; and Lewis, adding a more forcible contingency, hinted that our side feared a public trial. Comyn presently shut him up.

"Do you ride the horse after his Grace is thrown," says he, "and I agree to get on after and he does not kill you. 'Sdeath! I am not of the army," adds my Lord, cuttingly; "I am a seaman, and not supposed to know a stirrup from a snaffle."

"'Od's blood!" yelled the captain, "you question my horsemanship, my Lord? Do I understand your Lordship to question my courage?"

"After I am thrown!" cries his Grace, very ugly, and fingering the jewels on his hilt.

Sir John was awakened by the noise, and turning heavily spilled the whole of a pint of port on the duke's satin waistcoat and breeches. Whereat Chartersea in a rage flung the bottle at his head with a curse, which it seems was a habit with his Grace. But the servants coming in, headed by my old friend the chamberlain, they quieted down. And it was presently agreed that the horse was to be at noon in the King's Old Road, or Rotten Row (as it was then beginning to be called), in Hyde Park.

I shall carry to the grave the memory of the next day. I was up betimes, and over to the White Horse Cellar to see Pollux groomed, where I found a crowd about the opening into the stable court. "The young American!" called some one, and to my astonishment and no small annoyance I was greeted with a "Huzzay for you, sir!" "My groat's on your honour!" This good-will was owing wholly to the duke's unpopularity with all classes. Inside, sporting gentlemen in hunting-frocks of red and green, and velvet visored caps, were shouldering favoured 'ostlers from the different noblemen's stables; and there was a liberal sprinkling of the characters who attended the cock mains in Drury Lane and at Newmarket. At the moment of my arrival the head 'ostler was rubbing down the stallion's flank.

"Here's ten pounds to ride him, Saunders!" called one of the hunting-frocks.

"Umph!" sniffed the 'ostler; "ride '*im* is it, yere honour? Two hunner beant eno', an' a Portugal crown i' th' boot. Sooner take me chaunces o' Tyburn on 'Ounslow 'Eath. An' Miller waurna able to sit 'im, 'tis no for th' likes o' me to try. Th' bloody devil took th' shirt off Teddy's back this morn. I adwises th' young Buckskin t' order 's coffin." Just then he perceived me, and touched his cap, something abashed. "With submission, sir, y'r honour'll take an old man's adwise an' not go near 'im."

Pollux's appearance, indeed, was not calculated to reassure me. He looked ugly to exaggeration, his ears laid back and his nostrils as big as crowns, and his teeth bared time and time. Now and anon an impatient fling of his hoof would make the grooms start away from him. Since coming to the inn he had been walked a couple of miles each day, with two men with loaded whips to control him. I was being offered a deal of counsel, when big Mr. Astley came in from Lambeth, and silenced them all.

"These grooms, Mr. Carvel," he said to me, as we took a bottle in private inside, "these grooms are the very devil for superstition. And once a horse gets a bad name with them, good-by to him. Miller knew how to ride, of course, but

like many another of them, was too damned over-confident. I
warned him more than once for getting young horses into a
fret, and I'm willing to lay a ten-pound note that he angered
Pollux. 'Od's life! He is a vicious beast. So was his father,
Culloden, before him. But here's luck to you, sir!" says
Mr. Astley, tipping his glass; "having seen you ride, egad! I
have put all the money I can afford in your favour."

Before I left him he had given me several valuable hints as
to the manner of managing that kind of a horse: not to anger
him with the spurs unless it became plain that he meant to
kill me; to try persuasion first and force afterwards; and secondly, he taught me a little trick of twisting the bit which I
have since found very useful.

Leaving the White Horse, I was followed into Piccadilly by
the crowd, until I was forced to take refuge in a hackney chaise.
The noise of the affair had got around town, and I was heartily
sorry I had not taken the other and better method of trying
conclusions with the duke, and slapped his face. I found Jack
Comyn in Dover Street, and presently Mr. Fox came for us
with his chestnuts in his chaise, Fitzpatrick with him. At
Hyde Park Corner there was quite a jam of coaches, chaises,
and cabriolets and beribboned phaetons, which made way for
us, but kept us busy bowing as we passed among them. It
seemed as if everybody of consequence that I had met in London was gathered there. One face I missed, and rejoiced that
she was absent, for I had a degraded feeling like that of being
the favourite in a cudgel-bout. And the thought that her
name was connected with all this made my face twitch. I
heard the people clapping and saw them waving in the carriages as we passed, and some stood forward before the rest in
a haphazard way, without rhyme or reason. Mr. Walpole with
Lady Di Beauclerk, and Mr. Storer and Mr. Price and Colonel
St. John, and Lord and Lady Carlisle and Lady Ossory. These
I recognized. Inside, the railing along the row was lined with
people. And there stood Pollux, bridled, with a blanket thrown
over his great back and chest, surrounded still by the hunting-frocks, who had followed him from the White Horse. Mixed
in with these, swearing, conjecturing, and betting, were some

to surprise me, whose names were connected with every track in England: the Duke of Grafton and my Lords Sandwich and March and Bolingbroke, and Sir Charles Bunbury, and young Lords Derby and Foley, who, after establishing separate names for folly on the tracks, went into partnership. My Lord Baltimore descended listlessly from his cabriolet to join the group. They all sang out when they caught sight of our party, and greeted me with a zeal to carry me off my feet. And my Lord Sandwich, having done me the honour to lay something very handsome upon me, had his chief jockey on hand to give me some final advice. I believe I was the coolest of any of them. And at that time of all others the fact came up to me with irresistible humour that I, a young colonial Whig, who had grown up to detest these people, should be rubbing noses with them.

The duke put in an appearance five minutes before the hour, upon a bay gelding, and attended by Lewis and Sir John Brooke, both mounted. As a most particular evidence of the detestation in which Chartersea was held, he could find nothing in common with such notorious rakes as March and Sandwich. And it fell to me to champion these. After some discussion between Fox and Captain Lewis, March was chosen umpire. His Lordship took his post in the middle of the Row, drew forth an enamelled repeater from his waistcoat, and mouthed out the conditions of the match,—the terms, as he said, being private.

"Are you ready, Mr. Carvel?" he asked.

"I am, my Lord," I answered. The bells were pealing noon.

"Then mount, sir," said he.

The voices of the people dropped to a hum that brought to mind the long-forgotten sound of the bees swarming in the garden by the Chesapeake. My breath began to come quickly. Through the sunny haze I saw the cows and deer grazing by the Serpentine, and out of the back of my eye handkerchiefs floated from the carriages banked at the gate. They took the blanket off the stallion. Stall-fed, and excited by the crowd, he looked brutal indeed. The faithful Banks, in a new suit of the Carvel livery, held the stirrup, and whispered a husky "God keep you, sir!" Suddenly I was up. The murmur was hushed, and the Park became still as a peaceful farm in Devonshire. The grooms let go of the stallion's head.

He stood trembling like the throes of death. I gripped my knees as Captain Daniel had taught me, years ago, when some invisible force impelled me to look aside. From between the broad and hunching shoulders of Chartersea I met such a venomous stare as a cuttle-fish might use to freeze his prey. *Cuttle-fish!* The word kept running over my tongue. I thought of the snaky arms that had already caught Mr. Marmaduke, and were soon, perhaps, to entangle Dorothy. She had begged me not to ride, and I was risking a life which might save hers.

The wind rushing in my ears and beating against my face awoke me all at once. The trees ran madly past, and the water at my right was a silver blur. The beast beneath me snorted as he rose and fell. Fainter and fainter dropped the clamour behind me, which had risen as I started, and the leaps grew longer and longer. Then my head was cleared like a steamed window-pane in a cold blast. I saw the road curve in front of me, I put all my strength into the curb, and heeling at a fearful angle was swept into the busy Kensington Road. For the first time I knew what it was to fear a horse. The stallion's neck was stretched, his shoes rang on the cobbles, and my eyes were fixed on a narrow space between carriages coming together. In a flash I understood why the duke had insisted upon Hyde Park, and that nerved me some. I saw the frightened coachmen pulling their horses this way and that, I heard the cries of the foot-passengers, and then I was through, I know not how. Once more I summoned all my power, recalled the twist Astley had spoken of, and tried it. I bent his neck for an inch of rein. Next I got another inch, and then came a taste — the smallest taste — of mastery like elixir. The motion changed with it, became rougher, and the hoof-beats a fraction less frequent. He steered like a ship with sail reduced. In and out we dodged among the wagons, and I was beginning to think I had him, when suddenly, without a move of warning, he came down rigid with his feet planted together, and only a miracle and my tight grip restrained me from shooting over his head. There he stood shaking and snorting, nor any persuasion would move him. I resorted at last to the spurs.

He was up in the air in an instant, and came down across the road. Again I dug in to the rowels, and clung the tighter, and this time he landed with his head to London. A little knot of people had collected to watch me, and out stepped a strapping fellow in the King's scarlet, from the Guard's House near by.

"Hold him, sir!" he said, tipping. "Better dismount, sir. He means murder, y'r honour."

"Keep clear, curse you!" I cried, waving him off. "What time is it?"

He stepped back, no doubt thinking me mad. Some one spoke up and said it was five minutes past noon. I had the grace to thank him, I believe. To my astonishment I had been gone but four minutes; they had seemed twenty. Looking about me, I found I was in the open space before old Kensington Church, over against the archway there. Once more I dug in the spurs, this time with success. Almost at a jump the beast took me into the angle of posts to the east of the churchyard gate and tore up the footpath of Church Lane, terrified men and women ahead of me taking to the kennel. He ran irregularly, now on the side of the posts, now against the bricks, and then I gave myself up.

Heaven put a last expedient into my head, that I had once heard Mr. Dulany speak of. I braced myself for a pull that should have broken the stallion's jaw and released his mouth altogether. Incredible as it may seem, he jarred into a trot, and presently came down to a walk, tossing his head like fury, and sweating at every pore. I leaned over and patted him, speaking him fair, and (marvel of marvels!) when we had got to the dogs that guard the entrance of Camden House I had coaxed him around and into the street, and cantered back at easy speed to the church. Without pausing to speak to the bunch that stood at the throat of the lane, I started toward London, thankfulness and relief swelling within me. I understood the beast, and spoke to him when he danced aside at a wagon with bells or a rattling load of coals, and checked him with a word and a light hand.

Before I gained the Life Guard's House I met a dozen horsemen, amongst them Banks on a mount of Mr. Fox's. They shouted when they saw me, Colonel St. John calling out that he had won another hundred that I was not dead. Sir John Brooke puffed and swore he did not begrudge his losses to see me safe, despite Captain Lewis's sourness. Storer vowed he he would give a dinner in my honour, and, riding up beside me, whispered that he was damned sorry the horse was now broken, and his Grace's chance of being killed taken away. And thus escorted, I came in by the King's New Road to avoid the people running in the Row, and so down to Hyde Park Corner, and in among the chaises and the phaetons, where there was enough cheering and waving of hats and handkerchiefs to please the most exacting of successful generals. I rode up to my Lord March, and finding there was a minute yet to run I went up the Row a distance and back again amidst more huzzaing, Pollux prancing and quivering, and frothing his bit, but never once attempting to break.

When I had got down, they pressed around me until I could scarce breathe, crying congratulations, Comyn embracing me openly. Mr. Fox vowed he had never seen so fine a sight, and said many impolitic things which the duke must have overheard. . . . Lady Carlisle sent me a red rose for my buttonhole by his Lordship. Mr. Warner, the lively parson with my Lord March, desired to press my hand, declaring that he had won a dozen of port upon me, which he had set his best cassock against. My Lord Sandwich offered me snuff, and invited me to Hichinbroke. Indeed, I should never be through were I to continue. But I must not forget my old acquaintance Mr. Walpole, who protested that he must get permission to present me to Princess Amelia: that her Royal Highness would not rest content now, until she had seen me. I did not then know her Highness's sporting propensity.

Then my Lord March called upon the duke, who stood in

the midst of an army of his toadeaters. I almost pitied him then, tho' I could not account for the feeling. I think it was because a nobleman with so great a title should be so cordially hated and despised. There were high words along the railing among the duke's supporters, Captain Lewis, in his anger, going above an inference that the stallion had been broken privately. Chartersea came forward with an indifferent swagger, as if to say as much: and, in truth, no one looked for more sport, and some were even turning away. He had scarce put foot to the stirrup, when the surprise came. Two minutes were up before he was got in the saddle, Pollux rearing and plunging and dancing in a circle, the grooms shouting and dodging, and his Grace cursing in a voice to wake the dead: and Mr. Fox laughing, and making small wagers that he would never be mounted. But at last the duke was up and gripped, his face bloody red, giving vent to his fury with the spurs.

Then something happened, and so quickly that it cannot be writ fast enough. Pollux bolted like a shot out of a sling, vaulted the railing as easily as you or I would hop over a stick, and galloping across the lawn and down the embankment flung his Grace into the Serpentine. Precisely, as Mr. Fox afterwards remarked, as the swine with the evil spirits ran down the slope into the sea.

An indescribable bedlam of confusion followed, lords and gentlemen, tradesmen and grooms, hostlers and apprentices, all tumbling after, many crying with laughter. My Lord Sandwich's jockey pulled his Grace from the water in a most pitiable state of rage and humiliation. His side curls gone, the powder and pomatum washed from his hair, bedraggled and muddy and sputtering oaths, he made his way to Lord March, swearing by all divine that a trick was put on him, that he would ride the stallion to Land's End. His Lordship, pulling his face straight, gravely informed the duke that the match was over. With this his Grace fell flatly sullen, was pushed into a coach by Sir John and the captain, and drove rapidly off Kensington way, to avoid the people at the corner.

CHAPTER XXXVIII

IN WHICH I AM ROUNDLY BROUGHT TO TASK

I WOULD have gone to Arlington Street direct, but my friends had no notion of letting me escape. They carried me off to Brooks's Club, where a bowl of punch was brewed directly, and my health was drunk to three times three. Mr. Storer commanded a turtle dinner in my honour. We were not many, fortunately, — only Mr. Fox's little coterie. And it was none other than Mr. Fox who made the speech of the evening. "May I be strung as high as Haman," said he, amid a tempest of laughter, "if ever I saw half so edifying a sight as his Grace pitching into the Serpentine, unless it were his Grace dragged out again. Mr. Carvel's advent has been a Godsend to us narrow ignoramuses of this island, gentlemen. To the Englishmen of our colonies, sirs, and that we may never underrate or misunderstand them more!"

"Nay, Charles," cried my Lord Comyn. "Where is our gallantry? I give you first the Englishwomen of our colonies, and in particular the pride of Maryland, who has brought back to the old country all the graces of the new, — Miss Manners."

His voice was drowned by a deafening shout, and we charged our glasses to drain them brimming. And then we all went to Drury Lane to see Mrs. Clive romp through *The Wonder* in the spirit of the "immortal Peg." She spoke an epilogue that Mr. Walpole had writ especial for her, and made some witty and sarcastic remarks directed at the gentlemen in our stage-box. We topped off a very full day by a supper at the Bedford Arms, where I must draw the curtain.

The next morning I was abed at an hour which the sobriety of old age makes me blush to think of. Banks had just concluded a discreet discourse upon my accomplishment of the day before, and had left for my newspapers, when he came running back with the information that Miss Manners would see my honour that day. There was no note. Between us we made my toilet in a jiffy, and presently I was walking in at the Manners's door in an amazing hurry, and scarcely waited for a direction. But as I ran up the stairs, I heard the tinkle of the spinet, and the notes of an old, familiar tune fell upon my ears. The words rose in my head with the cadence.

> "Love me little, love me long,
> Is the burthen of my song,
> Love that is too hot and strong
> Runneth soon to waste."

That simple air, already mellowed by an hundred years, had always been her favourite. She used to sing it softly to herself as we roamed the woods and fields of the Eastern Shore. Instinctively I paused at the dressing-room door. Nay, my dears, you need not cry out, such was the custom of the times. A dainty bower it was, filled with the perfume of flowers, and rosy cupids disporting on the ceiling; and china and silver and gold filigree strewn about, with my tea-cups on the table. The sunlight fell like a halo round Dorothy's head, her hands strayed over the keys, and her eyes were far away. She had not heard me. I remember her dress, — a silk with blue cornflowers on a light ground, and the flimsiest of lace caps resting on her hair. I thought her face paler; but beyond that she did not show her illness.

She looked up, and perceived me, I thought, with a start. "So it is you!" she said demurely enough; "you are come at last to give an account of yourself."

"Are you better, Dorothy?" I asked earnestly.

"Why should you think that I have been ill?" she replied, her fingers going back to the spinet. "It is a mistake, sir. Dr. James has given me near a gross of his infamous powders, and is now exploiting another cure. I have been resting from the fatigues of London, while you have been wearing yourself out."

"Dr. James himself told me your condition was serious," I said.

"Of course," said she; "the worse the disease, the more remarkable the cure, the more sought after the physician. When will you get over your provincial simplicity?"

I saw there was nothing to be got out of her while in this baffling humour. I wondered what devil impelled a woman to write one way and talk another. In her note to me she had confessed her illness. The words I had formed to say to her were tied on my tongue. But on the whole I congratulated myself. She knew how to step better than I, and there were many awkward things between us of late best not spoken of. But she kept me standing an unconscionable time without a word, which on the whole was cruelty, while she played over some of Dibdin's ballads.

"Are you in a hurry, sir," she asked at length, turning on me with a smile, "are you in a hurry to join my Lord March or his Grace of Grafton? And have you writ Captain Clapsaddle and your Whig friends at home of your new intimacies, of Mr. Fox and my Lord Sandwich?"

I was dumb.

"Yes, you must be wishing to get away," she continued cruelly, picking up the newspaper. "I had forgotten this notice. When I saw it this morning I thought of you, and despaired of a glimpse of you to-day." (Reading.) "'At the Three Hats, Islington, this day, the 10th of May, will be played a grand match at that ancient and much renowned manly diversion called Double Stick by a sett of chosen young men at that exercise from different parts of the West Country, for two guineas given free; those who break the most heads to bear away the prize. Before the above-mentioned diversion begins, Mr. Sampson and his young German will display alternately on one, two, and three horses, various surprising and curious feats of famous horsemanship in like manner as at the Grand Jubilee at Stratford-upon-Avon. Admittance one shilling each person.' Before you leave, Mr. Richard," she continued, with her eyes still on the sheet, "I should like to talk over one or two little matters."

I AM ROUNDLY BROUGHT TO TASK

"Dolly —!"

"Will you sit, sir?"

I sat down uneasily, expecting the worst. She disappointed me, as usual.

"What an unspeakable place must you keep in Dover Street! I cannot send even a footman there but what he comes back reeling."

I had to laugh at this. But there was no smile out of my lady.

"It took me near an hour and a half to answer your note," I replied.

"And 'twas a masterpiece!" exclaimed Dolly, with withering sarcasm; "oh, a most amazing masterpiece, I'll be bound! His worship the French Ambassador is a kitten at diplomacy beside you, sir. An hour and a half, did you say, sir? Gemini, the Secretary of State and his whole corps could not have composed the like in a day."

"Faith!" I cried, with feeling enough; "and if that is diplomacy, I would rather make leather breeches than be given an embassy."

She fixed her eyes upon me so disconcertingly that mine fell.

"There was a time," she said, with a change of tone, "there was a time when a request of mine, and it were not granted outright, would have received some attention. This is my first experience at being ignored."

"I had made a wager," said I, "and could not retract with honour."

"So you had made a wager! Now we are to have some news at last. How stupid of you, Richard, not to tell me before. I confess I wonder what these wits find in your company. Here am I who have seen naught but dull women for a fortnight, and you have failed to say anything amusing in a quarter of an hour. Let us hear about the wager."

"There is little to tell," I answered shortly, considerably piqued. "I bet your friend, the Duke of Chartersea, some hundreds of pounds I could ride Lord Baltimore's Pollux for twenty minutes, after which his Grace was to get on and ride twenty more."

"Where did you see the duke?" Dolly interrupted, without much show of interest.

I explained how we had met him at Brooks's, and had gone to his house.

"You went to his house?" she repeated, raising her eyebrows a trifle; "and Comyn and Mr. Fox? And pray, how did this pretty subject come up?"

I related, very badly, I fear, Fox's story of young Wrottlesey and the tea-merchant's daughter. And what does my lady do but get up and turn her back, arranging some pinks in the window. I could have sworn she was laughing, had I not known better.

"Well?"

"Well, that was a reference to a little pleasantry Mr. Fox had put up on him some time before. His Grace flared, but tried not to show it. He said he had heard I could do something with a horse (I believe he made it up), and Comyn gave oath that I could; and then he offered to bet Comyn that I could not ride this Pollux, who had killed his groom. That made me angry, and I told the duke I was no jockey to be put up to decide wagers, and that he must make his offers to me."

"La!" said Dolly, "you fell in head over heels."

"What do you mean by that?" I demanded.

"Nothing," said she, biting her lip. "Come, you are as ponderous as Dr. Johnson."

"Then Mr. Fox proposed that his Grace should ride after me."

Here Dolly laughed in her handkerchief.

"I'll be bound," said she.

"Then the duke went to York," I continued hurriedly; "and when he came back we met him at the Star and Garter. He insisted that the match should come off in Hyde Park. I should have preferred the open roads north of Bedford House."

"Where there is no Serpentine," she interrupted, with the faintest suspicion of a twinkle about her eyes. "On, sir, on! You are as reluctant as our pump at Wilmot House in the dry season. I see you were not killed, as you richly deserved. Let us have the rest of your tale."

"There is very little more to it, save that I contrived to master the beast, and his Grace —"

"Was disgraced. A vastly fine achievement, surely. But where are you to stop? You will be shaming the King next by outwalking him. Pray, how did the duke appear as he was going into the Serpentine?"

"You have heard?" I exclaimed, the trick she had played me dawning upon me.

"Upon my word, Richard, you are more of a simpleton than I thought you. Have you not seen your newspaper this morning?"

I explained how it was that I had not. She took up the *Chronicle*.

"'This Mr. Carvel has made no inconsiderable noise since his arrival in town, and yesterday crowned his performances by defeating publicly a noble duke at a riding match in Hyde Park, before half the quality of the kingdom. His Lordship of March and Ruglen acted as umpire.' There, sir, was I not right to beg Sir John Fielding to put you in safe keeping until your grandfather can send for you?"

I made to seize the paper, but she held it from me.

"'If Mr. Carvel remains long enough in England, he bids fair to share the talk of Mayfair with a certain honourable young gentleman of Brooks's and the Admiralty, whose debts and doings now furnish most of the gossip for the clubs and the card tables. Their names are both connected with this contest. 'Tis whispered that the wager upon which the match was ridden arose —'" here Dolly stopped shortly, her colour mounting, and cried out with a stamp of her foot. "You are not content to bring publicity upon yourself, who deserve it, but must needs drag innocent names into the newspapers."

"What have they said?" I demanded, ready to roll every printer in London in the kennel.

"Nay, you may read for yourself," said she. And, flinging the paper in my lap, left the room.

They had not said much more, Heaven be praised. But I was angry and mortified as I had never been before, realizing for the first time what a botch I had made of my stay in London. In great dejection, I was picking up my hat to leave the house, when Mrs. Manners came in upon me, and insisted that I should stay for dinner. She was very white, and seemed troubled and preoccupied, and said that Mr. Manners had come back from York with a cold on his chest, but would insist upon joining the party to Vauxhall on Monday. I asked her when she was going to the baths, and suggested that the change would do her good. Indeed, she looked badly.

"We are not going, Richard," she replied; "Dorothy will not hear of it. In spite of the doctor she says she is not ill, and must attend at Vauxhall, too. You are asked?"

I said that Mr. Storer had included me. I am sure, from the way she looked at me, that she did not heed my answer. She appeared to hesitate on the verge of a speech, and glanced once or twice at the doors.

"Richard, I suppose you are old enough to take care of yourself, tho' you seem still a child to me. I pray you will be careful, my boy," she said, with something of the affection she had always borne me, "for your grandfather's sake, I pray you will run into no more danger. I — we are your old friends, and the only ones here to advise you."

She stopped, seemingly, to weigh the wisdom of what was to come next, while I leaned forward with an eagerness I could not hide. Was she to speak of the Duke of Chartersea? Alas, I was not to know. For at that moment Dorothy came back to inquire why I was not gone to the cudgelling at the Three Hats. I said I had been invited to stay to dinner.

"Why, I have writ a note asking Comyn," said she. "Do you think the house will hold you both?"

His Lordship came in as we were sitting down, bursting with some news, and he could hardly wait to congratulate Dolly on her recovery before he delivered it.

"Why, Richard," says the dog, "what do you think some wag has done now? They believe at Brooks's 'twas that jackanapes of a parson, Dr. Warner, who was there yesterday with March." He drew a clipping from his pocket. "Listen, Miss Dolly : —

> "'On Wednesday did a carter see
>   His Grace, the Duke of Ch-rt—s-a,
> As plump and helpless as a bag,
>   A-straddle of a big-boned nag.
> "Lord, Sam!" the carter loudly yelled,
>   On by this wondrous sight impelled,
> "We'll run and watch this noble gander
>   Master a steed, like Alexander."
> But, when the carter reached the Row,
>   His Grace had left it, long ago.
> Bucephalus had leaped the green,
>   The duke was in the Serpentine.
> The fervent wish of all good men
>   That he may ne'er come out again!'"

Comyn's impudence took my breath, tho' the experiment interested me not a little. My lady was pleased to laugh at the doggerel, and even Mrs. Manners. Its effect upon Mr. Marmaduke was not so spontaneous. His smile was half-hearted. Indeed, the little gentleman seemed to have lost his spirits, and said so little (for him), that I was encouraged to corner him that very evening and force him to a confession. But I might have known he was not to be caught. It appeared almost as if he guessed my purpose, for as soon as ever the claret was come on, he excused himself, saying he was promised to Lady Harrington, who wanted one.

Comyn and I departed early on account of Dorothy. She had denied a dozen who had left cards upon her.

"Egad, Richard," said my Lord, when we had got to my lodgings, "I made him change colour, did I not? Do you know how the little fool looks to me? 'Od's life, he looks hunted, and cursed near brought to earth. We must fetch this thing to a point, Richard. And I am wondering what Chartersea's next move will be," he added thoughtfully.

CHAPTER XXXIX

HOLLAND HOUSE

On the morrow, as I was setting out to dine at Brooks's, I received the following on a torn slip of paper: "Dear Richard, we shall have a good show to-day you may care to see." It was signed "Fox," and dated at St. Stephen's. I lost no time in riding to Westminster, where I found a flock of excited people in Parliament Street and in the Palace Yard. And on climbing the wide stone steps outside and a narrower flight within I was admitted directly into the august presence of the representatives of the English people. They were in a most prodigious and unseemly state of uproar.

What a place is old St. Stephen's Chapel, over St. Mary's in the Vaults, for the great Commons of England to gather! It is scarce larger or more imposing than our own assembly room in the Stadt House in Annapolis. St. Stephen's measures but ten yards by thirty, with a narrow gallery running along each side for visitors. In one of these, by the rail, I sat down suffocated, bewildered, and deafened. And my first impression out of the confusion was of the bewigged speaker enthroned under the royal arms, sore put to restore order. On the table in front of him lay the great mace of the Restoration. Three chandeliers threw down their light upon the mob of honourable members, and I wondered what had put them into this state of uproar.

Presently, with the help of a kind stranger on my right, who was occasionally making shorthand notes, I got a few bearings. That was the Treasury Bench, where Lord North sat (he was wide awake, now). And there was the Government side. He pointed out Barrington and Weymouth and

Jerry Dyson and Sandwich, and Rigby in the court suit of purple velvet with the sword thrust through the pocket. I took them all in, as some of the worst enemies my country had in Britain. Then my informant seemed to hesitate, and made bold to ask my persuasion. When I told him I was a Whig, and an American, he begged the favour of my hand.

"There, sir," he cried excitedly, "that stout young gentleman with the black face and eyebrows, and the blacker heart, I may say,— the one dressed in the fantastical costume called by a French name,— is Mr. Charles Fox. He has been sent by the devil himself, I believe, to ruin this country. 'Ods, sir, that devil Lord Holland begot him. He is but one and twenty, but his detestable arts have saved North's neck from Burke and Wedderburn on two occasions this year."

"And what has happened to-day?" I asked, smiling.

The stranger smiled, too.

"Why, sir," he answered, raising his voice above the noise; "if you have been in London any length of time, you will have read the account, with comment, of the Duke of Grafton's speech in the Lords, signed *Domitian*. Their Lordships well know it should have been over a greater signature. This afternoon his Grace of Manchester was talking in the Upper House about the Spanish troubles, when Lord Gower arose and desired that the place might be cleared of strangers, lest some Castilian spy might lurk under the gallery. That was directed against us of the press, sir, and their Lordships knew it. 'Ad's heart, sir, there was a riot, the house servants tumbling everybody out, and Mr. Burke and Mr. Dunning in the boot, who were gone there on the business of this house to present a bill. Those gentlemen are but just back, calling upon the commons to revenge them and vindicate their honour. And my Lord North looks troubled, as you will mark, for the matter is like to go hard against his Majesty's friends. But hush, Mr. Burke is to speak."

The house fell quiet to listen, and my friend began to ply his shorthand industriously. I leaned forward with a sharp curiosity to see this great friend of America. He was dressed in a well-worn suit of brown, and I recall a decided Irish face, and a more decided Irish accent, which presently I forgot under the spell of his eloquence. I have heard it said he had many defects of delivery. He had none that day, or else I was too little experienced to note them. Afire with indignation, he told how the deputy black rod had hustled him like a vagabond or a thief, and he called the House of Lords a bear garden. He was followed by Dunning, in a still more inflammatory mood, until it seemed as if all the King's friends in the Lower House must desert their confederates in the Upper. No less important a retainer than Mr. Onslow moved a policy of retaliation, and those that were left began to act like the Egyptians when they felt the Red Sea under them. They nodded and whispered in their consternation.

It was then that Mr. Fox got calmly up before the pack of frightened mercenaries and argued (God save the mark!) for moderation. He had the ear of the house in a second, and he spoke with all the confidence — this youngster who had just reached his majority — he had used with me before his intimates. I gaped with astonishment and admiration. The Lords, said he, had plainly meant no insult to this honourable house, nor yet to the honourable members. They had aimed at the common enemies of man, the printers. And for this their heat was more than pardonable. My friend at my side stopped his writing to swear under his breath. "Look at 'em!" he cried; "they are turning already. He could argue Swedenborg into popery!"

The deserters were coming back to the ranks, indeed, and North and Dyson and Weymouth had ceased to look haggard, and were wreathed in smiles. In vain did Mr. Burke harangue them in polished phrase. It was a language North and Company did not understand, and cared not to learn. Their young champion spoke the more worldly and cynical tongue of White's and Brooks's, with its shorter sentences and absence of formality. And even as the devil can quote Scripture to his purpose, Mr. Fox quoted history and the classics, with plenty more that was not above the heads of the booted and spurred country squires. And thus, for the third time, he earned the gratitude of his gracious Majesty.

"Well, Richard," said he, slipping his arm through mine as we came out into Parliament Street, "I promised you some sport. Have you enjoyed it?"

I was forced to admit that I had.

"Let us to the 'Thatched House,' and have supper privately," he suggested. "I do not feel like a company to-night." We walked on for some time in silence. Presently he said: "You must not leave us, Richard. You may go home to see your grandfather die, and when you come back I will see about getting you a little borough for what my father paid for mine. And you shall marry Dorothy, and perchance return in ten years as governor of a principality. That is, after we've ruined you at the club. How does that prospect sit?"

I wondered at the mood he was in, that made him choose me rather than the adulation and applause he was sure to receive at Brooks's for the part he had played that night. After we had satisfied our hunger,—for neither of us had dined,—and poured out a bottle of claret, he looked up at me quizzically.

"I have not heard you congratulate me," he said.

"Nor will you," I replied, laughing.

"I like you the better for it, Richard. 'Twas a damned poor performance, and that's truth."

"I thought the performance remarkable," I said honestly.

"Oh, but it was not," he answered scornfully. "The moment that dun-coloured Irishman gets up, the whole government pack begins to whine and shiver. There are men I went to school with I fear more than Burke. But you don't like to see the champion of America come off second best. Is that what you're thinking?"

"No. But I was wondering why you have devoted your talents to the devil," I said, amazed at my boldness.

He glanced at me, and half laughed again.

"You are cursed frank," said he; "damned frank."

"But you invited it."

"Yes," he replied, "so I did. Give me a man who is honest. Fill up again," said he; "and spit out all you would like to say, Richard."

"Then," said I, "why do you waste your time and your breath in defending a crew of political brigands and placemen, and a king who knows not the meaning of the word *gratitude*, and who has no use for a man of ability? You have honoured me with your friendship, Charles Fox, and I may take the liberty to add that you seem to love power more than spoils. You have originality. You are honest enough to think and act upon your own impulses. And pardon me if I say you have very little chance on that side of the house where you have put yourself."

"You seem to have picked up a trifle since you came into England," he said. "A damned shrewd estimate, I'll be sworn. And for a colonial! But, as for power," he added a little doggedly, "I have it in plenty, and the kind I like. The King and North hate and fear me already more than Wilkes."

"And with more cause," I replied warmly. "His Majesty perhaps knows that you understand him better, and foresees the time when a man of your character will give him cause to fear indeed."

He did not answer that, but called for a reckoning; and taking my arm again, we walked out past the sleeping houses.

"Have you ever thought much of the men we have in the colonies?" I asked.

"No," he replied; "Chatham stands for 'em, and I hate Chatham on my father's account. That is reason enough for me."

"You should come back to America with me," I said. "And when you had rested awhile at Carvel Hall, I would ride with you through the length of the provinces from Massachusetts to North Carolina. You will see little besides hard-working, self-respecting Englishmen, loyal to a king who deserves loyalty as little as Louis of France. But with their eyes open, and despite the course he has taken. They are men whose measure of resolution is not guessed at."

He was silent again until we had got into Piccadilly and opposite his lodgings.

"Are they all like you?" he demanded.

"Who?" said I. For I had forgotten my words.

"The Americans."

"The greater part feel as I do."

"I suppose you are for bed," he remarked abruptly.

"The night is not yet begun," I answered, repeating his favourite words, and pointing at the glint of the sun on the windows.

"What do you say to a drive behind those chestnuts of mine, for a breath of air? I have just got my new cabriolet Selwyn ordered in Paris."

Soon we were rattling over the stones in Piccadilly, wrapped in greatcoats, for the morning wind was cold. We saw the Earl of March and Ruglen getting out of a chair before his house, opposite the Green Park, and he stopped swearing at the chairmen to wave at us.

"Hello, March!" Mr. Fox said affably, "you're drunk."

His Lordship smiled, bowed graciously if unsteadily to me, and did not appear to resent the pleasantry. Then he sighed.

"What a pair of cubs it is," said he; "I wish to God I was young again. I hear you astonished the world again last night, Charles."

We left him being assisted into his residence by a sleepy footman, paid our toll at Hyde Park Corner, and rolled onward toward Kensington, Fox laughing as we passed the empty park at the thought of what had so lately occurred there. After the close night of St. Stephen's, nature seemed doubly beautiful. The sun slanted over the water in the gardens in bars of green and gold. The bright new leaves were on the trees, and the morning dew had brought with it the smell of the living earth. We passed the stream of market wagons lumbering along, pulled by sturdy, patient farm-horses, driven by smocked countrymen, who touched their caps to the fine gentlemen of the court end of town; who shook their heads and exchanged deep tones over the whims of quality, unaccountable as the weather. But one big-chested fellow arrested his salute, a scowl came over his face, and he shouted back to the wagoner whose horses were munching his hay: —

"Hi, Jeems, keep down yere hands. Mr. Fox is noo friend of we."

This brought a hard smile on Mr. Fox's face.

"I believe, Richard," he said, "I have become more detested than any man in Parliament."

"And justly," I replied; "for you have fought all that is good in you."

"I was mobbed once, in Parliament Street. I thought they would kill me. Have you ever been mobbed, Richard?" he asked indifferently.

"Never, I thank Heaven," I answered fervently.

"I think I would rather be mobbed than indulge in any amusement I know of," he continued. "Than confound Wedderburn, or drive a measure against Burke, — which is no bad sport, my word on't. I would rather be mobbed than have my horse win at Newmarket. There is a keen pleasure you wot not of, my lad, in listening to Billingsgate and Spitalfields howl maledictions upon you. And no sensation I know of is equal to that of the moment when the mud and sticks and oranges are coming through the windows of your coach, when the dirty weavers are clutching at your ruffles and shaking their filthy fists under your nose."

"It is, at any rate, strictly an aristocratic pleasure," I assented, laughing.

So we came to Holland House. Its wide fields of sprouting corn, its woods and pastures and orchards in blossom, were smiling that morning, as though Leviathan, the town, were not rolling onward to swallow them. Lord Holland had bought the place from the Warwicks, with all its associations and memories. The capped towers and quaint façades and projecting windows were plain to be seen from where we halted in the shaded park, and to the south was that Kensington Road we had left, over which all the glory and royalty of England at one time or another had rolled. Under these majestic oaks and cedars Cromwell and Ireton had stood while the beaten Royalists lashed their horses on to Brentford. Nor did I forget that the renowned Addison had lived here after his unhappy marriage with Lady Warwick, and had often ridden hence to Button's Coffee House in town, where my grandfather had had his dinner with Dean Swift.

We sat gazing at the building, which was bathed in the early sun, at the deer and sheep grazing in the park, at the changing colours of the young leaves as the breeze swayed them. The market wagons had almost ceased now, and there was little to break the stillness.

"You love the place?" I said.

He started, as though I had awakened him out of a sleep. And he was no longer the Fox of the clubs, the cynical, the reckless. He was no longer the best-dressed man in St. James's Street, or the aggressive youngster of St. Stephen's.

"Love it!" he cried. "Ay, Richard, and few guess how well. You will not laugh when I tell you that my happiest days have been passed here, when I was but a chit, in the long room where Addison used to walk up and down composing his *Spectators:* or trotting after my father through these woods and gardens. A kinder parent does not breathe than he. Well I remember how he tossed me in his arms under that tree when I had thrashed another lad for speaking ill of him. He called me his knight. In all my life he has never broken faith with me. When they were blasting down a wall where those palings now stand, he promised me I should see it done, and had it rebuilt and blown down again because I had missed the sight. All he ever exacted of me was that I should treat him as an elder brother. He had his own notion of the world I was going into, and prepared me accordingly. He took me from Eton to Spa, where I learned gaming instead of Greek, and gave me so much a night to risk at play."

I looked at him in astonishment. To say that I thought these relations strange would have been a waste of words.

"To be sure," Charles continued, "I was bound to learn, and could acquire no younger." He flicked the glossy red backs of his horses with his whip. "You are thinking it an extraordinary education, I know," he added rather sadly. "I have told you this—God knows why! Yes, because I like you damnably, and you would have heard worse elsewhere, both of him and of me. I fear you have listened to the world's opinion of Lord Holland."

Indeed, I had heard a deal of that nobleman's peculations of the public funds. But in this he was no worse than the bulk of his colleagues. His desertion of William Pitt I found hard to forgive.

"The best father in the world, Richard!" cried Charles. "If his former friends could but look into his kind heart, and see him in his home, they would not have turned their backs upon him. I do not mean such scoundrels as Rigby. And now my father is in exile half the year in Nice, and the other half at King's Gate. The King and Jack Bute used him for a tool, and then cast him out. You wonder why I am of the King's party?" said he, with something sinister in his smile; "I will tell you. When I got my borough I cared not a fig for parties or principles. I had only the one definite ambition, to revenge Lord Holland. Nay," he exclaimed, stopping my protest, "I was not too young to know rottenness as well as another. The times are rotten in England. You may have virtue in America, amongst a people which is fresh from a struggle with the earth and its savages. We have cursed little at home, in faith. The King, with his barley water and rising at six, and shivering in chapel, and his middle-class table, is rottener than the rest. The money he saves in his damned beggarly court goes to buy men's souls. His word is good with none. For my part I prefer a man who is drunk six days out of the seven to one who takes his pleasure so. And I am not so great a fool that I cannot distinguish justice from injustice. I know the wrongs of the colonies, which you yourself have put as clear as I wish to hear, despite Mr. Burke and his eloquence.[1] And perhaps, Richard," he concluded, with a last lingering look at the old pile as he turned his horses, "perhaps some day, I shall remember what you told us at Brooks's."

It was thus, boyishly, that Mr. Fox chose to take me into his confidence, an honour which I shall remember with a thrill to my dying day. So did he reveal to me the impulses of his early life, hidden forever from his detractors. How little does the censure of this world count, which cannot see the heart behind the embroidered waistcoat! When Charles Fox began

[1] My grandfather has made a note here, which in justice should be added, that he was not deceived by Mr. Fox's partiality. — D. C. C.

his career he was a thoughtless lad, but steadfast to such principles as he had formed for himself. They were not many, but, compared to those of the arena which he entered, they were noble. He strove to serve his friends, to lift the name of a father from whom he had received nothing but kindness, however misguided. And when he saw at length the error of his ways, what a mighty blow did he strike for the right!

"Here is a man," said Dr. Johnson, many years afterwards, "who has divided his kingdom with Cæsar; so that it was a doubt whether the nation should be ruled by the sceptre of George the Third or the tongue of Fox."

CHAPTER XL

VAUXHALL

MATTERS had come to a pretty pickle indeed. I was openly warned at Brooks's and elsewhere to beware of the duke, who was said upon various authority to be sulking in Hanover Square, his rage all the more dangerous because it was smouldering. I saw Dolly only casually before the party to Vauxhall. Needless to say, she flew in the face of Dr. James's authority, and went everywhere. She was at Lady Bunbury's drum, whither I had gone in another fruitless chase after Mr. Marmaduke. Dr. Warner's verse was the laughter of the company. And, greatly to my annoyance, — in the circumstances, — I was made a hero of, and showered with three times as many invitations as I could accept.

The whole story got abroad, even to the awakening of the duke in Covent Garden. And that clownish Mr. Foote, of the Haymarket, had added some lines to a silly popular song entitled *The Sights o' Lunnun*, with which I was hailed at Mrs. Betty's fruit-stall in St. James's Street. Here is one of the verses: —

> "In Maryland, he hunts the Fox
> From dewy Morn till Day grows dim;
> At Home he finds a Paradox, —
> From Noon till Dawn the Fox hunts him."

Charles Fox laughed when he heard it. But he was serious when he came to speak of Chartersea, and bade me look out for assassination. I had Banks follow me abroad at night with a brace of pistols under his coat, albeit I feared nothing save that I should not have an opportunity to meet the duke in a fair fight. And I resolved at all hazards to run Mr. Marmaduke down with despatch, if I had to waylay him.

Mr. Storer, who was forever giving parties, was responsible for this one at Vauxhall. We went in three coaches, and besides Dorothy and Mr. Marmaduke, the company included Lord and Lady Carlisle, Sir Charles and Lady Sarah Bunbury, Lady Ossory and Lady Julia Howard, two Miss Stanleys and Miss Poole, and Comyn, and Hare, and Price, and Fitzpatrick, the latter feeling very glum over a sum he had dropped that afternoon to Lord Harrington. Fox had been called to St. Stephen's on more *printer's* business.

Dolly was in glowing pink, as I loved best to see her, and looked divine. Comyn and I were in Mr. Manners's coach. The evening was fine and warm, and my lady in very lively spirits. As we rattled over Westminster Bridge, the music of the Vauxhall band came "throbbing through the still night," and the sky was bright with the reflection of the lights. It was the fashion with the quality to go late; and so eleven o'clock had struck before we had pulled up between Vauxhall stairs, crowded with watermen and rough mudlarks, and the very ordinary-looking house which forms the entrance of the great garden. Leaving the servants outside, single-file we trailed through the dark passage guarded by the wicket-gate.

"Prepare to be ravished, Richard," said my lady, with fine sarcasm.

"You were yourself born in the colonies, miss," I retorted. "I confess to a thrill, and will not pretend that I have seen such sights often enough to be sated."

"La!" exclaimed Lady Sarah, who had overheard; "I vow this is refreshing. Behold a new heaven and a new earth, Mr. Carvel!"

Indeed, much to the amusement of the company, I took no pains to hide my enthusiasm at the brilliancy of the scene which burst upon me. A great orchestra rose in the midst of a stately grove lined on all four sides with supper-boxes of brave colours, which ran in straight tiers or swept around in circles. These were filled with people of all sorts and conditions, supping and making merry. Other people were sauntering under the trees, keeping step with the music. Lamps of white and blue and red and green hung like luminous fruit from the branches, or clustered in stars and crescents upon the buildings.

"Why, Richard, you are as bad as Farmer Colin.

> "'O Patty! Soft in feature,
> I've been at dear Vauxhall;
> No paradise is sweeter,
> Not that they Eden call.'"

whispered Dolly, paraphrasing.

At that instant came hurrying Mr. Tom Tyers, who was one of the brothers, proprietors of the gardens. He was a very lively young fellow who seemed to know everybody, and he desired to know if we would walk about a little before being shown to the boxes reserved for us.

"They are on the right side, Mr. Tyers?" demanded Mr. Storer.

"Oh, to be sure, sir. Your man was most particular to stipulate the pink and blue flowered brocades, next the Prince of Wales's."

"But you must have the band stop that piece, Mr. Tyers," cried Lady Sarah. "I declare, it is too much for my nerves. Let them play Dibbin's *Ephesian Matron*."

"As your Ladyship wishes," responded the obliging Mr. Tyers, and sent off an uniformed warder to the band-master.

As he led us into the Rotunda, my Lady Dolly, being in one of her whimsical humours, began to recite in the manner of the guide-book, to the vast diversion of our party and the honest citizens gaping at us.

"This, my lords, ladies, and gentlemen," says the minx, "is that marvellous Rotunda commonly known as the 'umbrella,' where the music plays on wet nights, and where we have our masquerades and ridottos. Their Royal Highnesses are very commonly seen here on such occasions. As you see, it is decorated with mirrors and scenes and busts, and with gilded festoons. That picture was painted by the famous Hogarth. The organ in the orchestra cost — you must supply the figure,

Mr. Tyers,—and the ceiling is at least two hundred feet high. Gentlemen from the colonies and the country take notice."

By this time we were surrounded. Mr. Marmaduke was scandalized and crushed, but Mr. Tyers, used to the vagaries of his fashionable patrons, was wholly convulsed.

"Faith, Miss Manners, and you would consent to do this two nights more, we should have to open another gate," he declared. Followed by the mob, which it seems was part of the excitement, he led us out of the building into the Grand Walk; and offered to turn on the waterfall and mill, which (so Lady Sarah explained to me) the farmers and merchants fell down and worshipped every night at nine, to the tinkling of bells. She told Mr. Tyers there was diversion enough without "tin cascades." When we got to the Grand Cross Walk he pointed out the black "Wilderness" of tall elms and cedars looming ahead of us. And so we came to the South Walk, with its three triumphal arches framing a noble view of architecture at the far end. Our gentlemen sauntered ahead, with their spy-glasses, staring the citizens' pretty daughters out of countenance, and making cynical remarks.

"Why, egad!" I heard Sir Charles say, "the wig-makers have no cause to petition his Majesty for work. I'll be sworn the false hair this good staymaker has on cost a guinea."

A remark which caused the staymaker (if such he was) such huge discomfort that he made off with his wife in the opposite direction, to the time of jeers and cock-crows from the bevy of Vauxhall bucks walking abreast.

"You must show us the famous 'dark walks,' Mr. Tyers," says Dorothy.

"Surely you will not care to see those, Miss Manners."

"O lud, of course you must," chimed in the Miss Stanleys; "there is no spice in these flaps and flies."

He led us accordingly into Druid's Walk, overarched with elms, and dark as the shades, our gentlemen singing, "'Ods! Lovers will contrive," in chorus, the ladies exclaiming and drawing together. Then I felt a soft, restraining hold on my arm, and fell back instinctively, vibrating to the touch.

"Could you not see that I have been trying to get a word with you for ever so long?"

"I trust you to find a way, Dolly, if you but wish," I replied, admiring her stratagem.

"I am serious to-night." Indeed, her voice betrayed as much. How well I recall those rich and low tones! "I said I wished you shut up in the Marshalsea, and I meant it. I have been worrying about you."

"You make me very happy," said I; which was no lie.

"Richard, you are every bit as reckless and indifferent of danger as they say your father was. And I am afraid—"

"Of what?" I asked quickly.

"You once mentioned a name to me—"

"Yes?" I was breathing deep.

"I have forgiven you," she said gently. "I never meant to have referred to that incident more. You will understand whom I mean. You must know that he is a dangerous man, and a treacherous. Oh!" she exclaimed, "I have been in hourly terror ever since you rode against him in Hyde Park. There! I have said it."

The tense sweetness of that moment none will ever know.

"But you have more reason to fear him than I, Dorothy."

"Hush!" she whispered, catching her breath; "what are you saying?"

"That he has more cause to fear me than I to dread him."

She came a little closer.

"You stayed in London for me, Richard. Why did you? There was no need," she exclaimed; "there was no need, do you hear? Oh, I shall never forgive Comyn for his meddling! I am sure 'twas he who told you some ridiculous story. He had no foundation for it."

"Dorothy," I demanded, my voice shaking with earnestness, "will you tell me honestly there is no foundation for the report that the duke is intriguing to marry you?"

That question was not answered, and regret came the instant it had left my lips—regret and conviction both. Dorothy joined Lady Carlisle before our absence had been noted, and began to banter Fitzpatrick upon his losings.

We were in the lighted Grove again, and sitting down to a supper of Vauxhall fare: transparent slices of ham (which had been a Vauxhall joke for ages), and chickens and cheese cakes and champagne and claret, and arrack punch. Mr. Tyers extended the concert in our favour. Mrs. Weichsell and the beautiful Baddeley trilled sentimental ballads which our ladies chose; and Mr. Vernon, the celebrated tenor, sang *Cupid's Recruiting Sergeant* so happily that Storer sent him a bottle of champagne. After which we amused ourselves with catches until the space between our boxes and the orchestra was filled. In the midst of this Comyn came quietly in from the other box and took a seat beside me.

"Chartersea is here to-night," said he.

I started. "How do you know?"

"Tyers told me he turned up half an hour since. Tom asked his Grace to join our party," his Lordship laughed. "Duke said no — he was to be here only half an hour, and Tom did not push him. He told me as a joke, and thinks Chartersea came to meet some *petite*."

"Any one with him?" I asked.

"Yes. Tall, dark man, one eye cast, — that's Lewis. They have come on some dirty work, Richard. Watch little Marmaduke. He has been fidgety as a cat all night."

"That's true," said I. Looking up, I caught Dorothy's eyes upon us, her lips parted, uneasiness and apprehension plain upon her face. Comyn dropped his voice still lower.

"I believe she suspects something," he said, rising. "Chartersea is gone off toward the Wilderness, so Tom says. You must not let little Marmaduke see him. If Manners gets up to go, I will tune up *Black-eyed Susan*, and do you follow on some pretext. If you are not back in a reasonable time, I'll after you."

He had been gone scant three minutes before I heard his clear voice singing *All in the Downs*, and up I got, with a precipitation far from politic, and stepped out of the box. Our company stared in surprise. But Dorothy rose clear from her chair. The terror I saw stamped upon her face haunts me yet, and I heard her call my name.

I waited for nothing. Gaining the Grand Walk, I saw Mr. Marmaduke's insignificant figure dodging fearfully among the roughs, whose hour it was. He traversed the Cross Walk, and twenty yards farther on dived into an opening in the high hedge bounding the Wilderness. Before he had made six paces I had him by the shoulder, and he let out a shriek of fright like a woman's.

"It is I, Richard Carvel, Mr. Manners," I said shortly. I could not keep out the contempt from my tone. "I beg a word with you."

In his condition then words were impossible. His teeth rattled again, and he trembled like a hare caught alive. I kept my hold of him, and employed the time until he should be more composed peering into the darkness. For all I knew Chartersea might be within ear-shot. But I could see nothing but black trunks of trees.

"What is it, Richard?"

"You are going to meet Chartersea," I said.

He must have seen the futility of a lie, or else was scared out of all contrivance. "Yes," he said weakly.

"You have allowed it to become the talk of London that this filthy nobleman is blackmailing you for your daughter," I went on, without wasting words. "Tell me, is it, or is it not, true?"

As he did not answer, I retained a handful of the grained silk on his shoulder as a measure of precaution.

"Is this so?" I repeated.

"You must know, I suppose," he said, under his breath, and with a note of sullenness.

"I must," I said firmly. "The knowledge is the weapon I need, for I, too, am going to meet Chartersea."

He ceased quivering all at once.

"You are going to meet him!" he cried, in another voice. "Yes, yes, it is so, — it is so. I will tell you all."

"Keep it to yourself, Mr. Manners," I replied, with repugnance, "I have heard all I wish. Where is he?" I demanded.

"Hold the path until you come to him. And God bless —"

I shook my head.

"No, not that! Do you go back to the company and make some excuse for me. Do not alarm them. And if you get the chance, tell Lord Comyn where to come."

I waited until I saw him under the lights of the Grand Walk, and fairly running. Then I swung on my heel. I was of two minds whether to wait for Comyn, by far the wiser course. The unthinking recklessness I had inherited drove me on.

CHAPTER XLI

THE WILDERNESS

My eyes had become accustomed to the darkness, and presently I made out a bench ahead, with two black figures starting from it. One I should have known on the banks of the Styx. From each came a separate oath as I stopped abreast them, and called the duke by name.

"Mr. Carvel!" he cried; "what the devil do you here, sir?"

"I am come to keep an appointment for Mr. Manners," I said. "May I speak to your Grace alone?"

He made a peculiar sound by sucking in his breath, meant for a sneering laugh.

"No," says he, "damned if you shall! I have nothing in common with you, sir. So love for Miss Manners has driven you mad, my young upstart. And he is not the first, Lewis."

"Nor the last, by G—," says the captain.

"I have a score to settle with you, d—n you!" cried Chartersea.

"That is why I am here, your Grace," I replied; "only you have twisted the words. There has been foul play enough. I have come to tell you," I cried, boiling with anger, "I have come to tell you there has been foul play enough with a weakling that cannot protect himself, and to put an end to your blackmail."

In the place of an oath, a hoarse laugh of derision came out of him. But I was too angry then to note its significance. I slapped his face — nay, boxed it so that my palm stung. I heard his sword scraping out of the scabbard, and drew mine, stepping back to distance at the same instant. Then, with something of a shudder, I remembered young Atwater, and a brace of other instances of his villany. I looked for the captain. He was gone.

Our blades, the duke's and mine, came together with a ring, and I felt the strength of his wrist behind his, and of his short, powerful arm. The steel sung with our quick changes from *quarte* to *tierce*. 'Twas all by the feeling, without light to go by, and hatred between us left little space for skill. Our lunges were furious. 'Twas not long before I felt his point at my chest, but his reach was scant. All at once the music swelled up: voices and laughter were wafted faintly from the pleasure-world of lights beyond. But my head was filled, to the exclusion of all else, with a hatred and fury. And (God forgive me!) from between my teeth came a prayer that if I might kill this monster, I would die willingly.

Suddenly, as I pressed him, he shifted ground, and there was Lewis standing within range of my eye. His hands were nowhere — they were behind his back! God alone knows why he had not murdered me. To keep Chartersea between him and me I swung another quarter. The duke seemed to see my game, struggled against it, tried to rush in under my guard, made a vicious lunge that would have ended me then and there had he not slipped. We were both panting like wild beasts. When next I raised my eyes Lewis had faded into the darkness. Then I felt my head as wet as from a plunge, the water running on my brow, and my back twitching. Every second I thought the sting of his sword was between my ribs. But to forsake the duke would have been the maddest of follies.

In that moment of agony came footsteps beating on the path, and by tacit consent our swords were still. We listened.

"Richard! Richard Carvel!"

For the second time in my life I thanked Heaven for that brave and loyal English heart. I called back, but my throat was dry and choked.

"So they are at their d—d assassins' tricks again! You need have no fear of one murderer."

With that their steels rang out behind me like broadswords, Lewis wasting his breath in curses and blasphemies. I began to push Chartersea with all my might, and the wonder of it was that we did not fight with our fingers on each other's necks. His attacks, too, redoubled. Twice I felt the stings of his point, once in the hand, and once in the body, but I minded them as little as pin-pricks. I was sure I had touched him, too. I heard him blowing distressedly. The casks of wine he had drunk in his short life were telling now, and his thrusts grew weaker. That fiercest of all joys — of killing an enemy — was in me, when I heard a cry that rang in my ears for many a year afterward, and the thud of a body on the ground.

"I have done for him, your Grace," says Lewis, with an oath; and added immediately, "I think I hear people."

Before I had reached my Lord the captain repeated this, and excitedly begged the duke, I believe, to fly. Chartersea hissed out that he would not move a step until he had finished me, and as I bent over the body his point popped through my coat, and the pain shot under my shoulder. I staggered, and fell. A second of silence ensued, when the duke said with a laugh that was a cackle: —

"He won't marry her, d—n him!" (panting). "He had me cursed near killed, Lewis. Best give him another for luck."

I felt his heavy hand on the sword, and it tearing out of me. Next came the single word "Dover," and they were gone. I had not lost my senses, and was on my knees again immediately, ripping open Comyn's waistcoat with my left hand, and murmuring his name in an agony of sorrow. I was searching under his shirt, wet with blood, when I became aware of voices at my side. "A duel! A murder! Call the warders! Warders, ho!"

"A surgeon!" I cried. "A surgeon first of all!"

Some one had wrenched a lamp from the Grand Walk and held it, flickering in the wind, before his Lordship's face. Guided by its light, more people came running through the wood, then the warders with lanthorns, headed by Mr. Tyers, and on top of him Mr. Fitzpatrick and my Lord Carlisle. We carried poor Jack to the house at the gate, and closed the doors against the crowd.

By the grace of Heaven Sir Charles Blicke was walking in the gardens that night, and, battering at the door, was admitted along with the constable and the watch. Assisted by a young apothecary, Sir Charles washed and dressed the wound, which was in the left groin, and to our anxious questions replied that there was a chance of recovery.

"But you, too, are hurt, sir," he said, turning his clear eyes upon me. Indeed, the blood had been dripping from my hand and arm during the whole of the operation, and I began to be weak from the loss of it. By great good fortune Chartersea's thrust, which he thought had ended my life, passed under my armpit from behind and, stitching the skin, lodged deep in my right nipple. This wound the surgeon bound carefully, and likewise two smaller ones.

The constable was for carrying me to the Marshalsea. And so I was forced to tell that I had quarrelled with Chartersea; and the watch, going out to the scene of the fight, discovered the duke's sword which he had pulled out of me, and Lewis's laced hat; and also a trail of blood leading from the spot. Mr. Tyers testified that he had seen Chartersea that night, and Lord Carlisle and Fitzpatrick to the grudge the duke bore me. I was given my liberty.

Comyn was taken to his house in Brook Street, Grosvenor Square, in Sir Charles's coach, whither I insisted upon preceding him. 'Twas on the way there that Fitzpatrick told me Dorothy had fainted when she heard the alarm — a piece of news which added to my anxiety. We called up the dowager countess, Comyn's mother, and Carlisle broke the news to her, mercifully lightening me of a share of the blame. Her Ladyship received the tidings with great fortitude; and instead of the torrent of reproaches I looked for, and deserved, she implored me to go home and care for my injuries lest I get the fever. I believe that I burst into tears.

His Lordship was carried up the stairs with never a word or a groan from his lips, and his heart beating out slowly.

We reached my lodgings as the watchman was crying: "Past two o'clock, and a windy morning!"

Mr. Fitzpatrick stayed with me that night. And the next morning, save for the soreness of the cuts I had got, I found myself well as ever. I was again to thank the robustness of my health. Despite the protests of Banks and Fitzpatrick, and of Mr. Fox (who arrived early, not having been to bed at all), I jumped into a chaise and drove to Brook Street. There I had the good fortune to get the greatest load from my mind. Comyn was resting so much easier that the surgeon had left, and her Ladyship retired two hours since.

The day was misting and dark, but so vast was my relief that I imagined the sun was out as I rattled toward Arlington Street. If only Dolly were not ill again from the shock, I should be happy indeed. She must have heard, ere then, that I was not killed; and I had still better news to tell her than that of Lord Comyn's condition. Mr. Fox, who got every rumour that ran, had shouted after me that the duke and Lewis were set out for France. How he knew I had not waited to inquire. But the report tallied with my own surmise, for they had used the word "Dover" when they left us for dead in the Wilderness.

I dismissed my chaise at the door.

"Mr. Manners waits on you, sir, in the drawing-room," said the footman. "Your honour is here sooner than he looked for," he added gratuitously.

"Sooner than he looked for?"

"Yes, sir. James is gone to you but quarter of an hour since with a message, sir."

I was puzzled.

"And Miss Manners? Is she well?"

The man smiled.

"Very well, sir, thank your honour."

To add to my surprise, Mr. Marmaduke was pacing the drawing-room in a yellow night-gown. He met me with an expression I failed to fathom, and then my eye was held by a letter in his hand. He cleared his throat.

"Good morning, Richard," said he, very serious, — very pompous, I thought. "I am pleased to see that you are so well out of the deplorable affair of last night."

I had not looked for gratitude. In truth, I had done nothing for him, and Chartersea might have exposed him a highwayman for all I cared, — I had fought for Dolly. But this attitude astonished me. I was about to make a tart reply, and then thought better of it.

"Walter, a decanter of wine for Mr. Carvel," says he to the footman. Then to me: "I am rejoiced to hear that Lord Comyn is out of danger."

I merely stared at him.

"Will you sit?" he continued. "To speak truth, the Annapolis packet came in last night with news for you. Knowing that you have not had time to hear from Maryland, I sent for you."

My brain was in such a state that for the moment I took no meaning from this introduction. I was conscious only of indignation against him for sending for me, when for all he knew I might have been unable to leave my bed. Suddenly I jumped from the chair.

"You have heard from Maryland?" I cried. "Is Mr. Carvel dead? Oh, tell me, is Mr. Carvel dead?" And I clutched his arm to make him wince.

He nodded, and turned away. "My dear old friend is no more," he said. "Your grandfather passed away on the seventh of last month."

I sank into a chair and bowed my face, a flood of recollections overwhelming me, a thousand kindnesses of my grandfather coming to mind. One comfort alone stood forth, — even had I gone home with John Paul, I had missed him. But that he should have died alone with Grafton brought the tears brimming to my eyes. I had thought to be there to receive his last words and blessing, to watch over him, and to smooth his pillow. Who had he else in the world to bear him affection on his death-bed? The imagination of that scene drove me mad.

Mr. Manners aroused me by a touch, and I looked up quickly. So quickly that I surprised the trace of a smile about his weak mouth. Were I to die to-morrow, I would swear to this on the Evangels. Nor was it the smile which compels itself upon the weak in serious moments. Nay, there was in it something malicious. And Mr. Manners could not even act.

2 c

"There is more, Richard," he was saying; "there is worse to come. Can you bear it?"

His words and look roused me from my sorrow. I have ever been short of temper with those I disliked, and (alas!) with my friends also. And now all my pent-up wrath against this little man broke forth. I divined his meaning, and forgot that he was Dorothy's father.

"Worse?" I shouted, while he gave back in his alarm. "Do you mean that Grafton has got possession of the estate? Is that what you mean, sir?"

"Yes," he gasped, "yes. I pray you be calm."

"And you call that worse than losing my dearest friend on earth?" I cried. There must have been an infinite scorn in my voice. "Then your standards and mine are different, Mr. Manners. Your ways and mine are different, and I thank God for it. You have played more than one double part with me. You looked me in the face and denied me, and left me to go to a prison. I shall not repeat my grandfather's kindnesses to you, sir. Though you may not recall them, I do. And if your treatment of me was known in Maryland, you would be drummed out of the colony even as Mr. Hood was, and hung in effigy."

"As God hears me, Richard —"

"Do not add perjury to it," I said. "And have no uneasiness that I shall publish you. Your wife and daughter have saved you before, — they will save you now."

I paused, struck speechless by a suspicion that suddenly flashed into my head. A glance at the contemptible form cowering within the folds of the flowered gown clinched it to a conviction. In two strides I had seized him by the skin over his ribs, and he shrieked with pain and fright.

"You — you snake!" I cried, in uncontrollable anger. "You well knew Dorothy's spirit, which she has not got from you, and you lied to her. Yes, lied, I say. To force her to marry Chartersea you made her believe that your precious honour was in danger. And you lied to me last night, and sent me in the dark to fight two of the most treacherous villains in England. You wish they had killed me. The plot was between

"You ... would sell your daughter and your honour for a title"

you and his Grace. You, who have not a cat's courage, commit an indiscretion! You never made one in your life. Tell me," I cried, shaking him until his teeth smote together, "was it not put up between you?"

"Let me go! Let me go, and I will tell!" he wailed in the agony of my grip. I tightened it the more.

"You shall confess it first," I said, from between my teeth.

Scarce had his lips formed the word *yes*, when I had flung him half across the room. He tripped on his gown, and fell sprawling on his hands. So the servant found us when he came back with the tray. The lackey went out again hastily.

"My God!" I exclaimed, in bitterness and disgust; "you are a father, and would sell both your daughter and your honour for a title, and to the filthiest wretch in the kingdom?"

Without bestowing upon him another look, I turned on my heel and left the room. I had set my foot on the stair, when I heard the rustle of a dress, and the low voice which I knew so well calling my name.

"Richard."

There at my side was Dorothy, even taller in her paleness, with sorrow and agitation in her blue eyes.

"Richard, I have heard all, — I listened. Are you going away without a word for me?" Her breath came fast, and mine, as she laid a hand upon my arm. "Richard, I do not care whether you are poor. What am I saying?" she cried wildly. "Am I false to my own father? Richard, what have you done?"

And then, while I stood dazed, she tore open her gown, and drawing forth a little gold locket, pressed it in my palm. "The flowers you gave me on your birthday, — the lilies of the valley, do you remember? They are here, Richard. I have worn them upon my heart ever since."

I raised the locket to my lips.

"I shall treasure it for your sake, Dorothy," I said, "for the sake of the old days. God keep you!"

For a moment I looked into the depths of her eyes. Then she was gone, and I went down the stairs alone. Outside, the rain fell unheeded on my new coat. My steps bent southward, past Whitehall, where the martyr Charles had met death so nobly: past the stairs to the river, where she had tripped with me so gayly not a month since. Death was in my soul that day,—death and love, which is the mystery of life. God guided me into the great Abbey near by, where I fell on my knees before Him and before England's dead. He had raised them and cast them down, even as He was casting me, that I might come to know the glory of His holy name.

CHAPTER XLII

MY FRIENDS ARE PROVEN

At the door of my lodgings I was confronted by Banks, red with indignation and fidgety from uneasiness.

"O Lord, Mr. Carvel, what has happened, sir?" he cried. "Your honour's agent 'as been here since noon. Must I take orders from the likes o' him, sir?"

Mr. Dix was indeed in possession of my rooms, lounging in the chair Dolly had chosen, smoking my tobacco. I stared at him from the threshold. Something in my appearance, or force of habit, or both brought him to his feet, and wiped away the smirk from his face. He put down the pipe guiltily. I told him shortly that I had heard the news which he must have got by the packet: and that he should have his money, tho' it took the rest of my life: and the ten per cent I had promised him provided he would not press my Lord Comyn. He hesitated, and drummed on the table. He was the man of business again.

"What security am I to have, Mr. Carvel?" he asked.

"My word," I said. "It has never yet been broken, I thank God, nor my father's before me. And hark ye, Mr. Dix, you shall not be able to say that of Grafton." Truly I thought the principal and agent were now well matched.

"Very good, Mr. Carvel," he said; "ten per cent. I shall call with the papers on Monday morning."

"I shall not run away before that," I replied.

He got out, with a poor attempt at a swagger, without his customary protestations of duty and humble offers of service. And I thanked Heaven he had not made a scene, which in my state of mind I could not have borne, but must have laid hands upon him. Perhaps he believed Grafton not yet secure in his title. I did not wonder then, in the heat of my youth, that he should have accepted my honour as security. But since I have marvelled not a little at this. The fine gentlemen at Brooks's with whom I had been associating were none too scrupulous, and regarded money-lenders as legitimate prey. Debts of honour they paid but tardily, if at all. A certain nobleman had been owing my Lord Carlisle thirteen thousand pounds for a couple of years, that his Lordship had won at hazard. And tho' I blush to write it, Mr. Fox himself was notorious in such matters, and was in debt to each of the coterie of fashionables of which he was the devoted chief.

The faithful Banks vowed, with tears in his eyes, that he would never desert me. And in that moment of dejection the poor fellow's devotion brought me no little comfort. At such times the heart is bitter. We look askance at our friends, and make the task of comfort doubly hard for those that remain true. I had a great affection for the man, and had become so used to his ways and unwearying service that I had not the courage to refuse his prayers to go with me to America. I had not a farthing of my own — he would serve me for nothing — nay, work for me. "Sure," he said, taking off my coat and bringing me my gown, — "Sure, your honour was not made to work." To cheer me he went on with some foolish footman's gossip that there lacked not ladies with jointures who would marry me, and be thankful. I smiled sadly.

"That was when I was Mr. Carvel's heir, Banks."

"And your face and figure, sir, and masterful ways! Faith, and what more would a lady want!" Banks's notions of morality were vague enough, and he would have had me sink what I had left at hazard at Almack's. He had lived in this atmosphere. Alas! there was little chance of my ever regaining the position I had held but yesterday. I thought of the sponging-house, and my brow was moist. England was no place, in those days, for fallen gentlemen. With us in the Colonies the law offered itself. Mr. Swain, and other barristers of Annapolis, came to my mind, for God had given me courage. I would try the law. For I had small hopes of defeating my Uncle Grafton.

The Sunday morning dawned brightly, and the church bells ringing brought me to my feet, and out into Piccadilly, in the forlorn hope that I might see my lady on her way to morning service, — see her for the last time in life, perhaps. Her locket I wore over my heart. It had lain upon hers. To see her was the most exquisite agony in the world. But not to see her, and to feel that she was scarce quarter of a mile away, was beyond endurance. I stood beside an area at the entrance to Arlington Street, and waited for an hour, quite in vain; watching every face that passed, townsmen in their ill-fitting Sunday clothes, and fine ladies with the footmen carrying velvet prayer-books. And some that I knew only stared, and others gave me distant bows from their coach windows. For those that fall from fashion are dead to fashion.

Dorothy did not go to church that day.

It is a pleasure, my dears, when writing of that hour of bitterness, to record the moments of sweetness which lightened it. As I climbed up to my rooms in Dover Street, I heard merry sounds above, and a cloud of smoke blew out of the door when I opened it.

"Here he is," cried Mr. Fox. "You see, Richard, we have not deserted you when we can win no more of your money."

"Why, egad! the man looks as if he had had a calamity," said Mr. Fitzpatrick.

"And there is not a Jew here," Fox continued. "Tho' it is Sunday, the air in my Jerusalem chamber is as bad as in any crimp's den in St. Giles's. 'Slife, and I live to be forty, I shall have as many underground avenues as his Majesty Louis the Eleventh."

"He must have a place," put in my Lord Carlisle.

"We must do something for him," said Fox, "albeit he is an American and a Whig, and all the rest of the execrations. Thou wilt have to swallow thy golden opinions, my buckskin, when we put thee in office."

I was too overwhelmed even to protest.

"You are not in such a cursed bad way, when all is said,

Richard," said Fitzpatrick. "Charles, when he loses a fortune, immediately borrows another."

"If you stick to whist and quinze," said Charles, solemnly, giving me the advice they were forever thrusting upon him, "and play with system, you may make as much as four thousand a year, sir."

And this was how I was treated by those heathen and cynical macaronies, Mr. Fox's friends. I may not say the same for the whole of Brooks's Club, tho' I never darkened its doors afterwards. But I encountered my Lord March that afternoon, and got only a blank stare in place of a bow.

Charles had collected (Heaven knows how!) the thousand pounds which he stood in my debt, and Mr. Storer and Lord Carlisle offered to lend me as much as I chose. I had some difficulty in refusing, and more still in denying Charles when he pressed me to go with them to Richmond, where he had rooms for play over Sunday.

Banks brought me the news that Lord Comyn was sitting up, and had been asking for me that day; that he was recovering beyond belief. But I was resolved not to go to Brook Street until the money affairs were settled on Monday with Mr. Dix, for I knew well that his Lordship would insist upon carrying out with the agent the contract he had so generously and hastily made, rather than let me pay an abnormal interest.

On Monday I rose early, and went out for a bit of air before the scene with Mr. Dix. Returning, I saw a coach with his Lordship's arms on the panels, and there was Comyn himself in my great chair at the window, where he had been deposited by Banks and his footman. I stared as on one risen from the dead.

"Why, Jack, what are you doing here?" I cried.

He replied very offhand, as was his manner at such times:—

"Blicke vows that Chartersea and Lewis have qualified for the College of Surgeons," says he. "They are both born anatomists. Your job under the arm was the worst bungle of the two, egad, for Lewis put his sword, pat as you please, between two of my organs (cursed if I know their names), and not so much as scratched one."

"Look you, Jack," said I, "I am not deceived. You have no right to be here, and you know it."

"Tush!" answered his Lordship; "I am as well as you." And he took snuff to prove the assertion. "Why the devil was you not in Brook Street yesterday to tell me that your uncle had swindled you? I thought I was your friend," says he, "and I learn of your misfortune through others."

"It is because you are my friend, and my best friend, that I would not worry you when you lay next door to death on my account," I said, with emotion.

And just then Banks announced Mr. Dix.

"Let him wait," said I, greatly disturbed.

"Show him up!" said my Lord, peremptorily.

"No, no!" I protested; "he can wait. We shall have no business now."

But Banks was gone. And I found out, long afterward, that it was put up between them.

The agent swaggered in with that easy assurance he assumed whenever he got the upper hand. He was the would-be squire once again, in top-boots and a frock. I have rarely seen a man put out of countenance so easily as was Mr. Dix that morning when he met his Lordship's fixed gaze from the arm-chair.

"And so you are turned Jew?" says he, tapping his snuff-box. "Before you go ahead so fast again, you will please to remember, d—n you, that Mr. Carvel is the kind that does not lose his friends with his fortune."

Mr. Dix made a salaam, which was so ludicrous in a squire that my Lord roared with laughter, and I feared for his wound.

"A man must live, my Lord," sputtered the agent. His discomfiture was painful.

"At the expense of another," says Comyn, dryly. "That is your motto in Change Alley."

"If you will permit, Jack, I must have a few words in private with Mr. Dix," I cut in uneasily.

His Lordship would be damned first. "I am not accustomed to be thwarted, Richard, I tell you. Ask the dowager if I have not always had my way. I am not going to stand by

and see a man who saved my life fall into the clutches of an
usurer. Yes, I said *usurer*, Mr. Dix. My attorney, Mr. Ken-
nett, of Lincoln's Inn, has instructions to settle with you."

And, despite all I could say, he would not budge an inch.
At last I submitted under the threat that he would never after
have a word to say to me. By good luck, when I had paid
into Mr. Dix's hand the thousand pounds I had received from
Charles Fox, and cleared my outstanding bills, the sum I
remained in Comyn's debt was not greatly above seven hundred pounds. And that was the end of Mr. Dix for me; when
he had backed himself out in chagrin at having lost his ten
per centum, my feelings got the better of me. The water
rushed to my eyes, and I turned my back upon his Lordship.
To conceal his own emotions he fell to swearing like mad.

"Fox will get you something," he said at length, when he
was a little calmed.

I told him, sadly, that my duty took me to America.

"And Dorothy?" he said; "you will leave her?"

I related the whole miserable story (all save the part of the
locket), for I felt that I owed it him. His excitement grew
as he listened, until I had to threaten to stop to keep him
quiet. But when I had done, he saw nothing but good to
come of it.

"'Od's life! Richard, lad, come here!" he cried. "Give me
your hand. Why, you ass, you have won a thousand times
over what you lost. She loves you! Did I not say so? And
as for that intriguing little puppy, her father, you have pulled
his teeth, egad. She heard what you said to him, you tell me.
Then he will never deceive her again, my word on't. And
Chartersea may come back to London, and be damned."

CHAPTER XLIII

ANNAPOLIS ONCE MORE

THREE days after that I was at sea, in the *Norfolk* packet, with the farewells of my loyal English friends ringing in my ears. Captain Graham, the master of the packet, and his passengers found me but a poor companion. But they had heard of my misfortune, and vied with each other in heaping kindnesses upon me. Nor did they intrude on my walks in the night watches, to see me slipping a locket from under my waistcoat — ay, and raising it to my lips. 'Twas no doubt a blessing that I had lesser misfortunes to share my attention. God had put me in the way of looking forward rather than behind, and I was sure that my friends in Annapolis would help me to an honest living, and fight my cause against Grafton.

Banks was with me. The devoted soul did his best to cheer me, tho' downcast himself at leaving England. To know what to do with him gave me many an anxious moment. I doubted not that I could get him into a service, but when I spoke of such a thing he burst into tears, and demanded whether I meant to throw him off. Nor was any argument of mine of use.

After a fair and uneventful voyage of six weeks, I beheld again my native shores in the low spits of the Virginia capes. The sand was very hot and white, and the waters of the Chesapeake rolled like oil under the July sun. We were all day getting over to Yorktown, the ship's destination. A schooner was sailing for Annapolis early the next morning, and I barely had time to get off my baggage and catch her. We went up the bay with a fresh wind astern, which died down at night.

The heat was terrific after England and the sea-voyage, and we slept on the deck. And Banks sat, most of the day, exclaiming at the vast scale on which this new country was laid out, and wondering at the myriad islands we passed, some of them fair with grain and tobacco; and at the low-lying shores clothed with forests, and broken by the salt marshes, with now and then the manor-house of some gentleman-planter visible on either side. Late on the second day I beheld again the cliffs that mark the mouth of the Severn, then the sail-dotted roads and the roofs of Annapolis.

We landed, Banks and I, in a pinnace from the schooner, and so full was my heart at the sight of the old objects that I could only gulp now and then, and utter never a word. There was the dock where I had paced up and down near the whole night, when Dolly had sailed away; and Pryse the coachmaker's shop, and the little balcony upon which I had stood with my grandfather, and railed in a boyish tenor at Mr. Hood. The sun cast sharp, black shadows. And it being the middle of the dull season, when the quality were at their seats, and the dinner-hour besides, the town might have been a deserted one for its stillness, as tho' the inhabitants had walked out of it, and left it so. I made my way, Banks behind me, into Church Street, past the "Ship" tavern, which brought memories of the brawl there, and of Captain Clapsaddle forcing the mob, like chaff, before his sword. The bees were humming idly over the sweet-scented gardens, and Farris, the clock-maker, sat at his door, and nodded. He jerked his head as I went by with a cry of "Lord, it is Mr. Richard back!" and I must needs pause, to let him bow over my hand. Farther up the street I came to mine host of the Coffee House standing on his steps, with his hands behind his back.

"Mr. Claude," I said.

He looked at me as tho' I had risen from the dead.

"God save us!" he shouted, in a voice that echoed through the narrow street. "God save us!"

He seemed to go all to pieces. To my bated questions he replied at length, when he had got his breath, that Captain Clapsaddle had come to town but the day before, and was even then in the coffee-room at his dinner. Alone? Yes, alone. Almost tottering, I mounted the steps, and turned in at the coffee-room door, and stopped. There sat the captain at a table, the roast and wine untouched before him, his waistcoat thrown open. He was staring out of the open window into the inn garden beyond, with its shade of cherry trees. Mr. Claude's cry had not disturbed his reveries, nor our talk after it. I went forward. I touched him on the shoulder, and he sprang up and looked once into my face, and by some trick of the mind uttered the very words Mr. Claude had used.

"God save us! Richard!" And he opened his arms and strained me to his great chest, calling my name again and again, while the tears coursed down the furrows of his cheeks. For I marked the furrows for the first time, and the wrinkles settling in his forehead and around his eyes. What he said when he released me, nor my replies, can I remember now, but at last he called, in his ringing voice, to mine host: —

"A bottle from your choicest bin, Claude! Some of Mr. Bordley's. For he that was lost is found."

The hundred questions I had longed to ask were forgotten. A peace stole upon me that I had not felt since I had looked upon his face before. The wine was brought by Mr. Claude, and opened, and it was mine host who broke the silence, and the spell.

"Your very good health, Mr. Richard," he said; "and may you come to your own again!"

"I drink it with all my heart, Richard," replied Captain Daniel. But he glanced at me sadly, and his honest nature could put no hope into his tone. "We have got him back again, Mr. Claude. And God has answered our prayers. So let us be thankful." And he sat down in silence, gazing at me in pity and tenderness, while Mr. Claude withdrew. "I can give you but a sad welcome home, my lad," he said presently, with a hesitation strange to him. "'Tis not the first bad news I have had to break in my life to your family, but I pray it may be the last." He paused. I knew he was thinking of the black tidings he had once brought my mother. "Richard, your grandfather is dead," he ended abruptly.

I nodded wonderingly.

"What!" he exclaimed; "you have heard already?"

"Mr. Manners told me, in London," I said, completely mystified.

"London!" he cried, starting forward. "London and Mr. Manners! Have you been to London?"

"You had my letters to Mr. Carvel?" I demanded, turning suddenly sick.

His eye flashed.

"Never a letter. We mourned you for dead, Richard. This is Grafton's work!" he cried, springing to his feet and striking the table with his great fist, so that the dishes jumped. "Grafton Carvel, the prettiest villain in these thirteen colonies! Oh, we shall hang him some day."

"Then Mr. Carvel died without knowing that I was safe?" I interrupted.

"On that I'll lay all my worldly goods," replied Captain Daniel, emphatically. "If any letters came to Marlboro' Street from you, Mr. Carvel never dropped eyes on 'em."

"What a fool was I not to have written you!" I groaned.

He drew his chair around the table, and close to mine.

"Had the news that you escaped death been cried aloud in the streets, my lad, 'twould never have got to your grandfather's ear," he said, in lower tones. "I will tell you what happened, tho' I have it at second hand, being in the North, as you may remember. Grafton came in from Kent and invested Marlboro' Street. He himself broke the news to Mr. Carvel, who took to his bed. Leiden was not in attendance, you may be sure, but that quack-doctor Drake. Swain sent me a message, and I killed a horse getting here from New York. But I could no more gain admittance to your grandfather, Richard, than to King George the Third. I was met in the hall by that crocodile, who told me with too many fair words that I could not see my old friend; that for the present Dr. Drake denied him everybody. Then I damned Dr. Drake, and Grafton too. And I let him know my suspicions. He ordered me off, Richard — from that house which has been my only home for these twenty years." His voice broke.

"Mr. Carvel thought me dead, then."

"And most mercifully. Your black Hugo, when he was somewhat recovered, swore he had seen you killed and carried off. Sooth, they say there was blood enough on the place. But we spared no pains to obtain a clew of you. I went north to Boston, and Lloyd's factor south to Charleston. But no trace of the messenger who came to the Coffee House after you could we find. Hell had opened and swallowed him. And mark this for consummate villany: Grafton himself spent no less than five hundred pounds in advertising and the like."

"And he is not suspected?" I asked. This was the same question I had put to Mrs. Manners. It caused the captain to flare up again.

"'Tis incredible how a rogue may impose upon men of worth and integrity if he but know how to smirk piously, and never miss a service. And then he is an exceeding rich man. Riches cover a multitude of sins in the most virtuous community in the world. Your Aunt Caroline brought him a pretty fortune, you know. We had ominous times this spring, with the associations forming, and the *Good Intent* and the rest being sent back to England. His Excellency was at his wits' end for support. It was Grafton Carvel who helped him most, and spent money like tobacco for the King's cause, which, being interpreted, was for his own advancement. But I believe Colonel Lloyd suspects him, tho' he has never said as much to me. I have told Mr. Swain, under secrecy, what I think. He is one of the ablest lawyers that the colony owns, Richard, and a stanch friend of yours. He took your case of his own accord. But he says we have no foothold as yet."

When I asked if there was a will the captain rapped out an oath.

"'Sdeath! yes," he cried, "a will in favour of Grafton and his heirs, witnessed by Dr. Drake, they say, and another scoundrel. Your name does not occur throughout the length and breadth of it. You were dead. But you will have to ask Mr. Swain for those particulars. My dear old friend was sadly gone when he wrote it, I fear. For he never lacked shrewdness in his best days. Nor," added Captain Daniel, with force, "nor did he want for a proper estimation of Grafton."

"He has never been the same since that first sickness," I answered sadly.

When the captain came to speak of Mr. Carvel's death, the son and daughter he loved, and the child of his old age in the grave before him, he proceeded brokenly, and the tears blinded him. Mr. Carvel's last words will never be known, my dears. They sounded in the unfeeling ears of the serpent Grafton. 'Twas said that he was seen coming out of his father's house an hour after the demise, a smile on his face which he strove to hide with a pucker of sorrow. But by God's grace Mr. Allen had not read the prayers. The rector was at last removed from Annapolis, and had obtained the fat living of Frederick which he coveted.

"As I hope for salvation," the captain concluded, "I will swear there is not such another villain in the world as Grafton. The imagination of a fiend alone could have conceived and brought to execution the crime he has committed. And the Borgias were children to him. 'Twas not only the love of money that urged him, but hatred of you and of your father. That was his strongest motive, I believe. However, the days are coming, lad, when he shall have his reward, unless all signs fail. And we have had enough of sober talk," said he, pressing me to eat. "Faith, but just now, when you came in, I was thinking of you, Richard. And — God forgive me! — complaining against the lot of my life. And thinking, now that you were taken out of it, and your father and mother and grandfather gone, how little I had to live for. Now you are home again," says he, his eyes lighting on me with affection, "I count the gray hairs as nothing. Let us have your story, and be merry. Nay, I might have guessed you had been in London, with your fine clothes and your English servant."

'Twas a long story, as you know, my dears. He lighted his pipe and laid his big hand over mine, and filled my glass, and I told him most of that which had happened to me. But I left out the whole of that concerning Mr. Manners and the Duke of Chartersea, nor did I speak of the sponging-house. I believe my only motive for this omittance was a reluctance to dwell upon Dorothy, and a desire to shield her father for her sake. He dropped many a vigorous exclamation into my pauses, but when I came to speak of my friendship with Mr. Fox, his brow clouded over.

"'Ad's heart!" he cried, "'Ad's heart! And so you are turned Tory, and have at last been perverted from those principles for which I loved you most. In the old days my conscience would not allow me to advise you, Richard, and now that I am free to speak, you are past advice."

I laughed aloud.

"And what if I tell you that I made friends with his Grace of Grafton, and Lord Sandwich, and was invited to Hichinbroke, his Lordship's seat?" said I.

His honest face was a picture of consternation.

"Now the good Lord deliver us!" he exclaimed fervently. "Sandwich! Grafton! The devil!"

I gave myself over to the first real merriment I had had since I had heard of Mr. Carvel's death.

"And when Mr. Fox learned that I had lost my fortune," I went on, "he offered me a position under Government."

"Have you not friends enough at home to care for you, sir?" he said, his face getting purple. "Are you Jack Carvel's son, or are you an impostor?"

"I am Jack Carvel's son, dear Captain Daniel, and that is why I am here," I replied. "I am a stouter Whig than ever, and I believe I might have converted Mr. Fox himself had I remained at home sufficiently long," I added, with a solemn face. And, for my own edification, I related how I had bearded his Majesty's friends at Brooks's, whereat he gave a great, joyful laugh, and thumped me on the back.

"You dog, Richard! You sly rogue!" And he called to Mr. Claude for another bottle on the strength of that, and we pledged the Association. He peppered me with questions concerning *Junius*, and Mr. Wilkes, and Mr. Franklin of Philadelphia. Had I seen him in London? "I would not doubt a Carvel's word," says the captain, "(always excepting Grafton and his line, as usual), but you may duck me on the stool and

I comprehend why Mr. Fox and his friends took up with such a young rebel rapscallion as you — and after the speech you made 'em."

I astonished him vastly by pointing out that Mr. Fox and his friends cared a deal for place, and not a fig for principle; that my frankness had entertained rather than offended them; and that, having a taste for a bit of wild life and the money to gratify it, and being of a tolerant, easy nature withal, I had contrived to make many friends in that set, without aiming at influence. Whereat he gave me another lick between the shoulders.

"It was so with Jack," he cried; "thou art a replica. He would have made friends with the devil himself. In the French war, when all the rest of us Royal Americans were squabbling with his Majesty's officers out of England, and cursing them at mess, they could never be got to fight with Jack, tho' he gave them ample provocation. There was Tetherington, of the 22d foot, — who jeered us for damned provincials, and swaggered through three duels in a week, — would enter no quarrel with him. I can hear him say: 'Damn you, Carvel, you may slap my face and you will, or walk in ahead of me at the general's dinner and you will, but I like you too well to draw at you. I would not miss your company at table for all the world.' And when he was killed," Captain Daniel continued, lowering his voice, "some of them cried like women, — Tetherington among 'em, — and swore they would rather have lost their commissions at high play."

We sat talking until the summer's dusk grew on apace, and one thing this devoted lover of my family told me, which lightened my spirits of the greatest burden that had rested upon them since my calamity befell me. I had dwelt at length upon my Lord Comyn, and upon the weight of his services to me, and touched upon the sum which I stood in his debt. The captain interrupted me.

"One day, before your mother died, she sent for me," said he, "and I came to Carvel Hall. You were too young to remember. It was in September, and she was sitting on the seat under the oak she loved so well, — by Dr. Hilliard's study.

The lace shawl your father had given her was around her shoulders, and upon her face was the smile that gave me a pang to see. For it had something of heaven in it, Richard. She called me 'Daniel' then for the second time in her life. She bade me be seated beside her. 'Daniel,' she said, 'when I am gone, and father is gone, it is you who will take care of Richard. I sometimes believe all may not be well then, and that he will need you.' I knew she was thinking of Grafton," said the captain. "'I have a little money of my own, Daniel, which I have saved lately with this in view. I give it into your charge, and if trouble comes to him, my old friend, you will use it as you see fit.'

"It was a bit under a thousand pounds, Richard. And when she died I put it out under Mr. Carroll's direction at safe interest. So that you have enough to discharge your debt, and something saved against another emergency."

He fell silent, sunk into one of those reveries which the memory of my mother awoke in him. My own thoughts drifted across the sea. I was again at the top of the stairs in Arlington Street, and feeling the dearest presence in the world. The pale oval of Dorothy's face rose before me and the troubled depths of her blue eyes. And I heard once more the tremble in her voice as she confessed, in words of which she took no heed, that love for which I had sought in vain.

The summer dusk was gathering. Outside, under the cherry trees, I saw Banks holding forth to an admiring circle of negro 'ostlers. And presently Mr. Claude came in to say that Shaw, the town carpenter, and Sol Mogg, the ancient sexton of St. Anne's, and several more of my old acquaintances were without, and begged the honour of greeting me.

CHAPTER XLIV

NOBLESSE OBLIGE

I LAY that night in Captain Clapsaddle's lodgings opposite, and slept soundly. Banks was on hand in the morning to assist at my toilet, and was greatly downcast when I refused him this privilege, for the first time. Captain Daniel was highly pleased with the honest fellow's devotion in following me to America. To cheer him he began to question him as to my doings in London, and the first thing of which Banks must tell was of the riding-contest in Hyde Park, which I had omitted. It is easy to imagine how this should have tickled the captain, who always had my horsemanship at heart; and when it came to Chartersea's descent into the Serpentine, I thought he would go into apoplexy. For he had put on flesh with the years.

The news of my return had spread all over town, so that I had a deal more handshaking to do when we went to the Coffee House for breakfast. All the quality were in the country, of course, save only four gentlemen of the local Patriots' committee, of which Captain Daniel was a member, and with whom he had an appointment at ten. It was Mr. Swain who arrived first of the four.

This old friend of my childhood was a quiet man (I may not have specified), thin, and a little under stature, with a receding but thoughtful forehead. But he could express as much of joy and welcome in his face and manner as could Captain Daniel with his heartier ways.

"It does me good to see you, lad," he said, pressing my hand. "I heard you were home, and sent off an express to Patty and the mother last night."

"And are they not here?" I asked, with disappointment. Mr. Swain smiled.

"I have done a rash thing since I saw you, Richard, and bought a little plantation in Talbot, next to Singleton's. It will be my ruin," he added. "A lawyer has no business with landed ambitions."

"A little plantation!" echoed the captain. "'Od's life, he has bought one of his Lordship's own manors — as good an estate as there is in the province."

"You overdo it, Daniel," said he, reprovingly.

At that moment there was a stir in the doorway, and in came Mr. Carroll, the barrister, and Mr. Bordley and Colonel Lloyd. These gentlemen gave me such a welcome as those warm-hearted planters and lawyers knew how to bestow.

"What, ho!" cried Mr. Lloyd, "I'm stamped and taxed if it isn't young Richard Carvel himself. Well," says he, "I know one who will sleep easier o' nights now, — one Clapsaddle. The gray hairs are forgot, Daniel. We had more to-do over your disappearance than when Mr. Worthington lost his musical nigger. Where a deuce have you been, sir?"

"He shall tell us when we come back," said Mr. Bordley. "He has brought our worthy association to a standstill once, and now we must proceed about our business. Will you come, Richard? I believe you have proved yourself a sufficiently good patriot, and in this very house."

We went down Church Street, I walking behind with Colonel Lloyd, and so proud to be in such company that I cared not a groat whether Grafton had my acres or not. I remembered that the committee all wore plain and sober clothes, and carried no swords. Mr. Swain alone had a wig. I had been away but seven months, and yet here was a perceptible change. In these dignified and determined gentlemen England had more to fear than in all the mobs at Mr. Wilkes's back. How I wished that Charles Fox might have been with me.

The sun beat down upon the street. The shopkeepers were gathered at their doors, but their chattering was hushed as the dreaded committee passed. More than one, apparently, had tasted of its discipline. Colonel Lloyd whispered to me

to keep my countenance, that they were not after very large
game that morning, — only Chipchase, the butcher. And
presently we came upon the rascal putting up his shutters in
much precipitation, although it was noon. He had shed his
blood-stained smock and breeches, and donned his Sunday best,
— a white, thick-set coat, country cloth jacket, blue broadcloth
breeches, and white shirt. A grizzled cut wig sat somewhat
awry under his bearskin hat. When he perceived Mr. Carroll
at his shoulder, he dropped his shutter against the wall, and
began bowing frantically.

"You keep good hours, Master Chipchase," remarked Colonel Lloyd.

"And lose good customers," Mr. Swain added laconically.

The butcher wriggled.

"Your honours must know there be little selling when the
gentry be out of town. And I was to take a holiday to-day, to
see my daughter married."

"You will have a feast, my good man?" Captain Daniel
asked.

"To be sure, your honour, a feast."

"And any little ewe-lambs?" says Mr. Bordley, very
innocent.

Master Chipchase turned the colour of his meat, and his wit
failed him.

"'Fourthly,'" recited Mr. Carroll, with an exceeding sober
face, "'Fourthly, that we will not kill, or suffer to be killed, or
sell, or dispose to any person whom we have reason to believe
intends to kill, any ewe-lamb that shall be weaned before the
first day of May, in any year during the time aforesaid.' Have
you ever heard anything of that sound, Mr. Chipchase?"

Mr. Chipchase had. And if their honours pleased, he had a
defence to make, if their honours would but listen. And if
their honours but knew, he was as good a patriot as any in the
province, and sold his wool to Peter Psalter, and he wore the
homespun in winter. Then Mr. Carroll drew a paper from his
pocket, and began to read: "Mr. Thomas Hincks, personally
known to me, deposeth and saith, — "

Master Chipchase's knees gave from under him.

"And your honours please," he cried piteously, "I killed the lamb, but 'twas at Mr. Grafton Carvel's order, who was in town with his Excellency." (Here Mr. Swain and the captain glanced significantly at me.) "And I lose Mr. Carvel's custom, there is twelve pounds odd gone a year, your honours. And I am a poor man, sirs."

"Who is it owns your shop, my man?" asks Mr. Bordley, very sternly.

"Oh, I beg your honours will not have me put out —"

The wailing of his voice had drawn a crowd of idlers and brother shopkeepers, who seemed vastly to enjoy the knave's discomfiture. Amongst them I recognized my old acquaintance, Weld, now a rival butcher. He pushed forward boldly.

"And your honours please," said he, "he has sold lamb to half the Tory gentry in Annapolis."

"A lie!" cried Chipchase; "a lie, as God hears me!"

Now Captain Clapsaddle was one who carried his loves and his hatreds to the grave, and he had never liked Weld since the day, six years gone by, he had sent me into the Ship tavern. And when Weld heard the captain's voice he slunk away without a word.

"Have a care, Master Weld," says he, in a quiet tone that boded no good; "there is more evidence against you than you will like."

Master Chipchase, after being frightened almost out of his senses, was pardoned this once by Captain Daniel's influence. We went thence to Mr. Hildreth's shop; he was suspected of having got tea out of a South River snow; then to Mr. Jackson's; and so on. 'Twas after two when we got back to the Coffee House, and sat down to as good a dinner as Mr. Claude could prepare. "And now," cried Colonel Lloyd, "we shall have your adventures, Richard. I would that your uncle were here to listen to them," he added dryly.

I recited them very much as I had done the night before, and I warrant you, my dears, that they listened with more zest and eagerness than did Mr. Walpole. But they were all shrewd men, and kept their suspicions, if they had any, to themselves. Captain Daniel would have me omit nothing, — my intimacy with Mr. Fox, the speech at Brooks's Club, and the riding-match at Hyde Park.

"What say you to that, gentlemen?" he cried. "Egad, I'll be sworn he deserves credit, — an arrant young spark out of the Colonies, scarce turned nineteen, defeating a duke of the realm on horseback, and preaching the gospel of 'no taxation' at Brooks's Club! Nor the favour of Sandwich or March could turn him from his principles."

Modesty, my dears, does not permit me to picture the enthusiasm of these good gentlemen, who bore the responsibility of the colony of Maryland upon their shoulders. They made more of me than I deserved. In vain did I seek to explain that if a young man was but well-born, and had a full purse and a turn for high play, his principles might go hang, for all Mr. Fox cared. Colonel Lloyd commanded that the famous rose punch-bowl be filled to the brim with Mr. Claude's best summer brew, and they drank my health and my grandfather's memory. It mattered little to them that I was poor. They vowed I should not lose by my choice. Mr. Bordley offered me a home, and added that I should have employment enough in the days to come. Mr. Carroll pressed me likewise. And big-hearted Colonel Lloyd desired to send me to King's College, as was my grandfather's wish, where Will Fotheringay and my cousin Philip had been for a term. I might make a barrister of myself. Mr. Swain alone was silent and thoughtful, but I did not for an instant doubt that he would have done as much for me.

Before we broke up for the evening the gentlemen plied me with questions concerning the state of affairs in England, and the temper of his Majesty and Parliament. I say without vanity that I was able to enlighten them not a little, for I had learned a deeper lesson from the set into which I had fallen in London than if I had become the confidant of Rockingham himself. America was a long way from England in those days. I regretted that I had not arrived in London in time to witness Lord Chatham's dramatic return to politics in January, when he had completed the work of *Junius*, and broken up the Grafton ministry. But I told them of the debate I had heard in

St. Stephen's, and made them laugh over Mr. Fox's rescue of the King's friends, and the hustling of Mr. Burke from the Lords.

They were very curious, too, about Mr. Manners; and I was put to much ingenuity to answer their queries and not reveal my own connection with him. They wished to know if it were true that some nobleman had flung a bottle at his head in a rage because Dorothy would not marry him, as Dr. Courtenay's letter had stated. I replied that it was so. I did not add that it was the same nobleman who had been pitched into the Serpentine. Nor did I mention the fight at Vauxhall. I made no doubt these things would come to their ears, but I did not choose to be the one to tell them. Mr. Swain remained after the other gentlemen, and asked me if I would come with him to Gloucester Street; that he had something to say to me. We went the long way thither, and I was very grateful to him for avoiding Marlboro' Street, which must needs bring me painful recollections. He said little on the way.

I almost expected to see Patty come tripping down from the vine-covered porch with her needlework in her hand, and the house seemed strangely empty without her. Mr. Swain had his negro, Romney, place chairs for us under the apple tree, and bring out pipes and sangaree. The air was still, and heavy with the flowers' scent, and the sun was dipping behind the low eaves of the house. It was so natural to be there that I scarce realized all that had happened since last I saw the back gate in the picket fence. Alas! little Patty would never more be smuggled through it and over the wall to Marlboro' Street. Mr. Swain recalled my thoughts.

"Captain Clapsaddle has asked me to look into this matter of the will, Richard," he began abruptly. "Altho' we thought never to see you again, we have hoped against hope. I fear you have little chance for your property, my lad."

I replied that Captain Daniel had so led me to believe, and thanked him for his kindness and his trouble.

"'Twas no trouble," he replied quickly. "Indeed, I wish it might have been. I shall always think of your grandfather with reverence and with sorrow. He was a noble man, and was a friend to me, in spite of my politics, when other gentlemen of position would not invite me to their houses. It would be the greatest happiness of my life if I could restore his property to you, where he would have had it go, and deprive that villain, your uncle, of the fruits of his crime."

"Then there is nothing to be got by contesting the will?" I asked.

He shook his head soberly.

"I fear not at present," said he, "nor can I with honesty hold out any hope to you, Richard. Your uncle, by reason of his wealth, is a man of undue influence with the powers of the colony. Even if he were not so, I doubt greatly whether we should be the gainers. The will is undoubtedly genuine. Mr. Carvel thought you dead, and we cannot prove undue influence by Grafton unless we also prove that it was he who caused your abduction. Do you think you can prove that?"

"There is one witness," I exclaimed, "who overheard my uncle and Mr. Allen talking of South River and Griggs, the master of the slaver, in the stables at Carvel Hall."

"And who is that?" demanded Mr. Swain, with more excitement than I believed him capable of.

"Old Harvey."

"Your grandfather's coachman? Alas, he died the day after Mr. Carvel, and was buried the same afternoon. Have you spoken of this?"

"Not to a soul," said I.

"Then I would not. You will have to be very careful and say nothing, Richard. Let me hear what other reasons you have for believing that your uncle tried to do away with you."

I told him, lucidly as possible, everything I have related in these pages, and the admission of Griggs. He listened intently, shaking his head now and then, but not a word out of him.

"No," he said at length, "nothing is there which will be admitted, but enough to damn him if you yourself might be a witness. I will give you the law, briefly: descendible estates among us are of two kinds, estates in fee simple and estates in fee tail. Had your grandfather died without a will, his estate, which we suppose to be in fee simple, would have descended to you as the son of his eldest son, according to the fourth of the canons of descent in Blackstone. But with us fee simple estates are devisable, and Mr. Carvel was wholly within his right in cutting off the line of his eldest son. Do you follow me?"

I nodded.

"There is one chance," he continued, "and that is a very slim one. I said that Mr. Carvel's estate was *supposed* to be in fee simple. Estates tail are not devisable. Our system of registration is far from infallible, and sometimes an old family settlement turns up to prove that a property which has been willed out of the direct line, as in fee simple, is in reality entailed. Is there a possibility of any such document?"

I replied that I did not know. My grandfather had never brought up the subject.

"We must bend our efforts in that direction," said the barrister. "I shall have my clerks make a systematic search."

He ceased talking, and sat sipping his sangaree in the abstracted manner common to him. I took the opportunity to ask about his family, thinking about what Dolly had said of Patty's illness.

"The mother is as well as can be expected, Richard, and Patty very rosy with the country air. Your disappearance was a great shock to them both."

"And Tom?"

He went behind his reserve. "Tom is a d—d rake," he exclaimed, with some vehemence. "I have given him over. He has taken up with that macaroni Courtenay, who wins his money,—or rather my money,—and your cousin Philip, when he is home from King's College. How Tom can be son of mine is beyond me, in faith. I see him about once in two months, when he comes here with a bill for his satins and his ruffles, and a long face of repentance, and a lot of gaming debts to involve my honour. And that reminds me, Richard," said he, looking straight at me with his clear, dark eyes: "have you made any plans for your future?"

I ventured to ask his advice as to entering the law.

"As the only profession open to a gentleman," he replied, smiling a little. "No, you were no more cut out for an attorney, or a barrister, or a judge, than was I for a macaroni doctor. The time is not far away, my lad," he went on, seeing my shame and confusion, "when an American may amass money in any way he chooses, and still be a gentleman,— behind a counter, if he will."

"I do not fear work, Mr. Swain," I remarked, with some pride.

"That is what I have been thinking," he said shortly. "And I am not a man to make up my mind while you count three, Richard. I have the place in Talbot, and no one to look after it. And — and in short I think you are the man."

He paused to watch the effect of this upon me. But I was so taken aback by this new act of kindness that I could not say a word.

"Tom is fast going to the devil, as I told you," he continued. "He cannot be trusted. If I die, that estate shall be Patty's, and he may never squander it. Captain Daniel tells me, and Mr. Bordley also, that you managed at Carvel Hall with sense and ability. I know you are very young, but I think I may rely upon you."

Again he hesitated, eying me fixedly.

"Ah," said he, with his quiet smile, "it is the old *noblesse oblige*. How many careers has it ruined since the world began!"

CHAPTER XLV

THE HOUSE OF MEMORIES

I WAS greatly touched, and made Mr. Swain many awkward acknowledgments, which he mercifully cut short. I asked him for a while to think over his offer. This seemed to please rather than displease him. And my first impulse on reaching the inn was to ask the captain's advice. I thought better of it however, and at length resolved to thrash out the matter for myself.

The next morning, as I sat reflecting, an overwhelming desire seized me to go to Marlboro' Street. Hitherto I could not have borne the sight of the old place. I gulped down my emotion as the gate creaked behind me, and made my way slowly to the white seat under the big chestnut behind the house, where my grandfather had been wont to sit reading his prints, in the warm weather. The flowers and the hedges had grown to a certain wildness; and the smell of the American roses carried me back — as odours will — to long-forgotten and trivial scenes. Here I had been caned many a day for Mr. Daaken's reports, and for earlier offences. And I recalled my mother as she once ran out at the sound of my cries to beg me off. So vivid was that picture that I could hear Mr. Carvel say: "He is yours, madam, not mine. Take him!"

I started up. The house was still, the sun blistering the green paint of the shutters. My eye was caught by those on the room that had been hers, and which, by my grandfather's decree, had lain closed since she left it. The image of it grew in my mind: the mahogany bed with its poppy counterpane and creamy curtains, and the steps at the side by which she was wont to enter it; and the *prie-dieu*, whence her soul had been lifted up to God. And the dresser with her china and silver upon it, covered by years of dust. For I had once stolen the key from Willis's bunch, crept in, and crept out again, awed. That chamber would be profaned, now, and those dear ornaments, which were mine, violated. The imagination choked me.

I would have them. I must. Nothing easier than to pry open a door or window in the north wing, by the ball-room. When I saw Grafton I would tell him. Nay, I would write him that day. I was even casting about me for an implement, when I heard a step on the gravel beside me.

I swung around, and came face to face with my uncle.

He must have perceived me. And after the first shock of my surprise had passed, I remarked a bearing on him that I had not seen before. He was master of the situation at last, — so it read. The realization gave him an easier speech than ever.

"I thought I might find you here, Richard," he said, "since you were not at the Coffee House."

He did not offer me his hand. I could only stare at him, for I had expected anything but this.

"I came from Carvel Hall to get you," he proceeded smoothly enough. "I heard but yesterday of your return, and some of your miraculous adventures. Your recklessness has caused us many a trying day, Richard, and I believe killed your grandfather. You have paid dearly, and have made us pay dearly, for your mad frolic of fighting cut-throats on the highroad."

The wonder was that I did not kill him on the spot. I cannot think what possessed the man, — he must have known me better.

"My recklessness!" I shouted, fairly hoarse with anger. I paid no heed to Mr. Swain's warning. "You d—d scoundrel!" I cried, "it was you killed him, and you know it. When you had put me out of the way and he was in your power, you tortured him to death. You forced him to die alone with your sneering face, while your shrew of a wife counted cards downstairs. Grafton Carvel, God knows you better than I, who know you too well. And He will punish you as sure as the crack of doom."

He heard me through, giving back as I came forward, his face blanching only a little, and wearing all the time that yellow smile which so fitted it.

"You have finished?" says he.

"Ay, I have finished. And now you may order me from this ground you have robbed me of. But there are some things in that house you shall not steal, for they are mine despite you."

"Name them, Richard," he said, very sorrowful.

"The articles in my mother's room, which were hers."

"You shall have them this day," he answered.

It was his way never to lose his temper, tho' he were called by the vilest name in the language. He must always assume this pious grief which made me long to throttle him. He had the best of me, even now, as he took the great key from his pocket.

"Will you look at them before you go?" he asked.

At first I was for refusing. Then I nodded. He led the way silently around by the front; and after he had turned the lock he stepped aside with a bow to let me pass in ahead of him. Once more I was in the familiar hall with the stairs dividing at the back. It was cool after the heat, and musty, and a touch of death hung in the prisoned air. We paused for a moment on the landing, beside the high, triple-arched window which the branches tapped on windy winter days, while Grafton took down the bunch of keys from beside the clock. I thought of my dear grandfather winding it every Sunday, and his ruddy face and large figure as he stood glancing sidewise down at me. Then the sound of Grafton's feet upon the bare steps recalled the present.

We passed Mr. Carvel's room and went down the little corridor over the ball-room, until we came to the full-storied wing. My uncle flung open the window and shutters opposite and gave me the key. A delicacy not foreign to him held him where he was. Time had sealed the door, and when at last it gave before my strength, a shower of dust quivered in the ray of sunlight from the window. I entered reverently. I took only the silver-bound prayer-book, cast a lingering look at the old familiar ob-

jects dimly defined, and came out and locked the door again.
I said very quietly that I would send for the things that afternoon, for my anger was hushed by what I had seen.

We halted together on the uncovered porch in front of the
house, that had a seat set on each side of it. Marlboro'
Street was still, the wide trees which flanked it spreading their
shade over walk and roadway. Not a soul was abroad in the
midday heat, and the windows of the long house opposite were
sightless.

"Richard," said my uncle, staring ahead of him, "I came to
offer you a home, and you insult me brutally, as you have done
unreproved all your life. And yet no one shall say of me that
I shirk my duty. But first I must ask you if there is aught else
you desire of me."

"The black boy, Hugo, is mine," I said. I had no great love
for Hugo, save for association's sake, and I had one too many
servants as it was; but to rescue one slave from Grafton's
clutches was charity.

"You shall have him," he replied, "and your chaise, and your
wardrobe, and your horses, and whatever else I have that belongs
to you. As I was saying, I will not shirk my duty. The memory of my dear father, and of what he would have wished, will
not permit me to let you go a-begging. You shall be provided
for out of the estate, despite what you have said and done."

This was surely the quintessence of a rogue's imagination.
Instinctively I shrank from him. With a show of piety that
turned me sick he continued: —

"Let God witness that I carry out my father's will!"

"Stop there, Grafton Carvel!" I cried; "you shall not take
His name in vain. Under this guise of holiness you and your
accomplice have done the devil's own work, and the devil will
reward you."

This reference to Mr. Allen, I believe, frightened him. For
a second only did he show it.

"My — my accomplice, sir!" he stammered. And then
righting himself: "You will have to explain this, by Heaven."

"In ample time your plot shall be laid bare, and you and
his Reverence shall hang, or lie in chains."

"You threaten, Mr. Carvel?" he shouted, nearly stepping off the porch in his excitement.

"Nay, I predict," I replied calmly. And I went down the steps and out of the gate, he looking after me. Before I had turned the corner of Freshwater Lane, he was in the seat, and fanning himself with his hat.

I went straight to Mr. Swain's chambers in the Circle, where I found the good barrister and Captain Daniel in their shirt-sleeves, seated between the windows in the back room. Mr. Swain was grave enough when he heard of my talk with Grafton, but the captain swore I was my father's son (for the fiftieth time since I had come back), and that a man could no more help flying at Grafton's face than Knipe could resist his legs; or Cynthia his back, if he went into her stall. I had scarce finished my recital, when Mr. Renwick, the barrister's clerk, announced Mr. Tucker, which caused Mr. Swain to let out a whistle of surprise.

"So the wind blows from that quarter, Daniel," said he. "I thought so."

Mr. Tucker proved to be the pettifogger into whose hands Grafton had put his affairs, taking them from Mr. Dulany at Mr. Carvel's death. The man was all in a sweat, and had hardly got in the door before he began to talk. He had no less astonishing a proposition to make than this, which he enunciated with much mouthing of the honour and sense of duty of Mr. Grafton Carvel. His client offered to Mr. Richard Carvel the estate lying in Kent County, embracing thirty-three hundred acres more or less of arable land and woodland, with a fine new house, together with the indented servants and negroes and other chattels thereon. Mr. Richard Carvel would observe that in making this generous offer for the welfare of his nephew, Mr. Tucker's client was far beyond the letter of his obligations; wherefore Mr. Grafton Carvel made it contingent upon the acceptance of the estate that his nephew should sign a paper renouncing forever any claims upon the properties of the late Mr. Lionel Carvel. This condition was so deftly rolled up in law-Latin that I did not understand a word of it until Mr. Swain stated it very briefly in English. His quiet laugh prodigiously disconcerted the pettifogger, who had before been sufficiently ill at ease in the presence of the great lawyer. Mr. Tucker blew his nose loudly to hide his confusion.

"And what say you, Richard?" said Mr. Swain, without a shade of accent in his voice.

I bowed my head. I knew that the honest barrister had read my heart when he spoke of *noblesse oblige*. That senseless pride of cast, so deep-rooted in those born in our province, had made itself felt. To be a factor (so I thought, for I was young) was to renounce my birth. Until that moment of travail the doctrine of equality had seemed very pretty to me. Your fine gentleman may talk as nobly as he pleases over his Madeira, and yet would patronize Monsieur Rousseau if he met him; and he takes never a thought of those who knuckle to him every day, and clean his boots and collect his rents. But when he is tried in the fire, and told suddenly to collect some one else's rents and curse another's negroes, he is fainthearted for the experiment. So it was with me when I had to meet the issue. I might take Grafton's offer, and the chance to marry Dorothy was come again. For by industry the owner of the Kent lands would become rich.

The room was hot, and still save for the buzzing of the flies. When I looked up I discovered the eyes of all three upon me.

"You may tell your client, Mr. Tucker, that I refuse his offer," I said.

He got to his feet, and with the customary declaration of humble servitude bowed himself out.

The door was scarce closed on him when the captain had me by the hands.

"What said I, Henry?" he cried. "Did I not know the lad?"

Mr. Swain did not stir from his seat. He was still gazing at me with a curious expression. And then I saw the world in truer colour. This good Samaritan was not only taking me into his home, but would fight for my rights with the strong brain that had lifted him out of poverty and obscurity. I stood, humbled before him.

"I would accept your kindness, Mr. Swain," I said, vainly trying to steady my voice, "but I have the faithful fellow, Banks, who followed me here from England, dependant on me, and Hugo, whom I rescued from my uncle. I will make over the black to you and you will have him."

He rose, brushed his eyes with his shirt, and took me by the arm. "You and the captain dine with me to-day," says he. "And as for Banks, I think that can be arranged. Now I have an estate, I shall need a trained butler, egad. I have some affairs to keep me in town to-day, Richard. But we'll be off for *Gordon's Pride* in the morning, and I know of one little girl will be glad to see us."

We dined out under the apple tree in Gloucester Street. And the captain argued, in his hopeful way, that Tucker's visit betrayed a weak point in Grafton's position. But the barrister shook his head and said that Grafton was too shrewd a rogue to tender me an estate if he feared me. It was Mr. Swain's opinion that the motive of my uncle was to put himself in a good light; and perhaps, he added, there was a little revenge mixed therein, as the Kent estate was the one Mr. Carvel had given him when he cast him off.

A southerly wind was sending great rolls of fog before it as Mr. Swain and I, with Banks, crossed over to Kent Island on the ferry the next morning. We traversed the island, and were landed by the other ferry on the soil of my native county, Queen Anne's. In due time we cantered past Master Dingley's tavern, the sight of which gave me a sharp pang, for it is there that the by-road turns over the bridge to Carvel Hall and Wilmot House; and force of habit drew my reins to the right across the horse's neck, so that I swerved into it. The barrister had no word of comment when I overtook him again.

'Twas about two o'clock when we came to the gate Mr. Swain had erected at the entrance to his place; the land was a little rolling, and partly wooded, like that on the Wye. But the fields were prodigiously unkempt. He drew up, and glanced at me.

"You will see there is much to be done with such fallows as these," said he. "The lessees from his Lordship were sportsmen rather than husbandmen, and had an antipathy to a constable or a sheriff like a rat to a boar cat. That is the curse of some of your Eastern Shore gentlemen, especially in Dorchester," he added; "they get to be fishmongers."

Presently we came in sight of the house, long and low, like the one in Gloucester Street, with a new and unpainted wing just completed. That day the mist softened its outline and blurred the trees which clustered about it. Even as we swung into the circle of the drive a rounded and youthful figure appeared in the doorway, gave a little cry, and stood immovable. It was Patty, in a striped dimity gown with the sleeves rolled up, and her face fairly shone with joy as I leaped from my horse and took her hands.

"So you like my surprise, girl?" said her father, as he kissed her blushing face.

For answer she tore herself away, and ran through the hall to the broad porch in front.

"Our barrister is come, mother," we heard her exclaiming, "and whom do you think he has brought?"

"Is it Richard?" asked the gentler voice, more hastily than usual.

I stepped out on the porch, where the invalid sat in her armchair. She was smiling with joy, too, and she held out her wasted hands and drew me toward her, kissing me on both cheeks.

"I thank God for His goodness," said she.

"And the boy has come to stay, mother," said her husband, as he stooped over her.

"To stay!" cries Patty.

"Gordon's Pride is henceforth his home," replied the barrister. "And now I can return in peace to my musty law, and know that my plantation will be well looked after."

Patty gasped.

"Oh, I am so glad!" said she, "I could almost rejoice that his uncle cheated him out of his property. He is to be factor of Gordon's Pride?"

"He is to be *master* of Gordon's Pride, my dear," says her father, smiling and tilting her chin; "we shall have no such persons as factors here."

At that the tears forced themselves into my own eyes. I turned away, and then I perceived for the first time the tall form of my old friend, Percy Singleton.

"May I, too, bid you welcome, Richard," said he, in his manly way, "and rejoice that I have got such a neighbour?"

"Thank you, Percy," I answered. I was not in a state to say much more.

"And now," exclaims Patty, "what a dinner we shall have in the prodigal's honour! I shall make you all some of the Naples biscuit Mrs. Brice told me of."

She flew into the house, and presently we heard her clear voice singing in the kitchen.

CHAPTER XLVI

GORDON'S PRIDE

THE years of a man's life that count the most are often those which may be passed quickest in the story of it. And so I may hurry over the first years I spent as Mr. Swain's factor at Gordon's Pride. The task that came to my hand was heaven-sent.

That manor-house, I am sure, was the tidiest in all Maryland, thanks to Patty's New England blood. She was astir with the birds of a morning, and near the last to retire at night, and happy as the days were long. She was ever up to her elbows in some dish, and her butter and her biscuits were the best in the province. Little she cared to work samplers, or peacocks in pretty wools, tho' in some way she found the time to learn the spinet. As the troubles with the mother country thickened, she took to a foot-wheel, and often in the crisp autumn evenings I would hear the bumping of it as I walked to the house, and turn the knob to come upon her spinning by the twilight. She would have no English-made linen in that household. "If mine scratch your back, Richard," she would say, "you must grin and bear, and console yourself with your virtue." It was I saw to the flax, and learned from Ivie Rawlinson (who had come to us from Carvel Hall) the best manner to ripple and break and swingle it. And Mr. Swain, in imitation of the high example set by Mr. Bordley, had buildings put up for wheels and the looms, and in due time kept his own sheep.

If man or woman, white or black, fell sick on the place, it was Patty herself who tended them. She knew the virtue of every herb in the big chest in the storeroom. And at table she presided over her father's guests with a womanliness that won her more admiration than mine. Now that the barrister was become a man of weight, the house was as crowded as ever was Carvel Hall. Carrolls and Pacas and Dulanys and Johnsons, and Lloyds and Bordleys and Brices and Scotts and Jennings and Ridouts, and Colonel Sharpe, who remained in the province, and many more families of prominence which I have not space to mention, all came to Gordon's Pride. Some of these, as their names proclaim, were of the King's side; but the bulk of Mr. Swain's company were stanch patriots, and toasted Miss Patty instead of his Majesty. By this I do not mean that they lacked loyalty, for it is a matter of note that our colony loved King George.

I must not omit from the list above the name of my good friend, Captain Clapsaddle.

Nor was there lack of younger company. Betty Tayloe, who plied me with questions concerning Dorothy and London, but especially about the dashing and handsome Lord Comyn; and the Dulany girls, and I know not how many others. Will Fotheringay, when he was home from college, and Archie Brice, and Francis Willard (whose father was now in the Assembly) and half a dozen more to court Patty, who would not so much as look at them. And when I twitted her with this she would redden and reply: "I was created for a housewife, sir, and not to make eyes from behind a fan." Indeed, she was at her prettiest and best in the dimity frock, with the sleeves rolled up.

'Twas a very merry place, the manor of Gordon's Pride. A generous bowl of punch always stood in the cool hall, through which the south winds swept from off the water, and fruit and sangaree and lemonade were on the table there. The manor had no ball-room, but the negro fiddlers played in the big parlour. And the young folks danced till supper time. In three months Patty's suppers grew famous in a colony where there was no lack of good cooks.

The sweet-natured invalid enjoyed these festivities in her quiet way, and often pressed me to partake. So did Patty beg me, and Mr. Swain. Perhaps a false sense of pride restrained me, but my duties held me all day in the field, and often into the night when there was curing to be done, or some other matters of necessity. And for the rest, I thought I detected a change in the tone of Mr. Fotheringay, and some others, tho' it may have been due to sensibility on my part. I would put up with no patronage.

There was no change of tone, at least, with the elder gentlemen. They plainly showed me an added respect. And so I fell into the habit, after my work was over, of joining them in their suppers rather than the sons and daughters. There I was made right welcome. The serious conversation spiced with the wit of trained barristers and men of affairs better suited my changed condition of life. The times were sober, and for those who could see, a black cloud was on each horizon. 'Twas only a matter of months when the thunder-clap was to come — indeed, enough was going on within our own province to forebode a revolution. The Assembly to which many of these gentlemen belonged was in a righteous state of opposition to the Proprietary and the Council concerning the emoluments of colonial officers and of clergymen. Honest Governor Eden had the misfortune to see the justice of our side, and was driven into a seventh state by his attempts to square his conscience. Bitter controversies were waging in the *Gazette*, and names were called and duels fought weekly. For our cause "The First Citizen" led the van, and the able arguments and moderate language of his letters soon identified him as Mr. Charles Carroll of Carrollton, one of the greatest men Maryland has ever known. But even at Mr. Swain's, amongst his few intimate friends, Mr. Carroll could never be got to admit his *nom de guerre* until long after *Antilon* had been beaten.

I write it with pride, that at these suppers I was sometimes asked to speak; and, having been but lately to England, to give my opinion upon the state of affairs there. Mr. Carroll honoured me upon two occasions with his confidence, and I was made clerk to a little club they had, and kept the minutes in my own hand.

I went about in homespun, which, if good enough for Mr. Bordley, was good enough for me. I rode with him over the estate. This gentleman was the most accomplished and scientific farmer we had in the province. Having inherited his plantation on Wye Island, near Carvel Hall, he resigned his duties as judge, and a lucrative practice, to turn all his energies to the cultivation of the soil. His wheat was as eagerly sought after as was Colonel Washington's tobacco.

It was to Mr. Bordley's counsel that the greater part of my success was due. He taught me the folly of ploughing with a fluke, — a custom to which the Eastern Shore was wedded, — pointing out that a double surface was thus exposed to the sun's rays; and explained at length why there was more profit in small grain in that district than heavy tobacco. He gave me Dr. Eliot's "Essays on Field Husbandry," and Mill's "Husby," which I read from cover to cover. And I went from time to time to visit him at Wye Island, when he would canter with me over that magnificent plantation, and show me with pride the finished outcome of his experiments.

Mr. Swain's affairs kept him in town the greater part of the twelve months, and Mrs. Swain and Patty moved to Annapolis in the autumn. But for three years I was at Gordon's Pride winter and summer alike. At the end of that time I was fortunate enough to show my employer such substantial results as to earn his commendation — ay, and his confidence, which was the highest token of that man's esteem. The moneys of the estate he left entirely at my order. And in the spring of '73, when the opportunity was suddenly offered to buy a thousand acres of excellent wheat land adjoining, I made the purchase for him while he was at Williamsburg, and upon my own responsibility.

This connected the plantation on the east with Singleton's. It had been my secret hope that the two estates might one day be joined in marriage. For of all those who came a-courting Patty, Percy was by far the best. He was but a diffident suitor; he would sit with me on the lawn evening after evening, when company was there, while Fotheringay and Francis Willard made their compliments within, — silly flatteries, at which Patty laughed.

Percy kept his hounds, and many a run we had together in

the sparkling days that followed the busy summer, when the crops were safe in the bottoms; or a quiet pipe and bottle in his bachelor's hall, after a soaking on the duck points.

And this brings me to a subject on which I am loth to write. Where Mr. Singleton was concerned, Patty, the kindest of creatures, was cruelty itself. Once, when I had the effrontery to venture a word in his behalf, I had been silenced so effectively as to make my ears tingle. A thousand little signs led me to a conclusion which pained me more than I can express. Heaven is my witness that no baser feeling leads me to hint of it here. Every day while the garden lasted flowers were in my room, and it was Banks who told me that she would allow no other hands than her own to place them by my bed. He got a round rating from me for violating the pledge of secrecy he had given her. It was Patty who made my shirts, and on Christmas knitted me something of comfort; who stood on the horse-block in the early morning waving after me as I rode away, and at my coming her eyes would kindle with a light not to be mistaken.

None of these things were lost upon Percy Singleton, and I often wondered why he did not hate me. He was of the kind that never shows a hurt. Force of habit still sent him to Gordon's Pride, but for days he would have nothing to say to the mistress of it, or she to him.

CHAPTER XLVII

VISITORS

It was not often that Mr. Thomas Swain honoured Gordon's Pride with his presence. He vowed that the sober Whig company his father brought there gave him the vapours. He snapped his fingers at the articles of the Patriots' Association, and still had his cocked hats and his Brussels lace and his spyglass, and his top boots when he rode abroad, like any other Tory buck. His intimates were all of the King's side, — of the worst of the King's side, I should say, for I would not be thought to cast any slur on the great number of conscientious men of that party. But, being the son of one of the main props of the Whigs, Mr. Tom went unpunished for his father's sake. He was not uncondemned.

Up to 1774, the times that Mr. Swain mentioned his son to me might be counted on the fingers of one hand. It took not a great deal of shrewdness to guess that he had paid out many a pretty sum to keep Tom's honour bright: as bright, at least, as such doubtful metal would polish. Tho' the barrister sought my ear in many matters, I never heard a whimper out of him on this score.

Master Tom had no ambition beyond that of being a macaroni; his easy-going nature led him to avoid alike trouble and responsibility. Hence he did not bother his head concerning my position. He appeared well content that I should make money out of the plantation for him to spend. His visits to Gordon's Pride were generally in the late autumn, and he brought his own company with him. I recall vividly his third or fourth appearance, in October of '73. Well I may! The family was preparing to go to town, and this year I was to follow them, and take from Mr. Swain's shoulders some of his private business, for he had been ailing a little of late from overwork.

The day of which I have spoken a storm had set in, the rain falling in sheets. I had been in the saddle since breakfast, seeing to an hundred repairs that had to be made before the cold weather. 'Twas near the middle of the afternoon when I pulled up before the weaving house. The looms were still, and Patty met me at the door with a grave look, which I knew portended something. But her first words were of my comfort.

"Richard, will you ever learn sense? You have been wet all day long, and have missed your dinner. Go at once and change your clothes, sir!" she commanded severely.

"I have first to look at the warehouse, where the roof is leaking," I expostulated.

"You shall do no such thing," replied she, "but dry yourself, and march into the dining room. We have had the ducks you shot yesterday, and some of your experimental hominy; but they are all gone."

I knew well she had laid aside for me some dainty, as was her habit. I dismounted. She gave me a quick, troubled glance, and said in a low voice: —

"Tom is come. And oh, I dare not tell you whom he has with him now!"

"Courtenay?" I asked.

"Yes, of course. I hate the sight of the man. But your cousin, Philip Carvel, is here, Richard. Father will be very angry. And they are making a drinking-tavern of the house."

I gave Firefly a slap that sent her trotting stable-ward, and walked rapidly to the house. I found the three of them drinking in the hall, the punch spilled over the table, and staining the cards.

"Gad's life!" cries Tom, "here comes Puritan Richard, in his broad rim. How goes the crop, Richard? 'Twill have to go well, egad, for I lost an hundred at the South River Club last week!"

Next him sat Philip, whom I had not seen since before I was carried off. He was lately come home from King's College;

and very mysteriously, his father giving out that his health was not all it should be. He had not gained Grafton's height, but he was broader, and his face had something in it of his father. He had his mother's under lip and complexion. Grafton was sallow; Philip was a peculiar pink, — not the ruddy pink of heartier natures, like my grandfather's, nor yet had he the peach-like skin of Mr. Dix. Philip's was a darker and more solid colour, and I have never seen man or woman with it and not mistrusted them. He wore a red velvet coat embroidered with gold, and as costly ruffles as I had ever seen in London. But for all this my cousin had a coarse look, and his polished blue flints of eyes were those of a coarse man.

He got to his feet as Tom spoke, looking anywhere but at me, and came forward slowly. He was loyal to no one, was Philip, not even to his father. When he was got within three paces he halted.

"How do you, cousin?" says he.

"A little wet, as you perceive, Philip," I replied.

I left him and stood before the fire, my rough wool steaming in the heat. He sat down again, a little awkwardly; and the situation began to please me better.

"How do you?" I asked presently.

"I have got a devilish cold," said he. "Faith, I'll warrant the doctor will be sworn I have been but indifferent company since we left the Hall. Eh, doctor?"

Courtenay, with his feet stretched out, bestowed an amiable but languid wink upon me, as much as to say that I knew what Mr. Philip's company was at best. When I came out after my dinner, they were still sitting there, Courtenay yawning, and Tom and Philip wrangling over last night's play.

"Come, my man of affairs, join us a hand!" says the doctor to me. "I have known the time when you would sit from noon until supper."

"I had money then," said I.

"And you have a little now, or I am cursed badly mistook. Oons! what do you fear?" he exclaimed, "you that have played with March and Fox?"

"I fear nothing, doctor," I answered, smiling. "But a man

must have a sorry honour when he will win fifty pounds with but ten of capital."

"One of Dr. Franklin's maxims, I presume," says he, with sarcasm.

"And if it were, it could scarce be more pat," I retorted. "'Tis Poor Richard's maxim."

"O lud! O my soul!" cries Tom, with a hiccup and a snigger; "'tis time you made another grand tour, Courtenay. Here's the second Whig has got in on you within the week!"

"I thank God they have not got me down to osnabrig and bumbo yet," replies the doctor. Coming over to me by the fire, he tapped my sleeve and added in a low tone: "Forbearance with such a pair of asses is enough to make a man shed bitter tears. But a little of it is necessary to keep out of debt. You and I will play together, against both the lambs, Richard. One of them is not far from maudlin now."

"Thank you, doctor," I answered politely, "but I have a better way to make my living." In three years I had learned a little to control my temper.

He shrugged his thin shoulders. "*Eh bien, mon bon,*" says he, "I dare swear you know your own game better than do I." And he cast a look up the stairs, of which I quite missed the meaning. Indeed, I was wholly indifferent. The doctor and his like had passed out of my life, and I believed they were soon to disappear from our Western Hemisphere. The report I had heard was now confirmed, that his fortune was dissipated, and that he lived entirely off these young rakes who aspired to be macaronies.

"Since your factor is become a damned Lutheran, Tom," said he, returning to the table and stripping a pack, "it will have to be picquet. You promised me we could count on a fourth, or I had never left Inman's."

It was Tom, as I had feared, who sat down unsteadily opposite. Philip lounged and watched them sulkily, snuffing and wheezing and dipping into the bowl, and cursing the house for a draughty barn. I took a pipe on the settle to see what would come of it. I was not surprised that Courtenay lost at first, and that Tom drank the most of the punch. Nor was it above half an hour before the stakes were raised and the tide began to turn in the doctor's favour.

"A plague of you, Courtenay!" cries Mr. Tom, at length, flinging down the cards. His voice was thick, while the Selwyn of Annapolis was never soberer in his life. Tom appealed first to Philip for the twenty pounds he owed him.

"You know how damned stingy my father is, curse you," whined my cousin, in return. "I told you I should not have it till the first of the month."

Tom swore back. He thrust his hands deep in his pockets and sank into that attitude of dejection common to drunkards. Suddenly he pulled himself up.

"'Shblood! Here's Richard t' draw from. Lemme have fifty pounds, Richard."

"Not a farthing," I said, unmoved.

"You say wha' shall be done with my father's money!" he cried. "I call tha' damned cool — Gad's life! I do. Eh, Courtenay?"

Courtenay had the sense not to interfere.

"I'll have you dishcharged, Gad's death! so I will!" he shouted. "No damned airs wi' me, Mr. Carvel. I'll have you know you're not wha' you once were, but only a cursht oversheer."

He struggled to his feet, forgot his wrath on the instant, and began to sing drunkenly the words of a ribald air. I took him by both shoulders and pushed him back into his chair.

"Be quiet," I said sternly; "while your mother and sister are here you shall not insult them with such a song." He ceased, astonished. "And as for you, gentlemen," I continued, "you should know better than to make a place of resort out of a gentleman's house."

Courtenay's voice broke the silence that followed.

"Of all the cursed impertinences I ever saw, egad!" he drawled. "Is this your manor, Mr. Carvel? Or have you a seat in Kent?"

I would not have it in black and white that I am an advocate of fighting. But at that moment I was in the mood when it does not matter much one way or the other. The drunken man carried us past the point.

"The damned in-intriguing rogue'sh worked himself into my father's grashes," he said, counting out his words. "He'sh no more Whig than me. I know'sh game, Courtenay — he wants t' marry Patty. Thish place'll be hers."

The effect upon me of these words, with all their hideous implication of gossip and scandal, was for an instant benumbing. The interpretation of the doctor's innuendo struck me then. I was starting forward, with a hand open to clap over Tom's mouth, when I saw the laugh die on Courtenay's face, and him come bowing to his legs. I turned with a start.

On the stairs stood Patty herself, pale as marble.

"Come with me, Tom," she said.

He had obeyed her from childhood. This time he tried, and failed miserably.

"Beg pardon, Patty," he stammered, "no offensh meant. Thish factor thinks h' ownsh Gordon's now. I say, not'll h' marries you. Good fellow, Richard, but infernal forward. Eh, Courtenay?"

Philip turned away, while the doctor pretended to examine the silver punch-ladle. As for me, I could only stare. It was Patty who kept her head, and made us a stately curtsey.

"Will you do me the kindness, gentlemen," said she, "to leave me with my brother?"

We walked silently into the parlour, and I closed the door.

"'Slife!" cried Courtenay, "she's a vision. What say you, Philip? And I might see her in that guise again, egad, I would forgive Tom his five hundred crowns!"

"A buxom vision," agreed my cousin, "but I vow I like 'em so." He had forgotten his cold.

"This conversation is all of a piece with the rest of your conduct," said I, hotly.

The candles were burning brightly in the sconces. The doctor walked to the glass, took snuff, and brushed his waistcoat before he answered.

"Sure, a fortune lies under every virtue we assume," he

recited. "But she is not for you, Richard," says he, tapping his box.

"Mr. Carvel, if you please," I replied. I felt the demon within me. But I had the sense to realize that a quarrel with Dr. Courtenay, under the circumstances, would be far from wise. He had no intention of quarrelling, however. He made me a grand bow.

"Mr. Carvel, your very obedient. Hereafter I shall know better than to forget myself with an overseer." And he gave me his back. "What say you to a game of billiards, Philip?"

Philip seemed glad to escape. And soon I heard their voices, mingling with the click of the balls. There followed for me one of the bitterest half hours I have had in my life. Then Patty opened the hall door.

"Will you come in for a moment, Richard?" she said, quite calmly.

I followed her, wondering at the masterful spirit she had shown. For there was Tom all askew in his chair, his feet one way and his hands another, totally subdued. What was most to the point, he made me an elaborate apology. How she had sobered his mind I know not. His body was as helpless as the day he was born.

Long before the guests thought of rising the next morning, Patty came to me as I was having the mare saddled. The sun was up, and the clouds were being chased, like miscreants who have played their prank, and were now running for it. The sharp air brought the red into her cheeks. And for the first time in her life with me she showed shyness. She glanced up into my face, and then down at the leaves running on the ground.

"I hope they will go to-day," said she, when I was ready to mount.

I began to tighten the girths, venting my feelings on Firefly until the animal swung around and made a vicious pass at my arm.

"Richard!"

"Yes."

"You will not worry over that senseless speech of Tom's?"

"I see it in a properer light now, Patty," I replied. "We usually do — in the morning."

She sighed.

"You are so high-strung," she said, "I was afraid you would — "

"I would — ?"

She did not answer until I had repeated.

"I was very silly," she said slowly, her colour mounting even higher, "I was afraid that you would — leave us." Stroking the mare's neck, and with a little halt in her voice, "I do not know what we should do without you."

Indeed, I was beginning to think I would better leave, though where I should go was more than I could say. With a quick intuition she caught my hand as I put foot in the stirrup.

"You will not go away!" she cried. "Say you will not! What would poor father do? He is not so well as he used to be."

The wild appeal in her eyes frightened me. It was beyond resisting. In great agitation I put my foot to the ground again.

"Patty, I should be a graceless scamp in truth," I exclaimed. "I do not forget that your father gave me a home when mine was taken away, and has made me one of his family. I shall thank God if I can but lighten some of his burdens."

But they did not depart that day, nor the next; nor, indeed, for a week after. For Philip's cold brought on a high fever. He stuck to his bed, and Patty herself made broth and dainties for him, and prescribed him medicine out of the oak chest whence had come so much comfort. At first Philip thought he would die, and forswore wine and cards, and some other things the taste for which he had cultivated, and likewise worse vices that had come to him by nature.

I am greatly pleased to write that the stay profited the gallant Dr. Courtenay nothing. Patty's mature beauty and her manner of carrying off the episode in the hall had made a deep impression upon the Censor. I read the man's mind in his eye; here was a match to mend his fortunes, and do him credit besides. However, his wit and his languishing glances and double meanings fell on barren ground. No tire-woman on the plantation was busier than Patty during the first few days of his stay. After that he grew sulky and vented his spleen on poor Tom, winning more money from him at billiards and picquet. Since the doctor was too much the macaroni to ride to hounds and to shoot ducks, time began to hang exceeding heavy on his hands.

Patty and I had many a quiet laugh over his predicament. And, to add zest to the situation, I informed Singleton of what was going forward. He came over every night for supper, and to my delight the bluff Englishman was received in a fashion to make the doctor writhe and snort with mortification. Never in his life had he been so insignificant a person. And he, whose conversation was so sought after in the gay season in town, was thrown for companionship upon a scarce-grown boy whose talk was about as salted, and whose intellect as great, as those of the cockerouse in our fable. He stood it about a se'nnight, at the end of which space Philip was put on his horse, will-he-nill-he, and made to ride northward.

I sat with my cousin of an evening as he lay in bed. Not, I own, from any charity on my part, but from other motives which do me no credit. The first night he confessed his sins, and they edified me not a little. On the second he was well enough to sit up and swear, and to vow that Miss Swain was an angel; that he would marry her the very next week and his father Grafton were not such a stickler for family.

"Curse him," says his dutiful and loyal son, "he is so bally stingy with my stipend that I am in debt to half the province. And I say it myself, Richard, he has been a blackguard to you, tho' I allow him some little excuse. You were faring better now, my dear cousin, and you had not given him every reason to hate you. For I have heard him declare more than once — 'pon my soul, I have — that he would rather you were his friend than his enemy."

My contempt for Philip kept me silent here. I might quarrel with Grafton, who had sense enough to feel pain at a well-deserved thrust. Philip had not the intelligence to recognize insult from compliment. It was but natural he should mistake my attitude now. He leaned forward in his bed.

"Hark you, Richard," whispers he, with a glance at the door, "I might tell you some things and I chose, and — and it were worth my while."

"Worth your while?" I repeated vaguely.

He traced nervously the figures on the counterpane. Next came a rush of anger to redden his face.

"By Gad, I will tell you. Swear to Gad I will." Then, the little cunning inherited from his father asserting itself, he added, "Look you, Richard, I am the son of one of the richest men in the colony, and I get the pittance of a backwoods pastor. I tell you 'tis not to be borne with. And I am not of as much consideration at the Hall as Brady, the Irish convict, who has become overseer."

I little wondered at this. Philip sank back, and for some moments eyed me between narrowed lids. He continued presently with shortened breath: —

"I have evidence — I have evidence to get you back a good share of the estate, which my father will never miss. And I will do it," he cries, suddenly bold, "I will do it for three thousand pounds down when you receive it."

This was why he had come with Tom to Talbot! I was so dumfounded that my speech was quite taken away. Then I got up and began pacing the room. Was it not fair to fight a scoundrel with his own weapons? Here at last was the witness Mr. Swain had been seeking so long, come of his own free will. Then — Heaven help me! — my mind flew on. As time had passed I had more than once regretted refusing the Kent plantation, which had put her from whom my thought never wandered within my reach again. Good Mr. Swain had erred for once. 'Twas foolish, indeed, not to accept a portion of what was rightfully mine, when no more could be got. And now, if what Philip said was true (and I doubted it not), here at last was the chance come again to win her without whom I should never be happy. I glanced at my cousin.

"Gad's life!" says he, "it is cheap enough. I might have asked you double."

"So you might, and have been refused," I cried hotly. For I believe that speech of his recalled me to my senses. It has ever been an instinct with me that no real prosperity comes out of double-dealing. And commerce with such a sneak sickened me. " Go back to your father, Philip, and threaten him, and he may make you rich. Such as he live by blackmail. And you may add, and you will, that the day of retribution is coming for him."

CHAPTER XLVIII

MULTUM IN PARVO

I LOST no time after getting to Annapolis in confiding to Mr. Swain the conversation I had had with my cousin Philip. And I noticed, as he sat listening to my account in the library in Gloucester Street, that the barrister looked very worn. He had never been a strong man, and the severe strain he had been under with the patriots' business was beginning to tell.

He was very thoughtful when I had finished, and then told me briefly that I had done well not to take the offer. "Tucker would have made but short work of such evidence, my lad," said he, "and I think Master Philip would have lied himself in and out a dozen times. I cannot think what witness he would have introduced save Mr. Allen. And there is scarcely a doubt that your uncle pays him for his silence, for I am told he is living in Frederick in a manner far above what he gets from the parish. However, Philip has given us something more to work on. It may be that he can put hands on the messenger."

I rose to go.

"We shall bring them to earth yet, Richard, and I live," he added. "And I have always meant to ask you whether you ever regretted your decision in taking Gordon's Pride."

"And you live, sir!" I exclaimed, not heeding the question.

He smiled somewhat sadly.

"Of one thing I am sure, my lad," he continued, "which is that I have had no regrets about taking you. Mr. Bordley has just been here, and tells me you are the ablest young man in the province. You see that more eyes than mine are upon you. You have proved yourself a man, Richard, and there are very few macaronies would have done as you did. I am resolved to add another little mite to your salary."

The "little mite" was of such a substantial nature that I protested strongly against it. I thought of Tom's demands upon him.

"I could afford to give you double for what you have made off the place," he interrupted. "But I do not believe in young men having too much." He sighed, and turned to his work.

I hesitated. "You have spent time and labour upon my case, sir, and have asked no fee."

"I shall speak of the fee when I win it," he said dryly, "and not before. How would you like to be clerk this winter to the Committee of Correspondence?"

I suppose my pleasure was expressed in my face.

"Well," said he, "I have got you the appointment without much difficulty. There are many ways in which you can be useful to the party when not helping me with my affairs."

This conversation gave me food for reflection during a week. I was troubled about Mr. Swain, and what he had said as to not living kept running in my head as I wrote or figured. For I had enough to hold me busy.

In the meantime, the clouds fast gathering on both sides of the Atlantic grew blacker, and blacker still. I saw a great change in Annapolis. Men of affairs went about with grave faces, while gay and sober alike were touched by the spell. The Tory gentry, to be sure, rattled about in their gilded mahogany coaches, in spite of jeers and sour looks. My Aunt Caroline wore jewelled stomachers to the assemblies, — now become dry and shrivelled entertainments. She kept her hairdresser, had three men in livery to her chair, and a little negro in Turk's costume to wait on her. I often met her in the streets, and took a fierce joy in staring her in the eye. And Grafton! By a sort of fate I was continually running against him. He was a very busy man, was my uncle, and had a kind of dignified run, which he used between Marlboro' Street and the Council Chamber in the Stadt House, or the Governor's mansion. He never did me the honour to glance at me. The Rev. Mr. Allen, too, came a-visiting from Frederick, where he had grown stout as an alderman upon the living and its perquisites and Grafton's additional bounty. The gossips were busy with his doings, for he had his travelling-coach and servant now. He went to the Tory balls with my aunt. Once I all but encountered him on the Circle, but he ran into Northeast Street to avoid me.

Yes, that was the winter when the wise foresaw the inevitable, and the first sharp split occurred between men who had been brothers. The old order of things had plainly passed, and I was truly thankful that my grandfather had not lived to witness those scenes. The greater part of our gentry stood firm for America's rights, and they had behind them the best lawyers in America. After the lawyers came the small planters and most of the mechanics. The shopkeepers formed the backbone of King George's adherents; the Tory gentry, the clergy, and those holding office under the proprietor made the rest.

And it was all about *tea*, a word which, since '67, had been steadily becoming the most vexed in the language. The East India Company had put forth a complaint. They had Heaven knows how many tons getting stale in London warehouses, all by reason of our stubbornness, and so it was enacted that all tea paying the small American tax should have a rebate of the English duties. That was truly a master-stroke, for Parliament to give it us cheaper than it could be had at home! To cause his Majesty's government to lose revenues for the sake of being able to say they had caught and taxed us at last! The happy result is now history, my dears. And this is not a history, tho' I wish it were. What occurred at Boston, at Philadelphia, and Charleston, has since caused Englishmen, as well as Americans, to feel proud. The chief incident in Annapolis I shall mention in another chapter.

When it became known with us that several cargoes were on their way to the colonies, excitement and indignation gained a pitch not reached since the Stamp Act. Business came to a standstill, plantations lay idle, and gentry and farmers flocked to Annapolis, and held meetings and made resolutions anew. On my way of a morning from Mr. Swain's house to his chambers in the Circle I would meet as many as a dozen knots of people. Mr. Claude was one of the few patriots who reaped reward out of the disturbance, for his inn was crowded. The Assembly met, appointed committees to correspond with the other colonies, and was prorogued once and again. Many a night I sat up until the small hours copying out letters to the committees of Virginia, and Pennsylvania, and Massachusetts. The gentlemen were wont to dine at the Coffee House, and I would sit near the foot of the table, taking notes of their plans. 'Twas so I met many men of distinction from the other colonies. Colonel Washington came once. He was grown a greater man than ever, and I thought him graver than when I had last seen him. I believe a trait of this gentleman was never to forget a face.

"How do you, Richard?" said he. How I reddened when he called me so before all the committee. "I have heard your story, and it does you vast credit. And the gentlemen tell me you are earning laurels, sir."

That first winter of the tea troubles was cold and wet with us, and the sun, as if in sympathy with the times, rarely showed his face. Early in February our apprehensions concerning Mr. Swain's health were realized. One day, without a word to any one, he went to his bed, where Patty found him. And I ran all the way to Dr. Leiden's. The doctor looked at him, felt his pulse and his chest, and said nothing. But he did not rest that night, nor did Patty or I.

Thus I came to have to do with the good barrister's private affairs. I knew that he was a rich man, as riches went in our province, but I had never tried to guess at his estate. I confess the sums he had paid out in Tom's behalf frightened me. With the advice of Mr. Bordley and Mr. Lloyd I managed his money as best I could, but by reason of the non-importation resolutions there was little chance for good investments, — no cargoes coming and few going. I saw, indeed, that buying the Talbot estate had been a fortunate step, since the quantities of wheat we grew there might be disposed of in America.

When Dr. Leiden was still coming twice a day to Gloucester Street, Mr. Tom must needs get into a scrape with one of the ladies of the theatre, and come to me in the Circle chambers for one hundred pounds. I told him, in despair, that I had no authority to pay out his father's money.

"And so you have become master, sure enough!" he cried, in a passion. For he was desperate. "You have worked your way in vastly well, egad, with your Whig committee meetings and speeches. And now he is on his back, and you have possession, you choose to cut me off. 'Slife, I know what will be coming next."

I pulled him into Mr. Swain's private room, where we would be free of the clerks.

"Yes, I am master here," I replied, sadly enough, as he stood sullenly before me. "I should think you would be ashamed to own it. When I came to your father I was content to be overseer in Talbot, and thankful for his bounty. 'Tis no fault of mine, but your disgrace, that his son is not managing his business, and supporting him in the rights of his country. I am not very old, Tom. A year older than you, I believe. But I have seen enough of life to prophesy your end and you do not reform."

"We are turned preacher," he says, with a sneer.

"God forbid! But I have been in a sponging-house, and tasted the lowest dregs. And if this country becomes free, as I think it will some day, such as you will be driven to England, and die in the Fleet."

"Not while my father lives," retorts he, and throws aside the oiled silk cape with a London name upon it. The day was rainy.

I groaned. My responsibility lay heavy upon me. And this was not my first scene with him. He continued doggedly:—

"You have no right to deny me what is not yours. 'Twill be mine one day."

"You have no right to accuse me of thoughts that do not occur to men of honour," I replied. "I am slower to anger than I once was, but I give you warning now. Do you know that you will ruin your father in another year and you continue?"

He gave me no answer. I reached for the ledger, and turning the pages, called off to him the sums he had spent.

"Oh, have done, d—n it!" he cried, when I was not a third through. "Are you or are you not to give me the money?"

"And you are to spend it upon an actress?" I should have called her by a worse name.

"Actress!" he shouted. "Have you seen her in *The Orphan?* My soul, she is a divinity!" Then he shifted suddenly to whining and cringing. "I am ruined outright, Richard, if I do not get it."

Abjectly he confessed the situation, which had in it enough material for a scandal to set the town wagging for a month. And the weight of it would fall, as I well knew, upon those who deserved it least.

"I will lend you the money, or, rather, will pay it for you," I said, at last. For I was not so foolish as to put it into his hands. "You shall have the sum under certain conditions."

He agreed to them before they were out of my mouth, and swore in a dozen ways that he would repay me every farthing. He was heartily tired of the creature, and, true to his nature, afraid of her. That night when the play was over I went to her lodging, and after a scene too distressing to dwell upon, bought her off.

I sat with Mr. Swain many an hour that spring, with Patty sewing at the window open to the garden. Often, as we talked, unnoticed by her father she would drop her work and the tears glisten in her eyes. For the barrister's voice was not as strong as it once was, and the cold would not seem to lift from his chest. So this able man, who might have sat in the seats of Maryland's high reward, was stricken when he was needed most.

He was permitted two visitors a day: now 'twas Mr. Carroll and Colonel Lloyd, again Colonel Tilghman and Captain Clapsaddle, or Mr. Paca and Mr. Bordley. The gentlemen took turns, and never was their business so pressing that they missed their hour. Mr. Swain read all the prints, and on his easier days would dictate to me his views for the committee, or a letter signed *Brutus* for Mr. Green to put in the *Gazette*. So I became his mouthpiece at the meetings, and learned to formulate my thoughts and to speak clearly.

For fear of confusing this narrative, my dears, I have referred but little to her who was in my thoughts night and day, and whose locket I wore, throughout all those years, next my heart. I used to sit out under the stars at Gordon's Pride, with the river lapping at my feet, and picture her the shining centre of all the brilliant scenes I had left, and wonder if she still thought of me.

Nor have I mentioned that faithful correspondent, and more faithful friend, Lord Comyn. As soon as ever I had obtained from Captain Daniel my mother's little inheritance, I sent off the debt I owed his Lordship. 'Twas a year before I got him to receive it; he despatched the money back once, saying that I had more need of it than he. I smiled at this, for my Lord was never within his income, and I made no doubt he had signed a note to cover my indebtedness.

Every letter Comyn writ me was nine parts Dolly, and the rest of his sheet usually taken up with Mr. Fox and his calamities: these had fallen upon him very thick of late. Lord Holland had been forced to pay out a hundred thousand pounds for Charles, and even this enormous sum did not entirely free Mr. Fox from the discounters and the hounds. The reason for this sudden onslaught was the birth of a boy to his brother Stephen, who was heir to the title. "When they told Charles of it," Comyn wrote, "said he, coolly: 'My brother Ste's son is a second Messiah, born for the destruction of the Jews.'"

I saw no definite signs, as yet, of the conversion of this prodigy, which I so earnestly hoped for. He had quarrelled with North, lost his place on the Admiralty, and presently the King had made him a Lord of the Treasury, tho' more out of fear than love. Once in a while, when he saw Comyn at Almack's, he would desire to be remembered to me, and he always spoke of me with affection. But he could be got to write to no one, said my Lord, with kind exaggeration; nor will he receive letters, for fear he may get a dun.

Alas, I got no message from Dorothy! Nor had she ever mentioned my name to Comyn. He had not seen her for eight months after I left England, as she had been taken to the Continent for her health. She came back to London more ravishing than before, and (I use his Lordship's somewhat extravagant language) her suffering had stamped upon her face even more of character and power. She had lost much of her levity, likewise. In short, my Lord declared, she was more of the queen than ever, and the mystery which hung over the Vauxhall duel had served only to add to her fame.

Dorothy having become cognizant of Mr. Marmaduke's trickery, Chartersea seemed to have dropped out of the race. He now spent his time very evenly between Spa and Derresley and Paris. Hence I had so much to be thankful for,—that with all my blunders, I had saved her from his Grace. My Lord the Marquis of Wells was now most conspicuous amongst her suitors. Comyn had nothing particular against this nobleman, saying that he was a good fellow, with a pretty fortune. And here is a letter, my dears, in which he figures, that I brought to Gordon's Pride that spring:—

"10 SOUTH PARADE, BATH,
March 12, 1774.

"DEAR RICHARD:—Miss Manners has come to Bath, with a train behind her longer than that which followed good Queen Anne hither, when she made this Gehenna the fashion. Her triumphal entry last Wednesday was announced by such a peal of the abbey bells as must have cracked the metal (for they have not rung since) and started Beau Nash a-cursing where he lies under the floor. Next came her serenade by the band. Mr. Marmaduke swore they would never have done, and squirmed and grinned like Punch when he thought of the fee,— for he had hoped to get off with a crown, I warrant you. You should have seen his face when they would accept no fee at all for the beauty! Some wag has writ a verse about it, which was printed, and has set the whole pump-room laughing this morning.

"She was led out by Wells in the *Seasons* last night. As *Spring* she is too bewildering for my pen, — all primrose and white, with the flowers in her blue-black hair. Had Sir Joshua seen her, he would never rest content till he should have another portrait. The Duc de Lauzun, who contrived to get two dances, might give you a description in a more suitable language than English. And there was a prodigious deal of jealousy among the fair ones on the benches, you may be sure, and much jaundiced comment.

"Some half dozen of us adorers have a mess at the Bear, and have offered up a prize for the most appropriate toast on the beauty. This is in competition with Mrs. Miller. Have you not heard of her among your tobacco-hills? Horry calls her Mrs. 'Calliope' Miller. At her place near here, Bath Easton Villa, she has set up a Roman vase bedecked with myrtle, and into this we drop our *bouts-rimés*. Mrs. Calliope has a ball every Thursday, when the victors are crowned. T'other day the theme was 'A Buttered Muffin,' and her Grace of Northumberland was graciously awarded the prize. In faith, that theme taxed our wits at the Bear, — how to weave Miss Dolly's charms into a verse on a buttered muffin. I shall not tire you with mine. Storer's deserved to win, and we whisper that Mrs. Calliope ruled it out through spite. 'When Phyllis eats,' so it began, and I vow 'twas devilish ingenious.

"We do nothing but play lasquenet and tennis, and go to the assembly, and follow Miss Dolly into Gill's, the pastry-cook's, where she goes every morning to take a jelly. The ubiquitous Wells does not give us much chance. He writes *vers de société* with the rest, is high in Mr. Marmaduke's favour, which alone is enough to damn his progress. I think she is ill of the sight of him.

"Albeit she does not mourn herself into a tree, I'll take oath your Phyllis is true to you, Richard, and would live with you gladly in a thatched hut and you asked her. Write me more news of yourself.
     "Your ever affectionate
                "COMYN.

"P.S. I have had news of you through Mr. Worthington, of your colony, who is just arrived here. He tells me that you have gained a vast reputation for your plantation, and likewise that you are thought much of by the Whig wiseacres, and that you hold many seditious offices. He does not call them so. Since your modesty will not permit you to write me any of these things, I have been imagining you driving slaves with a rawhide, and sending runaway convicts to the mines. Mr. W. is even now paying his respects to Miss Manners, and I doubt not trumpeting your praises there, for he seems to like you. So I have asked him to join the Bear mess. One more unfortunate!

"P.S. I was near forgetting the news about Charles Fox. He sends you his love, and tells me to let you know that he has been turned out of North's house for good and all. He is sure you will be cursed happy over it, and says that you predicted he would go over to the Whigs. I can scarce believe that he will. North took a whole week to screw up his courage, h—s M—j—sty pricking him every day. And then he wrote this: 'Sir, his Majesty has thought proper to order a new Commission of the Treasury to be made out, in which I do not see your name.' Poor Charles! He is now without money or place, but as usual appears to worry least of all of us, and still reads his damned Tasso for amusement.

"C."

Perchance he was to be the Saint Paul of English politics, after all.

CHAPTER XLIX

LIBERTY LOSES A FRIEND

Mr. Bordley's sloop took Mr. Swain to Gordon's Pride in May, and placed him in the big room overlooking the widening river. There he would lie all day long, staring through the leaves at the water, or listening to the sweet music of his daughter's voice as she read from the pompous prints of the time. Gentlemen continued to come to the plantation, for the barrister's wisdom was sorely missed at the councils. One day, as I rode in from the field, I found Colonel Lloyd just arrived from Philadelphia, sipping sangaree on the lawn and mopping himself with his handkerchief. His jolly face was troubled. He waved his hand at me.

"Well, Richard," says he, "we children are to have our first whipping. At least one of us. And the rest are resolved to defy our parent."

"Boston, Mr. Lloyd?" I asked.

"Yes, Boston," he replied; "her port is closed, and we are forbid any intercourse with her until she comes to her senses. And her citizens must receive his gracious Majesty's troopers into their houses. And if a man kill one of them by any chance, he is to go to England to be tried. And there is more quite as bad."

"'Tis bad enough!" I cried, flinging myself down. And Patty gave me a glass in silence.

"Ay, but you must hear all," said he; "our masters are of a mind to do the thing thoroughly. Canada is given some score of privileges. Her French Roman Catholics, whom we fought not long since, are thrown a sop, and those vast territories between the lakes and the Ohio and Mississippi are given to Quebec as a price for her fidelity. And so, if the worst comes to worst, George's regiments will have a place to land against us."

Such was the news, and though we were some hundreds of miles from Massachusetts, we felt their cause as our own. There was no need of the appeal which came by smoking horses from Philadelphia, for the indignation of our people was roused to the highest pitch. Now Mr. Swain had to take to his bed from the excitement.

This is not a history, my dears, as I have said. And time is growing short. I shall pass over that dreary summer of '74. It required no very keen eye to see the breakers ahead, and Mr. Bordley's advice to provide against seven years of famine did not go unheeded. War was the last thing we desired. We should have been satisfied with so little, we colonies! And would have voted the duties ten times over had our rights been respected. Should any of you doubt this, you have but to read the "Address to the King" of our Congress, then sitting in Philadelphia. The quarrel was so petty, and so easy of mending, that you of this generation may wonder why it was allowed to run. I have tried to tell you that the head of a stubborn, selfish, and wilful monarch blocked the way to reconciliation. King George the Third is alone to blame for that hatred of race against race which already hath done so much evil. And I pray God that a great historian may arise whose pen will reveal the truth, and reconcile at length those who are, and should be, brothers.

By October, that most beautiful month of all the year in Maryland, we were again in Annapolis. One balmy day — 'twas a Friday, I believe, and a gold and blue haze hung over the Severn — Mr. Chase called in Gloucester Street to give the barrister news of the Congress, which he had lately left. As he came down the stairs he paused for a word with me in the library, and remarked sadly upon Mr. Swain's condition. "He looks like a dying man, Richard," said he, "and we can ill afford to lose him."

Even as we sat talking in subdued tones, the noise of a distant commotion arose. We had scarce started to our feet,

2 G

Mr. Chase and I, when the brass knocker resounded, and Mr. Hammond was let in. His wig was awry, and his face was flushed.

"I thought to find you here," he said to Mr. Chase. "The Anne Arundel Committee is to meet at once, and we desire to have you with us." Perceiving our blank faces, he added: "The *Peggy Stewart* is in this morning with over a ton of tea aboard, consigned to the Williams's."

The two jumped into a chaise, and I followed afoot, stopped at every corner by some excited acquaintance; so that I had the whole story, and more, ere I reached Church Street. The way was blocked before the committee rooms, and 'twas said that the merchants, Messrs. Williams, and Captain Jackson of the brig, were within, pleading their cause.

Presently the news leaked abroad that Mr. Anthony Stewart, the brig's owner, had himself paid the duty on the detested plant. Some hundreds of people were elbowing each other in the street, for the most part quiet and anxious, until Mr. Hammond appeared and whispered to a man at the door. In all my life before I had never heard the hum of an angry crowd. The sound had something ominous in it, like the first moanings of a wind that is to break off great trees at their trunks. Then some one shouted: "To Hanover Street! To Hanover Street! We'll have him tarred and feathered before the sun is down!" The voice sounded strangely like Weld's. They charged at this cry like a herd of mad buffalo, the weaker ones trampled under foot or thrust against the wall. The windows of Mr. Aikman's shop were shattered. I ran with the leaders, my stature and strength standing me in good stead more than once, and as we twisted into Northwest Street I took a glance at the mob behind me, and great was my anxiety at not being able to descry one responsible person.

Mr. Stewart's house stood, and stands to-day, amid trim gardens, in plain sight of the Severn. Arriving there, the crowd massed in front of it, some of the boldest pressing in at the gate and spreading over the circle of lawn enclosed by the driveway. They began to shout hoarsely, with what voices they had left, for Mr. Stewart to come out, calling him names not to be spoken, and swearing they would show him how traitors were to be served. I understood then the terror of numbers, and shuddered. A chandler, a bold and violent man, whose leather was covered with grease, already had his foot on the steps, when the frightened servants slammed the door in his face, and closed the lower windows. In vain I strained my eyes for some one who might have authority with them. They began to pick up stones, though none were thrown.

Suddenly a figure appeared at an upper window,—a thin and wasted woman dressed in white, with sad, sweet features. It was Mrs. Stewart. Without flinching she looked down upon the upturned faces; but a mob of that kind has no pity. Their leaders were the worst class in our province, being mostly convicts who had served their terms of indenture. They continued to call sullenly for "the traitor." Then the house door opened, and the master himself appeared. He was pale and nervous, and no wonder; and his voice shook as he strove to make himself heard. His words were drowned immediately by shouts of "Seize him! Seize the d—d traitor!" "A pot and a coat of hot tar!"

Those who were nearest started forward, and I with them. With me 'twas the decision of an instant. I beat the chandler up the steps, and took stand in front of the merchant, and I called out to them to fall back.

To my astonishment they halted. The skirts of the crowd were now come to the foot of the little porch. I faced them with my hand on Mr. Stewart's arm, without a thought of what to do next, and expecting violence. There was a second's hush. Then some one cried out:—

"Three cheers for Richard Carvel!"

They gave them with a will that dumfounded me.

"My friends," said I, when I had got my wits, "this is neither the justice nor the moderation for which our province is noted. You have elected your committee of your free wills, and they have claims before you."

"Ay, ay, the committee!" they shouted. "Mr. Carvel is right. Take him to the Committee!"

Mr. Stewart raised his hand.

"My friends," he began, as I had done, "when you have learned the truth, you will not be so hasty to blame me for an offence of which I am innocent. The tea was not for me. The brig was in a leaky and dangerous state and had fifty souls aboard her. I paid the duty out of humanity —"

He had come so far, when they stopped him.

"Oh, a vile Tory!" they shouted. "He is conniving with the Council. 'Twas put up between them." And they followed this with another volley of hard names, until I feared that his chance was gone.

"You would best go before the Committee, Mr. Stewart," I said.

"I will go with Mr. Carvel, my friends," he cried at once. And he invited me into the house whilst he ordered his coach. I preferred to remain outside.

I asked them if they would trust me with Mr. Stewart to Church Street.

"Yes, yes, Mr. Carvel, we know you," said several. "He has good cause to hate Tories," called another, with a laugh. I knew the voice.

"For shame, Weld," I cried. And I saw McNeir, who was a stanch friend of mine, give him a cuff to send him spinning.

To my vast satisfaction they melted away, save only a few of the idlest spirits, who hung about the gate, and cheered as we drove off. Mr. Stewart was very nervous, and profuse in his gratitude. I replied that I had acted only as would have any other responsible citizen. On the way he told me enough of his case to convince me that there was much to be said on his side, but I thought it the better part of wisdom not to commit myself. The street in front of the committee rooms was empty, and I was informed that a town meeting had been called immediately at the theatre in West Street. And I advised Mr. Stewart to attend. But through anxiety or anger, or both, he was determined not to go, and drove back to his house without me.

I had got as far as St. Anne's, halfway to the theatre, when it suddenly struck me that Mr. Swain must be waiting for news. With a twinge I remembered what Mr. Chase had said about the barrister's condition, and I hurried back to Gloucester Street, much to the surprise of those I met on their way to the meeting. I was greatly relieved, when I arrived, to find Patty on the porch. I knew she had never been there were her father worse. After a word with her and her mother, I went up the stairs.

It was the hour for the barrister's nap. But he was awake, lying back on the pillows, with his eyes half closed. He was looking out into the garden, which was part orchard, now beginning to shrivel and to brown with the first touch of frosts.

"That is you, Richard?" he inquired, without moving. "What is going forward to-day?"

I toned down the news, so as not to excite him, and left out the occurrence in Hanover Street. He listened with his accustomed interest, but when I had done he asked no questions, and lay for a long time silent. Then he begged me to bring my chair nearer.

"Richard,— my son," said he, with an evident effort, "I have never thanked you for your devotion to me and mine through the best years of your life. It shall not go unrewarded, my lad."

It seemed as if my heart stood still with the presage of what was to come.

"May God reward you, sir!" I said.

"I have wished to speak to you," he continued, "and I may not have another chance. I have arranged with Mr. Carroll, the barrister, to take your cause against your uncle, so that you will lose nothing when I am gone. And you will see, in my table in the library, that I have left my property in your hands, with every confidence in your integrity, and ability to care for my family, even as I should have done."

I could not speak at once. A lump rose in my throat, for I had come to look upon him as a father. His honest dealings, his charity, of which the world knew nothing, and his plain and unassuming ways had inspired in me a kind of worship. I answered, as steadily as I might:—

"I believe I am too inexperienced for such a responsibility,

Mr. Swain. Would it not be better that Mr. Bordley or Mr. Lloyd should act?"

"No, no," he said; "I am not a man to do things unadvisedly, or to let affection get the better of my judgment, where others dear to me are concerned. I know you, Richard Carvel. Scarce an action of yours has escaped my eye, though I have said nothing. You have been through the fire, and are of the kind which comes out untouched. You will have Judge Bordley's advice, and Mr. Carroll's. And they are too busy with the affairs of the province to be burdened as my executors. But," he added a little more strongly, "if what I fear is coming, Mr. Bordley will take the trust in your absence. If we have war, Richard, you will not be content to remain at home, nor would I wish it."

I did not reply.

"You will do what I ask?" he said.

"I would refuse you nothing, Mr. Swain," I answered. "But I have heavy misgivings."

He sighed. "And now, if it were not for Tom, I might die content," he said.

If it were not for Tom! The full burden of the trust began to dawn upon me then. Presently I heard him speaking, but in so low a voice that I hardly caught the words.

"In our youth, Richard," he was saying, "the wrath of the Almighty is but so many words to most of us. When I was little more than a lad, I committed a sin of which I tremble now to think. And I was the fool to imagine, when I amended my life, that God had forgotten. His punishment is no heavier than I deserve. But He alone knows what He has made me suffer."

I felt that I had no right to be there.

"That is why I have paid Tom's debts," he continued; "I cannot cast off my son. I have reasoned, implored, and appealed in vain. He is like Reuben,—his resolutions melt in an hour. And I have pondered day and night what is to be done for him."

"Is he to have his portion?" I asked. Indeed, the thought of the responsibility of Tom Swain overwhelmed me.

"Yes, he is to have it," cried Mr. Swain, with a violence to bring on a fit of coughing. "Were I to leave it in trust for a time, he would have it mortgaged within a year. He is to have his portion, but not a penny additional."

He lay for a long time breathing deeply, I watching him. Then, as he reached out and took my hand, I knew by some instinct what was to come. I summoned all my self-command to meet his eye. I knew that the malicious and unthinking gossip of the town had reached him, and that he had received it in the simple faith of his hopes.

"One thing more, my lad," he said, "the dearest wish of all — that you will marry Patty. She is a good girl, Richard. And I have thought," he added with hesitation, "I have thought that she loves you, though her lips have never opened on that subject."

So the blow fell. I turned away, for to save my life the words would not come. He missed the reason of my silence.

"I understand and honour your scruples," he went on. His kindness was like a knife.

"No, I have had none, Mr. Swain," I exclaimed. For I would not be thought a hypocrite.

There I stopped. A light step sounded in the hall, and Patty came in upon us. Her colour at once betrayed her understanding. To my infinite relief her father dropped my fingers, and asked cheerily if there was any news from the town meeting.

On the following Wednesday, with her flag flying and her sails set, the *Peggy Stewart* was run ashore on Windmill Point. She rose, a sacrifice to Liberty, in smoke to heaven, before the assembled patriots of our city.

That very night a dear friend to Liberty passed away. He failed so suddenly that Patty had no time to call for aid, and when the mother had been carried in, his spirit was flown. We laid him high on the hill above the creek, in the new lot he had bought and fenced around. The stone remains : —

HERE LIETH

HENRY SWAIN, BARRISTER.

BORN MAY 13, 1730 (O.S.);

DIED OCTOBER 19, 1774.

Fidus Amicis atque Patriæ.

The simple inscription, which speaks volumes to those who knew him, was cut after the Revolution. He was buried with the honours of a statesman, which he would have been had God spared him to serve the New Country which was born so soon after his death.

CHAPTER L

FAREWELL TO GORDON'S

I CANNOT bear to recall my misery of mind after Mr. Swain's death. One hope had lightened all the years of my servitude. For, when I examined my soul, I knew that it was for Dorothy I had laboured. And every letter that came from Comyn telling me she was still free gave me new heart for my work. By some mystic communion — I know not what — I felt that she loved me yet, and despite distance and degree. I would wake of a morning with the knowledge of it, and be silent for half the day with some particle of a dream in my head, lingering like the burden of a song with its train of memories.

So, in the days that followed, I scarce knew myself. For a while (I shame to write it) I avoided that sweet woman who had made my comfort her care, whose father had taken me when I was homeless. The good in me cried out, but the flesh rebelled.

Poor Patty! Her grief for her father was pathetic to see. Weeks passed in which she scarcely spoke a word. And I remember her as she sat in church Sundays, the whiteness of her face enhanced by the crape she wore, and a piteous appeal in her gray eyes. My own agony was nigh beyond endurance, my will swinging like a pendulum from right to wrong, and back again. Argue as I might that I had made the barrister no promise, conscience allowed no difference. I was in despair at the trick fate had played me; at the decree that of all women I must love her whose sphere was now so far removed from mine. For Patty had character and beauty, and every gift which goes to make man's happiness and to kindle his affections.

Her sorrow left her more womanly than ever. And after the first sharp sting of it was deadened, I noticed a marked reserve in her intercourse with me. I knew then that she must have strong suspicions of her father's request. Speak I could not soon after the sad event, but I strove hard that she should see no change in my conduct.

Before Christmas we went to the Eastern Shore. In Annapolis fife and drum had taken the place of fiddle and clarion; militia companies were drilling in the empty streets; despatches were arriving daily from the North; and grave gentlemen were hurrying to meetings. But if the war was to come, I must settle what was to be done at Gordon's Pride with all possible speed. It was only a few days after our going there, that I rode into Oxford with a black cockade in my hat Patty had made me, and the army sword Captain Jack had given Captain Daniel at my side. For I had been elected a lieutenant in the Oxford company, of which Percy Singleton was captain.

So passed that winter, the darkest of my life. One soft spring day, when the birds were twittering amid new-born leaves, and the hyacinths and tulips in Patty's garden were coming to their glory, Master Tom rode leisurely down the drive at Gordon's Pride. That was a Saturday, the 29th of April, 1775. The news which had flown southward, night and day alike, was in no hurry to run off his tongue; he had been lolling on the porch for half an hour before he told us of the bloodshed between the minute-men of Massachusetts and the British regulars, of the rout of Percy's panting redcoats from Concord to Boston. Tom added, with the brutal nonchalance which characterized his dealings with his mother and sister, that he was on his way to Philadelphia to join a company.

The poor invalid was carried up the stairs in a faint by Banks and Romney. Patty, with pale face and lips compressed, ran to fetch the hartshorn. But Master Tom remained undisturbed.

"I suppose you are going, Richard," he remarked affably. For he treated me with more consideration than his family. "We shall ride together," said he.

"We ride different ways, and to different destinations," I replied dryly. "I go to serve my country, and you to fight against it."

"I think the King is right," he answered sullenly.

"Oh, I beg your pardon," I remarked, and rose. "Then you have studied the question since last I saw you."

"No, by G—d!" he cried, "and I never will. I do not want to know your d—d principles — or grievances, or whatever they are. We were living an easy life, in the plenty of money, and nothing to complain of. You take it all away, with your cursed cant—"

I left him railing and swearing. And that was the last I saw of Tom Swain. When I returned from a final survey of the plantation, and a talk with Percy Singleton, he had ridden North again.

I found Patty alone in the parlour. Her work (one of my own stockings she was darning) lay idle in her lap, and in her eyes were the unshed tears which are the greatest suffering of women. I sat down beside her and called her name. She did not seem to hear me.

"Patty!"

She started. And my courage ebbed.

"Are you going to the war — to leave us, Richard?" she faltered.

"I fear there is no choice, Patty," I answered, striving hard to keep my own voice steady. "But you will be well looked after. Ivie Rawlinson is to be trusted, and Mr. Bordley has promised to keep an eye upon you."

She took up the darning mechanically.

"I shall not speak a word to keep you, Richard. *He* would have wished it," she said softly. "And every strong arm in the colonies will be needed. We shall think of you, and pray for you daily."

I cast about for a cheerful reply.

"I think when they discover how determined we are, they will revoke their measures in a hurry. Before you know it, Patty, I shall be back again making the rounds in my broad rim, and reading to you out of Captain Cook."

It was a pitiful attempt. She shook her head sadly. The tears were come now, and she was smiling through them. The sorrow of that smile!

"I have something to say to you before I go, Patty," I said. The words stuck. I knew that there must be no pretence in that speech. It must be true as my life after, the consequence of it. "I have something to ask you, and I do not speak without your father's consent. Patty, if I return, will you be my wife?"

The stocking slipped unheeded to the floor. For a moment she sat transfixed, save for the tumultuous swelling of her breast. Then she turned and gazed earnestly into my face, and the honesty of her eyes smote me. For the first time I could not meet them honestly with my own.

"Richard, do you love me?" she asked.

I bowed my head. I could not answer that. And for a while there was no sound save that of the singing of the frogs in the distant marsh.

Presently I knew that she was standing at my side. I felt her hand laid upon my shoulder.

"Is — is it Dorothy?" she said gently.

Still I could not answer. Truly, the bitterness of life, as the joy of it, is distilled in strong drops.

"I knew," she continued, "I have known ever since that autumn morning when I went to you as you saddled — when I dreaded that you would leave us. Father asked you to marry me, the day you took Mr. Stewart from the mob. How could you so have misunderstood me, Richard?"

I looked up in wonder. The sweet cadence in her tone sprang from a purity not of this earth. They alone who have consecrated their days to others may utter it. And the light upon her face was of the same source. It was no will of mine brought me to my feet. But I was not worthy to touch her.

"I shall make another prayer, beside that for your safety, Richard," she said.

In the morning she waved me a brave farewell from the block where she had stood so often as I rode afield, when the dawn was in the sky. The invalid mother sat in her chair within the door; the servants were gathered on the lawn, and Ivie Rawlinson and Banks lingered where they had held my stirrup. That picture is washed with my own tears.

The earth was praising God that Sunday as I rode to Mr. Bordley's. And as it is sorrow which lifts us nearest to heaven, I felt as if I were in church.

I arrived at Wye Island in season to dine with the good judge and his family, and there I made over to his charge the property of Patty and her mother. The afternoon we spent in sober talk, Mr. Bordley giving me much sound advice, and writing me several letters of recommendation to gentlemen in Congress. His conduct was distinguished by even more of kindness and consideration than he had been wont to show me.

In the evening I walked out alone, skirting the acres of Carvel Hall, each familiar landmark touching the quick of some memory of other days. Childhood habit drew me into the path to Wilmot House. I came upon it just as the sunlight was stretching level across the Chesapeake, and burning its windows molten red. I had been sitting long on the stone steps, when the gaunt figure of McAndrews strode toward me out of the dusk.

"God be gude to us, it is Mr. Richard!" he cried. "I hae na seen ye're bonny face these muckle years, sir, syne ye cam' back frae ae sight o' the young mistress." (I had met him in Annapolis then.) "An' will ye be aff to the wars?"

I told him yes. That I had come for a last look at the old place before I left.

He sighed. "Ye're vera welcome, sir." Then he added: "Mr. Bordley's gi'en me a fair notion o' yere management at Gordon's. The judge is thinking there'll be nane ither lad t' haud a candle to ye."

"And what news do you hear from London?" I asked, cutting him short.

"Ill uncos, sir," he answered, shaking his head with violence. He had indeed but a sorry tale for my ear, and one to make my heart heavier than it was. McAndrews opened his mind to me, and seemed the better for it. How Mr. Marmaduke was living with the establishment they wrote of was more than the honest Scotchman could imagine. There was a country place in Sussex now, said he, that was the latest. And drafts were coming in before the wheat was in the ear; and the plantations of tobacco on the Western Shore had been idle since the non-exportation, and were mortgaged to their limit to Mr. Willard. Money was even loaned on the Wilmot House estate. McAndrews had a shrewd suspicion that neither Mrs. Manners nor Miss Dorothy knew aught of this state of affairs.

"Mr. Richard," he said earnestly, as he bade me good-by, "I kennt Mr. Manners's mind when he lea'd here. There was a laird in't, sir, an' a fortune. An' unless these come soon, I'm thinking I can spae th' en'."

In truth, a much greater fool than McAndrews might have predicted that end.

On Monday Judge Bordley accompanied me as far as Dingley's tavern, and showed much emotion at parting.

"You need have no fears for your friends at Gordon's Pride, Richard," said he. "And when the General comes back, I shall try to give him a good account of my stewardship."

The General! That title brought old Stanwix's cobwebbed prophecy into my head again. Here, surely, was the war which he had foretold, and I ready to embark in it.

Why not the sea, indeed?

CHAPTER LI

HOW AN IDLE PROPHECY CAME TO PASS

CAPTAIN CLAPSADDLE not being at his lodgings, I rode on to the Coffee House to put up my horse. I was stopped by Mr. Claude.

"Why, Mr. Carvel," says he, "I thought you on the Eastern Shore. There is a gentleman within will be mightily tickled to see you, or else his protestations are lies, which they may very well be. His name? Now, 'pon my faith, it was Jones — no more."

This thing of being called for at the Coffee House stirred up unpleasant associations.

"What appearance does the man make?" I demanded.

"Merciful gad!" mine host exclaimed; "once seen, never forgotten, and once heard, never forgotten. He quotes me Thomson, and he tells me of his estate in Virginia."

The answer was not of a sort to allay my suspicions.

"Then he appears to be a landowner?" said I.

"'Ods! Blest if I know what he is," says Mr. Claude. "He may be anything, an impostor or a high-mightiness. But he's something to strike the eye and hold it, for all his Quaker clothes. He is swarth and thickset, and some five feet eight inches — full six inches under your own height. And he comes asking for you as if you owned the town between you. 'Send a fellow to Marlboro' Street for Mr. Richard Carvel, my good host!' says he, with a snap of his fingers. And when I tell him the news of you, he is prodigiously affected, and cries — but here's my gentleman now!"

I jerked my head around. Coming down the steps I beheld my old friend and benefactor, Captain John Paul!

"Ahoy, ahoy!" cries he. "Now Heaven be praised, I have found you at last."

Out of the saddle I leaped, and straight into his arms.

"Hold, hold, Richard!" he gasped. "My ribs, man! Leave me some breath that I may tell you how glad I am to see you."

"Mr. *Jones!*" I said, holding him out, "now where the devil got you that?"

"Why, I am become a gentleman since I saw you," he answered, smiling. "My poor brother left me his estate in Virginia. And a gentleman must have three names at the least."

I dropped his shoulders and shook with laughter.

"But *Jones!*" I cried. "'Ad's heart! could you go no higher? Has your imagination left you, captain?"

"Republican simplicity, sir," says he, looking a trifle hurt. But I laughed the more.

"Well, you have contrived to mix oil and vinegar," said I. "A landed gentleman and republican simplicity. I'll warrant you wear silk-knit under that gray homespun, and have a cameo in your pocket."

He shook his head, looking up at me with affection.

"You might have guessed better," he answered. "All of quality I have about me are an enamelled repeater and a gold brooch."

This made me suddenly grave, for McAndrews's words had been ringing in my ears ever since he had spoken them. I hitched my arm into the captain's and pulled him toward the Coffee House door.

"Come," I said, "you have not dined, and neither have I. We shall be merry to-day, and you shall have some of the best Madeira in the colonies." I commanded a room, that we might have privacy. As he took his seat opposite me I marked that he had grown heavier and more browned. But his eye had the same unfathomable mystery in it as of yore. And first I upbraided him for not having writ me.

"I took you for one who glories in correspondence, captain," said I; "and I did not think you could be so unfaithful. I directed twice to you in Mr. Orchardson's care."

"Orchardson died before I had made one voyage," he replied, "and the *Betsy* changed owners. But I did not forget you, Richard, and was resolved but now not to leave Maryland until I had seen you. But I burn to hear of you," he added. "I have had an inkling of your story from the landlord. So your grandfather is dead, and that *blastie*, your uncle, of whom you told me on the *John*, is in possession."

He listened to my narrative keenly, but with many interruptions. And when I was done, he sighed.

"You are always finding friends, Richard," said he; "no matter what your misfortunes, they are ever double discounted. As for me, I am like Fulmer in Mr. Cumberland's 'West Indian': 'I have beat through every quarter of the compass; I have bellowed for freedom; I have offered to serve my country; I have'—I am engaging to betray it. No, Scotland is no longer my country, and so I cannot betray her. It is she who has betrayed me."

He fell into a short mood of dejection. And, indeed, I could not but reflect that much of the character fitted him like a jacket. Not the betrayal of his country. He never did that, no matter how roundly they accused him of it afterward.

To lift him, I cried:—

"You were one of my first friends, Captain Paul" (I could not stomach the *Jones*); "but for you I should now be a West Indian, and a miserable one, the slave of some unmerciful hidalgo. Here's that I may live to repay you!"

"And while we are upon toasts," says he, bracing immediately, "I give you the immortal Miss Manners! Her beauty has dwelt unfaded in my memory since I last beheld her, aboard the *Betsy*." Remarking the pain in my face, he added, with a concern which may have been comical: "And she is not married?"

"Unless she is lately gone to Gretna, she is not," I replied, trying to speak lightly.

"Alack! I knew it," he exclaimed. "And if there's any prophecy in my bones, she'll be Mrs. Carvel one of these days."

"Well, captain," I said abruptly, "the wheel has gone

around since I saw you. Now it is you who are the gentleman, while I am a factor. Is it the bliss you pictured?"

I suspected that his acres were not as broad, nor his produce as salable, as those of Mount Vernon.

"To speak truth, I am heartily tired of that life," said he. "There is little glory in raising nicotia, and sipping bumbo, and cursing negroes. Ho for the sea!" he cried. "The salt sea, and the British prizes. Give me a tight frigate that leaves a singing wake. Mark me, Richard," he said, a restless gleam coming into his dark eyes, "stirring times are here, and a chance for all of us to make a name." For so it seemed ever to be with him.

"They are black times, I fear," I answered.

"Black!" he said. "No, *glorious* is your word. And we are to have an upheaval to throw many of us to the top."

"I would rather the quarrel were peacefully settled," said I, gravely. "For my part, I want no distinction that is to come out of strife and misery."

He regarded me quizzically.

"You are grown an hundred years old since I pulled you out of the sea," says he. "But we shall have to fight for our liberties. Here is a glass to the prospect!"

"And so you are now an American?" I said curiously.

"Ay, strake and keelson,—as good a one as though I had got my sap in the Maine forests. A plague of monarchs, say I. They are a blotch upon modern civilization. And I have here," he continued, tapping his pocket, "some letters writ to the Virginia printers, signed *Demosthenes*, which Mr. Randolph and Mr. Henry have commended. To speak truth, Richard, I am off to Congress with a portmanteau full of recommendations. And I was resolved to stop here even till I secured your company. We shall sweep the seas together, and so let George beware!"

I smiled. But my blood ran faster at the thought of sailing under such a captain. However, I made the remark that Congress had as yet no army, let alone a navy.

"And think you that gentlemen of such spirit and resources will lack either for long?" he demanded, his eye flashing.

HOW A PROPHECY CAME TO PASS 467

"Then I know nothing of a ship save the little I learned on the *John*," I said.

"You were born for the sea, Richard," he exclaimed, raising his glass high. "And I would rather have one of your brains and strength and handiness than any merchant's mate I ever sailed with. The more gentlemen get commissions, the better will be our new service."

At that instant came a knock at the door, and one of the inn negroes to say that Captain Clapsaddle was below, and desired to see me. I persuaded John Paul to descend with me. We found Captain Daniel seated with Mr. Carroll, the barrister, and Mr. Chase.

"Captain," I said to my old friend, "I have a rare joy this day in making known to you Mr. John Paul *Jones*, of whom I have spoken to you a score of times. He it is whose bravery sank the *Black Moll*, whose charity took me to London, and who got no other reward for his faith than three weeks in a debtors' prison. For his honour, as I have told you, would allow him to accept none, nor his principles to take the commission in the Royal Navy which Mr. Fox offered him."

Captain Daniel rose, his honest face flushing with pleasure. "Faith, Mr. Jones," he cried, when John Paul had finished one of his elaborate bows, "this is well met, indeed. I have been longing these many years for a chance to press your hand, and in the names of those who are dead and gone to express my gratitude."

"I have my reward now, captain," replied John Paul; "a sight of you is to have Richard's whole life revealed. And what says Mr. Congreve? —

"'For blessings ever wait on virtuous deeds,
And tho' a late, a sure reward succeeds.'

Tho' I would not have you believe that my deed was virtuous. And you, who know Richard, may form some notion of the pleasure I had out of his companionship."

I hastened to present my friend to the other gentlemen, who welcomed him with warmth, though they could not keep their amusement wholly out of their faces.

"Mr. Jones is now the possessor of an estate in Virginia, sirs," I explained.

"And do you find it more to your taste than seafaring, Mr. Jones?" inquired Mr. Chase.

This brought forth a most vehement protest, and another quotation.

"Why, sir," he cried, "to be

> "'Fixed like a plant on his peculiar spot,
> To draw nutrition, propagate, and rot,'

is an animal's existence. I have thrown it over, sir, with a right good will, and am now on my way to Philadelphia to obtain a commission in the navy soon to be born."

Mr. Chase smiled. John Paul little suspected that he was a member of the Congress.

"This is news indeed, Mr. Jones," he said. "I have yet to hear of the birth of this infant navy, for which we have not yet begun to make swaddling clothes."

"We are not yet an infant state, sir," Mr. Carroll put in, with a shade of rebuke. For Maryland was well content with the government she had enjoyed, and her best patriots long after shunned the length of secession. "I believe and pray that the King will come to his senses. And as for the navy, it is folly. How can we hope to compete with England on the sea?"

"All great things must have a beginning sir," replied John Paul, launching forth at once, nothing daunted by such cold conservatism. "What Israelite brickmaker of Pharaoh's dreamed of Solomon's temple? Nay, Moses himself had no conception of it. And God will send us our pillars of cloud and of fire. We must be reconciled to our great destiny, Mr. Carroll. No fight ever was won by man or nation content with half a victory. We have forests to build an hundred armadas, and I will command a fleet and it is given me."

The gentlemen listened in astonishment.

"I' faith, I believe you, sir," cried Captain Daniel, with admiration.

The others, too, were somehow fallen under the spell of this remarkable individuality. "What plan would you pursue, sir?" asked Mr. Chase, betraying more interest than he cared to show.

"What plan, sir!" said Captain John Paul, those wonderful eyes of his alight. "In the first place, we Americans build the fastest ships in the world,—yours of the Chesapeake are as fleet as any. Here, if I am not mistaken, one hundred and eighty-two were built in the year '71. They are idle now. To them I would issue letters of marque, to harry England's trade. From Carolina to Maine we have the wood and iron to build cruisers, in harbours that may not easily be got at. And skilled masters and seamen to elude the enemy."

"But a navy must be organized, sir. It must be an unit," objected Mr. Carroll. "And you would not for many years have force enough, or discipline enough, to meet England's navy."

"I would never meet it, sir," he replied instantly. "That would be the height of folly. I would divide our forces into small, swift-sailing squadrons, of strength sufficient to repel his cruisers. And I would carry the war straight into his unprotected ports of trade. I can name a score of such defenceless places, and I know every shoal of their harbours. For example, Whitehaven might be entered. That is a town of fifty thousand inhabitants. The fleet of merchantmen might with the greatest ease be destroyed, a contribution levied, and Ireland's coal cut off for a winter. The whole of the shipping might be swept out of the Clyde. Newcastle is another likely place, and in almost any of the Irish ports valuable vessels may be found. The Baltic and West Indian fleets are to be intercepted. I have reflected upon these matters for years, gentlemen. They are perfectly feasible. And I'll warrant you cannot conceive the havoc and consternation their fulfilment would spread in England."

If the divine power of genius ever made itself felt, 'twas on that May evening, at candle-light, in the Annapolis Coffee House. With my own eyes I witnessed two able and cautious statesmen of a cautious province thrilled to the pitch of enthusiasm by this strange young man of eight and twenty. As for good Captain Daniel, enthusiasm is but a poor word to express his feelings. A map was sent for and spread out upon the table. And it was a late hour when Mr. Chase and Mr. Carroll went home, profoundly impressed. Mr. Chase charged John Paul look him up in Congress.

The next morning I bade Captain Daniel a solemn good-by, and rode away with John Paul to Baltimore. Thence we took stage to New Castle on the Delaware, and were eventually landed by Mr. Tatlow's stage-boat at Crooked Billet wharf, Philadelphia.

A BRIEF SUMMARY, WHICH BRINGS THIS BIOGRAPHY TO THE FAMOUS FIGHT OF THE *BON HOMME RICHARD* AND THE *SERAPIS*

By Daniel Clapsaddle Carvel

Mr. Richard Carvel refers here to the narrative of his experiences in the War of the Revolution, which he had written in the year 1805 or 1806. The insertion of that account would swell this book, already too long, out of all proportion. Hence I take it upon myself, with apologies, to compress it.

Not until October of that year, 1775, was the infant navy born. Mr. Carvel was occupied in the interval in the acquirement of practical seamanship and the theory of maritime warfare under the most competent of instructors, John Paul Jones. An interesting side light is thrown upon the character of that hero by the fact that, with all his supreme confidence in his ability, he applied to Congress only for a first lieutenancy. This was in deference to the older men before that body. "I hoped," said he, "in that rank to gain much useful knowledge from those of more experience than myself." His lack of assertion for once cost him dear. He sailed on the New Providence expedition under Commodore Hopkins as first lieutenant of the *Alfred*, thirty; and he soon discovered that, instead of gaining information, he was obliged to inform others. He trained the men so thoroughly in the use of the great guns "that they went through the motions of broadsides and rounds exactly as soldiers generally perform the manual exercise."

Captain Jones was not long in fixing the attention and earning the gratitude of the nation, and of its Commander-in-Chief, General Washington. While in command of the *Providence*, twelve four-pounders, his successful elusions of the *Cerberus*, which hounded him, and his escape

HOW A PROPHECY CAME TO PASS

from the *Solebay*, are too famous to be dwelt upon here. Obtaining the *Alfred*, he captured and brought into Boston ten thousand suits of uniform for Washington's shivering army. Then, by the bungling of Congress, thirteen officers were promoted over his head. The bitterness this act engendered in the soul of one whose thirst for distinction was as great as Captain Jones's may be imagined. To his everlasting credit be it recorded that he remained true to the country to which he had dedicated his life and his talents. And it was not until 1781 that he got the justice due him.

That the rough and bluff captains of the American service should have regarded a man of Paul Jones's type with suspicion is not surprising. They resented his polish and accomplishments, and could not understand his language. Perhaps it was for this reason, as well as a reward for his brilliant services, that he was always given a separate command. In the summer of 1777 he was singled out for the highest gift in the power of the United States, nothing less than that of the magnificent frigate *Indien*, then building at Amsterdam. And he was ordered to France in command of the *Ranger*, a new ship then fitting at Portsmouth. Captain Jones was the admiration of all the young officers in the navy, and was immediately flooded with requests to sail with him. One of his first acts, after receiving his command, was to apply to the Marine Committee for Mr. Carvel. The favour was granted.

My grandfather had earned much commendation from his superiors. He had sailed two cruises as master's mate of the *Cabot*, and was then serving as master of the *Trumbull*, Captain Saltonstall. This was shortly after that frigate had captured the two British transports off New York.

Captain Jones has been at pains to mention in his letters the services rendered him by Mr. Carvel in fitting out the *Ranger*. And my grandfather gives a striking picture of the captain. At that time the privateers, with the larger inducements of profit they offered, were getting all the best seamen. John Paul had but to take two turns with a man across the dock, and he would sign papers.

Captain Jones was the first to raise the new flag of the stars and stripes over a man-o'-war. They got away on November 14, 1777, with a fair crew and a poor lot of officers. Mr. Carvel had many a brush with the mutinous first lieutenant Simpson. Family influence deterred the captain from placing this man under arrest, and even Dr. Franklin found trouble, some years after, in bringing about his dismissal from the service. To add to the troubles, the *Ranger* proved crank and slow-sailing; and she had only one barrel of rum aboard, which made the men discontented.

Bringing the official news of Burgoyne's surrender, which was to cause King Louis to acknowledge the independence of the United States, the *Ranger* arrived at Nantes, December 2. Mr. Carvel accompanied Captain Jones to Paris, where a serious blow awaited him. The American

Commissioners informed him that the *Indien* had been transferred to France to prevent her confiscation. That winter John Paul spent striving in vain for a better ship, and imbibing tactics from the French admirals. Incidentally, he obtained a salute for the American flag. The cruise of the *Ranger* in English waters the following spring was a striking fulfilment, with an absurdly poor and inadequate force, of the plan set forth by John Paul Jones in the Annapolis Coffee House. His descent upon Whitehaven spread terror and consternation broadcast through England, and he was branded as a pirate and a traitor. Mr. Carvel was fortunately not of the landing party on St. Mary's Isle, which place he had last beheld in John Paul's company, on the brigantine *John*, when entering Kirkcudbright. The object of that expedition, as is well known, was to obtain the person of the Earl of Selkirk, in order to bring about the rescue of the unfortunate Americans suffering in British prisons. After the celebrated capture of the sloop-of-war *Drake*, Paul Jones returned to France a hero.

If Captain Jones was ambitious of personal glory, he may never, at least, be accused of mercenary motives. The ragged crew of the *Ranger* was paid in part out of his own pocket, and for a whole month he supported the *Drake's* officers and men, no provision having been made for prisoners. He was at large expense in fitting out the *Ranger*, and he bought back at twice what it was worth the plate taken from St. Mary's Isle, getting but a tardy recognition from the Earl of Selkirk for such a noble and unheard-of action. And, I take pride in writing it, Mr. Carvel spent much of what he had earned at Gordon's Pride in a like honourable manner.

Mr. Carvel's description of the hero's reception at Versailles is graphic and very humorous. For all his republican principles John Paul never got over his love of courts, and no man was ever a more thorough courtier. He exchanged compliments with Queen Marie Antoinette, who was then in the bloom of her beauty, and declared that "she was a good girl, and deserved to be happy."

The unruly Simpson sailed for America in the *Ranger* in July, Captain Jones being retained in France "for a particular enterprise." And through the kindness of Dr. Franklin, Mr. Carvel remained with him. Then followed another period of heartrending disappointment. The fine ship the French government promised him was not forthcoming, though Captain Jones wrote a volume of beautiful letters to every one of importance, from her Royal Highness the Duchess of Chartres to his Most Christian Majesty, Louis, King of France and Navarre. At length, when he was sitting one day in unusual dejection and railing at the vanity of courts and kings, Mr. Carvel approached him with a book in his hand.

"What have you there, Richard?" the captain demanded.

"Dr. Franklin's Maxims," replied my grandfather. They were great favourites with him. The captain took the book and began mechanically to turn over the pages. Suddenly he closed it with a bang, jumped up, and put on his coat and hat. Mr. Carvel looked on in astonishment.

"Where are you going, sir?" says he.

"To Paris, sir," says the captain. "Dr. Franklin has taught me more wisdom in a second than I had in all my life before. 'If you wish to have any business faithfully and expeditiously performed, go and do it yourself; otherwise, send.'"

As a result of that trip he got the *Duras*, which he renamed the *Bon homme Richard* in honour of Dr. Franklin. The *Duras* was an ancient Indiaman with a high poop, which made my grandfather exclaim, when he saw her, at the remarkable fulfilment of old Stanwix's prophecy. She was perfectly rotten, and in the constructor's opinion not worth refitting. Her lowest deck (too low for the purpose) was pierced aft with three ports on a side, and six worn-out eighteen-pounders mounted there. Some of them burst in the action, killing their people. The main battery, on the deck above, was composed of twenty-eight twelve-pounders. On the uncovered deck eight nine-pounders were mounted. Captain Jones again showed his desire to serve the cause by taking such a ship, and not waiting for something better.

In the meantime the American frigate *Alliance* had brought Lafayette to France, and was added to the little squadron that was to sail with the *Bon homme Richard*. One of the most fatal mistakes Congress ever made was to put Captain Pierre Landais in command of her, out of compliment to the French allies. He was a man whose temper and vagaries had failed to get him a command in his own navy. His insulting conduct and treachery to Captain Jones are strongly attested to in Mr. Carvel's manuscript: they were amply proved by the written statements of other officers.

The squadron sailed from L'Orient in June, but owing to a collision between the *Bon homme Richard* and the *Alliance* it was forced to put back into the Groix roads for repairs. Nails and rivets were with difficulty got to hold in the sides of the old Indiaman. On August 14th John Paul Jones again set sail for English waters, with the following vessels: *Alliance*, thirty-six; *Pallas*, thirty; *Cerf*, eighteen; *Vengeance*, twelve; and two French privateers. Owing to the humiliating conditions imposed upon him by the French Minister of Marine, Commodore Jones did not have absolute command. In a gale on the 26th the two privateers and the *Cerf* parted company, never to return. After the most outrageous conduct off the coast of Ireland, Landais, in the *Alliance*, left the squadron on September 6th, and did not reappear until the 23d, the day of the battle.

Mr. Carvel was the third lieutenant of the *Bon homme Richard*, tho' he served as second in the action. Her first lieutenant (afterwards the celebrated Commodore Richard Dale) was a magnificent man, one worthy in every respect of the captain he served. When the hour of battle arrived, these two and the sailing master, and a number of raw midshipmen, were the only line-officers left, and two French officers of marines.

The rest had been lost in various ways. And the crew of the *Bon homme Richard* was as sorry a lot as ever trod a deck. Less than three score of the seamen were American born; near four score were British, inclusive of sixteen Irish; one hundred and thirty-seven were French soldiers, who acted as marines; and the rest of the three hundred odd souls to fight her were from all over the earth, — Malays and Maltese and Portuguese. In the hold were more than one hundred and fifty English prisoners.

This was a vessel and a force, truly, with which to conquer a fifty-gun ship of the latest type, and with a picked crew.

Mr. Carvel's chapter opens with Landais's sudden reappearance on the morning of the day the battle was fought. He shows the resentment and anger against the Frenchman felt by all on board, from cabin-boy to commodore. But none went so far as to accuse the captain of the *Alliance* of such supreme treachery as he was to show during the action. Cowardice may have been in part responsible for his holding aloof from the two duels in which the *Richard* and the *Pallas* engaged. But the fact that he poured broadsides into the *Richard*, and into her off side, makes it seem probable that his motive was to sink the commodore's ship, and so get the credit of saving the day, to the detriment of the hero who won it despite all disasters. To account for the cry that was raised when first she attacked the *Richard*, it must be borne in mind that the crew of the *Alliance* was largely composed of Englishmen. It was thought that these had mutinied and taken her.

CHAPTER LII

HOW THE GARDENER'S SON FOUGHT THE "SERAPIS"

When I came on deck the next morning our yards were a-drip with a clammy fog, and under it the sea was roughed by a southwest breeze. We were standing to the northward before it. I remember reflecting as I paused in the gangway that the day was Thursday, September the 23d, and that we were near two months out of Groix with this tub of an Indiaman. In all that time we had not so much as got a whiff of an English frigate, though we had almost put a belt around the British Isles. Then straining my eyes through the mist, I made out two white blurs of sails on our starboard beam. Honest Jack Pearce, one of the few good seamen we had aboard, was rubbing down one of the nines beside me.

"Why, Jack," said I, "what have we there? Another prize?" For that question had become a joke on board the *Bon homme Richard* since the prisoners had reached an hundred and fifty, and half our crew was gone to man the ships.

"Bless your 'art, no, sir," said he. "'Tis that damned Frenchy Landais in th' *Alliance*. She turns up with the *Pallas* at six bells o' the middle watch."

"So he's back, is he?"

"Ay, he's back," he returned, with a grunt that was half a growl; "arter three weeks breakin' o' liberty. I tell 'ee what, sir, them Frenchies is treecherous devils, an' not to be trusted the len'th of a lead line. An' they beant seamen eno' to keep a full an' by with all their *takteek*. Ez fer that Landais, I hearn him whinin' at the commodore in the round house when we was off Clear, an' sayin' as how he would tell Sartin on us when he gets back to Paree. An' jabberin to th' other Frenchmen as was there that this here butter-cask was er King's ship, an' that the commodore weren't no commodore nohow. They say as how Cap'n Jones be bound up in a hard knot by some articles of agreement, an' daresn't punish him. Be that so, Mr. Carvel?"

I said that it was.

"Shiver my bulkheads!" cried Jack, "I gave my oath to that same, sir. For I knowed the commodore was the lad t' string 'em to the yard-arm an' he had the say on it. Oh, the devil take the Frenchies," said Jack, rolling his quid to show his pleasure of the topic, "they sits on their bottoms in Brest and L'Oriong an' talks *takteek* wi' their han's and mouths, and daresn't as much as show the noses o' their three-deckers in th' Bay o' Biscay, while Cap'n Jones pokes his bowsprit into every port in England with a hulk the rats have left. I've had my bellyful o' Frenchies, Mr. Carvel, save it be to fight 'em. An' I tell 'ee 'twould give me the greatest joy in life t' leave loose *Scolding Sairy* at that there Landais. Th' gal ain't had a match on her this here cruise, an' t' my mind she couldn't be christened better, sir."

I left him patting the gun with a tender affection.

The scene on board was quiet and peaceful enough that morning. A knot of midshipmen on the forecastle were discussing Landais's conduct, and cursing the concordat which prevented our commodore from bringing him up short. Mr. Stacey, the sailing-master, had the deck, and the coasting pilot was conning; now and anon the boatswain's whistle piped for Garrett or Quito or Fogg to lay aft to the mast, where the first lieutenant stood talking to Colonel de Chamillard, of the French marines. The scavengers were sweeping down, and part of the after guard was bending a new bolt-rope on a storm staysail.

Then the fore-topmast crosstrees reports a sail on the weather quarter, the *Richard* is brought around on the wind, and away we go after a brigantine, "flying like a snow laden with English bricks," as Midshipman Coram jokingly remarks. A chase is not such a novelty with us that we crane our necks to windward.

At noon, when I relieved Mr. Stacey of the deck, the sun

had eaten up the fog, and the shores of England stood out boldly. Spurn Head was looming up across our bows, while that of Flamborough jutted into the sea behind us. I had the starboard watch piped to dinner, and reported twelve o'clock to the commodore. And had just got permission to "make it," according to a time-honoured custom at sea, when another "Sail, ho!" came down from aloft.

"Where away?" called back Mr. Linthwaite, who was midshipman of the forecastle.

"Starboard quarter, rounding Flamborough Head, sir. Looks like a full-rigged ship, sir."

I sent the messenger into the great cabin to report. He was barely out of sight before a second cry came from the masthead: "Another sail rounding Flamborough, sir!"

The officers on deck hurried to the taffrail. I had my glass, but not a dot was visible above the sea-line. The messenger was scarcely back again when there came a third hail: "Two more rounding the head, sir! Four in all, sir!"

Here was excitement indeed. Without waiting for instructions, I gave the command:—

"Up royal yards! Royal yardmen in the tops!"

We were already swaying out of the chains, when Lieutenant Dale appeared and asked the coasting pilot what fleet it was. He answered that it was the Baltic fleet, under convoy of the *Countess of Scarborough*, twenty guns, and the *Serapis*, forty-four.

"Forty-four," repeated Mr. Dale, smiling; "that means fifty, as English frigates are rated. We shall have our hands full this day, my lads," said he. "You have done well to get the royals on her, Mr. Carvel."

While he was yet speaking, three more sail were reported from aloft. Then there was a hush on deck, and the commodore himself appeared. As he reached the poop we saluted him and informed him of what had happened.

"The Baltic fleet," said he, promptly. "Call away the pilot-boat with Mr. Lunt to follow the brigantine, sir, and ease off before the wind. Signal 'General Chase' to the squadron, Mr. Mayrant."

The men had jumped to the weather braces before I gave the command, and all the while more sail were counting from the crosstrees, until their number had reached forty-one. The news spread over the ship; the starboard watch trooped up with their dinners half eaten. Then a faint booming of guns drifted down upon our ears.

"They've got sight of us, sir," shouted the lookout. "They be firing guns to windward, an' letting fly their topgallant sheets."

At that the commodore hurried forward, the men falling back to the bulwarks respectfully, and he mounted the fore-rigging as agile as any topman, followed by his aide with a glass. From the masthead he sung out to me to set our stu'nsails, and he remained aloft till near seven bells of the watch. At that hour the merchantmen had all scuttled to safety behind the head, and from the deck a great yellow King's frigate could be plainly seen standing south to meet us, followed by her smaller consort. Presently she hove to, and through our glasses we discerned a small boat making for her side, and then a man clambering up her sea-ladder.

"That be the bailiff of Scarborough, sir," said the coasting pilot, "come to tell her cap'n 'tis Paul Jones he has to fight."

At that moment the commodore lay down from aloft, and our hearts beat high as he walked swiftly aft to the quarter-deck, where he paused for a word with Mr. Dale. Meanwhile Mr. Mayrant hove out the signal for the squadron to form line of battle.

"Recall the pilot-boat, Mr. Carvel," said the commodore, quietly. "Then you may beat to quarters, and I will take the ship, sir."

"Ay, ay, sir." I raised my trumpet. "*All hands clear ship for action!*"

It makes me sigh now to think of the cheer which burst from that tatterdemalion crew. Who were they to fight the bone and sinew of the King's navy in a rotten ship of an age gone by? And who was he, that stood so straight upon the quarter-deck, to instil this scum with love and worship and fervour to blind them to such odds? But the bo'suns piped and sang out the command in fog-horn voices, the drums beat the long roll and the fifes whistled, and the decks became suddenly alive. Breechings were loosed and gun-tackles unlashed, rammer and sponge laid out, and pike and pistol and cutlass placed where they would be handy when the time came to rush the enemy's decks. The powder-monkeys tumbled over each other in their hurry to provide cartridges, and grape and canister and double-headed shot were hoisted up from below. The trimmers rigged the splinter nettings, got out spare spars and blocks and ropes against those that were sure to be shot away, and rolled up casks of water to put out the fires. Tubs were filled with sand, for blood is slippery upon the boards. The French marines, their scarlet and white very natty in contrast to most of our ragged wharf-rats at the guns, were mustered on poop and forecastle, and some were sent aloft to the tops to assist the tars there to sweep the British decks with handgrenade and musket. And, lastly, the surgeon and his mates went below to cockpit and steerage, to make ready for the grimmest work of all.

My own duties took me to the dark lower deck, a vile place indeed, and reeking with the smell of tar and stale victuals. There I had charge of the battery of old eighteens, while Mr. Dale commanded the twelves on the middle deck. We loaded our guns with two shots apiece, though I had my doubts about their standing such a charge, and then the men stripped until they stood naked to the waist, waiting for the fight to begin. For we could see nothing of what was going forward. I was pacing up and down, for it was a task to quiet the nerves in that dingy place with the gun-ports closed, when about three bells of the dog, Mr. Mease, the purser, appeared on the ladder.

"Lunt has not come back with the pilot-boat, Carvel," said he. "I have volunteered for a battery, and am assigned to this. You are to report to the commodore."

I thanked him, and climbed quickly to the quarterdeck. The *Bon homme Richard* was lumbering like a leaden ship before the wind, swaying ponderously, her topsails flapping and her heavy blocks whacking against the yards. And there was the commodore, erect, and with fire in his eye, giving sharp commands to the men at the wheel. I knew at once that no trifle had disturbed him. He wore a brand-new uniform; a blue coat with red lapels and yellow buttons, and slashed cuffs and stand-up collar, a red waistcoat with tawny lace, blue breeches, white silk stockings, and a cocked hat and a sword. Into his belt were stuck two brace of pistols.

It took some effort to realize, as I waited silently for his attention, that this was the man of whose innermost life I had had so intimate a view. Who had taken me to the humble cottage under Criffel, who had poured into my ear his ambitions and his wrongs when we had sat together in the dingy room of the Castle Yard sponging-house. Then some of those ludicrous scenes on the road to London came up to me, for which the sky-blue frock was responsible. And yet this commodore was not greatly removed from him I had first beheld on the brigantine *John*. His confidence in his future had not so much as wavered since that day. That future was now not so far distant as the horizon, and he was ready to meet it.

"You will take charge of the battery of nines on this deck, Mr. Carvel," said he, at length.

"Very good, sir," I replied, and was making my way down the poop ladder, when I heard him calling me, in a low voice, by the old name: "Richard!"

I turned and followed him aft to the taffrail, where we were clear of the French soldiers. The sun was hanging red over the Yorkshire Wolds, the Head of Flamborough was in the blue shadow, and the clouds were like rose leaves in the sky. The enemy had tacked and was standing west, with ensign and jack and pennant flying, the level light washing his sails to the whiteness of paper. 'Twas then I first remarked that the *Alliance* had left her place in line and was sailing swiftly ahead toward the *Serapis*. The commodore seemed to read my exclamation.

"Landais means to ruin me yet, by hook or crook," said he.

"But he can't intend to close with them," I replied. "He has not the courage."

"God knows what he intends," said the commodore, bitterly. "It is no good, at all events."

My heart bled for him. Some minutes passed that he did not speak, making shift to raise his glass now and again, and I knew that he was gripped by a strong emotion. 'Twas so he ever behaved when the stress was greatest. Presently he lays down the glass on the signal-chest, fumbles in his coat, and brings out the little gold brooch I had not set eyes on since Dolly and he and I had stood together on the *Betsy's* deck.

"When you see her, Richard, tell her that I have kept it as sacred as her memory," he said thickly. "She will recall what I spoke of you when she gave it me. You have been leal and true to me indeed, and many a black hour have you tided me over since this war began. Do you know how she may be directed to?" he concluded, with abruptness.

I glanced at him, surprised at the question. He was staring at the English shore.

"Mr. Ripley, of Lincoln's Inn, used to be Mr. Manners's lawyer," I answered.

He took out a little note-book and wrote that down carefully. "And now," he continued, "God keep you, my friend. We must win, for we fight with a rope around our necks."

"But you, Captain Paul," I said, "is — is there no one?"

His face took on the look of melancholy it had worn so often of late, despite his triumphs. That look was the stamp of fate.

"Richard," replied he, with an ineffable sadness, "I am naught but a wanderer upon the face of the earth. I have no ties, no kindred, — no real friends, save you and Dale, and some of these honest fellows whom I lead to slaughter. My ambition is seamed with a flaw. And all my life I must be striving, striving, until I am laid in the grave. I know that now, and it is you yourself who have taught me. For I have violently broken forth from those bounds which God in His wisdom did set."

I pressed his hand, and with bowed head went back to my station, profoundly struck by the truth of what he had spoken. Though he fought under the flag of freedom, the curse of the expatriated was upon his head.

Shortly afterward he appeared at the poop rail, straight and alert, his eye piercing each man as it fell on him. He was the commodore once more.

The twilight deepened, until you scarce could see your hands. There was no sound save the cracking of the cabins and the tumbling of the blocks, and from time to time a muttered command. An age went by before the trimmers were sent to the lee braces, and the *Richard* rounded lazily to. And a great frigate loomed out of the night beside us, half a pistol-shot away.

"What ship is that?" came the hail, intense out of the silence.

"I don't hear you," replied our commodore, for he had not yet got his distance.

Again came the hail: "What ship is that?"

John Paul Jones leaned forward over the rail.

"Pass the word below to the first lieutenant to begin the action, sir."

Hardly were the words out of my mouth before the deck gave a mighty leap, a hot wind that seemed half of flame blew across my face, and the roar started the pain throbbing in my ears. At the same instant the screech of shot sounded overhead, we heard the sharp crack-crack of wood rending and splitting,— as with a great broadaxe,— and a medley of blocks and ropes rattled to the deck with the thud of the falling bodies. Then, instead of stillness, moans and shrieks from above and below, oaths and prayers in English and French and Portuguese, and in the heathen gibberish of the East. As the men were sponging and ramming home in the first fury of hatred, the carpenter jumped out under the battle-lanthorn at the main hatch, crying in a wild voice that the old eighteens had burst, killing half their crews and blowing up the gun-deck above them. At this many of our men broke and ran for the hatches.

"*Back, back to your quarters! The first man to desert will be shot down!*"

It was the same strange voice that had quelled the mutiny on the *John,* that had awed the men of Kirkcudbright. The

WE MIGHT HAVE TOSSED A BISCUIT ABOARD THE "SERAPIS"

tackles were seized and the guns run out once more, and fired, and served again in an agony of haste. In the darkness shot shrieked hither and thither about us like demons, striking everywhere, sometimes sending casks of salt water over the nettings. Incessantly the quartermaster walked to and fro scattering sand over the black pools that kept running, running together as the minutes were tolled out, and the red flashes from the guns revealed faces in a hideous contortion. One little fellow, with whom I had had many a lively word at mess, had his arm taken off at the shoulder as he went skipping past me with the charge under his coat, and I have but to listen now to hear the patter of the blood on the boards as they carried him away to the cockpit below. Out of the main hatch, from that charnel house, rose one continuous cry. It was an odd trick of the mind or soul that put a hymn on my lips in that dreadful hour of carnage and human misery, when men were calling the name of their Maker in vain. But as I ran from crew to crew, I sang over and over again a long-forgotten Christmas carol, and with it came a fleeting memory of my mother on the stairs at Carvel Hall, and of the negroes gathered on the lawn without.

Suddenly, glancing up at the dim cloud of sails above, I saw that we were aback and making sternway. We might have tossed a biscuit aboard the big *Serapis* as she glided ahead of us. The broadsides thundered, and great ragged scantlings brake from our bulwarks and flew as high as the mizzen-top; and the shrieks and groans redoubled. Involuntarily my eyes sought the poop, and I gave a sigh of relief at the sight of the commanding figure in the midst of the whirling smoke. We shotted our guns with double-headed, manned our lee braces, and gathered headway.

"*Stand by to board!*"

The boatswains' whistles trilled through the ship, pikes were seized, and pistol and cutlass buckled on. But even as we waited with set teeth, our bows ground into the enemy's weather quarter-gallery. For the *Richard's* rigging was much cut away, and she was crank at best. So we backed and filled once more, passing the Englishman close aboard, himself being aback at the time. Several of his shot crushed through the bulwarks in front of me, shattering a nine-pounder and killing half of its crew. And it is only a miracle that I stand alive to be able to tell the tale. Then I caught a glimpse of the quartermaster whirling the spokes of our wheel, and over went our helm to lay us athwart the forefoot of the *Serapis,* where we might rake and rush her decks. Our old Indiaman answered but doggedly; and the huge bowsprit of the *Serapis,* towering over our heads, snapped off our spanker gaff and fouled our mizzen rigging.

"A hawser, Mr. Stacey, a hawser!" I heard the commodore shout, and saw the sailing-master slide down the ladder and grope among the dead and wounded and mass of broken spars and tackles, and finally pick up a smeared rope's end, which I helped him drag to the poop. There we found the commodore himself taking skilful turns around the mizzen with the severed stays and shrouds dangling from the bowsprit, the French marines looking on.

"Don't swear, Mr. Stacey," said he, severely; "in another minute we may all be in eternity."

I rushed back to my guns, for the wind was rapidly swinging the stern of the *Serapis* to our own bow, now bringing her starboard batteries into play. Barely had we time to light our matches and send our broadside into her at three fathoms before the huge vessels came crunching together, the disordered riggings locking, and both pointed northward to a leeward tide in a death embrace. The chance had not been given him to shift his crews or to fling open his starboard gun-ports.

Then ensued a moment's breathless hush, even the cries of those in agony lulling. The pall of smoke rolled a little, and a silver moonlight filtered through, revealing the weltering bodies twisted upon the boards. A stern call came from beyond the bulwarks.

"Have you struck, sir?"

The answer sounded clear, and bred hero-worship in our souls.

"*Sir, I have not yet begun to fight.*"

Our men raised a hoarse yell, drowned all at once by the popping of musketry in the tops and the bursting of grenades here and there about the decks. A mighty muffled blast sent the *Bon homme Richard* rolling to larboard, and the smoke eddied from our hatches and lifted out of the space between the ships. The Englishman had blown off his gun-ports. And next some one shouted that our battery of twelves was fighting them muzzle to muzzle below, our rammers leaning into the *Serapis* to send their shot home. No chance then for the thoughts which had tortured us in moments of suspense. That was a fearful hour, when a shot had scarce to leap a cannon's length to find its commission; when the belches of the English guns burned the hair of our faces; when Death was sovereign, merciful or cruel at his pleasure. The red flashes disclosed many an act of coolness and of heroism. I saw a French lad whip off his coat when a gunner called for a wad, and another, who had been a scavenger, snatch the rammer from Pearce's hands when he staggered with a grape-shot through his chest. Poor Jack Pearce! He did not live to see the work *Scolding Sairy* was to do that night. I had but dragged him beyond reach of the recoil when he was gone.

Then a cry came floating down from aloft. Thrice did I hear it, like one waking out of a sleep, ere I grasped its import. "The *Alliance!* The *Alliance!*" But hardly had the name resounded with joy throughout the ship, when a hail of grape and canister tore through our sails from aft forward. "She rakes us! She rakes us!" And the French soldiers tumbled headlong down from the poop with a wail of "*Les Anglais l'ont prise!*" "Her Englishmen have taken her, and turned her guns against us!" Our captain was left standing alone beside the staff where the stars and stripes waved black in the moonlight.

"The *Alliance* is hauling off, sir!" called the midshipman of the mizzen-top. "She is making for the *Pallas* and the *Countess of Scarborough.*"

"Very good, sir," was all the commodore said.

To us hearkening for his answer his voice betrayed no sign of dismay. Seven times, I say, was that battle lost, and seven times regained again. What was it kept the crews at their quarters and the officers at their posts through that hell of flame and shot, when a madman could scarce have hoped for victory? What but the knowledge that somewhere in the swirl above us was still that unswerving and indomitable man who swept all obstacles from before him, and into whose mind the thought of defeat could not enter. His spirit held us to our task, for flesh and blood might not have endured alone.

We had now but one of our starboard nine-pounders on its carriage, and word came from below that our battery of twelves was all but knocked to scrap iron, and their ports blown into one yawning gap. Indeed, we did not have to be told that sides and stanchions had been carried away, for the deck trembled and teetered under us as we dragged *Scolding Sairy* from her stand in the larboard waist, clearing a lane for her between the bodies. Our feet slipped and slipped as we hove, and burning bits of sails and splinters dropping from aloft fell unheeded on our heads and shoulders. With the energy of desperation I was bending to the pull, when the Malay in front of me sank dead across the tackle. But, ere I could touch him, he was tenderly lifted aside, and a familiar figure seized the rope where the dead man's hands had warmed it. Truly, the commodore was everywhere that night.

"Down to the surgeon with you, Richard!" he cried. "I will look to the battery."

Dazed, I put my hand to my hair to find it warm and wringing wet. When I had been hit, I knew not. But I shook my head, for the very notion of that cockpit turned my stomach. The blood was streaming from a gash in his own temple, to which he gave no heed, and stood encouraging that panting line until at last the gun was got across and hooked to the ring-bolts of its companion that lay shattered there. "Serve her with double-headed, my lads," he shouted, "and every shot into the Englishman's mainmast!"

"Ay, ay, sir," came the answer from every man of that little remnant.

The *Serapis*, too, was now beginning to blaze aloft, and choking wood-smoke eddied out of the *Richard's* hold and mingled with the powder fumes. Then the enemy's fire abreast us seemed to lull, and Mr. Stacey mounted the bulwarks, and cried out: "You have cleared their decks, my hearties!" Aloft, a man was seen to clamber from our mainyard into the very top of the Englishman, where he threw a hand-grenade, as I thought, down her main hatch. An instant after an explosion came like a clap of thunder in our faces, and a great quadrant of light flashed as high as the *Serapis's* trucks, and through a breach in her bulwarks I saw men running with only the collars of their shirts upon their naked bodies.

'Twas at this critical moment, when that fearful battle once more was won, another storm of grape brought the spars about our heads, and that name which we dreaded most of all was spread again. As we halted in consternation, a dozen round shot ripped through our unengaged side, and a babel of voices hailed the treacherous Landais with oaths and imprecations. We made out the *Alliance* with a full head of canvas, black and sharp, between us and the moon. Smoke hung above her rail. Getting over against the signal fires blazing on Flamborough Head, she wore ship and stood across our bows, the midshipman on the forecastle singing out to her, by the commodore's orders, to lay the enemy by the board. There was no response.

"Do you hear us?" yelled Mr. Linthwaite.

"Ay, ay," came the reply; and with it the smoke broke from her and the grape and canister swept our forecastle. Then the *Alliance* sailed away, leaving brave Mr. Caswell among the many Landais had murdered.

The ominous clank of the chain pumps beat a sort of prelude to what happened next. The gunner burst out of the hatch with blood running down his face, shouting that the *Richard* was sinking, and yelling for quarter as he made for the ensignstaff on the poop, for the flag was shot away. Him the commodore felled with a pistol-butt. At the gunner's heels were the hundred and fifty prisoners we had taken, released by the master at arms. They swarmed out of the bowels of the ship like a horde of Tartars, unkempt and wild and desperate with fear, until I thought that the added weight on the scarce-supported deck would land us all in the bilges. Words fail me when I come to describe the frightful panic of these creatures, frenzied by the instinct of self-preservation. They surged hither and thither as angry seas driven into a pocket of a storm-swept coast. They trampled rough-shod over the moaning heaps of wounded and dying, and crowded the crews at the guns, who were powerless before their numbers. Some fought like maniacs, and others flung themselves into the sea.

Those of us who had clung to hope lost it then. Standing with my back to the mast, beating them off with a pike, visions of an English prison-ship, of an English gallows, came before me. I counted the seconds until the enemy's seamen would be pouring through our ragged ports. The seventh and last time, and we were beaten, for we had not men enough left on our two decks to force them down again. Yes, — I shame to confess it, — the heart went clean out of me, and with that the pain pulsed and leaped in my head like a devil unbound. At a turn of the hand I should have sunk to the boards, had not a voice risen strong and clear above that turmoil, compelling every man to halt trembling in his steps.

"*Cast off, cast off! The Serapis is sinking. To the pumps, ye fools, if you would save your lives!*"

That unerring genius of the gardener's son had struck the only chord!

They were like sheep before us as we beat them back into the reeking hatches, and soon the pumps were heard bumping with a renewed and a desperate vigour. Then, all at once, the towering mainmast of the enemy cracked and tottered and swung this way and that on its loosened shrouds. The first intense silence of the battle followed, in the midst of which came a cry from our top: —

"Their captain is hauling down, sir!"

The sound which broke from our men could scarce be called a cheer. That which they felt as they sank exhausted on the blood of their comrades may not have been elation. My own feeling was of unmixed wonder as I gazed at a calm profile above me, sharp-cut against the moon.

THE "SERAPIS"

I was moved as out of a revery by the sight of Dale swinging across to the *Serapis* by the main brace pennant. Calling on some of my boarders, I scaled our bulwarks and leaped fairly into the middle of the gangway of the *Serapis*.

Such is nearly all of my remembrance of that momentous occasion. I had caught the one glimpse of our first lieutenant in converse with their captain and another officer, when a naked seaman came charging at me. He had raised a pike above his shoulder ere I knew what he was about, and my senses left me.

CHAPTER LIII

IN WHICH I MAKE SOME DISCOVERIES

THE room had a prodigious sense of change about it. That came over me with something of a shock, since the moment before I had it settled that I was in Marlboro' Street. The bare branches swaying in the wind outside should belong to the trees in Freshwater Lane. But beyond the branches were houses, the like of which I had no remembrance of in Annapolis. And then my grandfather should be sitting in that window. Surely, he was there! He moved! He was coming toward me to say: "Richard, you are forgiven," and to brush his eyes with his ruffles.

Then there was the bed-canopy, the pleatings of which were gone, and it was turned white instead of the old blue. And the chimney-place! That was unaccountably smaller, and glowed with a sea-coal fire. And the mantel was now but a bit of a shelf, and held many things that seemed scarce at home on the rough and painted wood,—gold filigree, and China and Japan, and a French clock that ought not to have been just there. Ah, the tea-cups! Here at last was something to touch a fibre of my brain, but a pain came with the effort of memory. So my eyes went back to my grandfather in the window. His face was now become black as Scipio's, and he wore a red turban and a striped cotton gown that was too large for him. And he was sewing. This was monstrous!

I hurried over to the tea-cups, such a twinge did that discovery give me. But they troubled me near as much, and the sea-coal fire held strange images. The fascination in the window was not to be denied, for it stood in line with the houses and the trees. Suddenly there rose up before me a gate. Yes,

I MAKE SOME DISCOVERIES

I knew that gate, and the girlish figure leaning over it. They were in Prince George Street. Behind them was a mass of golden-rose bushes, and out of these came forth a black face under a turban, saying, "Yes, mistis, I'se comin'."

"Mammy — Mammy Lucy!"

The figure in the window stirred, and the sewing fell into its ample lap.

"Now Lawd 'a mercy!"

I trembled with a violence unspeakable. Was this but one more of those thousand voices, harsh and gentle, rough and tender, to which I had listened in vain this age past? The black face was hovering over me now, and in an agony of apprehension I reached up and felt its honest roughness. Then I could have wept for joy.

"Mammy Lucy!"

"Yes, Marse Dick?"

"Where — where is Miss Dolly?"

"Now, Marse Dick, doctah done say you not t' talk, suh."

"Where is Miss Dolly?" I cried, seizing her arm.

"Hush, Marse Dick. Miss Dolly'll come terectly, suh. She's lyin' down, suh."

The door creaked, and in my eagerness I tried to lift myself. 'Twas Aunt Lucy's hand that restrained me, and the next face I saw was that of Dorothy's mother. But why did it appear so old and sorrow-lined? And why was the hair now of a whiteness with the lace of the cap? She took my fingers in her own, and asked me anxiously if I felt any pain.

"Where am I, Mrs. Manners?"

"You are in London, Richard."

"In Arlington Street?"

She shook her head sadly. "No, my dear, not in Arlington Street. But you are not to talk."

"And Dorothy? May I not see Dorothy? Aunt Lucy tells me she is here."

Mrs. Manners gave the old mammy a glance of reproof, a signal that alarmed me vastly.

"Oh, tell me, Mrs. Manners! You will speak the truth. Tell me if she is gone away?"

"My dear boy, she is here, and under this very roof. And you shall see her as soon as Dr. Barry will permit. Which will not be soon," she added with a smile, "if you persist in this conduct."

The threat had the desired effect. And Mrs. Manners quietly left the room, and after a while as quietly came back again and sat down by the fire, whispering to Aunt Lucy.

Fate, in some inexplicable way, had carried me into the enemy's country and made me the guest of Mr. Marmaduke Manners. As I lay staring upward, odd little bits of the past came floating to the top of my mind, presently to be pieced together. The injuries Mr. Marmaduke had done me were the first to collect, since I was searching for the cause of my resentment against him. The incidents arrived haphazard as magic lanthorn views, but very vivid. His denial of me before Mr. Dix, and his treachery at Vauxhall, when he had sent me to be murdered. Next I felt myself clutching the skin over his ribs in Arlington Street, when I had flung him across the room in his yellow night-gown. That brought me to the most painful scene of my life, when I had parted with Dorothy at the top of the stairs. Afterward followed scraps of the years at Gordon's Pride, and on top of them the talk with McAndrews. Here was the secret I sought. The crash had come. And they were no longer in Mayfair, but must have taken a house in some poorer part of London. This thought cast me down tremendously.

And Dorothy! Had time changed her? 'Twas with that query on my lips I fell asleep, to dream of the sun shining down on Carvel Hall and Wilmot House; of Aunt Hester and Aunt Lucy, and a lass and a lad romping through pleasant fields and gardens.

When I awoke it was broad day once more. A gentleman sat on the edge of my bed. He had a queer, short face, ruddy as the harvest moon, and he smiled good-humouredly when I opened my eyes.

"I bid you good morning, Mr. Carvel, for the first time since I have made your acquaintance," said he. "And how do you feel, sir?"

"I have never felt better in my life," I replied, which was the whole truth.

"Well, vastly well," says he, laughing, "prodigious well for a young man who has as many holes in him as have you. Do you hear him, Mrs. Manners?"

At that last word, I popped up to look about the room, and the doctor caught hold of me with ludicrous haste. A pain shot through my body.

"Avast, avast, my hearty," cries he. "'Tis a miracle you can speak, let alone carry your bed and walk for a while yet." And he turned to Dorothy's mother, whom I beheld smiling at me. "You will give him the physic, ma'am, at the hours I have chosen. Egad, I begin to think we shall come through. But pray remember, ma'am, if he talks, you are to put a wad in his mouth."

"He shall have no opportunity to talk, Dr. Barry," said Mrs. Manners.

"Save for a favour I have to ask you, doctor," I cried.

"'Od's bodkins! Already, sir? And what may that be?"

"That you will allow me to see Miss Manners."

He shook with laughter, and then winked at me very roguishly.

"Oh!" says he, "and faith, I should be worse than cruel. First she comes imploring me to see you, and so prettily that a man of oak could not refuse her. And now it is you begging to see her. Had your eyes been opened, sir, you might have had many a glimpse of Miss Dolly these three weeks past."

"What! She has been watching with me?" I asked, in a rapture not to be expressed.

"'Od's, but those are secrets. And the medical profession is close-mouthed, Mr. Carvel. So you want to see her? No," cries he, "'tis not needful to swear it on the Evangels. And I let her come in, will you give me your honour as a gentleman not to speak more than two words to her?"

"I promise anything, and you will not deny me looking at her," said I.

He shook again, all over. "You rascal! You sad dog, sir!

No, sir, faith, you must shut your eyes. Eh, madam, must he not shut his eyes?"

"They were playmates, doctor," answers Mrs. Manners. She was laughing a little, too.

"Well, she shall come in. But remember that I shall have my ear to the keyhole, and you go beyond your promise, out she's whisked. So I caution you not to spend rashly those two words, sir."

And he followed Mrs. Manners out of the room, frowning and shaking his fist at me in mock fierceness. I would have died for the man. For a space — a prodigious long space — I lay very still, my heart bumping like a gun-carriage broke loose, and my eyes riveted on the crack of the door. Then I caught the sound of a light footstep, the knob turned, and joy poured into my soul with the sweep of a Fundy tide.

"Dorothy!" I cried. "Dorothy!"

She put her finger to her lips.

"There, sir," said she, "now you have spoken them both at once!"

She closed the door softly behind her, and stood looking down upon me with such a wondrous love-light in her eyes as no man may describe. My fancy had not lifted me within its compass, my dreams even had not imagined it. And the fire from which it sprang does not burn in humbler souls. So she stood gazing, those lips which once had been the seat of pride now parted in a smile of infinite tenderness. But her head she still held high, and her body straight. Down the front of her dress fell a tucked apron of the whitest linen, and in her hand was a cup of steaming broth.

"You are to take this, Richard," she commanded. And added, with a touch of her old mischief, "Mind, sir, if I hear a sound out of you, I am to disappear like the fairy godmother."

I knew full well she meant it, and the terror of losing her kept me silent. She put down the cup, placed another pillow behind my head with a marvellous deftness, and then began feeding me in dainty spoonfuls something which was surely nectar. And mine eyes, too, had their feast. Never before had I seen my lady in this gentle guise, this task of nursing the sick, which her doing raised to a queenly art.

Her face had changed some. Years of trial unknown to me had left an ennobling mark upon her features, increasing their power an hundred fold. And the levity of girlish years was gone. How I burned to question her! But her lips were now tight closed, her glance now and anon seeking mine, and then falling with an exquisite droop to the coverlet. For the old archness, at least, would never be eradicated. Presently, after she had taken the cup and smoothed my pillow, I reached out for her hand. It was a boldness of which I had not believed myself capable; but she did not resist, and even, as I thought, pressed my fingers with her own slender ones, the red of our Maryland holly blushing in her cheeks. And what need of words, indeed! Our thoughts, too, flew coursing hand in hand through primrose paths, and the angels themselves were not to be envied.

A master might picture my happiness, waking and sleeping, through the short winter days that came and went like flashes of gray light. The memory of them is that of a figure tall and lithe, a little more rounded than of yore, and a chiselled face softened by a power that is one of the world's mysteries. Dorothy had looked the lady in rags, and housewife's cap and apron became her as well as silks or brocades. When for any reason she was absent from my side, I moped, to the quiet amusement of Mrs. Manners and the more boisterous delight of Aunt Lucy, who took her turn sewing in the window. I was near to forgetting the use of words, until at length, one rare morning when the sun poured in, the jolly doctor dressed my wounds with more despatch than common, and vouchsafed that I might talk awhile that day.

"Oh!" cries he, putting me as ever to confusion, "but I have a guess whom my gentleman will be wishing to talk with. But I'll warrant, sir, you have said a deal more than I have any notion of without opening your lips."

And he went away, intolerably pleased with his joke.

Alas for the perversity of maiden natures! It was not my dear nurse who brought my broth that morning, but Mrs.

Manners herself. She smiled at my fallen face, and took a chair at my bedside.

"Now, my dear boy," she said, "you may ask what questions you choose, and I will tell you very briefly how you have come here."

"I have been thinking, Mrs. Manners," I replied, "that if it were known that you harboured one of John Paul Jones's officers in London, very serious trouble might follow for you."

I thought her brow clouded a little.

"No one knows of it, Richard, or is likely to. Dr. Barry, like so many in England, is a good Whig and friend to America. And you are in a part of London far removed from Mayfair." She hesitated, and then continued in a voice that strove to be lighter: "This little house is in Charlotte Street, Mary-le-Bone, for the war has made all of us suffer some. And we are more fortunate than many, for we are very comfortable here, and though I say it, happier than in Arlington Street. And the best of our friends are still faithful. Mr. Fox, with all his greatness, has never deserted us, nor my Lord Comyn. Indeed, we owe them much more than I can tell you of now," she said, and sighed. "They are here every day of the world to inquire for you, and it was his Lordship brought you out of Holland."

And so I had reason once more to bless this stanch friend!

"Out of Holland?" I cried.

"Yes. One morning as we sat down to breakfast, Mr. Ripley's clerk brought in a letter for Dorothy. But I must say first that Mr. Dulany, who is in London, told us that you were with John Paul Jones. You can have no conception, Richard, of the fear and hatred that name has aroused in England. Insurance rates have gone up past belief, and the King's ships are cruising in every direction after the *traitor* and *pirate*, as they call him. We have prayed daily for your safety, and Dorothy — well, here is the letter she received. It had been opened by the inspector, and allowed to pass. And it is to be kept as a curiosity." She drew it from the pocket of her apron and began to read.

"'THE TEXEL, October 3, 1779.

"MY DEAR MISS DOROTHY: I would not be thought to flutter y'r Gentle Bosom with Needless Alarms, nor do I believe I have misjudged y'r Warm & Generous Nature when I write you that One who is held very High in y'r Esteem lies Exceeding Ill at this Place, who might by Tender Nursing regain his Health. I seize this Opportunity to say, my dear Lady, that I have ever held my too Brief Acquaintance with you in London as one of the Sacred Associations of my Life. From the Little I saw of you then I feel Sure that this Appeal will not pass in Vain. I remain y'r most Humble and Devoted Admirer,

"JAMES ORCHARDSON."

"And she knew it was from Commodore Jones?" I asked, in astonishment.

"My dear," replied Mrs. Manners, with a quiet smile, "we women have a keener instinct than men — though I believe your commodore has a woman's intuition. Yes, Dorothy knew. And I shall never forget the fright she gave me as she rose from the table and handed me the sheet to read, crying but the one word. She sent off to Brook Street for Lord Comyn, who came at once, and in half an hour the dear fellow was set out for Dover. He waited for nothing, since war with Holland was looked for at any day. And his Lordship himself will tell you about that rescue. Within the week he had brought you to us. Your skull had been trepanned, you had this great hole in your thigh, and your heart was beating but slowly. By Mr. Fox's advice we sent for Dr. Barry, who is a skilled surgeon, and a discreet man despite his manner. And you have been here for better than three weeks, Richard, hanging between life and death."

"And I owe my life to you and to Dorothy," I said.

"To Lord Comyn and Dr. Barry, rather," she replied quickly. "We have done little but keep the life they saved. And I thank God it was given me to do it for the son of your mother and father."

Something of the debt I owed them was forced upon me.

They were poor, doubtless driven to make ends meet, and yet they had taken me in, called upon near the undivided services of an able surgeon, and worn themselves out with nursing me. Nor did I forget the risk they ran with such a guest. For the first time in many years my heart relented toward Mr. Marmaduke. For their sakes I forgave him over and over what I had suffered, and my treatment of him lay like a weight upon me. And how was I to repay them? They needed the money I had cost them, of that I was sure. After the sums I had expended to aid the commodore with the *Ranger* and the *Bon homme Richard*, I had scarce a farthing to my name. With such leaden reflections was I occupied when I heard Mrs. Manners speaking to me.

"Richard, I have some news for you which the doctor thinks you can bear to-day. Mr. Dulany, who is exiled like the rest of us, brought them. It is a great happiness to be able to tell you, my dear, that you are now the master of Carvel Hall, and like to stay so."

The tears stole into her eyes as she spoke. And the enormity of those tidings, coming as they did on the top of my dejection, benumbed me. All they meant was yet far away from my grasp, but the one supreme result that was first up to me brought me near to fainting in my weakness.

"I would not raise your hopes unduly, Richard," the good lady was saying, "but the best informed here seem to think that England cannot push the war much farther. If the Colonies win, you are secure in your title."

"But how is it come about, Mrs. Manners?" I demanded, with my first breath.

"You doubtless have heard that before the Declaration was signed at Philadelphia your Uncle Grafton went to the committee at Annapolis and contributed to the patriot cause, and took very promptly the oath of the Associated Freemen of Maryland, thus forsaking the loyalist party —"

"Yes, yes," I interrupted, "I heard of it when I was on the *Cabot*. He thought his property in danger."

"Just so," said Mrs. Manners, laughing; "he became the best and most exemplary of patriots, even as he had been the

I MAKE SOME DISCOVERIES

best of Tories. He sent wheat and money to the army, and went about bemoaning that his only son fought under the English flag. But very little fighting has Philip done, my dear. Well, when the big British fleet sailed up the bay in '77, your precious uncle made the first false step in his long career of rascality. He began to correspond with the British at Philadelphia, and one of his letters was captured near the Head of Elk. A squad was sent to the Kent estate, where he had been living, to arrest him, but he made his escape to New York. And his lands were at once confiscated by the state."

"Then they belong to the state," I said, with misgiving.

"Not so fast, Richard. At the last session of the Maryland Legislature a bill was introduced, through the influence of Mr. Bordley and others, to restore them to you, their rightful owner. And insomuch as you were even then serving the country faithfully and bravely, and had a clean and honourable record of service, the whole of the lands were given to you. And now, my dear, you have had excitement enough for one day."

CHAPTER LIV

MORE DISCOVERIES

ALL that morning I pondered over the devious lane of my life, which had led up to so fair a garden. And one thing above all kept turning and turning in my head, until I thought I should die of waiting for its fulfilment. Now was I free to ask Dorothy to marry me, to promise her the ease and comfort that had once been hers, should God bring us safe back to Maryland. The change in her was little less than a marvel to me, when I remembered the wilful miss who had come to London bent upon pleasure alone. Truly, she was of that rare metal which refines, and then outshines all others. And there was much I could not understand. A miracle had saved her from the Duke of Chartersea, but why she had refused so many great men and good was beyond my comprehension. Not a glimpse of her did I get that day, though my eyes wandered little from the knob of the door. And even from Aunt Lucy no satisfaction was to be had as to the cause of her absence.

"'Clare to goodness, Marse Dick," said she, with great solemnity, "'clare to goodness, I'se nursed Miss Dolly since she was dat high, and neber one minnit ob her life is I knowed what de chile gwine t' do de next. She ain't neber yit done what I calcelated on."

The next morning, after the doctor had dressed my wounds and bantered me to his heart's content, enters Mr. Marmaduke Manners. I was prodigiously struck by the change in him, and pitied him then near as much as I had once despised him. He was arrayed in finery, as of old. But the finery was something shabby; the lace was frayed at the edges, there was a neat but obvious patch in his small-clothes, and two more in his coat. His air was what distressed me most of all, being that of a man who spends his days seeking favours and getting none. I had seen too many of the type not to know the sign of it.

He ran forward and gave me his hand, which I grasped as heartily as my weakness would permit.

"They would not let me see you until to-day, my dear Richard," he exclaimed. "I bid you welcome to what is left of our home. 'Tis not Arlington Street, my lad."

"But more of a home than was that grander house, Mr. Manners."

He sighed heavily.

"Alas!" said he, "poverty is a bitter draught, and we have drunk deep of it since last we beheld you. My great friends know me no more, and will not take my note for a shilling. They do not remember the dinners and suppers I gave them. Faith, this war has brought nothing but misery, and how we are to get through it, God knows!"

Now I understood it was not the war, but Mr. Marmaduke himself, which had carried his family to this pass. And some of my old resentment rekindled.

"I know that I have brought you great additional anxiety and expense, Mr. Manners," I answered somewhat testily. "The care I have been to Mrs. Manners and Dorothy I may never repay. But it gives me pleasure to feel, sir, that I am in a position to reimburse you, and likewise to loan you something until your lands begin to pay again."

"There the Carvel speaks," he cried, "and the true son of our generous province. You can have no conception of the misfortunes come to me out of this quarrel. The mortgages on my Western Shore tobacco lands are foreclosed, and Wilmot House itself is all but gone. You well know, of course, that I would do the same by you, Richard."

I smiled, but more in sadness than amusement. Hardship had only degraded Mr. Marmaduke the more, and even in trouble his memory was convenient as is that of most people in prosperity. I was of no mind to jog his recollection. But

I wanted badly to ask about his Grace. Where had my fine nobleman been at the critical point of his friend's misfortunes? For I had had many a wakeful night over that same query since my talk with McAndrews.

"So you have come to your own again, Richard, my lad," said Mr. Marmaduke, breaking in upon my train. "I have felt for you deeply, and talked many a night with Margaret and Dorothy over the wrong done you. Between you and me," he whispered, "that uncle of yours is an arrant knave, whom the patriots have served with justice. To speak truth, sir, I begin myself to have a little leaning to that cause which you have so bravely espoused."

This time I was close to laughing outright. But he was far too serious to remark my mirth. He commenced once more, with an *ahem*, which gave me a better inkling than frankness of what bothered him.

"You will have an agent here, Richard, I take it," said he. "Your grandfather had one. Ahem! Doubtless this agent will advance you all you shall have need of, when you are well enough to see him. Fact is, he might come here."

"You forget, Mr. Manners, that I am a pirate and an outlaw, and that you are the shielder of such."

That thought shook the pinch of Holland he held all over him. But he recovered.

"My dear Richard, men of business are of no faction and of no nation. Their motto is discretion. And to obtain the factorship in London of a like estate to yours one of them would wear a plaster over his mouth, I'll warrant you. You have but to summon one of the rascals, promise him a bit of war interest, and he will leave you as much as you desire, and nothing spoken."

"To talk plainly, Mr. Manners," I replied, "I think 'twould be the height of folly to resort to such means. When I am better, we shall see what can be done."

His face plainly showed his disappointment.

"To be sure," he said, in a whining tone, "I had forgotten your friends, Lord Comyn and Mr. Fox. They may do something for you, now you own your estate. My dear sir, I dislike to say aught against any man. Mrs. Manners will tell you of their kindness to us, but I vow I have not been able to see it. With all the money at their command they will not loan me a penny in my pressing need. And I shame to say it, my own daughter prevents me from obtaining the money to keep us out of the Fleet. I know she has spoken to Dulany. Think of it, Richard, my own daughter, upon whom I lavished all when I had it, who might have made a score of grand matches when I gave her the opportunity, and now we had all been rolling in wealth. I'll be sworn I don't comprehend her, nor her mother either, who abets her. For they prefer to cook Maryland dainties for a living, to put in the hands of the footmen of the ladies whose houses they once visited. And how much of that money do you suppose I get, sir? Will you believe it that I" (he was shrieking now), "that I, the man of the family, am allowed only my simple meals, a farthing for snuff, and not a groat for chaise-hire? At my age I am obliged to walk to and from their lordships' side entrances in patched clothes, egad, when a new suit might obtain us a handsome year's income!"

I turned my face to the wall, completely overcome, and the tears scalding in my eyes, at the thought of Dorothy and her mother bending over the stove cooking delicacies for their livelihood, and watching at my bedside night and day despite their weariness of body. And not a word out of these noble women of their sacrifice, nor of the shame and trouble and labour of their lives, who always had been used to every luxury! Nothing but cheer had they brought to the sick-room, and not a sign of their poverty and hardship, for they knew that their broths and biscuit and jellies must have choked me. No. It remained for this contemptible cur of a husband and father to open my eyes.

He had risen when I had brought myself to look at him. And as I hope for heaven he took my emotion for pity of himself.

"I have worried you enough for one day with my troubles, my lad," said he. "But they are very hard to bear, and once in a while it does me good to speak of them."

I did not trust myself to reply.

It was Aunt Lucy who spent the morning with me, and Mrs. Manners brought my dinner. I observed a questioning glance as she entered, which I took for an attempt to read whether Mr. Marmaduke had spoke more than he ought. But I would have bitten off my tongue rather than tell her of my discoveries, though perhaps my voice may have betrayed an added concern. She stayed to talk on the progress of the war, relating the gallant storming of Stony Point by Mad Anthony in July, and the latest Tory insurrection on our own Eastern Shore. She passed from these matters to a discussion of General Washington's new policy of the defensive, for Mrs. Manners had always been at heart a patriot. And whilst I lay listening with a deep interest, in comes my lady herself. So was it ever, when you least expected her, even as Mammy had said. She curtseyed very prettily, with her chin tilted back and her cheeks red, and asked me how I did.

"And where have you been these days gone, Miss Will-o'-the-Wisp, since the doctor has given me back my tongue?" I cried.

"I like you better when you are asleep," says she. "For then you are sometimes witty, though I doubt not the wit is other people's."

So I saw that she had tricked me, and taken her watch at night. For I slept like a trooper after a day's forage. As to what I might have said in my dreams — that thought made me red as an apple.

"Dorothy, Dorothy," says her mother, smiling, "you would provoke a saint."

"Which would be better fun than teasing a sinner," replies the minx, with a little face at me. "Mr. Carvel, a gentleman craves the honour of an audience from your Excellency."

"A gentleman!"

"Even so. He presents a warrant from your Excellency's physician."

With that she disappeared, Mrs. Manners going after her. And who should come bursting in at the door but my Lord Comyn? He made one rush at me, and despite my weakness bestowed upon me a bear's hug.

"Oh, Richard," cried he, when he had released me, "I give you my oath that I never hoped to see you rise from that bed when we laid you there. But they say that love works wondrous cures, and, egad, I believe that now. 'Tis love is curing you, my lad."

He held me off at arm's length, the old-time affection beaming from his handsome face.

"What am I to say to you, Jack?" I answered. And my voice was all but gone, for the sight of him revived the memory of every separate debt of the legion I owed him. "How am I to piece words enough together to thank you for this supreme act of charity?"

"'Od's, you may thank your own devilish thick head," said my Lord Comyn. "I should never have bothered my own about you were it not for *her*. Had it not been for her happiness do you imagine I would have picked you out of that crew of half-dead pirates in the Texel fort?"

I must needs brush my cheek, then, with the sleeve of my night-rail.

"And will you give me some account of this last prodigious turn you have done *her?*" I said.

He laughed, and pinched me playfully.

"Now are you coming to your senses," said he. "There was cursed little to the enterprise, Richard, and that's the truth. I got down to Dover, and persuaded the master of a schooner to carry me to Rotterdam. That was not so difficult, since your Terror of the Seas was locked up safe enough in the Texel. In Rotterdam I had a travelling-chaise stripped, and set off at the devil's pace for the Texel. You must know that the whole Dutch nation was in an uproar — as much of an uproar as those boors ever reach — over the arrival of your infamous squadron. The Court Party and our ambassador were for having you kicked out, and the Republicans for making you at home. I heard that their High Mightinesses had given Paul Jones the use of the Texel fort for his wounded and his prisoners, and thither I ran. And I was even cursing the French sentry at the drawbridge in his own tongue, when up comes your commodore himself. You may quarter me if I wasn't knocked off my feet when I recognized the identical peacock of a sea-captain we had pulled out of Castle Yard along with you, and offered a commission in the Royal Navy."

"Dolly hadn't told you?"

"Dolly tell me!" exclaimed his Lordship, scornfully. "She was in a state to tell me nothing the morning I left, save only to bring you to England alive, and repeat it over and over. But to return to your captain,— he, too, was taken all aback. But presently he whipt out my name, and I his, without the *Jones*. And when I told him my errand, he wept on my neck, and said he had obtained unlimited leave of absence for you from the Paris commissioners. He took me up into a private room in the fort, where you were; and the surgeon, who was there at the time, said that your chances were as slim as any man's he had ever seen. Faith, you looked it, my lad. At sight of your face I took one big gulp, for I had no notion of getting you back to her. And rather than come without you, and look into her eyes, I would have drowned myself in the Straits of Dover.

"Despite the host of troubles he had on his hands, your commodore himself came with us to Rotterdam. Now I protest I love that man, who has more humanity in him than most of the virtuous people in England who call him hard names. If you could have seen him leaning over you, and speaking to you, and feeling every minute for your heart-beats, egad, you would have cried. And when I took you off to the schooner, he gave me an hundred directions how to care for you, and then his sorrow bowled him all in a heap."

"And is the commodore still at the Texel?" I asked, after a space.

"Ay, that he is, with our English cruisers thick as gulls outside waiting for a dead fish. But he has spurned the French commission they have offered him, saying that of the Congress is good enough for him. And he declares openly that when he gets ready he will sail out in the *Alliance* under the Stars and Stripes. And for this I honour him," added he, "and Charles honours him, and so must all Englishmen honour him when they come to their senses. And by Gad's life, I believe he will get clear, for he is a marvel at seamanship."

"I pray with all my heart that he may," said I, fervently.

"God help him if they catch him!" my Lord exclaimed. "You should see the bloody piratical portraits they are scattering over London."

"Has the risk you ran getting me into England ever occurred to you, Jack?" I asked, with some curiosity.

"Faith, not until the day after we got back, Richard," says he, "when I met Mr. Attorney General on the street. 'Sdeath, I turned and ran the other way like the devil was after me. For Charles Fox vows that conscience makes cowards of the best of us."

"So that is some of Charles's wisdom!" I cried, and laughed until I was forced to stop from pain.

"Come, my hearty," says Jack, "you owe me nothing for fishing you out of Holland — that is *her* debt. But I declare that you must one day pay me for saving her for you. What! have I not always sworn that she loved you? Did I not pull you into the coffee-room of the Star and Garter years ago, and tell you that same?"

My face warmed, though I said nothing.

"Oh, you sly dog! I'll warrant there has been many a tender talk just where I'm sitting."

"Not one," said I.

"'Slife, then, what have you been doing," he cries, "seeing her every day and not asking her to marry you, my master of Carvel Hall?"

"Since I am permitted to use my tongue, she has not come near me, save when I slept," I answered ruefully.

"Nor will she, I'll be sworn," says he, shaken with laughter. "'Ods, have you no invention? Egad, you must feign sleep, and seize her unawares."

I did not inform his Lordship how excellent this plan seemed to me.

"And I possessed the love of such a woman, Richard," he said, in another tone, "I think I should die of happiness. *She will* never tell you how these weeks past she has scarce left your side. The threats combined of her mother and the doctor, and Charles and me, would not induce her to take any sleep. And time and time have I walked from here to Brook Street without recognizing a step of the way, lifted clear out of myself by the sight of her devotion."

What was my life, indeed, that such a blessing should come into it!

"When the crash came," he continued, "'twas she took command, and 'tis God's pity she had not done so long before. Mr. Marmaduke was pushed to the bottom of the family, where he belongs, and was given only snuff-money. She would give him no opportunity to contract another debt, and even charged Charles and me to loan him nothing. Nor would she receive aught from us, but" (he glanced at me uneasily) — "but she and Mrs. Manners must take to cooking delicacies —"

"Yes, yes, I know," I faltered.

"What! has the puppy told you?" cried he.

I nodded. "He was in here this morning, with his woes."

"And did he speak of the bargain he tried to make with our old friend, his Grace of Chartersea?"

"He tried to sell her again?" I cried, my breath catching. "I have feared as much since I heard of their misfortunes."

"Yes," replied Comyn, "that was the first of it. 'Twas while they were still in Arlington Street, and before Mrs. Manners and Dorothy knew. Mr. Marmaduke goes posting off to Nottinghamshire, and comes back inside the duke's own carriage. And his Grace goes to dine in Arlington Street for the first time in years. Dorothy had wind of the trouble then, Charles having warned her. And not a word would she speak to Chartersea the whole of the dinner, nor look to the right or left of her plate. And when the servants are gone, up gets my lady with a sweep and confronts him.

"'Will your Grace spare me a minute in the drawing-room?' says she.

"He blinked at her in vast astonishment, and pushed back his chair. When she was come to the door, she turns with another sweep on Mr. Marmaduke, who was trotting after.

"' You will please to remain here, father,' she said; 'what I am to say is for his Grace's ear alone.'

"Of what she spoke to the duke I can form only an estimate, Richard," my Lord concluded, "but I'll lay a fortune 'twas greatly to the point. For in a little while Chartersea comes stumbling down the steps. And he has never darkened the door since. And the cream of it is," said Comyn, "that her father gave me this himself, with a face a foot long, for me to sympathize. The little beast has strange bursts of confidence."

"And stranger confidants," I ejaculated, thinking of the morning, and of Courtenay's letter, long ago.

But the story had made my blood leap again with pride of her. The picture in my mind had followed his every sentence, and even the very words she must have used were ringing in my ears.

Then, as we sat talking in low tones, the door opened, and a hearty voice cried out:—

"Now where is this rebel, this traitor? They tell me one lies hid in this house. 'Slife, I must have at him!"

"Mr. Fox!" I exclaimed.

He took my hands in his, and stood regarding me.

"For the convenience of my friends, I was christened Charles," said he.

I stared at him in amazement. He was grown a deal stouter, but my eye was caught and held by the blue coat and buff waistcoat he wore. They were frayed and stained and shabby, yet they seemed all of a piece with some new grandeur come upon the man.

"Is all the world turning virtuous? Is the millennium arrived?" I cried.

He smiled, with his old boyish smile.

"You think me changed some since that morning we drove together to Holland House — do you remember it — after the night at St. Stephen's?"

"Remember it!" I repeated, with emphasis, "I'll warrant I can give you every bit of our talk."

"I have seen many men since, but never have I met your equal for a most damnable frankness, Richard Carvel. Even

Jack, here, is not half so blunt and uncompromising. But you took my fancy — God knows why! — that first night I clapped eyes on you in Arlington Street, and I loved you when your simplicity made us that speech at Brooks's Club. So you have not forgotten that morning under the trees, when the dew was on the grass. Faith, I am glad of it. What children we were!" he said, and sighed.

"And yet you were a Junior Lord," I said.

"Which is more than I am now," he answered. "Somehow — you may laugh — somehow I have never been able to shake off the influence of your words, Richard. Your cursed earnestness scared me."

"Scared you?" I cried, in astonishment.

"Just that," said Charles. "Jack will bear witness that I have said so to Dolly a score of times. For I had never imagined such a single character as yours. You know we were all of us rakes at fifteen, to whom everything good in the universe was a joke. And do you recall the teamster we met by the Park, and how he arrested his salute when he saw who it was? At another time I should have laughed over that, but it cut me to have it happen when you were along."

"And I'll lay an hundred guineas to a farthing the fellow would put his head on the block for Charles now," cut in his Lordship, with his hand on Mr. Fox's shoulder. "Behold, O Prophet," he cried, "one who is become the champion of the People he reviled! Behold the friend of Rebellion and *Lèse Majesté*, the viper in Britannia's bosom!"

"Oh, have done, Jack," said Mr. Fox, impatiently, "you have no more music in your soul than a cow. Damned little virtue attaches to it, Richard," he went on. "North threw me out, and the king would have nothing to do with me, so I had to pick up with you rebels and traitors."

"You will not believe him, Richard," cried my Lord; "you have only to look at him to see that he lies. Take note of the ragged uniform of the rebel army he carries, and then think of him *en petit maître*, with his cabriolet and his chestnuts. Egad, he might be as rich as Rigby were it not for those principles which he chooses to deride. And I have seen him reduced to a crown for them. I tell you, Richard," said my Lord, "by espousing your cause Charles is become greater than the King. For he has the hearts of the English people, which George has not, and the allegiance of you Americans, which George will never have. And if you once heard him in Parliament, you should hear him now, and see the Speaker wagging his wig like a man bewitched, and hear friends and enemies calling out for him to go on whenever he gives the sign of a pause."

This speech of his Lordship's may seem cold in the writing, my dears, and you who did not know him may wonder at it. It had its birth in an admiration few men receive, and which in Charles Fox's devoted coterie was dangerously near to idolatry. During the recital of it Charles walked to the window, and there stood looking out upon the gray prospect, seemingly paying but little attention. But when Comyn had finished, he wheeled on us with a smile.

"Egad, he will be telling you next that I have renounced the devil and all his works, Richard," said he.

"'Oons, that I will not," his Lordship made haste to declare. "For they were born in him, and will die with him."

"And you, Jack," I asked, "how is it that you are not in arms for the King, and commanding one of his frigates?"

"Why, it is Charles's fault," said my Lord, smiling. "Were it not for him I should be helping Sir George Collier lay waste to your coast towns."

CHAPTER LV

"THE LOVE OF A MAID FOR A MAN"

THE next morning, when Dr. Barry had gone, Mrs. Manners propped me up in bed and left me for a little, so she said. Then who should come in with my breakfast on a tray but my lady herself, looking so fresh and beautiful that she startled me vastly.

"A penny for your thoughts, Richard," she cried. "Why, you are as grave as a screech-owl this brave morning."

"To speak truth, Dolly," said I, "I was wondering how the commodore is to get away from the Texel, with half the British navy lying in wait outside."

"Do not worry your head about that," said she, setting down the tray; "it will be mere child's play to him. Oh, but I should like to see your commodore again, and tell him how much I love him."

"I pray that you may have the chance," I replied.

With a marvellous quickness she had tied the napkin beneath my chin, not so much as looking at the knot. Then she stepped to the mantel and took down one of Mr. Wedgwood's cups and dishes, and wiping them with her apron, filled the cup with fragrant tea, which she tendered me with her eyes sparkling.

"Your Excellency is the first to be honoured with this service," says she, with a curtsey.

I was as a man without a tongue, my hunger gone from sheer happiness — and fright. And yet eating the breakfast with a relish because she had made it. She busied herself about the room, dusting here and tidying there, and anon throwing a glance at me to see if I needed anything. My eyes followed her hither and thither. When I had finished, she undid the napkin, and brushed the crumbs from the coverlet.

"You are not going?" I said, with dismay.

"Did you wish anything more, sir?" she asked.

"Oh, Dorothy," I cried, "it is you I want, and you will not come near me."

For an instant she stood irresolute. Then she put down the tray and came over beside me.

"Do you really want me, sir?"

"Dorothy," I began, "I must first tell you that I have some guess at the sacrifice you are making for my sake, and of the trouble and danger which I bring you."

Without more ado she put her hand over my mouth.

"No," she said, reddening, "you shall tell me nothing of the sort."

I seized her hand, however it struggled, and holding it fast, continued:—

"And I have learned that you have been watching with me by night, and working by day, when you never should have worked at all. To think that you should be reduced to that, and I not know it!"

Her eyes sought mine for a fleeting second.

"Why, you silly boy, I have made a fortune out of my cookery. And fame, too, for now am I known from Mary-lebone to Chelsea, while before my name was unheard of out of little Mayfair. Indeed, I would not have missed the experience for a lady-in-waiting-ship. I have learned a deal since I saw you last, sir. I know that the world, like our Continental money, must not be taken for the price that is stamped upon it. And as for the watching with you," said my lady, "that had to be borne with as cheerfully as might be. Since I had sent off for you, I was in duty bound to do my share toward your recovery. I was even going to add that this watching was a pleasure,—our curate says the sense of duty performed is sure to be. But you used to cry out the most terrifying things to frighten me: the pattering of blood and the bumping of bodies on the decks, and the black rivulets that

2 L

ran and ran and ran and never stopped; and strange, rough commands I could not understand; and the name of your commodore whom you love so much. And often you would repeat over and over: '*I have not yet begun to fight, I have not yet begun to fight!*'"

"Yes, 'twas that he answered when they asked him if he had struck," I exclaimed.

"It must have been an awful scene," she said, and her shoulders quivered. "When you were at your worst you would talk of it, and sometimes of what happened to you in London, of that ride in Hyde Park, or — or of Vauxhall," she continued hurriedly. "And when I could bear it no longer, I would take your hand and call you by name, and often quiet you thus."

"And did I speak of aught else?" I asked eagerly.

"Oh, yes. When you were calmer, it would be of your childhood, of your grandfather and your birthdays, of Captain Clapsaddle, and of Patty and her father."

"And never of Dolly, I suppose."

She turned away her head.

"And never of Dolly?"

"I will tell you what you said once, Richard," she answered, her voice dropping very low. "I was sitting by the window there, and the dawn was coming. And suddenly I heard you cry: 'Patty, when I return will you be my wife?' I got up and came to your side, and you said it again, twice."

The room was very still. And the vision of Patty in the parlour of Gordon's Pride, knitting my woollen stocking, rose before me.

"Yes," I said at length, "I asked her that the day before I left for the war. God bless her! She has the warmest heart in the world, and the most generous nature. Do you know what her answer was, Dorothy?"

"No." 'Twas only her lips moving that formed the word. She was twisting absently the tassel of the bed curtain.

"She asked me if I loved her."

My lady glanced up with a start, then looked me searchingly through and through.

"And you?" she said, in the same inaudible way.

"I could answer nothing. 'Twas because of her father's dying wish I asked her, and she guessed that same. I would not tell her a lie, for only the one woman lives whom I love, and whom I have loved ever since we were children together among the strawberries. Need I say that that woman is you, Dorothy? I loved you before we sailed to Carvel Hall between my grandfather's knees, and I will love you till death claims me."

Then it seemed as if my heart had stopped beating. But the snowy apron upon her breast fluttered like a sail stirring in the wind, her head was high, and her eyes were far away. Even my voice sounded in the distance as I continued: —

"Will you be the mistress of Carvel Hall, Dorothy? Hallowed is the day that I can ask it."

What of this earth may excell in sweetness the surrender of that proud and noble nature! And her words, my dears, shall be sacred to you, too, who are descended from her. She bent forward a little, those deep blue eyes gazing full into my own with a fondness to make me tremble.

"Dear Richard," she said, "I believe I have loved you always. If I have been wilful and wicked, I have suffered more than you know — even as I have made you suffer."

"And now our suffering is over, Dorothy."

"Oh, don't say that, my dear!" she cried, "but let us rather make a prayer to God."

Down she got on her knees close beside me, and I took both of her hands between my own. But presently I sought for a riband that was around my neck, and drew out a locket. Within it were pressed those lilies of the valley I had picked for her long years gone by on my birthday. And she smiled, though the tears shone like dewdrops on her lashes.

"When Jack brought you to us for dead, we did not take it off, dear," she said gently. "I wept with sorrow and joy at sight of it, for I remembered you as you were when you picked those flowers, and how lightly I had thought of leaving you as I wound them into my hair. And then, when I had gone aboard the *Annapolis*, I knew all at once that I would have given anything to stay, and I thought my heart would break when we left the Severn cliffs behind. But that, sir, has been a secret until this day," she added, smiling archly through her tears.

She took out one of the withered flowers, and then as caressingly put it back beside the others, and closed the locket.

"I forbade Dr. Barry to take it off, Richard, when you lay so white and still. I knew then that you had been true to me, despite what I had heard. And if you were to die —" her voice broke a little as she passed her hand over my brow, "if you were to die, my single comfort would have been that you wore it then."

"And you heard rumours of me, Dorothy?"

"George Worthington and others told me how ably you managed Mr. Swain's affairs, and that you had become of some weight with the thinking men of the province. Richard, I was proud to think that you had the courage to laugh at disaster and to become a factor. I believe," she said shyly, "'twas that put the cooking into my head, and gave me courage. And when I heard that Patty was to marry you, Heaven is my witness that I tried to be reconciled and think it for the best. Through my own fault I had lost you, and I knew well she would make you a better wife than I."

"And you would not even let Jack speak for me!"

"Dear Jack!" she cried; "were it not for Jack we should not be here, Richard."

"Indeed, Dolly, two people could scarce fall deeper in debt to another than are you and I to my Lord Viscount," I answered, with feeling. "His honesty and loyalty to us both saved you for me at the very outset."

"Yes," she replied thoughtfully, "I believed you dead. And I should have married him, I think. For Dr. Courtenay had sent me that piece from the *Gazette* telling of the duel between you over Patty Swain —"

"Dr. Courtenay sent you that!" I interrupted.

"I was a wild young creature then, my dear, with little beside vanity under my cap. And the notion that you could admire and love any girl but me was beyond endurance. Then his Lordship arrived in England, brimming with praise of you, to assure me that the affair was not about Patty at all. This was far from making me satisfied that you were not in love with her, and I may say now that I was miserable. Then, as we were setting out for Castle Howard, came the news of your death on the road to Upper Marlboro'. I could not go a step. Poor Jack, he was very honest when he proposed," she added, with a sigh.

"He loved you, Dorothy."

She did not hear me, so deep was she in thought.

"'Twas he who gave me news of you, when I was starving at Gordon's."

"And I—I starved, too, Richard," she answered softly. "Dearest, I did very wrong. There are some matters that must be spoken of between us, whatever the pain they give. And my heart aches now when I think of that dark day in Arlington Street when I gave you the locket, and you went out of my life. I knew that I had done wrong then, Richard, as soon as ever the door closed behind you. I should have gone with you, for better for worse, for richer for poorer. I should have run after you in the rain and thrown myself at your feet. And that would have been best for my father and for me."

She covered her face with her hands, and her words were stifled by a sob.

"Dorothy, Dorothy!" I cried, drawing her to me. "Another time. Not now, when we are so happy."

"Now, and never again, dear," she said. "Yes, I saw and heard all that passed in the drawing-room. And I did not blame, but praised you for it. I have never spoken a word beyond necessity to my father since. God forgive me!" she cried, "but I have despised him from that hour. When I knew that he had plotted to sell me to that detestable brute, working upon me to save his honour, of which he has not the smallest spark; that he had recognized and denied you, friendless before our house, and sent you into the darkness at Vauxhall to be murdered, then he was no father of mine. I would that you might know what my mother has suffered from such a man, Richard."

"My dear, I have often pitied her from my soul," I said.

"And now I shall tell you something of the story of the Duke of Chartersea," she went on, and I felt her tremble as she spoke that name. "I think of all we have Lord Comyn to thank for, next to saving your life twice, was his telling you of the danger I ran. And, Richard, after refusing you that day on the balcony over the Park, I had no hope left. You may thank your own nobility and courage that you remained in London after that. Richard," she said, "do you recall my asking you in the coach, on the way from Castle Yard, for the exact day you met my father in Arlington Street?"

"Yes," I replied, in some excitement, "yes." For I was at last to come at the bottom of this affair.

"The duke had made a formal offer for me when first we came to London. I think my father wrote of that to Dr. Courtenay." (I smiled at the recollection, now.) "Then his Grace persisted in following me everywhere, and vowed publicly that he would marry me. I ordered him from our house, since my father would not. At last one afternoon he came back to dine with us, insolent to excess. I left the table. He sat with my father two hours or more, drinking and singing, and giving orders to the servants. I shut my door, that I might not hear. After a while my mother came up to me, crying, saying that Mr. Manners would be branded with dishonour and I did not consent to marry his Grace,—a most terrible dishonour, of which she could not speak. That the duke had given my father a month to win my consent. And that month was up, Richard, the very afternoon you appeared with Mr. Dix in Arlington Street."

"And you agreed to marry him, Dolly?" I asked breathlessly.

"By the grace of Heaven, I did not," she answered quickly. "The utmost that I would consent to was a two months' respite, promising to give my hand to no one in that interval. And so I was forced to refuse you, Richard. You must have seen even then that I loved you, dear, though I was so cruel when you spoke of saving me from his Grace. I could not bear to think that you knew of any stain upon our family. I think

—I think I would rather have died, or have married him. That day I threw Chartersea's presents out of the window, but my father made the servants gather them all which escaped breaking, and put them in the drawing-room. Then I fell ill."

She was silent, I clinging to her, and shuddering to think how near I had been to losing her.

"It was Jack who came to cheer me," I said presently. "His faith in you was never shaken, sweetheart. But I went to Newmarket and Ampthill, and behaved like the ingrate I was. I richly deserved the scolding he had for me when I got back to town, which sent me running to Arlington Street. There I met Dr. James coming out, who asked me if I was Mr. Carvel, and told me that you had called my name."

"And, you goose, you never suspected," says she, smiling.

"How was I to suspect that you loved a provincial booby like me, when you had the choice of so many accomplished gentlemen with titles and estates?"

"How were you to perceive, indeed, that you had qualities which they lacked?"

"And you were forever vowing that you would marry a nobleman, my lady. For you said to me once that I should call you so, and ride in the coach with the coroneted panels when I came home on a visit."

"And I said, too," retorted Dolly, with mischief in her eyes, "do you remember what I told you the New Year's eve when we sat out by the sundial at Carvel Hall, when I was so proud of having fixed Dr. Courtenay's attentions? I said that I should never marry you, sir, who was so rough and masterful, and thrashed every lad that did not agree with you."

"Alas, so you did, and a deal more!" I exclaimed.

With that she broke away from me and, getting to her feet, made me a low curtsey with the grace that was hers alone.

"You are my Lord and my King, sir," she said, "and my rough Patriot squire, all in one."

"Are you happy, Dolly?" I asked, tremulous from my own joy.

"I have never been happy in all my life before, Richard dear," she said.

In truth, she was a being transformed, and more wondrous fair than ever. And even then I pictured her in the brave gowns and jewels I would buy her when times were mended, when our dear country would be free. All at once, ere I could draw a breath, she had stooped and kissed me ever so lightly on the forehead.

The door opened upon Aunt Lucy. She had but to look at us, and her black face beamed at our blushes. My lady threw her arms about her neck, and hid her face in the ample bosom.

"Now praise de good Lawd!" cried Mammy; "I knowed it dis longest time. What's I done tole you, Miss Dolly? What's I done tole you, honey?"

But my lady flew from the room. Presently I heard the spinet playing softly, and the words of that air came out of my heart from long ago.

> "Love me little, love me long,
>   Is the burthen of my song.
>   Love that is too hot and strong
>   Burneth soon to waste.
>   Still, I would not have thee cold,
>   Nor too backward, nor too bold.
>   Love that lasteth till 'tis old
>   Fadeth not in haste."

CHAPTER LVI

HOW GOOD CAME OUT OF EVIL

'Twas about candlelight when I awoke, and Dorothy was sitting alone beside me. Her fingers were resting upon my arm, and she greeted me with a smile all tenderness.

"And does my Lord feel better after — after his excitement to-day?" she asked.

"Dorothy, you have made me a whole man again. I could walk to Windsor and back."

"You must have your dinner, or your supper first, sir," she answered gayly, "and do you rest quiet until I come back to feed you. Oh, Richard dear," she cried, "how delightful that you should be the helpless one, and dependent on me!"

As I lay listening for the rustle of her gown, the minutes dragged eternally. Every word and gesture of the morning passed before my mind, and the touch of her lips still burned on my forehead. At last, when I was getting fairly restless, the distant tones of a voice, deep and reverberating, smote upon my ear, jarring painfully some long-forgotten chord. That voice belonged to but one man alive, and yet I could not name him. Even as I strained, the tones drew nearer, and they were mixed with sweeter ones I knew well, and Dorothy's mother's voice. Whilst I was still searching, the door opened, the voices fell calm, and Dorothy came in bearing a candle in each hand. As she set them down on the table, I saw an agitation in her face, which she strove to hide as she addressed me.

"Will you see a visitor, Richard?"

"A visitor!" I repeated, with misgiving. 'Twas not so she had announced Comyn.

"Will you see Mr. Allen?"

"Mr. Allen, who was the rector of St. Anne's? Mr. Allen in London, and *here?*"

"Yes." Her breath seemed to catch at the word. "He says he must see you, dear, and will not be denied. How he discovered you were with us I know not."

"See him!" I cried. "And I had but the half of my strength I would fling him downstairs, and into the kennel. Will you tell him so for me, Dorothy?"

And I raised up in bed, shaken with anger against the man. In a trice she was holding me, fearfully.

"Richard, Richard, you will open your wound. I pray you be quiet."

"And Mr. Allen has the impudence to ask to see me!"

"Listen, Richard. Your anger makes you forget many things. Remember that he is a dangerous man, and now that he knows you are in London he holds your liberty, perhaps your life, in his hands."

It was true. And not mine alone, but the lives and liberty of others.

"Do you know what he wishes, Dorothy?"

"No, he will not tell us. But he is greatly excited, and says he must see you at once, for your own good. *For your own good, Richard!*"

"I do not trust the villain, but he may come in," I said, at length.

She gave me the one lingering, anxious look, and opened the door.

Never had I beheld such a change in mortal man as there was in Mr. Allen, my old tutor, and rector of St. Anne's. And 'twas a baffling, intangible change. 'Twas as if the mask had been torn from his face, for he was now just a plain adventurer that need not have imposed upon a soul. The coarse wine and coarse food of the lower coffee-houses of London had replaced the rich and abundant fare of Maryland. The next day was become one of the terrors of his life. His clothes were of poor stuff, but aimed at the fashion. And yet — and yet, as I looked upon him, a something was in his face to puzzle me entirely. I had seen many stamps of men, but this thing I could not recognize.

He stepped forward with all of his old confidence, and did not regard a farthing my cold stare.

"'Tis like gone days to see you again, Richard," he cried. "And I perceive you have as ever fallen into the best of hands."

"I am *Mr. Carvel* to my enemies, if they must speak to me at all," I said.

"But, my dear fellow, I am not your enemy, or I should not be here this day. And presently I shall prove that same." He took snuff. "But first I must congratulate you on coming alive out of that great battle off Flamborough. You look as though you had been very near to death, my lad. A deal nearer than I should care to get."

What to say to the man! What to do save to knock him down, and I could not do that.

"There can be no passing the time of day between you and me, Mr. Allen," I answered hotly. "You, whose machinations have come as near to ruining me as a man's can."

"And that was your own fault, my dear sir," said he, as he brushed himself. "You never showed me a whit of consideration, which is very dear to men in my position."

My head swam. Then I saw Dolly by the door regarding me curiously, with something of a smile upon her lips, but anxiety still in her eyes. With a "by your leave, ma'am," to her, Mr. Allen took the chair abreast me.

"You have but to call me when you wish, Richard," said she.

"Nay, Dorothy, Mr. Allen can have nothing to say to me that you may not hear," I said instantly. "And you will do me a favour to remain."

She sat down without a word, where I could look at her. Mr. Allen raised his eyebrows at the revelation in our talk, but by the grace of God he kept his mouth shut.

"And now, Mr. Allen," I said, "to what do I owe the pain of this visit?"

"The pain!" he exclaimed, and threw back his head and gave way to a fit of laughter. "By the mass! your politeness drowns me. But I like you, Richard, as I have said more than once. I believe your brutal straight-dealing has more to do with my predilection than aught else. For I have seen a deal of rogues in my day."

"And they have seen a deal of you, Mr. Allen."

"So they have," he cried, and laughed the more. "Egad, Miss Dorothy, you have saved all of him, I think." Then he swung round upon me, very careless. "Has your Uncle Grafton called to express his sympathies, Richard?" he asked.

That name brought a cry out of my head, Dolly seizing the arm of her chair.

"Grafton Carvel in London?" I exclaimed.

"Ay, in very pretty lodgings in Jermyn Street, for he has put by enough, I'll warrant you, despite the loss of his lands. Your aunt is with him, and his dutiful son, Philip, now broken of his rank in the English army. They arrived, before yesterday, from New York."

"And to what is this an introduction?" I demanded.

"I merely thought it strange," said Mr. Allen, imperturbably, "that he had not called to inquire after his nephew's health."

Dolly was staring at him, with eyes wide open.

"And pray, how did he discover I was in London, sir?" I said. "I was about to ask how you knew of it, but that is one and the same thing."

He shot at me a look not to be solved.

"It is not well to bite the hand that lifts you out of the fire, Richard," said he.

"You had not gained admission to this house were I not on my back, Mr. Allen."

"And that same circumstance is a blessing for you," he cried.

'Twas then I saw Dorothy making me mute signals of appeal.

"I cannot think why you are here, Mr. Allen," I said. "When you consider all the harm you have done me, and all the double-dealing I may lay at your door, can you blame me for my feelings?"

"No," he answered, with more soberness than he had yet used; "I honour you for them. And perchance I am here to atone for some of that harm. For I like you, my lad, and that's God's truth."

"All this is neither here nor there, Mr. Allen," I exclaimed, wholly out of patience. "If you have come with a message, let me have it. If not, I beg you get out of my sight, for I have neither the will nor the desire for palavering."

"Oh, Richard, do keep your temper!" implored Dorothy. "Can you not see that Mr. Allen desires to do us — to do you — a service?"

"Of that I am not so sure," I replied.

"It is his way, Miss Manners," said the rector, "and I hold it not against him. To speak truth, I looked for a worse reception, and came steeled to withstand it. And had my skin been thin, I had left ere now." He took more snuff. "It was Mr. Dix," he said to me slowly, "who informed Mr. Carvel of your presence in London."

"And how the devil did Mr. Dix know?"

He did not reply, but glanced apprehensively at Dorothy. And I have wondered since at his consideration.

"Miss Manners may not wish to hear," he said uneasily.

"Miss Manners hears all that concerns me," I answered.

He shrugged his shoulders in comprehension.

"It was Mr. Manners, then, who went to Mr. Dix, and told him under the pledge of secrecy."

Not a sound came from Dorothy, nor did I dare to look at her face. The whole matter was clear to me now. After his conversation with me, Mr. Marmaduke had lost no time in seeing Mr. Dix, in order to raise money on my prospects. And the man of business had gone straight to Grafton with the intelligence. The suspicion flashed through me that Mr. Allen had been sent to spy, but his very next words disarmed it.

"And now, Richard," he continued, "before I say what I have come to say, and since you cannot now prosecute me, I mean to confess to you something which you probably know almost to a certainty. I was in the plot to carry you off and deprive you of your fortune. I have been paid for it, though

not very handsomely. Fears for my own safety alone kept me
from telling you and Mr. Swain. And I swear to you that I
was sorry for the venture almost before I had embarked, and
ere I had received a shilling. The scheme was laid out before
I took you for a pupil; indeed, that was part of it, as you no
doubt have guessed. As God hears me, I learned to love you,
Richard, in those days at the rectory. You were all of a man,
and such an one as I might have hoped to be had I been born
like you. You said what you chose, and spoke from your
own convictions, and catered to no one. You did not whine
when the luck went against you, but lost like a gentleman,
and thought no more of it. You had no fear of the devil himself. Why should you? While your cousin Philip, with his
parrot talk and sneaking ways, turned my stomach. I was
sick of him, and sick of Grafton, I tell you. But dread of
your uncle drove me on, and I had debts to frighten me."

He paused. 'Twas with a strange medley of emotions I
looked at him. And Dorothy, too, was leaning forward, her
lips parted and her eyes riveted upon his face.

"Oh, I am speaking the truth," he said bitterly. "And I
assume no virtue for the little justice it remains in my power
to do. It is the lot of my life that I must be false to some
one always, and even now I am false to your uncle. Yes, I
am come to do justice, and 'tis a strange errand for me. I
know that estates have been restored to you by the Maryland
Legislature, Richard, and I believe in my heart that you will
win this war." Here he fetched a memorandum from his
pocket. "But to make you secure," said he, "in the year
1710, and on the 9th of March, old style, your great-grandfather, Mr. George Carvel, drew up a document entailing the
lands of Carvel Hall. By this they legally pass to you."

"The family settlement Mr. Swain suspected!" I exclaimed.

"Just so," he answered.

"And what am I to pay for this information?" I asked.

Hardly were the words spoken, when Dorothy ran to my
bedside, and seizing my hand, faced him.

"He — he is not well, Mr. Allen," she cried.

The rector had risen, and stood gazing down at us with the

whole of his life written on his face. That look was fearful to see, and all of hell was expressed therein. For what is hell if it is not hope dead and buried, and galling regret for what might have been? With mine own great happiness so contrasted against his torture, my heart melted.

"I am not well, indeed, Mr. Allen," I said. "God knows how hard it is for me to forgive, but I forgive you this night."

One brief instant he stared at me, and then tumbled suddenly down into his chair, his head falling forward on his arms. And the long sobs by which his frame was shaken awed our very souls. Dorothy drew back against me, clasping my shoulder, the tears wet upon her cheeks. What we looked on, there in the candlelight, was the Revelation itself.

How long it endured none of us might say. And when at last he raised his face, it was haggard and worn in truth, but the evil of it seemed to have fled. Again and again he strove to speak. The words would not obey. And when he had mastered himself, his voice was shattered and gone.

"Richard, I have sinned heavily in my time, and preached God's holy word with a sneer and unbelief in my heart. He knows what I have suffered, and what I shall yet suffer before His judgment comes for us all. But I beg it is no sin to pray to Him for your happiness and Miss Dorothy's."

He stumbled there, and paused, and then continued with more steadiness: —

"I came here to-night to betray you, and might have gone hence to your uncle to claim my pieces of silver. I remain to tell you that Grafton has an appointment at nine with his Majesty's chief Secretary of State. I need not mention his motives, nor dwell upon your peril. For the King's sentiments toward Paul Jones are well known. You must leave London without delay, and so must Mr. Manners and his family."

Is it the generations which decide? When I remember how Dorothy behaved that night, I think so. Scarce had the rector ceased when she had released me and was standing erect before him. Pity was in her eyes, but in her face that courage which danger itself begets in heroic women.

"You have acted a noble part this day, Mr. Allen," she said, "to atone for the wrongs you have done Richard. May God forgive you, and make you happier than you have been!"

He struggled to his feet, listening as to a benediction. Then, with a single glance to give me confidence, she was gone. And for a minute there was silence between us.

"How may you be directed to?" I asked.

He leaped as out of a trance.

"Just 'the world,' Richard," said he. "For I am adrift again, and not very like to find a harbour, now."

"You were to have been paid for this, Mr. Allen," I replied. "And a man must live."

"*A man must live!*" he cried. "The devil coined that line, and made it some men's history."

"I have you on my conscience, Mr. Allen," I went on, "for I have been at fault as well as you. I might have treated you better, even as you have said. And I command you to assign a place in London whence you may be reached."

"A letter to the *Mitre* coffee-house will be delivered," he said.

"You shall receive it," I answered. "And now I bid you good-by, and thank you."

He seized and held my hand. Then walked blindly to the door and turned abruptly.

"I do not tell you that I shall change my life, Richard, for I have said that too many times before. Indeed, I warn you that any money you may send will be spent in drink, and — and worse. I will be no hypocrite to you. But I believe that I am better this hour than I have been since last I knelt at my mother's knee in the little Oxfordshire cottage where I was born."

*   *   *   *   *   *

When Dorothy returned to me, there was neither haste in her step nor excitement in her voice. Her very coolness inspired me.

"Do you feel strong enough for a journey, Richard?" she asked.

"To the world's end, Dolly, if you will but go with me."

She smiled faintly. "I have sent off for my Lord and Mr. Fox, and pray that one of them may be here presently."

Scarcely greater were the visible signs of apprehension upon Mrs. Manners. Her first care, and Dorothy's, was to catechise me most particularly on my state. And whilst they were so occupied Mr. Marmaduke entered, wholly frenzied from fright, and utterly oblivious to his own blame in the matter. He was sent out again directly. After that, with Aunt Lucy to assist, they hurriedly packed what few things might be taken. The costly relics of Arlington Street were untouched, and the French clock was left on the mantel to tick all the night, and for days to come, in a silent and forsaken room; or perhaps to greet impassively the King's officers when they broke in at the door. But I caught my lady in the act of wrapping up the Wedgwood cups and dishes.

In the midst of these preparations Mr. Fox was heard without, and was met at the door by Dorothy. Two sentences sufficed her to tell him what had occurred, and two seconds for this man of action to make his decision.

"In an hour you shall have travelling chaises here, Dorothy," he said. "You must go to Portsmouth, and take ship for Lisbon. And if Jack does not arrive, I will go with you."

"No, Charles, you must not!" she cried, her emotion conquering her for the nonce. "That might be to ruin your career, and perchance to lose your life. And suppose we were to escape, what would they say of you!"

"Pish!" Charles retorted, to hide some feelings of his own; "once our rebel is out of the country, they may speak their minds. They have never lacked for names to call me, and I have been dubbed a traitor before now, my dear lady."

He stepped hastily to the bed, and laid his hand on me with affection.

"Charles," I said, "this is all of a piece with your old recklessness. You were ever one to take any risk, but I will not hear of such a venture as this. Do you think I will allow the hope of all England to be staked for a pirate? And would you break our commander of her rank? All that Dorothy need do at Portsmouth is to curtsey to the first skipper

2 M

she meets, and I'll warrant he will carry us all to the antipodes."

"Egad, but that is more practical than it sounds," he replied, with a glance of admiration at my lady, as she stood so tall before us. "She has a cool head, Richard Carvel, and a long head, and — and I'm thinking you are to come out of this the best of all of us. You cannot get far off your course, my lad, with her at the helm."

It was there his voice belied the jest in his words, and he left us with precipitation.

They lifted me out of my sheets (I was appalled to discover my weakness), and bundled me with tender care in a dozen shawls and blankets. My feet were thrust into two pairs of heavy woollen stockings, and Dorothy bound her own silk kerchief at my throat, whispering anxious questions the while. And when her mother and mammy went from the room, her arms flew around my neck in a passion of solicitude. Then she ran away to dress for the journey, and in a surprising short time was back again, with her muff and her heavy cloak, and bending over me to see if I gave any signs of failure.

Fifty and five minutes had been registered by the French clock, when the rattle of wheels and the clatter of hoofs sounded below, and Charles Fox panted up the stairs, muffled in a huge wrap-rascal. 'Twas he and Aunt Lucy carried me down to the street, Dorothy walking at my side, and propped me up in the padded corner of one of the two vehicles in waiting. This was an ample travelling-carriage with a lamp hanging from its top, by the light of which my lady tucked me in from head to foot, and then took her place next me. Aunt Lucy filled most of the seat opposite. The baggage was hoisted up behind, and Charles was about to slam the door, when a hackney-chaise turned the corner at a gallop and pulled up in the narrow street abreast, and the figure of my Lord Comyn suddenly leaped within the compass of the lanthorn's rays. He was dressed as for a ball, with only a thin rain-cloak over his shoulders, for the night was thick with mist. He threw at us a startled look that was a question.

"Jack, Richard is to be betrayed to-night by his uncle,"

said Charles, shortly. "And I am taking them to Portsmouth to get them off for Lisbon."

"Charles," said his Lordship, sternly, "give me that greatcoat."

It was just the one time that ever I saw uncertainty on Mr. Fox's face. He threw an uneasy glance into the chaise.

"I have brought money," his Lordship went on rapidly; "'twas that kept me, for I guessed at something of this kind. Give me the coat, I say."

Mr. Fox wriggled out of it, and took the oiled cape in return. "Thank you, Jack," he said simply, and stepped into the carriage. "Who is to mend my waistcoats now?" he cried. "Faith, I shall treasure this against you, Richard. Good-by, my lad, and obey your rebel general. Alas! I must even ask your permission to salute her."

And he kissed the unresisting Dorothy on both her cheeks. "God keep the two of you," he said, "for I love you with all my heart."

Before we could answer he was gone into the night; and my Lord, standing without, had closed the carriage door. And that was the last I saw of this noble man, the true friend of America, who devoted his glorious talents and his life to fighting the corruption that was rotting the greatness of England. He who was followed by the prayers of the English race was ever remembered in our own humble ones.

CHAPTER LVII

I COME TO MY OWN AGAIN

'Twas a rough, wild journey we made to Portsmouth, my dears, and I think it must have killed me had not my lady been at my side. We were no sooner started than she pulled the curtains and opened her portmanteau, which I saw was near filled with things for my aid and comfort. And I was made to take a spoonful of something. Never, I believe, was medicine swallowed with a greater willingness. Talk was impossible, so I lay back in the corner and looked at her; and now and anon she would glance at my face, with a troubled guess in her own as to how I might stand the night. For we were still in London. That I knew by the trot of our horses, and by the granite we traversed from time to time. But at length we rumbled over a bridge, there was a sharp call back from our post-boy to him of the chaise behind, and then began that rocking and pitching and swaying and creaking, which was to last the whole night long, save for the brief stops at the post-houses.

After an hour of it, I was holding my breath against the lurches, like a sea-sick man against that bottomless fall of the ship's bows on the ocean. I had no pain,—only an overwhelming exhaustion,—but the joy of her touch and her presence kept me from failing. And though Aunt Lucy dozed, not a wink of sleep did my lady get through all of those weary twelve hours. Always alert was she, solicitous beyond belief, scanning ever the dial of her watch to know when to give me brandy and physic; or reaching across to feel my temples for the fever. The womanliness of that last motion was a thing for a man to wonder at. But most marvellous of all was the

I COME TO MY OWN AGAIN

instinct which told her of my chief sickening discomfort,— of the leathery, travelled smell of the carriage. As a relief for this she charged her pocket-napkin with a most delicate perfume, and held it to my face.

When we drew up to shift horses, Jack would come to the door to inquire if there was aught she wanted, and to know how I was bearing up. And often Mrs. Manners likewise. At first I was for talking with them, but this Dorothy would not allow. Presently, indeed, it was beyond my power, and I could only smile feebly at my Lord when I heard Dolly asking him that the hostlers might be more quiet. Toward morning a lethargy fell upon me. Once I awoke when the lamp had burned low, to perceive the curtains drawn back, a black blotch of trees without, and the moonlight streaming in on my lady's features. With the crack of a whip I was off again.

When next consciousness came, the tarry, salt smell of a ship was in my nostrils, and I knew that we were embarked. I lay in a clean bunk in a fair-sized and sun-washed cabin, and I heard the scraping of ropes and the tramp of feet on the deck above my head. Framed against the irregular glass of the cabin window, which was greened by the water beyond, Dorothy and my Lord stood talking in whispers.

"Jack!" I said.

At the sound they turned and ran toward me, asking how I felt.

"I feel that words are very empty, Jack, to express such a gratitude as mine," I answered. "Twice you have saved me from death, you have paid my debts, and have been stanch to us both in our troubles. And —" The effort was beyond me, and I glanced appealingly at Dolly.

"And it is to you, dear Jack," she finished, "it is to you alone that we owe the great joy of our lives."

Her eyes were shining through her tears, and her smile was like the sun out of a rain-swept sky. His Lordship took one of her hands in his own, and one of mine. He scanned our faces in a long, lingering look.

"You will cherish her, Richard," he said brokenly, "for her like is not to be found in this world. I knew her worth when first she came to London, as arrant a baggage as ever led man a dance. I saw then that a great love alone was needed to make her the highest among women, and from the night I fought with you at the Coffee House I have felt upon whom that love would fall. O thou of little faith," he cried, "what little I may have done has been for her. No, Richard, you do not deserve her, but I would rather think of her as your wife than that of any man living."

* * * * * *

I shall not dwell upon that painful farewell which wrung our hearts, and made us silent for a long, long while after the ship was tossing in the short seas of the Channel.

Nor is it my purpose to tell you of that long voyage across the Atlantic. We reached Lisbon in safety, and after a week of lodgings in that city by the best of fortune got passage in a swift bark bound for Baltimore. For the Chesapeake commerce continued throughout the war, and kept alive the credit of the young nation. There were many excitements ere we sighted the sand-spits of Virginia, and off the Azores we were chased for a day and a night by a British sloop of war. Our captain, however, was a cool man and a seaman, and slipped through the cruisers lying in wait off the Capes very triumphantly.

But the remembrance of those fair days at sea fills my soul with longing. The weather was mild and bright for the season, and morning upon morning two stout topmen would carry me out to a sheltered spot on the deck, always chosen by my lady herself. There I sat by the hour, swathed in many layers of wool, and tended by her hands alone. Every nook and cranny of our lives were revealed to the other. She loved to hear of Patty and my years at Gordon's, and would listen with bated breath to the stories of the *Ranger* and the *Bon homme Richard*, and of that strange man whom we both loved, whose genius had made those cruises famous. Sometimes, in low voices, we talked of our future; but often, when the wind blew and the deck rocked and the sun flashed upon the waters, a silence would fall between us that needed no words to interpret.

Mrs. Manners yielded to my wish for us all to go to Carvel Hall. It was on a sparkling morning in February that we sighted the familiar toe of Kent Island, and the good-natured skipper put about and made for the mouth of our river. Then, as of old, the white cupola of Carvel House gleamed a signal of greeting, to which our full hearts beat a silent response. Once again the great windmill waved its welcome, and the same memory was upon us both as we gazed. Of a hale old gentleman in the sheets of a sailing pinnace, of a boy and a girl on his knees quivering with excitement of the days to come. Dorothy gently pressed my hand as the bark came into the wind, and the boat was dropped into the green water. Slowly they lowered me into it, for I was still helpless, Dorothy and her mother and Aunt Lucy were got down, and finally Mr. Marmaduke stepped gingerly from the sea-ladder over the gunwale. The cutter leaped under the strong strokes up the river with the tide. Then, as we rounded the bend, we were suddenly astonished to see people gathered on the landing at the foot of the lawn, where they had run, no doubt, in a flurry at sight of the ship below. In the front of the group stood out a strangely familiar figure.

"Why," exclaimed Dolly, "it is Ivie Rawlinson!"

Ivie it was, sure enough. And presently, when we drew a little closer, he gave one big shout and whipped off the hat from his head; and off, too, came the caps from the white heads of Scipio and Chess and Johnson behind him. Our oars were tossed, Ivie caught our bows, and reached his hand to Dorothy. It was fitting that she should be the first to land at Carvel Hall.

"'Twas yere bonny face I seed first, Miss Dolly," he cried, the tears coursing down the scars of his cheeks. "An' syne I kennt weel the young master was here. Noo God be praised for this blythe day, that Mr. Richard's cam to his ain at last!"

But Scipio and Chess could only blubber as they helped him to lift me out, Dolly begging them to be careful. As they carried me up the familiar path to the pillared porch, the first I asked Ivie was of Patty, and next why he had left Gordon's. She was safe and well, despite the Tories, and herself had sent him to take charge of Carvel Hall as soon as ever Judge Bordley had brought her the news of its restoration to me. He had supplied her with another overseer. Thanks to the good judge and to Colonel Lloyd, who had looked to my interests since Grafton was fled, Ivie had found the old place in good order, all the negroes quiet, and impatient with joy against my arrival.

It is time, my children, to bring this story to a close. I would I might write of those delicious spring days I spent with Dorothy at Carvel Hall, waited on by the old servants of my grandfather. At our whim my chair would be moved from one to another of the childhood haunts; on cool days we sat in the sun by the dial, where the flowers mingled their odours with the salt breezes off the Chesapeake; or anon, when it was warmer, in the summer-house my mother loved, or under the shade of the great trees on the lawn, looking out over the river. And once my lady went off very mysteriously, her eyes brimful of mischief, to come back with the first strawberries of the year staining her apron.

We were married on the fifteenth of June, already an anniversary for us both, in the long drawing-room. General Clapsaddle was there from the army to take Dorothy in his arms, even as he had embraced another bride on the same spot in years gone by. She wore the wedding gown that was her mother's, but when the hour was come to dress her Aunt Lucy and Aunt Hester failed in their task, and it was Patty who performed the most of that office, and hung the necklace of pearls about her neck.

Dear Patty! She hath often been with us since. You have heard your mothers and fathers speak of Aunt Patty, my dears, and they will tell you how she spoiled them when they went a-visiting to Gordon's Pride.

Ere I had regained my health, the war for Independence was won. I pray God that time may soften the bitterness it caused, and heal the breach in that noble race whose motto is Freedom. That the Stars and Stripes and the Union Jack may one day float together to cleanse this world of tyranny!

WITH THE FIRST STRAWBERRIES OF THE YEAR

AFTERWORD

The author makes most humble apologies to any who have, or think they have, an ancestor in this book. He has drawn the foregoing with a very free hand, and in the Maryland scenes has made use of names rather than of actual personages. His purpose, however poorly accomplished, was to give some semblance of reality to this part of the story. Hence he has introduced those names in the setting, choosing them entirely at random from the many prominent families of the colony.

No one may read the annals of these men, who were at once brave and courtly, and of these women, who were ladies by nature as well as by birth, and not love them. The fascination of that free and hospitable life has been so strong on the writer of this novel that he closes it with a genuine regret and the hope that its perusal may lead others to the pleasure he has derived from the history of Maryland.

As few liberties as possible have been taken with the lives of Charles James Fox and of John Paul Jones. The latter hero actually made a voyage in the brigantine *John* about the time he picked up Richard Carvel from the *Black Moll*, after the episode with Mungo Maxwell at Tobago. The Scotch scene, of course, is purely imaginary. Accuracy has been aimed at in the account of the fight between the *Bon homme Richard* and the *Serapis*, while a little different arrangement might have been better for the medium of the narrative. To be sure, it was Mr. Mease, the purser, instead of Richard Carvel, who so bravely fought the quarter-deck guns; and in reality Midshipman Mayrant, Commodore Jones's aide, was wounded by a pike in the thigh after the surrender. No injustice is done to the second and third lieutenants, who were absent from the ship during the action.

The author must acknowledge that the only good anecdote in the book and the only verse worth printing are stolen. The story on page 340 concerning Mr. Garrick and the Archbishop of York may be found in Fitzgerald's life of the actor, much better told. The verse on page 99 is by an unknown author in the Annapolis *Gazette*, and is republished in Mr. Elihu Riley's excellent "History of Annapolis."

www.ingramcontent.com/pod-product-compliance
Lightning Source LLC
Chambersburg PA
CBHW031941290426
44108CB00011B/634